Advances in Computer Vision and Pattern Recognition

For further volumes:
www.springer.com/series/4205

A. Criminisi · J. Shotton

Editors

Decision Forests for Computer Vision and Medical Image Analysis

 Springer

Editors
A. Criminisi
Microsoft Research Ltd.
Cambridge, UK

J. Shotton
Microsoft Research Ltd.
Cambridge, UK

Series Editors
Prof. Sameer Singh
Research School of Informatics
Loughborough University
Loughborough
UK

Dr. Sing Bing Kang
Microsoft Research
Microsoft Corporation
Redmond, WA
USA

ISSN 2191-6586   ISSN 2191-6594 (electronic)
Advances in Computer Vision and Pattern Recognition
ISBN 978-1-4471-4928-6   ISBN 978-1-4471-4929-3 (eBook)
DOI 10.1007/978-1-4471-4929-3
Springer London Heidelberg New York Dordrecht

Library of Congress Control Number: 2013930423

In memory of Josh, a wonderful brother, dearly missed

Foreword

We are grateful to the authors for inviting us to comment on the evolution of random decision forests. We will begin by recounting our participation in the history (and hope that the evoked memories are not randomized), continue with the recent and dramatic advances in both research and scholarship reported in the book, and finish with some speculative remarks.

For us, the story starts in the Spring of 1994 when we were failing to accurately classify handwritten digits using a decision tree. We were pretty confident that the features, which posed questions about the spatial relationship among local patterns, were discriminating. But we could not ask nearly enough of them and the best classification rate was just above 90 %. The NIST dataset had about 6,000 training images per digit, but as anybody knows who has induced a decision tree from data, the sample size goes down fast and estimation errors take over. So we could not ask more than say ten questions along any branch. We tried the recipes for pruning in [45] and elsewhere, and other ways to mitigate over-fitting, but no amount of fiddling made much of a difference.

Although building multiple trees was the "obvious" thing to do, it hadn't occurred to us until then. The first effort, which involved making ten trees by dividing the pool of questions among the trees, worked splendidly and lifted us well above 95 %. We sensed a breakthrough. Subsequently, we explored different randomization procedures and rather quickly settled on generating a small random sample of the question pool at every node of every tree, eventually exceeding 99 % accuracy with a forest of many trees.

The features were binary queries about the relative locations of local features and hence did not require any normalization or preprocessing of the image. The space of relational graphs is very large and provided a very rich source of linked queries. Each tree probed some aspects of an essentially infinite graph of relationships, with each new question refining the accumulated structure. In this way, growing the trees provided a greedy mechanism to explore this space of representations. We also explored clustering shape space by growing generic trees with unlabeled data [5], as well as initially growing trees with a small number of classes and then reestimating leaf node distributions and possibly deepening the trees with additional data from new classes. The work on trees for density estimation and manifold learning described in this book develops these ideas in multiple, fascinating directions.

In October 1994 we both went to a workshop on statistics and information theory [169], where we met Leo Breiman. One of us (DG) spoke about "randomized trees" at the workshop; this was the name we used in a technical report [4]. At the workshop, and continuing over dinner, we discussed trees with Leo, who described "bagging" (re-sampling the training set). We were all excited about advancing inductive learning with randomized classifiers. Soon after we became aware of two closely related lines of research. One was boosting, introduced earlier by Freund and Shapire. The other was the work of Ho [165], also published in the mid-1990s, which independently introduced a variation on randomization. In 1999 DG spent time with Leo at another conference [298] discussing the tradeoffs between single-tree accuracy and tree-to-tree correlation as the degree of randomness was varied.

From our perspective the source of success of both boosting and randomization was the ability to create moderately accurate trees that are weakly correlated conditional on the class. Boosting achieves this through the increased weights on the mis-classified training samples, and is largely insensitive to the particular re-weighting protocol. Randomization achieves this through sparse sampling from a large space of queries. In fact, both methods effectively sample the trees from some distribution on the space of trees; randomized trees do this explicitly and boosting in the limit cycle of a deterministic tree-generating process (see the discussion [113] of Breiman's 1997 paper on ARCing). By the way, back in 1994 we had speculated with Leo that bagging might be too stable, *i.e.* the distribution over trees resulting from mere re-sampling of the data might be too concentrated. With well-separated classes boosting can achieve lower error rates, but there is a risk of over-fitting; as discussed in [3], a combination of boosting and randomization is effective with multiple classes.

Random forests had very strong competition during the nineties from support vector machines. Whereas in practice the results on standard problems are about the same, SVMs had the appeal of a clean optimization framework, well-understood algorithms and an array of theoretical results. More recently, random forests have become popular in computational genomics, probably due to the relative transparency of the decision rules. Random forests have two other important advantages: speed and minimal storage. Nonlinear SVMs require storing large numbers of training samples, and computing large numbers of inner products. In contrast, it is hard to find something more efficient than storing and answering a series of simple questions.

This brings us to recent applications of decision and regression forests. Surely the best known is now the Kinect skeleton tracker; it is impressive how well simple depth-based comparison questions work. The Kinect solution is particularly interesting in that it synthesizes randomization with relational shape queries, the generalized Hough transform and shape context, which has proven very powerful in shape recognition. The main problem with the original formulation of shape context in [24] was the intense computation; exploring the neighborhood of a pixel using randomized trees provides a very efficient alternative. Also related is the application of regression forests to anatomy detection in 3D computed tomography (CT) images; using a form of generalized Hough transform that is trained with a predictive machine such as random forests opens up many interesting possibilities. The many other applications presented in this book further and convincingly demonstrate that sequential, adaptive learning and testing can provide a unifying framework for many of the major tasks of modern computational learning.

Looking ahead, we hope these efficient and versatile tools will spread into more applications. Many theoretical questions also remain open, such as determining conditions under which randomized forests really provide an advantage, as well as guidelines for selecting parameters such as tree depth, forest size and sampling density. Finally, whereas a decision forest efficiently integrates evidence by asking a great many questions in total, it still does not capture the full discriminating power of "20 questions" because the "line of reasoning" is broken with each new tree. In principle a single tree can develop a long series of linked questions which continue building on each other, progressing systematically from coarse to fine and exploring some aspect of the object under study in depth. For example, in computer vision, one might need 100 questions to accumulate a detailed understanding about a complex event in the scene involving multiple agents and actions. However, this is impossible in practice with current methodology: how would one store such a deep tree even if there was enough time and data to learn it or a model under which probabilities could be updated and new queries scored? Perhaps the answer is *online construction*. After all, at run time (*e.g.* during scene parsing), only one branch of each tree is traversed—the one dictated by the data being processed. Consequently, online learning might be feasible in some cases; a tracking example, which does not scale up to the complex problems treated in this book, was explored in [123]. Going further will require learning how to maintain a probability distribution over states of interest conditional on *all* the accumulated evidence.

Baltimore, USA
Yali Amit
Donald Geman

Preface

This book discusses the theoretical underpinnings of decision forests[1] as well as their practical applications in many automatic image analysis tasks typical of computer vision and medical image analysis.

Decision forests have recently become an indispensable tool for automatic image analysis, as demonstrated by the vast literature on the subject. This book attempts to organize the existing literature within a shared, flexible forest model that is capable of addressing a large and diverse set of image analysis tasks. The versatility of decision forests is also reflected in the provided research code: a compact, flexible and user friendly software library aimed at helping the reader to experiment with forests in a hands-on manner.

This book is directed at both students who wish to learn the basics of decision forests, more established researchers who wish to become more familiar with forest-based learning, and finally practitioners who wish to explore modern and efficient image analysis techniques. The book is divided into three parts:

- Part I presents our coherent model of forests, its theoretical foundations, and its applications to various tasks such as classification, regression, density estimation, manifold learning and semi-supervised classification.
- Part II contains a number of invited chapters that demonstrate the application of forests to practical tasks such as pedestrian tracking, human body pose estimation, pixel-wise semantic segmentation of images and videos, automatic parsing of medical 3D scans, and detection and delineation of brain lesions.
- Part III discusses practical implementation details, describes the provided software library, and presents concluding remarks.

We truly hope that this book can serve as a springboard to further exciting research in automatic image and video understanding.

Cambridge, UK

Antonio Criminisi
Jamie Shotton

---

[1]Throughout the book we use the terms "random forests", "randomized trees", "decision forests" or "random decision forests" interchangeably.

Acknowledgements

The authors would like to thank A. Blake, E. Konukoglu, J. Winn, D. Robertson, B. Glocker, D. Zikic, P. Kohli, S. Nowozin, I. Munasinghe, A. Fitzgibbon, C. Rother, M. Cook, A. Zisserman and N. Ayache for the many, inspiring and often animated conversations on decision forests and their theoretical and practical issues. In particular, E. Konukoglu co-authored with us the original article [80] upon which much of this book is based.

We would like to thank all the chapter contributors for their ability to push the boundaries of research in automatic image understanding. Their innovative use of decision forests is of inspiration to all young scientists in the field.

We are indebted to D. Robertson for his careful implementation of the Sherwood code library accompanying this book and made available as a free download from http://research.microsoft.com/projects/decisionforests.

We are grateful to Y. Amit and D. Geman for having agreed to write an inspiring foreword for the book, but more importantly for having pioneered the idea of randomised trees in 1994.

Many people have proof-read this book and helped us spot inaccuracies. The careful work of G. Ottaviano, C. Zach, B. Glocker, D. Zikic and S. Nowozin has helped improve the readability and correctness of the book enormously.

Finally, we are hugely indebted to A. Blake for running a research lab where ground-breaking research is allowed to happen and grow into hugely successful new products.

Contents

1   **Overview and Scope**   1
A. Criminisi and J. Shotton

2   **Notation and Terminology**   3
A. Criminisi and J. Shotton

Part I   The Decision Forest Model

3   **Introduction: The Abstract Forest Model**   7
A. Criminisi and J. Shotton

4   **Classification Forests**   25
A. Criminisi and J. Shotton

5   **Regression Forests**   47
A. Criminisi and J. Shotton

6   **Density Forests**   59
A. Criminisi and J. Shotton

7   **Manifold Forests**   79
A. Criminisi and J. Shotton

8   **Semi-supervised Classification Forests**   95
A. Criminisi and J. Shotton

Part II   Applications in Computer Vision and Medical Image Analysis

9   **Keypoint Recognition Using Random Forests and Random Ferns** . .   111
V. Lepetit and P. Fua

10 **Extremely Randomized Trees and Random Subwindows for Image
Classification, Annotation, and Retrieval**   125
R. Marée, L. Wehenkel, and P. Geurts

11 Class-Specific Hough Forests for Object Detection 143
J. Gall and V. Lempitsky

12 Hough-Based Tracking of Deformable Objects 159
M. Godec, P.M. Roth, and H. Bischof

13 Efficient Human Pose Estimation from Single Depth Images 175
J. Shotton, R. Girshick, A. Fitzgibbon, T. Sharp, M. Cook,
M. Finocchio, R. Moore, P. Kohli, A. Criminisi, A. Kipman, and A. Blake

14 Anatomy Detection and Localization in 3D Medical Images 193
A. Criminisi, D. Robertson, O. Pauly, B. Glocker, E. Konukoglu,
J. Shotton, D. Mateus, A. Martinez Möller, S.G. Nekolla, and N. Navab

15 Semantic Texton Forests for Image Categorization and Segmentation 211
M. Johnson, J. Shotton, and R. Cipolla

16 Semi-supervised Video Segmentation Using Decision Forests 229
V. Badrinarayanan, I. Budvytis, and R. Cipolla

**17 Classification Forests for Semantic Segmentation of Brain Lesions
in Multi-channel MRI** 245
E. Geremia, D. Zikic, O. Clatz, B.H. Menze, B. Glocker, E. Konukoglu,
J. Shotton, O.M. Thomas, S.J. Price, T. Das, R. Jena, N. Ayache, and
A. Criminisi

**18 Manifold Forests for Multi-modality Classification of Alzheimer's
Disease** 261
K.R. Gray, P. Aljabar, R.A. Heckemann, A. Hammers, and D. Rueckert

19 Entanglement and Differentiable Information Gain Maximization . 273
A. Montillo, J. Tu, J. Shotton, J. Winn, J.E. Iglesias, D.N. Metaxas, and
A. Criminisi

**20 Decision Tree Fields: An Efficient Non-parametric Random Field
Model for Image Labeling** 295
S. Nowozin, C. Rother, S. Bagon, T. Sharp, B. Yao, and P. Kohli

Part III Implementation and Conclusion

21 Efficient Implementation of Decision Forests 313
J. Shotton, D. Robertson, and T. Sharp

22 The Sherwood Software Library 333
D. Roberston, J. Shotton, and T. Sharp

23 Conclusions 343
A. Criminisi and J. Shotton

References 347

Index 367

Contributors

P. Aljabar Imperial College London, London, UK; King's College London, London, UK

N. Ayache Asclepios Research Project, Inria, Sophia-Antipolis, France

V. Badrinarayanan University of Cambridge, Cambridge, UK

S. Bagon Weizmann Institute of Science, Rehovot, Israel

H. Bischof Graz University of Technology, Graz, Austria

A. Blake Microsoft Research Ltd., Cambridge, UK

I. Budvytis University of Cambridge, Cambridge, UK

R. Cipolla University of Cambridge, Cambridge, UK

O. Clatz Asclepios Research Project, Inria, Sophia-Antipolis, France

M. Cook Microsoft Research Ltd., Cambridge, UK

A. Criminisi Microsoft Research Ltd., Cambridge, UK

T. Das Cambridge University Hospitals, Cambridge, UK

M. Finocchio Microsoft Corporation, Redmond, WA, USA

A. Fitzgibbon Microsoft Research Ltd., Cambridge, UK

P. Fua Ecole Polytechnique Fédérale de Lausanne, Lausanne, Switzerland

J. Gall Max Planck Institute for Intelligent Systems, Tübingen, Germany

E. Geremia Asclepios Research Project, Inria, Sophia-Antipolis, France

P. Geurts University of Liège, Liège, Belgium

R. Girshick University of California, Berkeley, CA, USA

B. Glocker Microsoft Research Ltd., Cambridge, UK

M. Godec Graz University of Technology, Graz, Austria

K.R. Gray Imperial College London, London, UK

A. Hammers Imperial College London, London, UK; Fondation Neurodis, Lyon, France

R.A. Heckemann Imperial College London, London, UK; Fondation Neurodis, Lyon, France

J.E. Iglesias Massachusetts General Hospital, Harvard Medical School, Boston, MA, USA

R. Jena Cambridge University Hospitals, Cambridge, UK

M. Johnson Unicorn Media, Temple, USA

A. Kipman Microsoft Corporation, Redmond, WA, USA

P. Kohli Microsoft Research Ltd., Cambridge, UK

E. Konukoglu Microsoft Research Ltd., Cambridge, UK

V. Lempitsky Skolkovo Institute of Science and Technology, Moscow, Russia

V. Lepetit Ecole Polytechnique Fédérale de Lausanne, Lausanne, Switzerland

R. Marée University of Liège, Liège, Belgium

A. Martinez Möller Nuklearmedizin, Klinikum rechts der Isar, Technische Universität München, München, Germany

D. Mateus Institute of Biomathematics and Biometry, Helmholtz Zentrum München, München, Germany; Computer Aided Medical Procedures, Technische Universität München, München, Germany

B.H. Menze ETH Zurich, Zurich, Switzerland

D.N. Metaxas Rutgers, Piscataway, NJ, USA

A. Montillo General Electric Global Research, Niskayuna, NY, USA

R. Moore ST-Ericsson, Redmond, WA, USA

N. Navab Computer Aided Medical Procedures, Technische Universität München, München, Germany

S.G. Nekolla Nuklearmedizin, Klinikum rechts der Isar, Technische Universität München, München, Germany

S. Nowozin Microsoft Research, Cambridge, UK

O. Pauly Institute of Biomathematics and Biometry, Helmholtz Zentrum München, München, Germany; Computer Aided Medical Procedures, Technische Universität München, München, Germany

S.J. Price Cambridge University Hospitals, Cambridge, UK

D. Roberston Redimension Ltd., Cambridge, UK

P.M. Roth Graz University of Technology, Graz, Austria

C. Rother Microsoft Research, Cambridge, UK

D. Rueckert Imperial College London, London, UK

T. Sharp Microsoft Research Ltd., Cambridge, UK

J. Shotton Microsoft Research Ltd., Cambridge, UK

O.M. Thomas Cambridge University Hospitals, Cambridge, UK

J. Tu General Electric Global Research, Niskayuna, NY, USA

L. Wehenkel University of Liège, Liège, Belgium

J. Winn Microsoft Research Ltd., Cambridge, UK

B. Yao Stanford University, Stanford, USA

D. Zikic Microsoft Research Ltd., Cambridge, UK

Chapter 1
Overview and Scope

A. Criminisi and J. Shotton

This book presents a unified, efficient model of decision forests which can be used in a number of applications such as scene recognition from photographs, object recognition in images and automatic diagnosis from radiological scans. Such applications have traditionally been addressed by different, supervised or unsupervised machine learning techniques.

However, in this book, diverse learning tasks including regression, classification and semi-supervised learning are all seen as instances of the same general decision forest model. The unified framework further extends to novel uses of forests in tasks such as density estimation and manifold learning. This unification carries both theoretical and practical advantages. For instance, the underlying single model gives us the opportunity to implement and optimize the general algorithm for all these tasks only once, and then easily adapt it to individual applications with relatively small changes.

Part I describes the general forest model which unifies classification, regression, density estimation, manifold learning, semi-supervised learning and active learning under the same flexible framework. The proposed model may be used both in a discriminative or generative way and may be applied to discrete or continuous, labeled or unlabeled data. It is based on a conventional training–testing framework, with the training phase trying to optimize a well defined energy function. Tasks such as classification or density estimation, supervised or unsupervised problems can all be addressed by setting a specific model for the objective function as well as the output prediction function.

Part II is a collection of invited chapters. Here various researchers show how it is possible to build different applications on top of the general forest model. Kinect-based player segmentation, semantic segmentation of photographs and automatic diagnosis of brain lesions are amongst the many applications discussed here.

Part III presents implementation details, documentation for the provided research software library, and some concluding remarks.

A. Criminisi (✉) · J. Shotton
Microsoft Research Ltd., 7 J.J. Thomson Avenue, Cambridge CB3 0FB, UK

A. Criminisi, J. Shotton (eds.), *Decision Forests for Computer Vision and Medical Image Analysis*, Advances in Computer Vision and Pattern Recognition, DOI 10.1007/978-1-4471-4929-3_1, © Springer-Verlag London 2013

Before diving into Part I, we present a roughly chronological, non-exhaustive survey of decision trees and forests, and their use in the past two decades. Further references will be available in the relevant chapters.

A Chronological Literature Review   One of the earlier works on decision trees is the seminal "Classification and Regression Trees (CART)" book by Breiman et al. [45], where the authors describe the basics of decision trees and their use in both classification and regression problems. Following that publication researchers focused on algorithms for constructing (learning) optimal decision trees for different tasks using available training data. For this purpose, one of the most popular algorithms is "C4.5" of Quinlan [302]. Although decision trees were proven to be useful, their application remained limited to relatively low dimensional data.

In the 1990s, researchers discovered how using ensembles of learners (*e.g.* generic "weak" classifiers) yields greater accuracy and generalization. This seems particulary true for high dimensional data, as often encountered in real life applications. One of the earliest references to ensemble methods is the boosting algorithm of Schapire [320], where the author discusses how iterative re-weighting of training data can be used to build "strong" classifiers as linear combination of many weak ones.

Combining decision trees with ensemble methods gave rise to decision forests, *i.e.* ensembles of randomly trained decision trees. The idea of constructing and using ensembles of trees with randomly generated node tests was introduced for the first time in the work of Amit and Geman [4, 5] for handwritten digit recognition. In that work the authors also proposed using the mean of the tree probabilities as output of the tree ensemble.

In the subsequent work of Ho [165] tree training via randomized partitioning of the feature space is studied further, and in [166] forests are shown to yield superior generalization to both boosting and pruned C4.5-trained trees, on some tasks. The author also shows comparisons between different split functions in the tree nodes.

Breiman's later work in [43, 44] introduced the term "random forests" and further popularized their use. Breiman proposes a different way of injecting randomness in the forest, by randomly sampling the labeled training data (namely "bagging"). The author also describes techniques for predicting the forest test error based on measures of tree strength and correlation.

In computer vision, ensemble methods became popular with the seminal face and pedestrian detection papers of Viola and Jones [389, 390]. Random decision forests where used in [235] for image classification and in [213] for keypoint tracking in videos. Recent years have seen an explosion of forest-based techniques in the machine learning, vision and medical imaging literature [36, 56, 78, 102, 117, 126, 211, 212, 246, 251–253, 271, 287, 333, 341, 355, 413]. Decision forests compare favorably with respect to other techniques [56] and have lead to one of the biggest success stories of computer vision in recent years: the body part recognition system of Microsoft Kinect [247, 343, 344].

Chapter 2
Notation and Terminology

A. Criminisi and J. Shotton

2.1 Notation

The tables below provides a quick reference of the notation and terminology followed in this book. The details will become clear in the following chapters. The invited chapters in Part II follow this convention as closely as possible, but inevitably contain a few minor differences.

Throughout the book, we denote vectors with boldface lowercase symbols (*e.g.* $\mathbf{v}$), matrices with teletype uppercase letters (*e.g.* $\mathtt{M}$) and sets in calligraphic notation (*e.g.* $\mathcal{S}$).

Forest notation	
maximum tree depth	D
number of trees in forest	T
index of tree within forest	t
index of split node within a tree	j
sets of data points reaching jth node	$\mathcal{S}_j$
sets of data points reaching children of jth node	$\mathcal{S}_j^{\mathrm{L}}, \mathcal{S}_j^{\mathrm{R}}$
weak learner (split node) parameters	$\boldsymbol{\theta}$
set of all possible weak learner parameters	$\mathcal{T}$
subset of params. available at jth node	$\mathcal{T}_j \subseteq \mathcal{T}$
information gain	$I(\mathcal{S}_j, \boldsymbol{\theta})$
node weak learner/split function	$h(\mathbf{v}, \boldsymbol{\theta}) \in \{0, 1\}$
randomness parameter	ρ
leaf predictor model (categorical)	$p(c\|\mathbf{v})$
leaf predictor model (continuous)	$p(\mathbf{y}\|\mathbf{v})$

A. Criminisi (✉) · J. Shotton
Microsoft Research Ltd., 7 J.J. Thomson Avenue, Cambridge CB3 0FB, UK

A. Criminisi, J. Shotton (eds.), *Decision Forests for Computer Vision and Medical Image Analysis*, Advances in Computer Vision and Pattern Recognition, DOI 10.1007/978-1-4471-4929-3_2, © Springer-Verlag London 2013

Data notation	
image	$J : \mathbb{N}^2 \to \mathbb{R}$ ($J : \mathbb{N}^3 \to \mathbb{R}$ for 3D volumes)
pixel position	$\mathbf{p} \in \mathbb{N}^2$ ($\mathbf{p} \in \mathbb{N}^3$ for 3D volumes)
data unit (feature vector)	$\mathbf{v} = (x_1, \ldots, x_d) \in \mathbb{R}^d$
individual feature response	v_i, or $x_i \in \mathbb{R}$
feature response at a given pixel	$\mathbf{v}(\mathbf{p})$
feature selector function	$\boldsymbol{\phi} : \mathbb{R}^d \to \mathbb{R}^{d'}$ with $d' \ll d$
output label (categorical)	c
output label (continuous)	$\mathbf{y}$

2.2 Common Terms

Decision forests have a rich literature, and as a result there are several important concepts that are commonly described using multiple terms. These terms will be used somewhat interchangeably in this book, although we will try to focus our attention on one 'primary' term for each concept. The table below summarizes a few of these terms.

Our primary term	Other common terms in use
decision forest	randomized forest, random forest, randomized decision forest
decision tree	randomized tree, randomized decision tree
split node	internal node, decision node, branch node
leaf node	terminal node
weak learner	split function, test function, feature
selector function	filter function

Part I
The Decision Forest Model

Part I discusses the abstract decision forest model and then presents its specializations to the tasks of: supervised classification and regression, density estimation, manifold learning, and semi-supervised classification.

Chapter 3
Introduction: The Abstract Forest Model

A. Criminisi and J. Shotton

Problems related to the automatic or semi-automatic analysis of complex data such as photographs, videos, medical scans, text or genomic data can all be categorized into a relatively small set of prototypical machine learning tasks. For instance:

- Recognizing the type (or category) of a scene captured in a photograph can be cast as a *classification* task, where the desired output is a discrete, categorical label (*e.g.* a beach scene, a cityscape, indoor, outdoor).
- Predicting the price of a house as a function of its distance from a good school may be thought of as a *regression* problem. In this case the output is a continuous variable.
- Detecting abnormalities in a medical scan can be achieved by evaluating the image under a probability *density* function learned from scans of healthy individuals.
- Correlating the size and shape of some key brain structures in magnetic resonance images with a patient's age and health level may be cast as *manifold learning*.
- Interactive image segmentation may be thought of as a *semi-supervised* problem, where the user's brush strokes define labeled data and the rest of image pixels provide *already available* unlabeled data.
- Learning a general rule for detecting tumors in images using minimal amount of manual annotations is an *active learning* problem, where expensive expert annotations can be optimally acquired in the most economical fashion.

The popularity of decision forests is mostly due to their recent success in *classification* tasks. However, forests are a more general tool which can be applied to many additional problems. This chapter presents a unified model of decision forests which can be used to tackle *all* the common learning tasks outlined above: classification, regression, density estimation, manifold learning, semi-supervised learning and active learning. The unification we present, yields both theoretical and practical advantages. In fact, we show how multiple prototypical machine learning problems

A. Criminisi (✉) · J. Shotton
Microsoft Research Ltd., 7 J.J. Thomson Avenue, Cambridge CB3 0FB, UK

A. Criminisi, J. Shotton (eds.), *Decision Forests for Computer Vision and Medical Image Analysis*, Advances in Computer Vision and Pattern Recognition, DOI 10.1007/978-1-4471-4929-3_3, © Springer-Verlag London 2013

can all be mapped onto the same general model by means of different parameterizations. As a result, properties of the general framework are inherited by the specific instantiations. The major practical advantage of such unification is that one can implement and optimize the associated inference algorithms only once and then use them, with relatively small modifications, in many applications. Such flexibility is demonstrated in the software library presented in Part III which can be used to undertake the exercises from the various chapters in Part I.

This chapter presents the model definitions and components in an abstract manner. Some brief concrete examples for different tasks are presented here, with further details in the subsequent chapters. Before delving into the model description we first provide an intuitive explanation of the basic principles of decision trees. Then we introduce the general mathematical notation that will be used throughout the manuscript. Finally, we extend the tree formalism to the decision forest model.

3.1 Decision Tree Basics

Decision trees have been around for a number of years [45, 302]. Their recent revival is mostly due to the discovery that higher accuracy on previously unseen data, a phenomenon known as *generalization* [4, 5, 44, 165], can be achieved by ensembles of slightly different trees. Ensembles of trees will be discussed extensively throughout this document. But let us first focus on individual trees.

3.1.1 Tree Data Structure

A tree is a special type of graph. It is a data structure made of a collection of nodes and edges organized in a hierarchical fashion (Fig. 3.1a). Nodes are divided into internal (or split) nodes and terminal (or leaf) nodes. We denote internal nodes with circles and terminal ones with squares. All nodes (except the root) have exactly one incoming edge. In contrast to general graphs a tree cannot contain loops. In this book we focus only on binary trees where each internal node has exactly two outgoing edges.[1]

3.1.2 Decision Tree

One can think of trying to solve a complex problem by running a series of simpler tests. For instance, when trying to figure out if a patient has cancer one can

---

[1] In this work we focus only on binary decision trees because they are simpler than n-ary ones, and any n-ary tree can be transformed into an equivalent binary tree. In our experiments we have not found big accuracy differences when using non-binary trees.

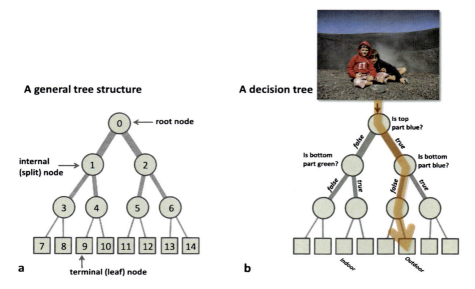

Fig. 3.1 Decision tree. (**a**) A tree is a set of nodes and edges organized in a hierarchical fashion. A tree is a graph with no loops. Internal nodes are denoted with *circles* and terminal nodes with *squares*. (**b**) A decision tree is a tree where each internal node stores a split (or test) function to be applied to the incoming data. Each leaf stores the final answer (predictor). Here we show an illustrative decision tree used to figure out whether a photo represents an indoor or outdoor scene

ask whether she smokes, or has a balanced diet; the doctor can run a blood test; *etc.* In a decision tree this set of diagnostic tests is organized hierarchically in a tree structure. For a given input object, a decision tree estimates an unknown property of the object by asking successive questions about its known properties. Which question to ask next depends on the answer of the previous question and this relationship is represented graphically as a path through the tree which the object follows. The decision is then made based on the terminal node reached by the input object.

For example, imagine we have a photograph and we need to construct an algorithm for figuring out automatically whether it represents an indoor or an outdoor scene. We have no other information but the image pixels. We can start by looking at the top part of the image and ask whether it is blue or not. If it is then that might be the sky. Based on this, we ask another question, for instance whether the bottom part is also blue. If it is not then our belief that this photograph displays an outdoor scene increases. However, if the bottom part of the photo is also blue then perhaps it is an indoor scene and we are looking at a blue wall.

All these questions/tests help our decision making move towards the correct region of the decision space. Also, the more questions asked, the higher the confidence we should expect in the response. The tests can be represented hierarchically via a decision tree structure. In a decision tree, each internal node is associated with one such question. In our example, we can think of the image as being injected at the

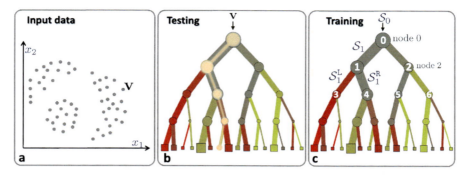

Fig. 3.2 Basic notation. (**a**) Input data are represented as a collection of points in the d-dimensional space defined by their feature responses (2D in this example). (**b**) A decision tree is a hierarchical structure of connected nodes. During testing, a split (internal) node applies a test to the input data **v** and sends it to the appropriate child. The process is repeated until a leaf (terminal) node is reached (beige path). (**c**) Training a decision tree involves sending the entire training set S_0 into the tree and optimizing the parameters of the split nodes so as to optimize a chosen energy function. See text for details

root node, and a test being applied to it (see Fig. 3.1b). Based on the result of this first test the whole image data is then sent to the left or right child. There, a new test is applied and so on until the image reaches a leaf. The leaf contains the most probable answer based on the answers to all the questions asked during the tree descent (*e.g.* "outdoor"). Therefore, key to the good functioning of a decision tree is to establish: (i) the tests associated with each internal node and (ii) the decision-making predictors associated with each leaf.

A decision tree can also be thought of as a technique for splitting complex problems into a set of simpler ones. It is a hierarchical piece-wise model. Its parameters (the node tests, the leaves predictors, *etc.*) could be selected by hand for simple problems. In more complex problems (such as vision related ones) the tree parameters and structure should be learned automatically from available training data.

Next we introduce some notation which will help us formalize these concepts.

3.2 Mathematical Notation and Basic Definitions

We now introduce several important concepts and their mathematical notation used in this book.

3.2.1 Data Point and Features

A generic object, called a *data point*, is denoted by a vector $\mathbf{v} = (x_1, x_2, \ldots, x_d) \in \mathbb{R}^d$, where the components x_i represent some attributes of the data point, called *features*. See Fig. 3.2a for an illustration. These features may vary from application

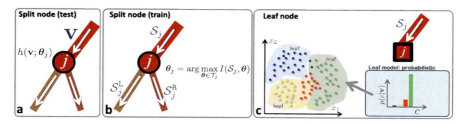

Fig. 3.3 Split and leaf nodes. (**a**) Split node (testing). A split node is associated with a weak learner (or split function, or test function). (**b**) Split node (training). Training the parameters $\boldsymbol{\theta}_j$ of node j involves optimizing a chosen objective function (maximizing the information gain I in this example). (**c**) A leaf node is associated with a predictor model. For example, in classification we may wish to estimate the conditional $p(c|\mathbf{v})$ with c indicating a discrete class index

to application. For instance, in a computer vision application, $\mathbf{v}$ may correspond to a pixel in an image and the x_is represent the responses of a chosen filter bank at that particular pixel.

The number of features naturally depends on the type of the data point as well as the application. In theory, the dimensionality d of the feature space can be extremely large, even infinite. In practice, often it is not possible, and further not necessary, to extract all d dimensions of $\mathbf{v}$ ahead of time. Instead we extract only a small portion of d on an as-needed basis. Let us formulate the features of interest that are computed at any single time to be a subset selected from the set of all possible features as $\boldsymbol{\phi}(\mathbf{v}) = (x_{\phi_1}, x_{\phi_2}, \ldots, x_{\phi_{d'}}) \in \mathbb{R}^{d'}$, where d' denotes the dimensionality of the subspace and $\phi_i \in [1, d]$ denote the selected dimensions. In most applications, d can be very large but the dimension d' of the subspace is much smaller $d' \ll d$; in many cases, d' is as small as 1 or 2.

3.2.2 Test Functions, Split Functions and Weak Learners

As explained above a decision tree is a set of tests that are hierarchically organized. In this book we use the terms "split function", "test function" and "weak learner" interchangeably. Each node has a different associated test function. We formulate a test function at a split node j as a function with binary outputs

$$h(\mathbf{v}, \boldsymbol{\theta}_j) : \mathbb{R}^d \times \mathcal{T} \to \{0, 1\}, \tag{3.1}$$

where 0 and 1 can be interpreted as "false" and "true", respectively, $\boldsymbol{\theta}_j \in \mathcal{T}$ denote the split parameters associated with the jth node, and $\mathcal{T}$ represents the space of all split parameters. The data point $\mathbf{v}$ arriving at the split node is sent to its left or right child node according to the result of the test function (see Fig. 3.3a).

3.2.3 Training Points and Training Sets

The last definitions we introduce here are the *training point* and the *training set*. A training point is a data point for which the attributes we are seeking for may be known and used to compute tree parameters. In the example of the previous section a training set would be a set of photos with associated "indoor" or "outdoor" labels. Based on this definition, a training set, denoted by S_0, is a collection of different training data points.

In a supervised learning task a training point is a pair $(\mathbf{v}, \mathbf{y})$ where $\mathbf{v}$ is the input data point (feature vector) and $\mathbf{y}$ here represents a generic, known label. In an unsupervised training task the training points are represented only by their feature response and there is no associated label.

When discussing trees it is convenient to think of subsets of training points as being associated with different tree branches. For instance S_1 denotes the subset of training points reaching node 1 (we number nodes in breadth-first order starting from 0 for the root; see Fig. 3.2c), and S_1^{L}, S_1^{R} denote the subsets going to the left and to the right children of node 1, respectively. In binary trees the following properties apply:

$$S_j = S_j^{\mathrm{L}} \cup S_j^{\mathrm{R}}, \qquad S_j^{\mathrm{L}} \cap S_j^{\mathrm{R}} = \emptyset, \qquad S_j^{\mathrm{L}} = S_{2j+1}, \qquad S_j^{\mathrm{R}} = S_{2j+2} \qquad (3.2)$$

for each split node j.

3.3 Randomly Trained Decision Trees

At a high level, the functioning of decision trees can be separated into an 'off-line' phase (training) and an 'on-line' phase (testing). Here we describe these two phases as well as the other components of random decision trees. We take a general approach and keep definitions and explanations at an abstract level. The subsequent chapters will describe and analyze specific variants of these definitions for different learning tasks.

3.3.1 Tree Testing (On-line Phase)

Given a previously unseen data point $\mathbf{v}$ a decision tree hierarchically applies a number of previously selected tests (see Fig. 3.2b). Note that the node tests have been selected during training (explained later) and remain fixed during testing. Starting at the root, each split node applies its associated test function $h(\cdot, \cdot)$ to $\mathbf{v}$. Depending on the result of this binary test, the data point $\mathbf{v}$ is sent to the left or right child. This process is repeated until the data point reaches a leaf node. The leaf nodes contain a predictor/estimator (*e.g.* a classifier or a regressor) which associates an output (*e.g.* a class label or a continuous value) with the input $\mathbf{v}$.

3.3.2 Tree Training (Off-line Phase)

The split functions stored at the internal nodes are key for the functioning of the tree. One may think of designing these functions manually. However, this approach would only be possible for very simple problems. For more realistic problems the test functions need to be learned automatically, from example data. Thus, the training phase takes care of selecting the type and parameters of the test function $h(\mathbf{v}, \boldsymbol{\theta})$ associated with each split node (indexed by j) by optimizing a chosen objective function defined on an available training set.[2]

In general, the optimization of the split functions proceeds in a greedy manner. At each node j, depending on the subset of the incoming training set $\mathcal{S}_j$ we *learn* the function that "best" splits $\mathcal{S}_j$ into $\mathcal{S}_j^{\mathrm{L}}$ and $\mathcal{S}_j^{\mathrm{R}}$. As before, the symbols $\mathcal{S}_j, \mathcal{S}_j^{\mathrm{L}}, \mathcal{S}_j^{\mathrm{R}}$ denote the sets of training points before and after the split (see Fig. 3.2c and Fig. 3.3b). This problem is formulated as the maximization of an objective function I at the jth split node

$$\boldsymbol{\theta}_j = \arg \max_{\boldsymbol{\theta} \in \mathcal{T}} I(\mathcal{S}_j, \boldsymbol{\theta}). \qquad (3.3)$$

Typically this optimization is performed as a simple search over a discrete set of samples of possible parameter settings $\boldsymbol{\theta}$ (though see Chap. 19 for an alternative).

Given the set $\mathcal{S}_j$ and the split parameters $\boldsymbol{\theta}$, the corresponding left and right sets are uniquely determined as

$$\begin{aligned}
\mathcal{S}_j^{\mathrm{L}}(\mathcal{S}_j, \boldsymbol{\theta}) &= \left\{ (\mathbf{v}, \cdot) \in \mathcal{S}_j \mid h(\mathbf{v}, \boldsymbol{\theta}) = 0 \right\} \\
\mathcal{S}_j^{\mathrm{R}}(\mathcal{S}_j, \boldsymbol{\theta}) &= \left\{ (\mathbf{v}, \cdot) \in \mathcal{S}_j \mid h(\mathbf{v}, \boldsymbol{\theta}) = 1 \right\}.
\end{aligned} \qquad (3.4)$$

We use the notation $(\mathbf{v}, \cdot)$ as $\cdot$ can stand for either $\mathbf{y}$ for continuous labels used in regression problems, or discrete labels c in classification problems.

The objective function I is then computed using those three sets as input. The children sets $\mathcal{S}_j^{\mathrm{L}}$ and $\mathcal{S}_j^{\mathrm{R}}$ are functions of the parent set $\mathcal{S}_j$ and the splitting parameters $\boldsymbol{\theta}$; however, in the rest of the book we do not make this dependency explicit to avoid cluttering the notation. The objective function $I(\mathcal{S}_j, \boldsymbol{\theta})$ is of an abstract form here. Its precise definition and the meaning of "best" depends on the task at hand (*e.g.* supervised or unsupervised, continuous or categorical output). For instance, for binary classification, the term "best" can be defined as splitting the training subset $\mathcal{S}_j$ such that the resulting child nodes are as pure as possible, *i.e.* containing mostly training points of a single class. In this case the objective function can, for instance, be defined as a standard information gain. Precise definitions and more task-specific details will be given in later chapters.

During training we also need to choose the tree structure (its size and shape). Training starts at the root node, $j = 0$, where the optimum split parameters are found

---

[2]Throughout the book we use the terms "maximizing an objective function" or "minimizing an energy" interchangeably.

as described earlier. Thus, we construct two child nodes, each receiving a different disjoint subset of the training set. This procedure is then applied recursively to all the newly constructed nodes and the training phase continues until a stopping criterion is met.

Tree Structure   The structure of the tree depends on how and when we decide to stop growing various branches of the tree. Diverse stopping criteria can be applied. For example it is common to stop the tree when a maximum number of levels D has been reached. Alternatively, one can impose a minimum value of the information gain at the node, in other words we stop when the sought-for attributes of the training points within the leaf node are similar to one another. Tree growing may also be stopped when a node contains too few training points. Avoiding growing full trees[3] has been demonstrated to have positive effects in terms of generalization [44]. In this work we avoid further post-hoc operations such as tree pruning [154] to keep the training process as simple as possible.

At the end of the training phase we obtain: (i) the (greedily) optimum weak learners (split functions) associated with each node, (ii) a learned tree structure, and (iii) a different set of training points at each leaf.

3.3.3 Weak Learner Models

The split functions play a crucial role both in training and testing. An early analysis of the effect of split functions is found in [223]. Until now we have refrained from defining a specific form for the split node models. In this section, we provide a simple geometric parametrization and a few derived formulations, which will be used throughout this book. We denote the parameters of the weak learner model as $\theta = (\phi, \psi, \tau)$ where the 'filter' (or 'selector') function $\phi = \phi(\mathbf{v})$ selects some features of choice out of the entire vector $\mathbf{v}$; ψ defines the geometric primitive used to separate the data (*e.g.* an axis-aligned hyperplane, an oblique hyperplane [158, 246, 410], or a general surface); and the parameter vector τ captures thresholds for the inequalities used in the binary test. The optimization given in (3.3) is then defined over all these three sets of parameters. Figure 3.4 illustrates a few possible weak learner models, for example:

Linear Data Separation   The first parametrization we define is the linear model

$$h(\mathbf{v}, \theta) = \left[\tau_1 > \phi(\mathbf{v}) \cdot \psi > \tau_2 \right], \tag{3.5}$$

where $[\cdot]$ is the indicator function.[4] For instance, in the 2D example in Fig. 3.4b $\phi(\mathbf{v}) = (x_1 \; x_2 \; 1)^\top$, and $\psi \in \mathbb{R}^3$ denotes a generic line in homogeneous coordinates.

---

[3]The term "full tree" here means a tree where each leaf contains only one training point.

[4]The indicator $[\cdot]$ returns 1 if the argument is true and 0 if it is false.

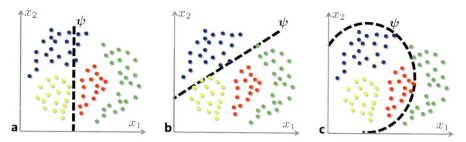

Fig. 3.4 Example weak learners. In this illustration the colors attached to each data point (*circles*) indicate different classes. (**a**) Axis-aligned hyperplane weak learner. (**b**) General oriented hyperplane. (**c**) Quadratic surface (conic in 2D). For ease of visualization here we have $\mathbf{v} = (x_1\ x_2)^\top \in \mathbb{R}^2$ and $\boldsymbol{\phi}(\mathbf{v}) = (x_1\ x_2\ 1)^\top$ in homogeneous coordinates. In general, a data point $\mathbf{v}$ may have a much higher dimensionality and $\boldsymbol{\phi}(\mathbf{v})$ still a dimensionality ≤ 2

In (3.5) setting $\tau_1 = \infty$ or $\tau_2 = -\infty$ corresponds to using a single-inequality test function. Another special case of this weak learner model is one where the line $\boldsymbol{\psi}$ is aligned with one of the axes of the feature space (*e.g.* $\boldsymbol{\psi} = (1\ 0\ \psi_3)$ or $\boldsymbol{\psi} = (0\ 1\ \psi_3)$), as in Fig. 3.4a). Such axis-aligned weak learners are often used in the boosting literature and they are referred to as *decision stumps* [389].

Please note that the axis-aligned case is over-parameterized in (3.5). We choose this parametrization because it highlights the role of the geometric model $\boldsymbol{\psi}$ and it generalizes to more complex cases. Also, in later chapters sometimes the dot product in (3.5) is denoted $f(\mathbf{v}; \boldsymbol{\phi}, \boldsymbol{\psi}) = \boldsymbol{\phi}(\mathbf{v}) \cdot \boldsymbol{\psi}$.

Non-linear Data Separation   More complex weak learners are obtained by replacing hyperplanes with higher degree of freedom surfaces. For instance, in 2D one could use conic sections as

$$h(\mathbf{v}, \boldsymbol{\theta}) = \left[\tau_1 > \boldsymbol{\phi}^\top(\mathbf{v})\ \boldsymbol{\psi}\ \boldsymbol{\phi}(\mathbf{v}) > \tau_2 \right] \tag{3.6}$$

with $\boldsymbol{\psi} \in \mathbb{R}^{3 \times 3}$ a matrix representing the conic section in homogeneous coordinates (Fig. 3.4c).

Note that low-dimensional weak learners of this type can be used even for data that originally reside in a very high dimensional space ($d \gg 2$). In fact, the selector function $\boldsymbol{\phi}$ can select a different, small set of features (*e.g.* just one or two) and they can be different for different nodes.

Here we discuss simple weak learner models. But one may use more complex split functions such as SVM, boosting, *etc.* [374, 410, 413]. However, care must be taken in selecting the complexity of such function. In fact, as shown later, the number of degrees of freedom of the weak learner influences heavily the forest generalization properties.

3.3.4 Energy Models

The objective function used during training is essential in constructing decision trees that will perform the desired task. In fact, the result of the optimization problem in (3.3) determines the parameters of the weak learners, which, in turn, determine the path followed by a data point and thus its associated prediction. In summary, through its influence on the choice of weak learners, the energy model determines the prediction and estimation behavior of a decision tree.

Developing task-specific energy models is a very active area of research. In this section we propose to use a generic definition of information gain as our abstract objective function. Later chapters will implement different instantiations of such function to deal with specific tasks such as classification, regression and density estimation. The definition of such flexible energy function constitutes the "glue" of this book as it allows us to employ essentially the same learning model to address multiple, diverse tasks.

Entropy and Information Gain   The tree training phase is driven by the statistics of the training set. The basic building blocks of the training objective function are the concepts of *entropy* and *information gain*. These concepts are usually discussed in information theory or probability courses. Here we briefly explain them from the point of view of the decision trees and illustrate them with toy examples in Figs. 3.5 and 3.6.

In information theory the information gain associated with a tree split node is defined as the reduction in uncertainty achieved by splitting the training data arriving at the node into multiple child subsets. Information gain is commonly defined as follows:

$$I = H(\mathcal{S}) - \sum_{i \in \{L,R\}} \frac{|\mathcal{S}^i|}{|\mathcal{S}|} H(\mathcal{S}^i). \tag{3.7}$$

Here the dataset $\mathcal{S}$ is split into two subsets $\mathcal{S}^L$ and $\mathcal{S}^R$ (here we focus on binary trees). In the definition above H is the entropy, *e.g.* a measure of the uncertainty associated with the random variable we wish to predict. In (3.7) $|\cdot|$ indicates cardinality for set arguments. Weighting the entropy by the cardinality of the child sets avoids splitting off children containing very few points.

Example 1 (Information gain for classification) Figure 3.5 illustrates a toy classification example. The graph in Fig. 3.5a shows a number of training points on a 2D space, where each coordinate denotes a feature value and the colors indicate the known classes (four in this case). In this example our objective is to separate different classes as much as possible. The aim of the training phase is to learn the parameters that best split the training data. For instance, splitting the training data horizontally (as shown in Fig. 3.5b) produces two sets of data. Each set now contains points from three classes while before the split the dataset had all four classes. Thus, if we use the children (rather than the parent node) we would have more chances of correct prediction; we have reduced the *uncertainty* of prediction.

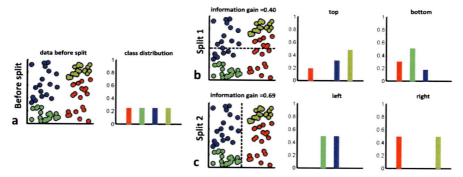

Fig. 3.5 Information gain for non-parametric distributions over categorical variables. (**a**) Dataset S before a split. (**b**) After a horizontal split. (**c**) After a vertical split. In this example the vertical split produces purer class distributions in the two child nodes

This intuitive explanation can be formulated using the quantitative measure of information gain in (3.7). For discrete probability distributions we use the Shannon entropy (see also [268] for alternatives), defined as

$$H(S) = -\sum_{c \in C} p(c) \log(p(c)), \qquad (3.8)$$

where S is the set of training points and c indicates the class label. The set of all classes is denoted C, and $p(c)$ indicates the empirical distribution extracted from the training points within the set S. This distribution can be easily computed as just a normalized histogram of the class labels. The empirical distribution over classes in Fig. 3.5a is uniform since in this example we have exactly the same number of points for each class (color). This corresponds to a large entropy for the training set. When applying a horizontal split such as the one in Fig. 3.5b we see that the empirical distributions of the resulting two sets are no longer uniform. The children distributions are more pure, their entropy has decreased and their information content increased. This improvement is reflected in the information gain.

In this example, the split has produced an information gain $I = 0.4$. However, the vertical split shown in Fig. 3.5c separates the training set better, because the resulting children each contain only two colors (classes). This corresponds to lower child entropies and a higher information gain ($I = 0.69$). This simple example shows how we can use the information gain as a training objective function. Maximizing the information gain helps select the split parameters which produce the highest *confidence* (lowest uncertainty) in the final distributions. This concept is at the basis of decision tree training.

Example 2 (Information gain for clustering) The previous example focused on discrete, categorical distributions. But entropy and information gain can also be defined for continuous-valued labels and continuous distributions. In fact, the definition of

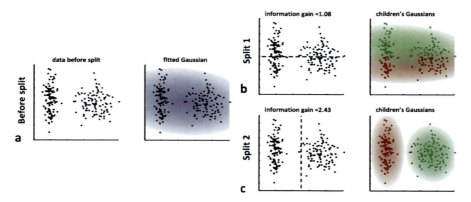

Fig. 3.6 Information gain for parametric densities over continuous variables. (**a**) Dataset $\mathcal{S}$ before a split. (**b**) After a horizontal split. (**c**) After a vertical split. A vertical split produces better separation and a correspondingly higher information gain

the information gain remains the same (3.7), but this time the differential (continuous) entropy is used in place of the Shannon entropy, as follows:

$$H(\mathcal{S}) = -\int_{\mathbf{y} \in \mathcal{Y}} p(\mathbf{y}) \log\big(p(\mathbf{y})\big)\, d\mathbf{y}. \tag{3.9}$$

Here y is a continuous label of interest and p is the probability density function estimated from the training points in the set $\mathcal{S}$. From a practical point of view, in the discrete case, the distribution $p(c)$ was defined as the empirical distribution computed from the training set. Similarly, in the continuous case the distribution $p(\mathbf{y})$ can be defined either using parametric distributions or non-parametric methods.

One of the most popular choices in various applications is to use Gaussian-based models to approximate the density $p(\mathbf{y})$ due to their simplicity. The differential entropy of a d-variate Gaussian can be derived analytically as

$$H(\mathcal{S}) = \frac{1}{2} \log\big((2\pi e)^d |\Lambda(\mathcal{S})|\big). \tag{3.10}$$

Figure 3.6 illustrates the role of the continuous information gain in training, with another toy example. This time we wish to cluster similar points according to their features (again, depicted as the coordinates in a 2D space). In this example the data are unlabeled. Given an arbitrary input data point we wish the tree to predict its associated cluster. In Fig. 3.6a we have a set $\mathcal{S}$ of training data points represented in a continuous 2D space. Fitting a Gaussian to the entire initial set $\mathcal{S}$ produces the density shown in blue, which has a high differential entropy. Splitting the data horizontally (Fig. 3.6b) produces two largely overlapping and slightly smaller Gaussians (in red and green). The large overlap indicates a suboptimal separation and is associated with a relatively low information gain ($I = 1.08$). Splitting the data points vertically (Fig. 3.6c) yields better separation, with peakier Gaussians and a correspondingly higher value of information gain ($I = 2.43$). The fact that the information gain measure can be defined flexibly, for discrete or continuous distributions and for labeled or unlabeled data points, is a useful property which is at the basis of our unified forest model.

3.3.5 Leaf Prediction Models

The training phase is in charge of estimating "optimal" weak learners and tree structures. Furthermore, it also has to learn good prediction models to be stored at the terminal nodes.

In the supervised case, after training, each leaf node remains associated with a subset of (labeled) training data. During testing, a previously unseen point traverses the tree until it reaches a leaf. Since the split nodes act on features, the input test point is likely to end up in a leaf associated with training points which are all similar to itself. Thus, it is reasonable to assume that the associated label must also be similar to that of the training points in that leaf. This justifies using the label statistics gathered in that leaf to predict the label associated with the input test point.

In the most general sense the leaf statistics can be captured using the conditional distributions

$$p(c|\mathbf{v}) \quad \text{or} \quad p(\mathbf{y}|\mathbf{v}), \tag{3.11}$$

where c and $\mathbf{y}$ represent the categorical and continuous labels, respectively. $\mathbf{v}$ is the data point that is being tested in the tree and the conditioning denotes the fact that the distributions depend on the specific leaf node reached by the test point (see Fig. 3.3c). Different leaf predictors can be used. For instance, a Maximum A-Posteriori (MAP) estimate may be obtained as

$$c^* = \arg\max_c p(c|\mathbf{v}) \quad \text{or} \quad \mathbf{y}^* = \arg\max_{\mathbf{y}} p(\mathbf{y}|\mathbf{v}) \tag{3.12}$$

for the categorical and continuous cases, respectively. However, in general it is preferable to keep the entire distribution around until the final moment where a decision must be taken, rather than taking an early point estimate. This allows us to reason about prediction uncertainty.

3.3.6 The Randomness Model

Randomness is injected into the trees during the training phase.[5] Two of the most popular ways of doing so are:

---

[5]Testing is instead almost always considered to be deterministic. Perhaps a more descriptive name for forests would therefore be 'randomly *trained* decision forests'.

- random training set sampling [42, 44] (*e.g.* bagging), and
- randomized node optimization [4, 166].

3.3.6.1 Bagging

In [42, 44] bagged training was introduced as a way of reducing possible overfitting and improving the generalization capabilities of random forests. The idea is to train each tree in a forest on a different training subset, sampled at random from the same labeled database. This strategy helps avoid specializing the selected parameters to a single training set and has been shown to improve generalization. Another advantage is that training is faster than having to use the entire labeled set. However, not being able to use all available training data for all trees seems wasteful. An alternative way of introducing randomness and reduce overfitting is described next.

3.3.6.2 Randomized Node Optimization (RNO)

In (3.3) at each node the optimization is done with respect to the entire parameter space $\mathcal{T}$. However, this has a major drawback: efficiency. For large dimensional problems, the size of $\mathcal{T}$ can be extremely large. Therefore, optimizing (3.3) by searching over $\mathcal{T}$ is not feasible in practice, nor desirable (for reasons that will become clearer later). Instead, when training the jth node we only make available a small random subset $\mathcal{T}_j \subset \mathcal{T}$ of parameter values. Thus, under the randomness model, training a tree is achieved by optimizing each split node j as

$$\boldsymbol{\theta}_j = \arg\max_{\boldsymbol{\theta} \in \mathcal{T}_j} I(\mathcal{S}_j, \boldsymbol{\theta}). \qquad (3.13)$$

Again, typically this maximization is performed as a simple search over the smaller, discrete set $\mathcal{T}_j$.

Note that in some cases we may have $|\mathcal{T}| = \infty$. At this point it is convenient to introduce a parameter $\rho = |\mathcal{T}_j|$. The parameter $\rho \in \{1, \ldots, |\mathcal{T}|\}$ controls the degree of randomness in a tree and (usually) its value is fixed for all nodes. At the limit, for $\rho = |\mathcal{T}|$ all the split nodes use all the information available and therefore there is no randomness in the system. Vice versa, when $\rho = 1$ each split node take only a single randomly chosen set of values for its parameter $\boldsymbol{\theta}$. Thus, there is no real optimization and we get maximum randomness.

In practical applications, one may wish to randomize none, some, or all of the parameters $\boldsymbol{\phi}$, $\boldsymbol{\psi}$, and $\boldsymbol{\tau}$. For example, one might want to randomize the $\boldsymbol{\phi}$ selector function parameters and the $\boldsymbol{\psi}$ parameters that define the orientation of a weak learner hyperplane, but search over a predefined set of thresholds $\boldsymbol{\tau}$. Certain variants of training in which particular choices of training parameters are randomized have been called 'totally randomized' and 'extremely randomized' trees; see Chap. 10 for more details. Also, parameter values do not necessarily need be sampled from

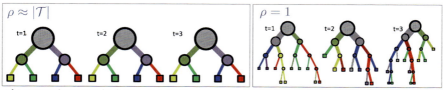

a) Low randomness, high tree correlation   **b) High randomness, low tree correlation**

Fig. 3.7 Controlling the amount of randomness and tree correlation. (**a**) Large values of ρ correspond to little randomness and thus large tree correlation. In this case the forest behaves very much as if it was made of a single tree. (**b**) Small values of ρ correspond to large randomness in the training process. Thus the forest component trees are all very different from one another

a uniform distribution; see Chap. 19. The interested reader is referred to [223] for further models of randomness.

Bagging and randomized node optimization are not mutually exclusive and could be used together. However, in this book we focus on the second alternative which: (i) enables us to train trees on the entire training data, and (ii) yields margin-maximization properties for the ensemble models (details in Chap. 4). On the other hand, bagging yields greater training efficiency.

Alternative randomness models exist. For example, in [64, 89] the authors discuss different *Bayesian* decision tree models where a tree is thought of as a random sample from a well defined tree prior distribution. A variety of different choices for such prior are discussed, which control *e.g.* the shape and size of trees probabilistically. "Good" trees are generated via the Metropolis-Hastings algorithm [156].

Having discussed randomized decision trees we next describe how those components are merged together to form decision forests.

3.4 Combining Trees into a Forest Ensemble

A random decision forest is an ensemble of *randomly trained* decision trees. The key aspect of the forest model is the fact that its component trees are all randomly different from one another. This leads to de-correlation between the individual tree predictions and, in turn, results in improved generalization and robustness. The forest model is characterized by the same components as the decision trees. The family of weak learners (test functions), energy model, the leaf predictors and the type of randomness influence the prediction/estimation properties of the forests. Furthermore, the randomness parameter ρ controls not only the amount of randomness within each tree but also the amount of correlation between different trees in the forest. In fact, as illustrated in Fig. 3.7, when $\rho = |\mathcal{T}|$ all the trees will be identical to one another, and as ρ decreases the trees become more decorrelated (different from one another).

In a forest with T trees we use the variable $t \in \{1, \ldots, T\}$ to index each component tree. All trees are trained independently (and possibly in parallel). During testing, each test point $\mathbf{v}$ is simultaneously pushed through all trees (starting at the

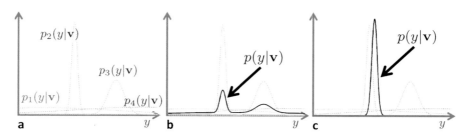

Fig. 3.8 Ensemble model. (**a**) The posteriors of four different regression trees (shown with different colors). Some correspond to higher confidence (peakier density curves) than others. (**b**) An ensemble posterior $p(y|\mathbf{v})$ obtained by averaging all tree posteriors. (**c**) The ensemble posterior $p(y|\mathbf{v})$ obtained as a product of all tree posteriors. Both in (**b**) and (**c**) the ensemble output is influenced more by the more informative trees

root) until it reaches the corresponding leaves. Tree testing can also often be done in parallel, thus achieving high computational efficiency on modern parallel CPU or GPU hardware (see Chap. 21). Combining all tree predictions into a single forest prediction may be done by a simple averaging operation [44]. For instance, in classification we have

$$p(c|\mathbf{v}) = \frac{1}{T} \sum_{t=1}^{T} p_t(c|\mathbf{v}), \tag{3.14}$$

where $p_t(c|\mathbf{v})$ denotes the posterior distribution obtained by the tth tree. Alternatively one could also multiply the tree outputs together (though the trees are not statistically independent), that is,

$$p(c|\mathbf{v}) = \frac{1}{Z} \prod_{t=1}^{T} p_t(c|\mathbf{v}) \tag{3.15}$$

with the partition function Z ensuring probabilistic normalization.

Figure 3.8 illustrates fusion of multiple tree outputs for a simple example where the attribute we want to predict is the continuous variable y. Imagine that we have trained a forest with $T = 4$ trees. For a test data point $\mathbf{v}$ we get the corresponding tree posteriors $p_t(y|\mathbf{v})$ modeled here as Gaussians, with $t \in \{1, \ldots, 4\}$. As illustrated, some trees produce peakier (more confident) predictions than others. Both the averaging and the product operations produce combined distributions (shown in black) which are heavily influenced by the most confident, most informative trees. Therefore, such simple operations have the effect of selecting (softly) the more confident trees out of the forest. This selection is carried out at a leaf-by-leaf level and the more confident trees may be different for different leaves. Averaging many tree posteriors also has the advantage of reducing the effect of possibly noisy tree contributions. In general, the product based ensemble model produces sharper distributions [163] and may be less robust to noise. Alternative ensemble models are possible, where for instance one may choose to select individual trees in a hard way. Also Chap. 9 discusses the use of a Naïve-Bayes strategy for combining tree outputs.

3.4.1 Key Model Parameters

The decision forests, their construction and prediction abilities depend on the model parameters. The parameters that most influence the behavior of a decision forest are:

- the maximum allowed tree depth D;
- the amount of randomness (controlled by ρ) and its type;
- the forest size T;
- the choice of weak learner model;
- the training objective function;
- the choice of features in practical applications.

Those choices directly affect the forest predictive accuracy, the *quality of its confidence*, its generalization and its computational efficiency.

For instance, several papers have pointed out how the testing accuracy increases monotonically with the forest size T [78, 341, 413], how learning very deep trees can lead to overfitting, as well as the importance of using very large amounts of training data [343]. In his seminal work Breiman [44] has also shown the importance of randomness and its effect on tree correlation. Additionally later chapters will show how the choice of randomness model affects a forest's generalization.

The choice of stopping criteria has a direct influence on the shape of the trees, *e.g.* whether they are well balanced or not. In general, very unbalanced trees should be avoided. At the limit they may become just chains of weak learners, with little feature sharing [370] and thus little generalization. A less studied issue is how the weak learners influence the forest's accuracy and its estimated uncertainty. To this end, later chapters will show the effect of the randomness parameter ρ on the forest behavior with some simple toy examples and compare the results with existing alternatives. When training a forest it is important to visualize its trees as well as other intermediate variables (*e.g.* the features and parameters chosen at each node), to make sure the forest has the expected behavior.

3.5 Summary

This chapter has defined our generic decision forest model. In the following chapters of Part I we discuss its specializations for the different tasks of interest. The explanations will be accompanied by a number of synthetic examples in the hope of increasing clarity and helping understand the forests' general properties. In Part II we then present many ways in which researchers around the world are employing decision forests in diverse practical applications.

Chapter 4
Classification Forests

A. Criminisi and J. Shotton

This chapter discusses the most common use of decision forests, *i.e.* classification. The goal here is to automatically associate an input data point **v** with a discrete class $c \in \{c_k\}$. Classification forests enjoy a number of useful properties:

- they naturally handle problems with more than two classes;
- they provide a probabilistic output;
- they can generalize well to previously unseen data;
- they are efficient thanks to a small set of tests that are applied to each data point, and the ease in which forests can be implemented in parallel.

In addition to these known properties the work in [80] also shows that:

- under certain conditions classification forests exhibit margin-maximizing behavior, and
- the quality of the posterior and associated confidence can be controlled via the choice of the specific parameters.

We begin with an overview of general classification methods and then discuss a possible way of specializing the generic forest model presented in the previous chapter for the classification task. A number of experiments on toy data is presented in order to provide the reader with some basic intuition about the behavior of classification forests. A small number of exercises is also provided to study the effect of various forest parameters and help the reader familiarize with the available code.

4.1 Classification Algorithms in the Literature

Classification (of pixels, regions, or whole images) is at the heart of modern computer vision and image understanding, as demonstrated by the large interest in the PASCAL Visual Object Class (VOC) recognition challenge [100].

A. Criminisi (✉) · J. Shotton
Microsoft Research Ltd., 7 J.J. Thomson Avenue, Cambridge CB3 0FB, UK

A. Criminisi, J. Shotton (eds.), *Decision Forests for Computer Vision and Medical Image Analysis*, Advances in Computer Vision and Pattern Recognition, DOI 10.1007/978-1-4471-4929-3_4, © Springer-Verlag London 2013

One of the most widely used classification algorithms is the support vector machine (SVM) [380] whose popularity is mostly due to the fact that in binary classification problems (two target classes) it guarantees maximum margin separation. In turn, this property yields good generalization with relatively little training data.

Another popular technique is boosting [112] which builds strong classifiers as linear combination of many weak classifiers. A boosted classifier is trained iteratively, where at each iteration the training examples for which the classifier works less well are "boosted" by increasing their associated training weight. Cascaded boosting was used in [389] for efficient face detection and localization in images, a task nowadays handled even by entry-level digital cameras and webcams.

Despite the success of SVMs and boosting, these techniques do not extend naturally to multiple class problems [74, 371]. In principle, classification trees and forests work unmodified, with any number of classes. For instance, they have been tested on ∼20 classes in [341] and ∼30 classes in [343].

Abundant literature has shown the advantage of fusing together multiple simple learners of different types [230, 352, 374, 413, 427]. Classification forests represent a simple, yet effective way of combining randomly trained classification trees. A thorough comparison of forests with respect to other binary classification algorithms has been presented in [56]. That work suggests that classification forests yield good generalization, even in problems with high dimensionality.

Classification forests have also been employed successfully in a number of practical vision and medical applications such as: tracking of keypoints in videos [213], human pose estimation [62, 311, 344], gaze estimation [25], anatomy detection in CT scans [77], semantic segmentation of photos and videos [341], and 3D delineation of brain lesions [126, 428]. Many such applications are described in detail in Part II of this book. Finally, recent new techniques are emerging which demonstrate the power of performing joint classification *and* regression within the same forest framework [131, 134].

4.2 Specializing the Decision Forest Model for Classification

This section specializes the abstract forest model introduced in Chap. 3 for use in classification.

Problem Statement   The classification task may be summarized as follows:

> *Given a labeled set of training data learn a general mapping which associates previously unseen test data with their corresponding classes.*

The need for a general rule that can be applied to "not-yet-available" test data is typical of *inductive* tasks.[1] In classification the desired output is of discrete, categorical, unordered type. Consequently, so is the nature of the training labels. Each

---

[1] As opposed to *transductive* tasks. The distinction will become clearer later.

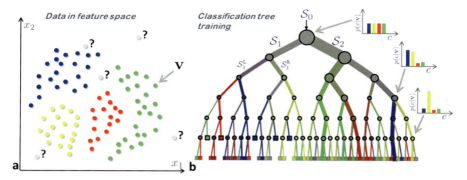

Fig. 4.1 Classification: training data and tree training. (**a**) Input data points are denoted with *circles* in their 2D feature space. Different colors denote different ground truth class labels. There are four classes here. *Gray circles* indicate unlabeled, previously unseen test data. (**b**) A binary classification tree. The edge thickness is proportional to the amount of training data going through it. Edge colors are a mix of the colors of the four classes, weighted in proportion to the associated class probabilities. During training a set of labeled training points $\mathcal{S}_0$ is used to optimize the parameters of the tree. In a classification tree the entropy of the class distributions associated with different nodes decreases (the confidence increases) when going from the root towards the leaves. Note the gray-ish color of the root node and the more distinct colors of the leaves

training point is denoted as a pair $(\mathbf{v}, c)$. In Fig. 4.1a data points are denoted with circles, with different colors indicating different training labels. Testing points (not available during training) are indicated in gray (their class label is not known in advance).

More formally, during testing we are given an input test data $\mathbf{v}$ and we wish to infer a class label c such that $c \in \mathcal{C}$, with $\mathcal{C} = \{c_k\}_{k=1}^{|\mathcal{C}|}$. More generally we wish to compute the whole distribution $p(c|\mathbf{v})$. As usual the input is represented as a multi-dimensional vector of feature responses $\mathbf{v} = (x_1, \ldots, x_d) \in \mathbb{R}^d$. Training happens by optimizing an energy over a training set $\mathcal{S}_0$ of data and associated ground truth labels. Next we specify the precise nature of this energy.

4.2.1 The Training Objective Function

Forest training happens by optimizing the parameters of the weak learner at each split node j via:

$$\boldsymbol{\theta}_j = \underset{\boldsymbol{\theta} \in \mathcal{T}_j}{\arg\max}\, I(\mathcal{S}_j, \boldsymbol{\theta}). \tag{4.1}$$

For classification the objective function I takes the form of a classical information gain defined for discrete distributions:

$$I(\mathcal{S}_j, \boldsymbol{\theta}) = H(\mathcal{S}_j) - \sum_{i \in \{\text{L,R}\}} \frac{|\mathcal{S}_j^i|}{|\mathcal{S}_j|} H\big(\mathcal{S}_j^i\big) \tag{4.2}$$

with i indexing the two child nodes. The two child sets are a function of the parent set and split parameters $\boldsymbol{\theta}$, but this dependency is left implicit in (4.2) to avoid cluttering the notation. The entropy for a generic set S of training points is defined as

$$H(S) = -\sum_{c \in C} p(c) \log p(c) \qquad (4.3)$$

where $p(c)$ is calculated as the normalized empirical histogram of labels corresponding to the training points in S. As illustrated in Fig. 4.1b training a classification tree by maximizing the information gain has the tendency to produce trees where the entropy of the class distributions associated with the nodes decreases (the prediction confidence increases) when going from the root towards the leaves. In turn, this yields increasing certainty of prediction.

Although the above definitions of information gain and entropy are very popular, viable alternative instantiations exist. For example in [268] the author presents both an information gain measure which is built upon more robust, unbiased estimates of entropy, and also non-parametric entropy estimators for both classification and regression tasks. In this book we also stick with using an information gain-like objective function. As will be clearer later, this choice aids unification of diverse tasks under the same forest framework.

4.2.2 Class Re-balancing

Note that in some applications one has an unbalanced distribution of classes in the training set S_0. For instance, when performing semantic image segmentation the number of "background" pixels may dominate other "object" pixels. This may have a detrimental effect on forest training. This problem may be mitigated by resampling the training data so as to have roughly uniform training distributions. An alternative is to use the known prior class distribution to weight the contribution of each class by its inverse frequency when computing the information gain at each split node.

4.2.3 Randomness

In (4.1) randomness is injected via randomized node optimization, with as before $\rho = |\mathcal{T}_j|$ controlling the amount of randomness. For instance, before starting to train node j we can randomly sample $\rho = 1000$ parameter values (*e.g.* randomly selecting 1000 features) out of possibly billions or even infinite possibilities. Information gain maximization is then carried out by exhaustive search on this reduced set of possibilities. It is important to point out that it is not necessary to have the entire set $\mathcal{T}$ computed in advance and stored. We can generate each random subset $\mathcal{T}_j$ as needed before starting training the corresponding node.

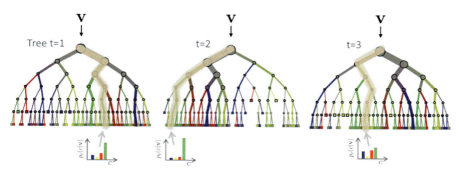

Fig. 4.2 Classification forest testing. During testing the same unlabeled test input data **v** is pushed through each component tree. At each internal node a test is applied and the data point sent to the appropriate child. The process is repeated until a leaf is reached. At the leaf the stored posterior $p_t(c|\mathbf{v})$ is read off. The forest class posterior $p(c|\mathbf{v})$ may be obtained as the average of all tree posteriors (4.4)

4.2.4 The Leaf and Ensemble Prediction Models

Classification forests produce probabilistic output as they return not just a single class point prediction but an entire class distribution. In fact, during testing, each tree leaf yields the posterior $p_t(c|\mathbf{v})$. Then, the forest output is defined as

$$p(c|\mathbf{v}) = \frac{1}{T} \sum_{t=1}^{T} p_t(c|\mathbf{v}) \tag{4.4}$$

(this is the same as (3.14) from the previous chapter). This is illustrated with a small, three-tree forest in Fig. 4.2. Averaging tree posteriors is only one possible choice of ensemble model, one which will be used in the examples in this book. However, alternatives are possible.

4.3 Effect of Model Parameters

The choices made in terms of the form of the objective function and that of the prediction model directly affect a classification forest accuracy and generalization. This section studies the effect of further parameters such as the forest size, its depth, the amount of randomness and the weak learner type. We use many illustrative, synthetic examples designed to bring to life various properties of classification forests. Chapter 13 demonstrates such properties further with a real-world, commercial application.

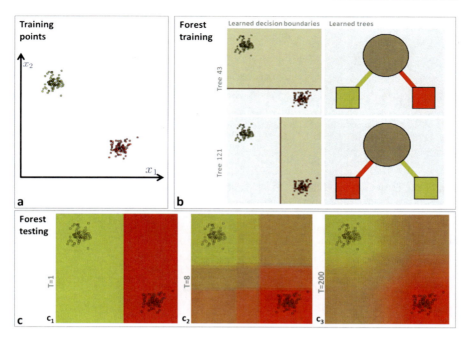

Fig. 4.3 A toy example illustrating the effect of forest size T. (**a**) Training points belonging to two classes (identified by the *red* and *yellow colors*). (**b**) Different training trees produce different partitions and thus different leaf predictors. The color of tree nodes and edges indicates the class probability of training points going through them. (**c**) In testing, increasing the forest size T produces smoother class posteriors. All experiments were run with $D = 2$ and axis-aligned weak learners

4.3.1 The Effect of the Forest Size on Generalization

Figure 4.3 shows a first synthetic example. Training points belonging to two different classes (shown in yellow and red) are randomly drawn from two well separated Gaussian distributions (Fig. 4.3a). The points are represented as 2-vectors, where each dimension represents a different feature.

A forest of shallow trees ($D = 2$) and varying size T is trained on those points. In this example simple axis-aligned weak learners are used. In such degenerate trees (stumps) there is only one split node, the root itself (Fig. 4.3b). The trees are all randomly different from one another and each defines a slightly different partition of the data. In this simple (linearly separable) example, each tree defines a "perfect" partition since the training data is separated perfectly. However, the partitions themselves are still randomly different from one another.

Figure 4.3c shows the classification posteriors resulting from testing the forest for all non-training points across a square portion of the feature space (the white testing pixels in Fig. 4.3a). In this visualization the color associated with each test point is a linear combination of the colors corresponding to the two classes, where the mixing weights are proportional to the class posteriors. Thus, intermediate, mixed colors (orange in this case) correspond to regions of high uncertainty and low predictive confidence.

We observe that each individual tree produces *overconfident* predictions (sharp probabilities in Fig. 4.3c_1). This is undesirable. In fact, intuitively one would expect the confidence of classification to be reduced for test data which is "different" than the training data. The larger the difference, the larger the uncertainty. Thanks to all trees being different from one another, increasing the forest size from $T = 1$ to $T = 200$ produces much smoother posteriors (Fig. 4.3c_3). Now we observe higher confidence near the training points and lower confidence away from training regions of space; a more intuitive generalization behavior.

For few trees (*e.g.* $T = 8$) the forest posterior shows strong box-like artifacts. This is due to the use of an axis-aligned weak learner model. Such artifacts yield low quality confidence estimates (especially when extrapolating away from training regions) and ultimately imperfect generalization. In the remainder of this paper we will always keep an eye on the *quality of the uncertainty* as this is key for inductive generalization away from (possibly little) training data.

4.3.2 Multiple Classes and Training Noise

One major advantage of decision forests over *e.g.* support vector machines and boosting is that the same classification model can handle both binary and multi-class problems. This is illustrated in Fig. 4.4 with both two- and four-class examples, and different levels of noise in the training data.

The top row of the figure shows the input training points (two classes in Fig. 4.4a and four classes in Fig. 4.4b, c). The middle row shows corresponding testing class posteriors. The bottom row also shows the entropy associated with each pixel. Note how points in between spiral arms or further away from training points are associated with larger uncertainty (orange pixels in Fig. 4.4a' and gray-ish ones in Fig. 4.4b', c'). This behavior is very much in agreement with our intuition of uncertainty.

In this case we have employed a richer *conic section* weak learner model (see Sect. 3.3.3) which reduces the artifacts observed in the previous example and yields smoother posteriors. Notice for instance in Fig. 4.4b' how the curve separating the red and the green spiral arms is nicely continued away from training points (with increasing uncertainty).

If the noise in the position of training points increases (*cf.* Fig. 4.4b and Fig. 4.4c) then training points for different classes are more intermingled with one another. As expected, this increase in training noise yields a larger overall uncertainty in the testing posterior (represented by less saturated colors in Fig. 4.4c'). Next we delve further into the issue of training noise and mixed training data.

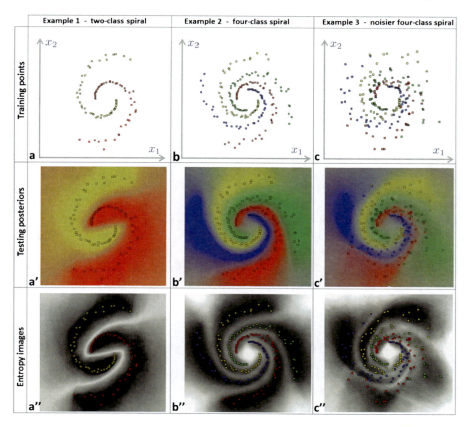

Fig. 4.4 Handling multiple classes and the effect of training noise. (**a, b, c**) Training points for three different experiments: 2-class spiral, 4-class spiral and another 4-class spiral with noisier point positions, respectively. (**a′, b′, c′**) Corresponding testing posteriors. (**a″, b″, c″**) Corresponding entropy images (brighter for larger entropy). The classification forest can handle both binary and multi-class problems. With larger training noise the classification uncertainty increases (less saturated colors in **c′** and less sharp entropy map in **c″**). All experiments in this figure were run with $T = 200$, $D = 6$, and a conic section weak learner model

4.3.3 The Effect of the Tree Depth

The experiment in Fig. 4.5 illustrates the behavior of classification forests on a four-class training set where there is both mixing of labels (in feature space) and large gaps. Here three different forests have been trained with the same number of trees $T = 200$ and varying maximum depth D. We observe that as the tree depth increases the overall prediction confidence also increases. Furthermore, in large gaps (*e.g.* between red and blue regions), the optimal separating surface tends to be placed roughly in the middle of the gap.[2]

---

[2]This effect will be analyzed further in the next section.

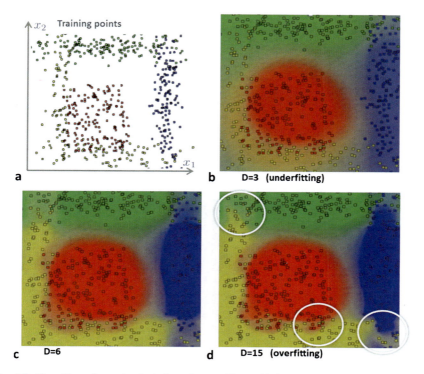

Fig. 4.5 The effect of tree depth. A four-class problem with both mixing of training labels and large gaps. (**a**) Training points. Notice the mixing of *e.g. yellow* and *red points* due to noisy training data. (**b, c, d**) Testing posteriors for different tree depths. All experiments were run with $T = 200$ and a conic weak learner model. The tree depth is a crucial parameter in avoiding under- or over-fitting

Finally, we notice that a large value of D (in the example $D = 15$) tends to produce *overfitting*, *i.e.* the posterior tends to split off isolated clusters of noisy training data (denoted with white circles in the figure). In fact, changing the maximum tree depth parameter D is one way to control the amount of overfitting. By the same token, too shallow trees produce washed-out, low-confidence posteriors. Thus, while using multiple trees alleviates the overfitting problem of individual trees, it does not cure it completely. In practice one has to be very careful to select the most appropriate value of D as its optimal value is a function of the problem complexity.

4.3.4 The Effect of the Weak Learner

Another important issue that has perhaps been overlooked in the literature is the effect of a particular choice of weak learner model on the forest behavior.

The experiment in Fig. 4.6 illustrates this point. We are given four sets of well separated point clusters, one cluster per class. We train three forests on those points

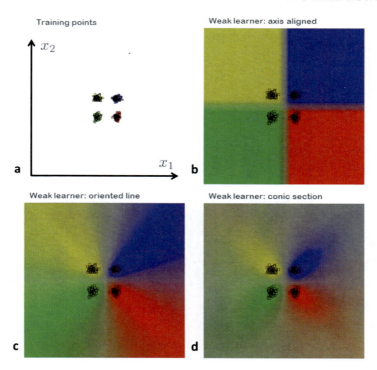

Fig. 4.6 The effect of the weak learner model. (**a**) A four-class training set. (**b**) The testing posterior for a forest with axis-aligned weak learners. In regions far from the training points the posterior is overconfident (illustrated by saturated, rich colors). (**c**) The testing posterior for a forest with oriented line weak learners. (**d**) The testing posterior for a forest with conic section weak learners. The uncertainty of class prediction increases with distance from the training data points. Here we use $D = 3$ and $T = 200$ for all examples

with different choices of weak learner. The goal is to study the effect of the weak learner on the confidence in regions far from the training data. By comparing Fig. 4.6b, Fig. 4.6c and Fig. 4.6d we observe that an axis-aligned weak learner produces overconfident predictions in the corners of the space. In this case the confidence value is independent of the distance from training points. In contrast, the curved nature of the conic sections yield a possibly more intuitive decrease of confidence with distance from training data. However, it is difficult to say which behavior is best in general, as this is really application dependent. Here we just wish to highlight the fact that decision forests are flexible enough to produce different confidence behaviors and show how to control them.

Another experiment is shown in Fig. 4.7 where we are given a set of training points arranged in four spirals, one for each of the four classes. Six different forests have been trained on the same training data, for two different values of tree depth and three different weak learners. The 2×3 arrangement of images shows the output

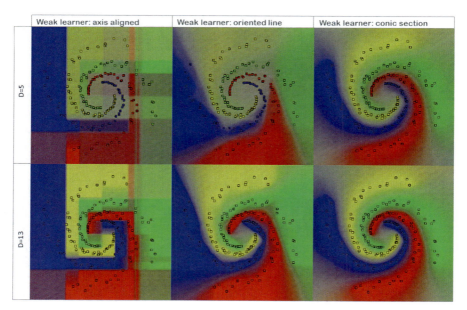

Fig. 4.7 The effect of the weak learner model. The same set of 4-class training data is used to train six different forests, for two different values of D three different weak learner types. For fixed weak learner deeper trees produce higher confidence. For constant D non-linear weak learners produce the most visually pleasing results (though not necessarily the best for all applications). The axis-aligned weak learner model produces blocky artifacts while the curvilinear model tends to extrapolate the shape of the spiral arms in a more "natural" way. Training has been achieved with $\rho = 500$ (*i.e.* randomly sampling 500 lines/curves) at all split nodes. The forest size is kept fixed at $T = 400$

test posterior for varying D (in different rows) and varying weak learner model (in different columns). All experiments are conducted with a very large number of trees ($T = 400$) to remove the effect of forest size and reach close to the maximum possible smoothness under the chosen model.

This experiment confirms again that increasing D increases the confidence of the output (for a fixed choice of weak learner). This is illustrated by the more intense colors going from the top row to the bottom row. Furthermore, we observe that the axis-aligned model may still separate the training data well, but produces large blocky artifacts in the test regions. This tends to indicate bad generalization. The oriented line model [158, 246] is a clear visual improvement, and better still is the non-linear model as it extrapolates the shape of the spiral arms in a more naturally curved manner.

On the flip side, of course, we should also consider the fact that axis-aligned tests are extremely efficient to compute. So the choice of the specific weak learner has to be based on considerations of both accuracy and efficiency and depends on

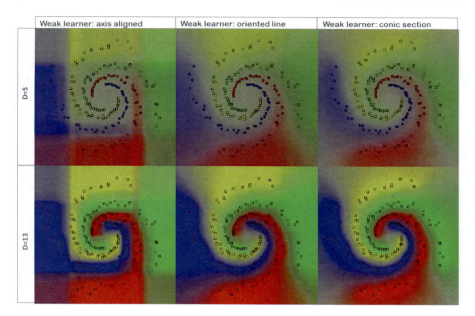

Fig. 4.8 The effect of randomness. The same set of 4-class training data is used to train six different forests, two different values of D three different weak learners. This experiment is identical to that in Fig. 4.7 except that we have used much more training randomness. In fact $\rho = 5$ for all split nodes. The forest size is kept fixed at $T = 400$. More randomness reduces the artifacts of the axis-aligned weak learner a little, as well as reducing overall prediction confidence too

the specific application at hand. Next we study the effect of randomness by running exactly the same experiment but with a much larger amount of training randomness.

4.3.5 The Effect of Randomness

Figure 4.8 shows the same experiment as in Fig. 4.7 with the only difference that now we set $\rho = 5$ as opposed to $\rho = 500$. Thus, much fewer separating lines/curves were made available to each node during training. This increases the randomness of each tree and reduces their correlation.

Larger randomness reduces the blocky artifacts of the axis-aligned weak learner and produces more rounded decision boundaries (first column in Fig. 4.8). Furthermore, larger randomness yields a much lower overall confidence. This is noticeable especially in shallower trees (the washed-out colors in the top row).

A disadvantage of the more complex weak learners is that they are sampled from a larger parameters space. Thus finding discriminative sets of parameter values may be time consuming. However, in this toy example the more complex conic section learner model works well for deeper trees ($D = 13$) even for small values of ρ (large randomness). The results reported here are only indicative. In fact, which specific weak learner to use depends on considerations of efficiency as well as accuracy, and these considerations are application dependent.

4.4 Maximum Margin Classification with Forests

The hallmark of support vector machines is their ability to separate data belonging to different classes via a margin-maximizing surface. This, in turn, yields good generalization even with relatively little training data. This section shows how this important property is replicated in random classification forests and under which conditions. Margin-maximizing properties of random forests were discussed in [211]. Here we show a different, simpler formulation, analyze the conditions that lead to margin maximization, and discuss how this property is affected by different choices of model parameters.

Imagine we are given a linearly separable 2-class training data set such as that shown in Fig. 4.9a. For simplicity here we assume $d = 2$ (only two features describe each data point), an axis-aligned weak learner model and $D = 2$ (trees are simple binary stumps). As usual randomness is injected via randomized node optimization.

When training the root node of the first tree, if we use enough candidate features/parameters (i.e. $|\mathcal{T}_0|$ is large) the selected separating line tends to be placed somewhere within the gap (see Fig. 4.9a) so as to separate the training data perfectly (achieving maximum information gain). Any position within the gap is associated with exactly the same, maximum information gain. Thus, a collection of randomly trained trees produces a set of separating lines randomly placed within the gap.

If the candidate separating lines are sampled from a uniform distribution (as is usually the case) then this would yield forest class posteriors that vary within the gap as a linear ramp, as shown in Fig. 4.9b, c. If we are interested in a hard separation then the optimal separating surface (assuming equal loss) is such that the posteriors for the two classes are identical. This corresponds to a line placed right in the middle of the gap, i.e. the maximum margin solution. Next, we describe the same concepts more formally.

We are given the two-class training points in Fig. 4.9a. In this simple example the training data is not only linearly separable, but it is perfectly separable via vertical stumps on x_1. So we constrain our weak learners to be vertical lines only, i.e.

$$h(\mathbf{v}, \boldsymbol{\theta}_j) = \left[\phi(\mathbf{v}) > \tau\right] \quad \text{with } \phi(\mathbf{v}) = x_1. \tag{4.5}$$

Under these conditions we can define the gap Δ as $\Delta = x_1'' - x_1'$, with x_1' and x_1'' corresponding to the first feature of the two "support vectors",[3] i.e. the yellow point with largest x_1 and the red point with smallest x_1. For a fixed value of x_2 the classification forest produces the posterior $p(c|x_1)$ for the two classes c_1 and c_2. The

---

[3] Analogous to support vectors in SVM.

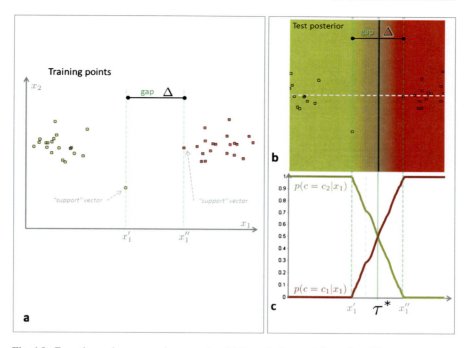

Fig. 4.9 Forest's maximum margin properties. (**a**) Input 2-class training points. They are separated by a gap of dimension Δ. (**b**) Forest posterior. Note that all of the uncertainty band resides within the gap. (**c**) Cross-sections of class posteriors along the horizontal, white dashed line in (**b**). Within the gap the class posteriors are linear functions of x_1. Since they have to sum to 1 they meet right in the middle of the gap. In these experiments we use $\rho = 500$, $D = 2$, $T = 500$ and axis aligned weak learners

optimal separating line (vertical) is at position τ^* such that

$$\tau^* = \arg\min_{\tau} \left| p(c = c_1 | x_1 = \tau) - p(c = c_2 | x_1 = \tau) \right|. \tag{4.6}$$

We make the additional assumption that when training a node its available test parameters (in this case just τ) are sampled from a uniform distribution, then the forest posteriors behave linearly within the gap region, *i.e.*

$$\lim_{\rho \to |\mathcal{T}|, T \to \infty} p(c = c_1 | x_1) = \frac{x_1 - x_1'}{\Delta}, \quad \forall x_1 \in \left[x_1', x_1'' \right] \tag{4.7}$$

(see Fig. 4.9b, c). Consequently, since $\sum_{c \in \{c_1, c_2\}} p(c | x_1) = 1$ we have

$$\lim_{\rho \to |\mathcal{T}|, T \to \infty} \tau^* = x_1' + \Delta/2 \tag{4.8}$$

which shows that the optimal separation is placed right in the middle of the gap. This demonstrates the forest's margin-maximization properties for this simple example.

Note that each individual tree is *not* guaranteed to produce maximum margin separation; it is instead the combination of multiple trees that at the limit $T \to \infty$ produces the desired max-margin behavior. In practice it suffices to have T and ρ "large enough". Furthermore, as observed earlier, for perfectly separable data each tree produces overconfident posteriors. Once again, their combination in a forest yields fully probabilistic and smooth posteriors (in contrast to SVM).

The simple mathematical derivation above provides us with some intuition on how model choices such as the amount of randomness or the type of weak learner affect the placement of the forest's separating surface. The next sections should clarify these concepts further.

4.4.1 The Effect of Randomness on Optimal Separation

The experiment in Fig. 4.9 has used a large value of ρ ($\rho \to |\mathcal{T}|$, little randomness, large tree correlation) to make sure that each tree decision boundary fell within the gap. When using more randomness (smaller ρ) then the individual trees are not guaranteed to split the data perfectly and thus they may yield a sub-optimal information gain. In turn, this yields a lower confidence in the posterior. Now, the locus of points where $p(c = c_1|x_1) = p(c = c_2|x_1)$ is no longer placed right in the middle of the gap. This is shown in the experiment in Fig. 4.10 where we can observe that by increasing the randomness (decreasing ρ) we obtain smoother and more spread-out posteriors. The optimal separating surface is less sharply defined. The effect of individual training points is weaker as compared to the entire mass of training data; and in fact, it is no longer possible to identify individual support vectors. This may be advantageous in the presence of "sloppy" or inaccurate training data.

The role of the parameter ρ is very similar to that of "slack" variables in SVM [380]. In SVM the slack variables control the influence of individual support vectors versus the rest of training data. Appropriate values of slack variables yield higher robustness with respect to training noise.

4.4.2 Influence of the Weak Learner Model

Figure 4.11 shows how more complex weak learners affect the shape and orientation of the optimal, hard classification surface (as well as the uncertain region, in orange). Once again, the position and orientation of the separation boundary is more or less sensitive to individual training points depending on the value of ρ. Little randomness produces a behavior closer to that of support vector machines.

In classification forests, using linear weak learners still produces (in general) globally non-linear classification (see the black curves in Fig. 4.10c and Fig. 4.11b). This is due to the fact that multiple simple linear split nodes are organized in a hierarchical fashion.

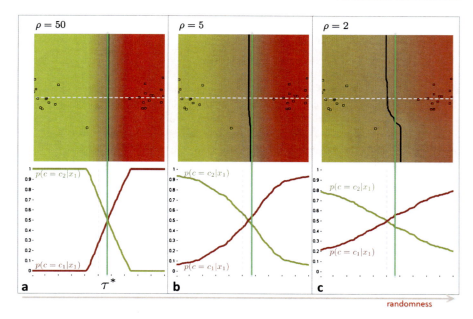

Fig. 4.10 The effect of randomness on the forest margin. (**a**) Forest posterior for $\rho = 50$ (small randomness). (**b**) Forest posterior for $\rho = 5$. (**c**) Forest posterior for $\rho = 2$ (highest randomness). These experiments have used $D = 2, T = 400$ and axis-aligned weak learners. The *bottom row* shows 1D posteriors computed along the white dashed line. Increasing randomness produces less well defined separating surfaces. The optimal separating surface, *i.e.* the loci of points where the class posteriors are equal (shown in *black*) moves towards the left of the margin-maximizing line (shown in *green* in all three experiments). As randomness increases individual training points have less influence on the separating surface

4.4.3 Maximum Margin with Multiple Classes

Since classification forests can naturally apply to more than 2 classes how does this affect their maximum margin properties? We illustrate this point with a multi-class synthetic example. In Fig. 4.12a we have a linearly separable four-class training set. On it we have trained two forests with $|\mathcal{T}_j| = 50$, $D = 3$, $T = 400$. The only difference between the two forests is the fact that the first one uses an oriented line weak learner and the second a conic weak learner. Figure 4.12b, c show the corresponding testing posteriors. As usual gray pixels indicate regions of higher posterior entropy and lower confidence. They roughly delineate the four optimal hard classification regions. Note that in both cases their boundaries are roughly placed half-way between neighboring classes. As in the 2-class case the influence of individual training points is dictated by the randomness parameter ρ.

Finally, when comparing Fig. 4.12c and Fig. 4.12b we notice that for conic learners the shape of the uncertainty region evolves in a curved fashion when moving away from training data.

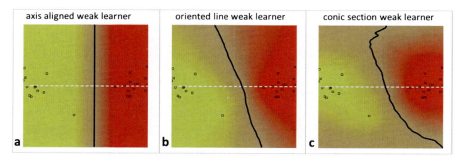

Fig. 4.11 The effect of the weak learner on forest margin. (**a**) Forest posterior for axis aligned weak learners. (**b**) Forest posterior for oriented line weak learners. (**c**) Forest posterior for conic–section weak learners. In these experiments we have used $\rho = 50$, $D = 2$, $T = 500$. The choice of weak learner affects the optimal, hard separating surface (in *black*). Individual training points influence the surface differently depending on the amount of randomness in the forest

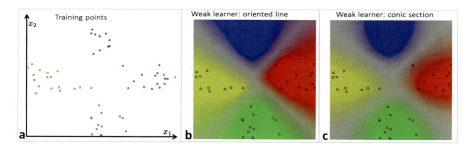

Fig. 4.12 Forest's max-margin properties for multiple classes. (**a**) Input four-class training points. (**b**) Forest posterior for oriented line weak learners. (**c**) Forest posterior for conic section weak learners. Regions of high entropy are shown as *gray bands* and correspond to loci of optimal separation. In these experiments we have used the following parameter settings: $\rho = 50$, $D = 3$, $T = 400$

4.4.4 The Effect of the Randomness Model

This section shows a direct comparison between the randomized node optimization and the bagging model.

In bagging, randomness is injected by randomly sampling different subsets of training data. So, each tree sees a different training subset. Its node parameters are then fully optimized on this set. This means that specific "support vectors" may not be available in some of the trees. The posterior associated with those trees will then tend to move the optimal separating surface away from the maximum margin one.

This is illustrated in Fig. 4.13 where we have trained two forests with $\rho = 500$, $D = 2$, $T = 400$ and two different randomness models. The forest tested in Fig. 4.13a uses randomized node optimization (RNO). The one in Fig. 4.13b uses

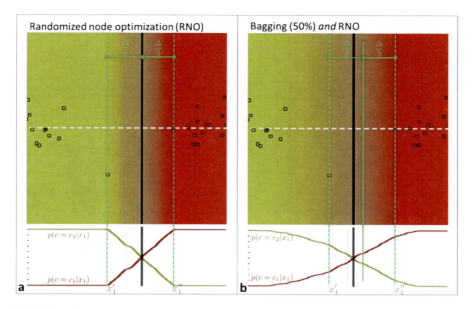

Fig. 4.13 Max-margin: bagging v randomized node optimization. (**a**) Posterior for forest trained with randomized node optimization. (**b**) Posterior for forest trained with bagging. In bagging, for each tree we use 50 % random selection of training data with replacement. Loci of optimal separation are shown as *black lines*. In these experiments we use $\rho = 500$, $D = 2$, $T = 400$ and axis-aligned weak learners. Areas of high entropy are shown in *gray* to highlight the separating surfaces

bagging (randomly selecting 50 % training data with replacement) on exactly the same training data. In bagging, when training a node, there may be a whole range of values of a certain parameter which yield maximum information gain (*e.g.* the range $[\tau_1', \tau_1'']$ for the threshold τ_1). In such a case we could decide to always select one value out of the range (*e.g.* τ_1'). But this would probably be an unfair comparison. Thus we chose to randomly select a parameter value uniformly within that range. In effect here we are combining bagging and random node optimization together. The effect is shown in Fig. 4.13b. In both cases we have used a large value of ρ to make sure that each tree achieves decent optimality in parameter selection. We observe that the introduction of training set randomization leads to smoother posteriors whose optimal boundary (shown as a vertical black line) does *not* coincide with the maximum margin (green, solid line). Of course this behavior is controlled by how much (training set) randomness we inject in the system. If we were to take all training data then we would reproduce a max-margin behavior (but it would not be bagging). One advantage of bagging is increased training speed (due to reduced training set size). More experiments and comparisons are available in [79]. In the rest of the paper we use the RNO randomness model because it allows us to use all available training data and enables us to control the maximum margin behavior simply, by means of changing ρ.

4.5 Summary

This chapter has taken the abstract decision forest model introduced in Chap. 3 and specialized it for multi-class classification. Toy experiments have illustrated the effects of various parameters on the accuracy and confidence of the predicted output, as well as the forest maximum margin classification properties. The experiments are only on synthetic data to convey the main principles of classification forests at an intuitive level. Chapters in Part II will demonstrate the use of classification forests in various practical applications. Furthermore, additional details regarding classification forests in comparison with alternative techniques such as boosting and support vector machines may be found in [80]. The reader is also invited to browse the many more examples, animations and demo videos available at [79].

4.6 Exercises and Experiments

In this section and at the end of other chapters in Part I we present a number of exercises. To complete them you need to download, compile and run the 'Sherwood' software library accompanying the book. This library can be downloaded for free from: http://research.microsoft.com/projects/decisionforests. Please refer to Chap. 22 for instructions on how to build and use the library.

Exercise 4.1

To begin, type `sw clas` in a command window to get a list of instructions.
The results of Fig. 4.3c (for $T = 8$) can be reproduced by running the following command:
```
sw clas exp1_n2.txt /d 2 /t 8
```
Note that parameter values $D = 2$ and $T = 8$ are supplied via the command line switches /d and /t. By default, $\rho = 10$ and axis-aligned split functions are used.

- Try varying the number of trees T:
  ```
  sw clas exp1_n2.txt /d 2 /t 1
  sw clas exp1_n2.txt /d 2 /t 200
  ```
  What happens? Why?
- Try running these commands several times.
  Are the results consistent across multiple runs? Why?
- Try using linear instead of axis-aligned weak learners:
  ```
  sw clas exp1_n2.txt /d 2 /t 1 /split linear
  sw clas exp1_n2.txt /d 2 /t 8 /split linear
  sw clas exp1_n2.txt /d 2 /t 200 /split linear
  ```
  What is the impact on the uncertainty region?

Exercise 4.2

Reproduce the zoomed out 4-class experiment of Fig. 4.6 by running the following command:

```
sw clas exp1_n4.txt /d 3 /t 10 /padx 2.0 /pady 2.0
```

Note that the /padx and /pady switches are used to increase the range of the plot beyond the range of the training data. The arguments are interpreted as a proportion of the training data range along the x and y axes. The plot extent is computed so as to completely contain the (padded) data.

- Try using different value for D, the maximum tree depth:
```
sw clas exp1_n4.txt /d 1 /t 1 /padx 2.0 /pady 2.0
sw clas exp1_n4.txt /d 2 /t 1 /padx 2.0 /pady 2.0
sw clas exp1_n4.txt /d 10 /t 1 /padx 2.0 /pady 2.0
```
  How many tree levels are necessary? Why?
- Try running these commands several times.
  What is the impact of varying T?
- Try using linear instead of axis aligned features:
```
          sw clas exp1_n4.txt /d 3 /t 200 /padx 2.0 /pady 2.0
/split linear
```
  What is the effect of the weak learner on the confidence region?

Exercise 4.3

Reproduce the results of Fig. 4.4a′ by running the command:
```
sw clas exp5_n2.txt /d 6 /t 200
```

- How does the confidence change when using linear split functions? What is the effect away from training points?
```
sw clas exp5_n2.txt /d 6 /t 200 /split linear
```
- What is the impact of reducing D?
```
sw clas exp5_n2.txt /d 3 /t 200 /split linear
```
- Try other values for D, both large and small.
  What do you notice about the impact of D on underfitting? Do you notice overfitting?

Exercise 4.4

Let us run the classification forest on a 4-arm spiral data:
```
sw clas exp5_n4.txt /d 8 /t 200 /split linear
```

- What is the impact of reducing D?
```
sw clas exp5_n4.txt /d 6 /t 200 /split linear
sw clas exp5_n4.txt /d 4 /t 200 /split linear
```
- Try other values for D, both large and small.
  What do you notice about the impact of D on underfitting and overfitting?

Exercise 4.5

Figures 4.7 and 4.8 illustrate the effect of varying the amount of training randomness via the parameter ρ (in Sherwood, ρ corresponds to the switch /f). Compare the results of the following two experiments:

```
sw clas exp5_n4.txt /d 8 /t 400 /f 500 /split linear
sw clas exp5_n4.txt /d 8 /t 400 /f 3 /split linear
```

What is the likely impact on generalization of increased randomness (*i.e.* small ρ)?

- Now run the experiments again using axis-aligned split functions
  ```
  sw clas exp5_n4.txt /d 8 /t 400 /f 500
  sw clas exp5_n4.txt /d 8 /t 400 /f 3
  ```
  How does the choice of weak learner interact with randomness?
- Try different values of other parameters such as T and D.

Chapter 5
Regression Forests

A. Criminisi and J. Shotton

This chapter discusses the use of decision forests for the probabilistic estimation of continuous variables. Regression forests are used for the non-linear regression of dependent variables given independent input, where both input and output may be multi-dimensional.

Regression forests are related to but less popular than their classification counterpart. Regression forests share many of the advantages of classification forests such as efficiency and flexibility. The main difference between regression and classification is that the output label to be associated with an input data point is continuous in the regression task. Therefore, the training labels also need to be continuous. Consequently, the objective function has to be adapted appropriately.

As with the other chapters we start with a brief literature survey of linear and non-linear regression techniques. We then describe the regression forest model, and finally we demonstrate its properties with a number of illustrative examples. Exercises are presented in the final section.

5.1 Non-linear Regression in the Literature

Given a set of noisy input data and associated continuous measurements, least squares techniques [30] can be used to fit a regressor, perhaps of a specified functional form (*e.g.* polynomial), which minimizes an error computed over all training points. Under this model, given a new test input the corresponding output can be estimated efficiently. The simplest incarnation of this technique is *linear* regression which, however, is not appropriate when trying to model most natural phenomena which are often non-linear [326]. Another well known issue with linear regression techniques is their sensitivity to input noise.

A. Criminisi (✉) · J. Shotton
Microsoft Research Ltd., 7 J.J. Thomson Avenue, Cambridge CB3 0FB, UK

A. Criminisi, J. Shotton (eds.), *Decision Forests for Computer Vision and
Medical Image Analysis*, Advances in Computer Vision and Pattern Recognition,
DOI 10.1007/978-1-4471-4929-3_5, © Springer-Verlag London 2013

In geometric computer vision, a popular technique for achieving robust regression via randomization is RANSAC [109, 153]. For instance the estimation of multi-view epipolar geometry and image registration transformations can be achieved in this way [153]. One disadvantage of conventional RANSAC is that its output is non-probabilistic. As will become clearer later, regression forests may be thought of as an extension of RANSAC, with little RANSAC regressors associated with each leaf node.

In machine learning, the success of support vector classification has encouraged the development of support vector regression (SVR [199, 351]). Similar to RANSAC, SVR can deal successfully with large amounts of noise. In [398] regression of clinically useful variables is achieved via ensembles of relevance vector machines (RVMs). In [420] boosted ridge regression was employed for the segmentation of the left ventricle in ultrasound images. In Bayesian machine learning, Gaussian processes [28, 305] have enjoyed much success due to their simplicity, elegance and their rigorous uncertainty modeling.

Although (non-probabilistic) regression forests were described in [44] they have only recently started to be used in computer vision and medical image analysis [70, 78, 82, 102, 133, 180, 224, 251, 309]. Recently, new techniques are emerging which demonstrate the power of performing joint classification *and* regression within the same forest framework [131, 134]. Other recent papers [84, 360] have simultaneously and independently extended regression forests by conditioning the output prediction on global variables. This gives rise to powerful *conditional* regression forests.

Next, we discuss how to specialize the generic forest model described in Chap. 3 to efficiently achieve probabilistic, non-linear regression.

5.2 Specializing the Decision Forest Model for Regression

We start with a definition of the goal of supervised regression.

Problem Statement   The regression task can be summarized as follows:

> *Given a labeled set of training data, learn a general mapping which associates previously unseen, independent test data points with their dependent, continuous output prediction.*

Like classification, the regression task is inductive, with the main difference being the continuous nature of the output. In general, a training point is denoted as a pair $(\mathbf{v}, \mathbf{y})$. Figure 5.1a provides an illustrative example of training data and associated continuous ground truth labels. A previously unseen test input (unavailable during training) is shown as a light gray circle on the x axis.

Formally, given a multivariate input $\mathbf{v}$ we wish to associate a continuous multivariate label $\mathbf{y} \in \mathbb{R}^n$. More generally, we wish to estimate the probability density

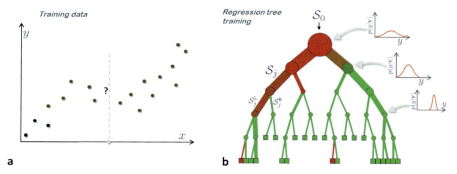

Fig. 5.1 Regression: training data and tree training. (**a**) Training data points are shown as *dark circles*. The input feature space is one-dimensional in this example, $\mathbf{v} = (x)$. The associated continuous ground truth label is denoted by their position along the direction of the y axis. The variable x is the independent input and y is the dependent output variable. A previously unseen test input (for which y is unknown) is indicated with a *light gray circle* and the *dashed gray line*. (**b**) A binary regression tree. The edge thickness is proportional to the amount of training data going through it. *Red* indicates high entropy, *green* denotes low entropy. During training a set of labeled training points $\mathcal{S}_0$ is used to optimize the parameters of the tree. In a regression tree the entropy of the continuous densities associated with different nodes decreases (their confidence increases) when going from the root towards the leaves

function $p(\mathbf{y}|\mathbf{v})$. As usual the input is represented as a multi-dimensional feature response vector $\mathbf{v} = (x_1, \ldots, x_d) \in \mathbb{R}^d$.

What Are Regression Forests?   A regression forest is a collection of randomly trained regression trees (Fig. 5.2). As with classification, it can be shown that in general a random regression forest generalizes better than a single fully optimized regression tree.

A regression tree (Fig. 5.1b) splits a complex non-linear regression problem into a set of smaller problems which can be more easily handled by simpler models (*e.g.* linear ones; see also Fig. 5.3). Next, we specify the precise nature of each model component.

5.2.1 The Prediction Model

The first job of a decision tree is to decide to which branch to direct the incoming data. But when the data reach a terminal node then that leaf needs to make a prediction.

The actual form of the prediction depends on the leaf prediction model. In classification we have used the pre-stored empirical class posterior as the model. In regression forests we have a few alternatives, as illustrated in Fig. 5.3. For instance we could use a polynomial function of the input $\mathbf{v}$. In the low-dimensional example shown in the figure, a generic polynomial model corresponds to $y(x) = \sum_{i=0}^{n} w_i x^i$. This simple model also captures the linear and constant models (see Fig. 5.3a, b).

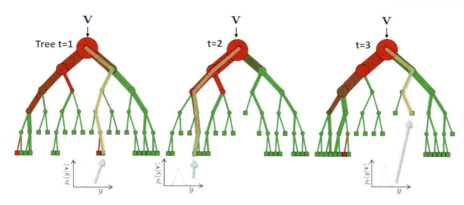

Fig. 5.2 Regression forest: the ensemble model. The regression forest posterior is simply the average of all individual tree posteriors: $p(\mathbf{y}|\mathbf{v}) = \frac{1}{T} \sum_{t=1}^{T} p_t(\mathbf{y}|\mathbf{v})$

In this book we are interested in output confidence as well as its actual value. Thus for prediction we can use a probability density function over the continuous variable $\mathbf{y}$. Given the tth tree in a forest and an input point $\mathbf{v}$, the associated leaf output takes the form $p_t(\mathbf{y}|\mathbf{v})$. In the low-dimensional example in Fig. 5.3c we assume an underlying linear model of type $y = w_0 + w_1 x$ and each leaf yields the conditional $p(y|x)$ (see below). Note that in general the leaf probability $p_t(\mathbf{y}|\mathbf{v})$ can be multi-modal. For example it might be obtained by fitting a Gaussian Mixture Model (GMM) to the training data arriving at that leaf.

5.2.2 The Ensemble Model

Just like in classification, the forest output is the average of all tree outputs (Fig. 5.2):

$$p(\mathbf{y}|\mathbf{v}) = \frac{1}{T} \sum_{t}^{T} p_t(\mathbf{y}|\mathbf{v}). \tag{5.1}$$

A practical justification for this averaging model was presented in Sect. 3.4, and viable alternatives exist.

5.2.3 Randomness Model

As for classification, here we also use a randomized node optimization model. Therefore, the amount of randomness is controlled during training by the parameter $\rho = |\mathcal{T}_j|$. The random subsets of split parameters $\mathcal{T}_j$ can be generated on the fly when training the jth node.

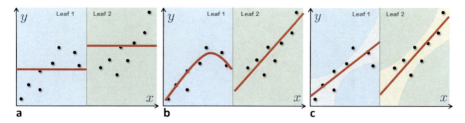

Fig. 5.3 Example predictor models. (**a**) Constant function. (**b**) Polynomial and linear functions. (**c**) Probabilistic linear model, which returns the conditional distribution $p(y|x)$. The confidence of the prediction is denoted with the *shaded area*

5.2.4 The Training Objective Function

Forest training is achieved by optimizing an energy function defined over a training set $\mathcal{S}_0$ of data and associated continuous labels. Therefore, restating (3.13), a split node j is optimized as

$$\boldsymbol{\theta}_j = \arg\max_{\boldsymbol{\theta} \in \mathcal{T}_j} I(\mathcal{S}_j, \boldsymbol{\theta}). \tag{5.2}$$

The main difference between classification and regression forests is in the form of the objective function I.

In [45] regression trees are trained by minimizing a least-squares or least-absolute error function. Here, for consistency with our general forest model we employ a continuous formulation of information gain which makes use of the functional form of the differential entropy of a Gaussian density.

In a generic decision forest the information gain associated with the jth split node is

$$I(\mathcal{S}_j, \boldsymbol{\theta}) = H(\mathcal{S}_j) - \sum_{i \in \{\mathrm{L,R}\}} \frac{|\mathcal{S}_j^i|}{|\mathcal{S}_j|} H(\mathcal{S}_j^i). \tag{5.3}$$

As usual, $\mathcal{S}_j$ indicates the set of training data arriving at node j, and $\mathcal{S}_j^{\mathrm{L}}, \mathcal{S}_j^{\mathrm{R}}$ the left and right split sets.

Next, we derive the specific form of *regression* information gain for the case of 1D input x and 1D output y. We use uni-variate variables for simplicity of exposition (see also Fig. 5.4). Given a training set $\mathcal{S}_0$, the average entropy for a generic training subset $\mathcal{S}$ is defined as

$$H(\mathcal{S}) = -\frac{1}{|\mathcal{S}|} \sum_{x \in \mathcal{S}} \int_y p(y|x) \log p(y|x) \, dy. \tag{5.4}$$

We model the conditional probability $p(y|x)$ as the following Gaussian distribution:

$$p(y|x) = N\big(y; \overline{y}(x), \sigma_y^2(x)\big). \tag{5.5}$$

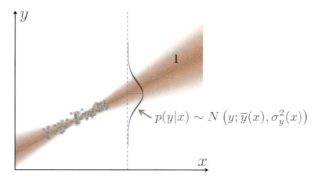

Fig. 5.4 Probabilistic line fitting. Given a set of training points we can fit a line **l** to them, *e.g.* by least squares or RANSAC. In this example $\mathbf{l} \in \mathbb{R}^2$. Matrix perturbation theory enables us to estimate a probabilistic model of **l** from where we can derive $p(y|x)$ (modeled here as a Gaussian) [80]. Training a regression tree involves minimizing the uncertainty of the prediction $p(y|x)$ over the training set. Therefore, the training objective is a function of σ_y^2 evaluated at the training points

As an example, the function $\bar{y}(x)$ could be linear. By substituting (5.5) in (5.4) we obtain

$$H(\mathcal{S}) = \frac{1}{|\mathcal{S}|} \sum_{x \in \mathcal{S}} \frac{1}{2} \log\big((2\pi e)^2 \sigma_y^2(x)\big) \tag{5.6}$$

which when plugged into (5.3) yields the following form of information gain:

$$I(\mathcal{S}_j, \boldsymbol{\theta}) \propto \sum_{x \in \mathcal{S}_j} \log\big(\sigma_y(x)\big) - \sum_{i \in \{\text{L,R}\}} \left(\sum_{x \in \mathcal{S}_j^i} \log\big(\sigma_y(x)\big) \right) \tag{5.7}$$

up to a constant scale factor which has no influence over the node optimization procedure and can be ignored for the purposes of forest training. The variance σ_y^2 is the conditional variance computed from probabilistic linear fitting (see also Fig. 5.4).

Above, we have derived the regression information gain for the simpler case of 1D input and output. It is easy to upgrade the derivation to multivariate variables, yielding the more general regression information gain below:

$$I(\mathcal{S}_j, \boldsymbol{\theta}) = \sum_{\mathbf{v} \in \mathcal{S}_j} \log\big(|\Lambda_{\mathbf{y}}(\mathbf{v})|\big) - \sum_{i \in \{\text{L,R}\}} \left(\sum_{\mathbf{v} \in \mathcal{S}_j^i} \log\big(|\Lambda_{\mathbf{y}}(\mathbf{v})|\big) \right) \tag{5.8}$$

with $\Lambda_{\mathbf{y}}$ the conditional covariance matrix computed from probabilistic linear fitting. Note that (5.8) is valid only for the case of a probabilistic linear prediction model (Fig. 5.3c and Fig. 5.4).

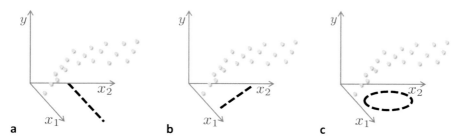

Fig. 5.5 Example weak learners. The (x_1, x_2) plane represents the d-dimensional input domain (independent). The y space represents the n-dimensional continuous output (dependent). The example types of weak learner are like in classification: (**a**) axis-aligned hyperplane; (**b**) generic oriented hyperplane; (**c**) conic section. Alternative weak learners may be considered

By comparison, the "error or fit" energy function used in [45] (for single-variate output y) is

$$\sum_{v \in \mathcal{S}_j} (y - \overline{y}_j)^2 - \sum_{i \in \{L, R\}} \left(\sum_{v \in \mathcal{S}_j^i} (y - \overline{y}_j^i)^2 \right), \tag{5.9}$$

with $\overline{y}_j$ indicating the (constant) mean value of y for all training points reaching the jth node. Note that (5.9) is closely related to (5.8) but limited to constant predictors. The formulation in (5.9) is related to the trace of the covariance matrix rather than its determinant, and thus it may be more robust in the case of very small variances. However, (5.9) produces a point estimate of y rather than a fully probabilistic output. Finally, in (5.8) using an information theoretic formulation allows us to view classification and regression forests as instances of the same, abstract forest model.

To fully characterize our regression forest model we still need to decide how to split the data arriving at an internal node.

5.2.5 The Weak Learner Model

As usual, the data arriving at a split node j are separated into its left and right children (see Fig. 5.1b) according to a binary weak learner of the following form:

$$h(\mathbf{v}, \boldsymbol{\theta}_j) \in \{0, 1\}, \tag{5.10}$$

with 0 indicating "false" (*e.g.* go left) and 1 indicating "true" (*e.g.* go right). Like in classification here we consider three types of weak learners: (i) axis-aligned hyperplanes, (ii) oriented hyperplanes, (iii) conic sections (see Fig. 5.5 for an illustration on 2D→1D regression). Many alternative weak learner models may be considered.

Next, a number of experiments will illustrate how regression forests work in practice and the effect of different model choices.

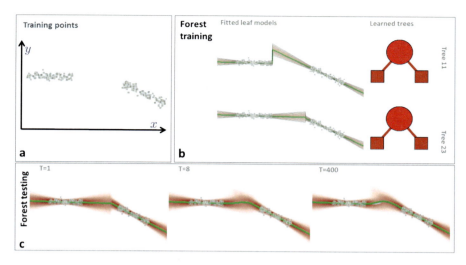

Fig. 5.6 The effect of the forest size T. (**a**) Training points. (**b**) Two different shallow trained trees ($D = 2$) split the data into two portions and produce disjoint piece-wise probabilistic linear predictions. (**c**) Testing posteriors evaluated for all values of x and increasing number of trees. The *green curve* denotes the conditional mean $\mathcal{E}[y|x] = \int y \cdot p(y|x)\,dy$. The mean curve corresponding to a single tree ($T = 1$) shows a sharp change of direction in the gap. Increasing the forest size produces smoother class posteriors $p(y|x)$ and smoother mean curves in the interpolated region. All examples have been run with $D = 2$, axis-aligned weak learners and probabilistic linear prediction models

5.3 Effect of Model Parameters

This section discusses the effect of model choices such as the tree depth D, the forest size T, and the weak learner model on the forest output.

5.3.1 The Effect of the Forest Size

Figure 5.6 shows a first, simple example. We are given the training points shown in Fig. 5.6a. We can think of those as being randomly drawn from two segments with different orientations. Each point has a one-dimensional input feature x and a corresponding scalar, continuous output label y.

A forest of shallow trees ($D = 2$) and varying size T is trained on those points. We use axis-aligned weak learners, and probabilistic linear predictor models. The trained trees are all slightly different from each other as they produce different leaf models (Fig. 5.6b). During training, as expected each leaf model produces smaller uncertainty near the training points and larger uncertainty away from them. In the gap, the actual split happens in different places (due to randomness) along the x axis for different trees.

The bottom row (Fig. 5.6c) shows the regression posteriors evaluated for *all* test positions along the x axis. For each x position we plot the entire distribution $p(y|x)$, where darker red indicates larger values of the posterior. Thus, compact, dark red regions correspond to higher prediction confidence. Washed out, lighter colors correspond to higher uncertainty.

The mean prediction curve is computed as

$$\overline{y}(x) = \mathcal{E}[y|x] = \int y \cdot p(y|x)\, dy, \tag{5.11}$$

with $\mathcal{E}$ denoting expectation. The curve $\overline{y}(\cdot)$ is shown in green in the figure. Note how a single tree produces a sharp change in direction of the mean curve in the large gap between the training clusters. However, as the number of trees increases both the prediction mean curve and its uncertainty become smoother. Thus smoothness of the interpolating curve is controlled here by the forest size T. We can also observe how the uncertainty increases as we move away from the training data (both in the interpolated gap and in the extrapolated regions).

5.3.2 The Effect of the Tree Depth

Figure 5.7 shows the effect of varying the maximum allowed tree depth D on the same training set as in Fig. 5.6. A regression forest with $D = 1$ (top row in figure) corresponds to conventional linear regression (with additional confidence estimation). In this case the training data are more complex than a single line and thus such a degenerate forest under-fits. In contrast, a forest of depth $D = 5$ (bottom row in the figure) yields over-fitting. This is highlighted in the figure by the high-frequency variations in the predicted mean $\overline{y}(\cdot)$ and the associated confidence.

5.3.3 Spatial Smoothness and Testing Uncertainty

Figure 5.8 shows four more experiments. Here we plot both the mean prediction (in green) and the mode

$$\hat{y}(x) = \arg\max_{y} p(y|x) \tag{5.12}$$

in gray. These experiments highlight the smooth interpolating behavior of the mean prediction in contrast to the more jagged nature of the mode.[1] The uncertainty increases away from training data. Finally, notice how in the gaps the regression forest can correctly capture multi-modal posteriors. This is highlighted by the difference between mode and mean predictions. In all experiments we used a probabilistic linear predictor with axis-aligned weak learner, $T = 400$ and $D = 7$.

---

[1]The smoothness of the mean curve is a function of T. In general, the larger the forest size the smoother the mean prediction curve.

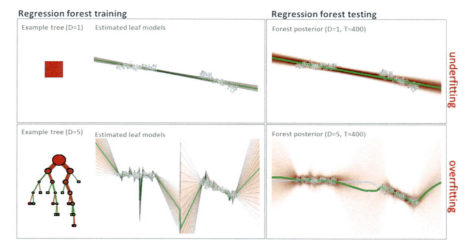

Fig. 5.7 The effect of tree depth. (*Top row*) Regression forest trained with $D = 1$. Trees are degenerate (each tree corresponds only to their root node). This corresponds to conventional linear regression. In this case the data cannot be explained well by a single linear model and thus this forest under-fits. (*Bottom row*) Regression forest trained with $D = 5$. Much deeper trees produce the opposite effect, *i.e.* over-fitting. This is evident in the high-frequency, spiky nature of the testing posterior. In both experiments we use $T = 400$, axis-aligned weak learners, and probabilistic linear prediction models

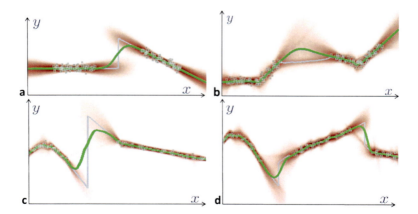

Fig. 5.8 Regression smoothness, multi-modal posteriors and testing confidence. Four more regression experiments. The *gray squares* indicate labeled training data points. The *green curve* is the estimated conditional mean $\overline{y}(x) = \mathcal{E}[y|x] = \int y \cdot p(y|x) \, dy$ and the *light gray curve* the estimated mode $\hat{y}(x) = \arg\max_y p(y|x)$. Note the smooth interpolating behavior of the mean over large gaps and increased uncertainty away from training data. The forest is capable of capturing multi-modal behavior in the gaps

5.4 Summary

This chapter has taken the abstract decision forest model introduced in Chap. 3 and specialized it for regression. Toy experiments have illustrated the effects of various parameters on the accuracy and confidence of the predicted output. The experiments are only on synthetic data to convey the main principles of regression forests at an intuitive level. A more thorough investigation of regression forests is beyond the scope of Part I, though the chapters in Part II of this book will demonstrate the use of regression forests in various practical applications. The reader is also invited to refer to [80], which contains further analysis of the properties of regression forests, as well as a direct comparison with alternative regression techniques such as Gaussian processes. Many more examples, animations, and videos are available at [79].

5.5 Exercises and Experiments

Here are a few exercises to allow the reader to gain familiarity with regression forests. The Sherwood library necessary for the experiments may be downloaded from http://research.microsoft.com/projects/decisionforests, and is described in Chap. 22.

Exercise 5.1

To begin, type `sw regression` in a command window to get a list of instructions.
To reproduce the results of Fig. 5.6 run the following command:

```
sw regression exp2.txt /d 2 /t 100
```

- What is the effect of varying T?

```
sw regression exp2.txt /d 2 /t 1
sw regression exp2.txt /d 2 /t 5
```

- What is the effect of changing D (with fixed $T = 100$)?

```
sw regression exp2.txt /d 1 /t 100
sw regression exp2.txt /d 4 /t 100
sw regression exp2.txt /d 6 /t 100
```

When do you observe under- or over-fitting?

Exercise 5.2

Reproduce the results in Fig. 5.8a by running the command:

```
sw regression exp3.txt /d 2 /t 200
```

- Try to answer the same questions as in Exercise 5.1.
- Try using a similar but more noisy training dataset:

```
sw regression exp4.txt /d 2 /t 200
```

How does the prediction confidence change?

Exercise 5.3

Reproduce Fig. 5.8b and Fig. 5.8d by running the following commands:

```
sw regression exp7.txt /d 4 /t 200
sw regression exp8.txt /d 4 /t 200
sw regression exp9.txt /d 4 /t 200
sw regression exp10.txt /d 4 /t 200
```

- Again, explore using different parameter values for D and T.
  What impact do these parameters have on over- and under-fitting?

Exercise 5.4

Now run the following command:

```
sw regression exp11.txt /d 4 /t 200
```

and try various parameters values.

Is there a set of parameters for which the regression forest works well in the central part of this "S"-shaped dataset?

Why do you think this regression model does not work properly in the central part?

How is the confidence different between the sides (noisy but unambiguous training data) and the central part (ambiguous training data)?

How could one improve on this current regression model, *e.g.* by fitting multiple lines at each leaf node?

You can refer to [80] for answers to some of these questions.

Chapter 6
Density Forests

A. Criminisi and J. Shotton

Chapters 4 and 5 have discussed the use of decision forests in supervised tasks, *i.e.* when *labeled* training data are available. In contrast, this chapter discusses the use of forests in unlabeled scenarios. For instance, one important task is that of discovering the "intrinsic nature" and structure of large sets of unlabeled data. This task can be tackled via another probabilistic model, the density forest.

Density forests are explained here as an instantiation of our abstract decision forest model as described in Chap. 3. Given some observed unlabeled data which we assume have been generated from an underlying probabilistic density function, we wish to estimate the unobserved generative model itself. More formally, one wishes to learn the probability density function $p(\mathbf{v})$ which has generated the data. The problem of density estimation is closely related to that of data clustering. Although much research has gone into tree-based clustering algorithms, to our knowledge this is the first time that ensembles of randomized trees have been used for density estimation.

We begin with a brief literature survey, then we show how to adapt the generic forest model to the density estimation task and then illustrate advantages and disadvantages of density forests. The experiments presented in this chapter are only illustrative and they do not claim to prove the superiority of density forests with respect to more established techniques. However, they suggest density estimation as a possible use of forests, in addition to its more common classification and regression applications. The flexibility of our decision forest model is one of its major strengths and a key message in this book.

6.1 Density Estimation in the Literature

Here we discuss only a few representative papers out of the vast literature on density estimation.

A. Criminisi (✉) · J. Shotton
Microsoft Research Ltd., 7 J.J. Thomson Avenue, Cambridge CB3 0FB, UK

A. Criminisi, J. Shotton (eds.), *Decision Forests for Computer Vision and Medical Image Analysis*, Advances in Computer Vision and Pattern Recognition, DOI 10.1007/978-1-4471-4929-3_6, © Springer-Verlag London 2013

A successful and commonly used probabilistic density model is the Gaussian mixture model (GMM), where complex distributions can be approximated via a collection of simple (multivariate) Gaussian components [28, 195]. Typically, the parameters of a Gaussian mixture are estimated via the well known Expectation Maximization (EM) algorithm [28, 88]. EM can be thought of as a probabilistic variant of the popular k-means clustering algorithm [227]. There is a close relationship between the problem of data clustering and that of density estimation.

Popular, non-parametric density estimation techniques are kernel-based algorithms such as the Parzen–Rosenblatt windows estimator [282]. The advantage of kernel-based estimation over *e.g.* more crude histogram-based techniques is in the added smoothness of the reconstruction which can be controlled by the kernel parameters. Closely related is the k-nearest neighbor density estimation algorithm [28].

In Breiman's seminal work on forests the author mentions using forests for clustering unsupervised data [44]. However, this goal is achieved via classification, by introducing dummy additional classes (see also [335]). In contrast, here we use a well defined information gain-based optimization, which fits well within our unified forest model. The work in [258] uses an information-theoretic, single-tree-based clustering approach. Forest-based data clustering has been discussed in [253, 341] for computer vision applications and will be discussed further in Part II.

A closely related paper is the one in [304], where the authors use single trees for non-parametric density estimation. There, tree training is achieved by minimizing an Integrated Squared Error loss function. The binary tree constructed this way produces an asymptotically consistent and efficient density estimator. Our work on density forests can be seen as an extension of the ideas set out in [304] to ensembles of trees. In the spirit of our general forest model the training objective function is an information-theoretical one, and overfitting is mitigated by the use of multiple randomly trained trees.

For further reading on general density estimation techniques the reader is invited to explore the material in [28, 347].

6.2 Specializing the Forest Model for Density Estimation

This section specializes the generic forest model of Chap. 3 for use in density estimation.

Problem Statement   The density estimation task can be summarized as follows:

> *Given a set of unlabeled observations we wish to estimate the probability density function from which such data have been generated.*

Each input data point $\mathbf{v}$ is represented as usual as a multi-dimensional feature response vector $\mathbf{v} = (x_1, \ldots, x_d) \in \mathbb{R}^d$. The desired output is the entire probability density function $p(\mathbf{v}) \geq 0$ s.t. $\int p(\mathbf{v})\,d\mathbf{v} = 1$, for any generic input $\mathbf{v}$. An explanatory illustration is shown in Fig. 6.1a. Unlabeled training data points are denoted with dark circles, while white circles indicate previously unseen test data.

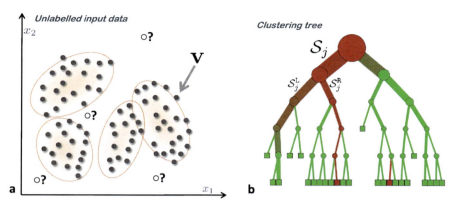

Fig. 6.1 Input data and density forest training. (**a**) Unlabeled data points used for training a density forest are shown as *dark circles*. *White circles* indicate previously unseen test data. The *red ellipses* indicate clusters associated with leaves in a clustering tree. (**b**) Density forests are ensembles of clustering trees. As usual the edge thickness is proportional to the amount of training data through the edge itself. The *red* and *green colors* denote large or small entropy, respectively

What Are Density Forests?   A density forest is a collection of randomly trained clustering trees (Fig. 6.1b). The tree leaves contain simple prediction models such as Gaussians. So, loosely speaking a density forest can be thought of as a generalization of Gaussian mixture models (GMM) with two differences: (i) multiple hard clustered data partitions are created, one for each tree. This is in contrast to the single soft clustering generated by the EM algorithm. (ii) The forest posterior is a combination of tree posteriors. So, each input data point is explained by multiple clusters (one per tree). This is in contrast to the single linear combination of Gaussians in a GMM. These concepts will become clearer later. Next, we delve into a detailed description of the model components, starting with the objective function.

6.2.1 The Training Objective Function

Given a collection of points $\mathcal{S}_0 = \{\mathbf{v}\}$ (note the absence of training labels here), we train each individual tree in the forest independently. As usual we employ randomized node optimization. Thus, restating (3.13) and (3.7), optimizing the jth split node is done as the following maximization:

$$\boldsymbol{\theta}_j = \arg\max_{\boldsymbol{\theta} \in \mathcal{T}_j} I(\mathcal{S}_j, \boldsymbol{\theta}) \qquad (6.1)$$

with the generic information gain I defined as

$$I(\mathcal{S}_j, \boldsymbol{\theta}) = H(\mathcal{S}_j) - \sum_{i=\{\mathrm{L,R}\}} \frac{|\mathcal{S}_j^i|}{|\mathcal{S}_j|} H(\mathcal{S}_j^i). \qquad (6.2)$$

Now we need to define the exact form of the entropy $H(S)$ of a set of points S. Unlike classification and regression, here the are no ground truth labels. Thus, we need to define an *unsupervised* entropy, *i.e.* one which applies to unlabeled data. As with a GMM, we use the working assumption of multivariate Gaussian distributions at the nodes of a clustering tree. Then, the differential (continuous) entropy of a d-dimensional Gaussian can be shown to be

$$H(S) = \frac{1}{2} \log\big((2\pi e)^d |\Lambda(S)|\big) \qquad (6.3)$$

with Λ the associated $d \times d$ covariance matrix. Consequently, the information gain in (6.2) reduces to

$$I(S_j, \boldsymbol{\theta}) = \log\big(|\Lambda(S_j)|\big) - \sum_{i \in \{L,R\}} \frac{|S_j^i|}{|S_j|} \log\big(|\Lambda(S_j^i)|\big) \qquad (6.4)$$

with $|\cdot|$ indicating a determinant for matrix arguments, or cardinality for set arguments.

Discussion For a set of data points in feature space, the determinant of the covariance matrix is a function of the volume of the ellipsoid corresponding to that cluster. Therefore, by maximizing (6.4) the tree training procedure tends to split the original dataset S_0 into a number of compact clusters (see Fig. 6.1a). The centers of those clusters tends to be placed in areas of high data density, while the separating surfaces are placed along regions of low density.

Finally, our derivation of density-based information gain in (6.4) builds upon an assumption of Gaussian distribution at the nodes. Of course, this is not realistic as real data may be distributed in much more complex ways. However, this assumption is useful in practice as it yields a simple and efficient objective function. Furthermore, the hierarchical nature of the trees allows us to construct very complex distributions by mixing the individual Gaussians base functions associated at the leaves. Alternative measures of "cluster compactness" may also be employed.

6.2.2 The Prediction Model

The set of leaves in the tth tree in a forest defines a partition of the data such that

$$l(\mathbf{v}) : \mathbb{R}^d \to \mathcal{L} \subset \mathbb{N} \qquad (6.5)$$

where $l(\mathbf{v})$ denotes the leaf reached (deterministically) by the input point $\mathbf{v}$, and $\mathcal{L}$ the set of all leaves in a given tree (the tree index t is not shown here to avoid cluttering the notation). The statistics of all training points arriving at each leaf node

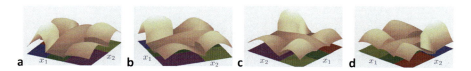

Fig. 6.2 A tree density is piece-wise Gaussian. (**a**, **b**, **c**, **d**) Different views of a tree density $p_t(\mathbf{v})$ defined over an illustrative 2D feature space. Each individual Gaussian component is defined over the bounded partition cell associated with the corresponding tree leaf. See text for details

are summarized by a single multivariate Gaussian distribution $\mathcal{N}(\mathbf{v}; \boldsymbol{\mu}_{l(\mathbf{v})}, \Lambda_{l(\mathbf{v})})$ estimated here via maximum likelihood.[1] Then, the output of the tth tree is

$$p_t(\mathbf{v}) = \frac{\pi_{l(\mathbf{v})}}{Z_t} \, \mathcal{N}(\mathbf{v}; \boldsymbol{\mu}_{l(\mathbf{v})}, \Lambda_{l(\mathbf{v})}). \qquad (6.6)$$

The vector $\boldsymbol{\mu}_l$ denotes the mean of all points reaching the leaf l and Λ_l the associated covariance matrix. The scalar π_l is the proportion of all training points that reach the leaf l, *i.e.* $\pi_l = \frac{|S_l|}{|S_0|}$. Thus (6.6) defines a piece-wise Gaussian density (see Fig. 6.2 for an illustration).

The Partition Function   Note that in (6.6) each Gaussian is truncated by the boundaries of the partition cell associated with the corresponding leaf (see Fig. 6.2). Thus, in order to ensure probabilistic normalization we need to incorporate the partition function Z_t, which is defined as follows:

$$Z_t = \int_{\mathbf{v}} \left(\sum_l \pi_l \mathcal{N}(\mathbf{v}; \boldsymbol{\mu}_l, \Lambda_l) p(l|\mathbf{v}) \right) d\mathbf{v}. \qquad (6.7)$$

However, in a density forest each data point reaches exactly *one* terminal node per tree. Thus, the conditional $p(l|\mathbf{v})$ is a delta function $p(l|\mathbf{v}) = \delta(l = l(\mathbf{v}))$ and consequently (6.7) becomes

$$Z_t = \int_{\mathbf{v}} \pi_{l(\mathbf{v})} \mathcal{N}(\mathbf{v}; \boldsymbol{\mu}_{l(\mathbf{v})}, \Lambda_{l(\mathbf{v})}) \, d\mathbf{v}. \qquad (6.8)$$

As it is often the case when dealing with generative models, computing Z_t in high dimensions may be challenging.

In the case of axis-aligned weak learners it is possible to compute the partition function via the cumulative multivariate normal distribution function. In fact, the partition function Z_t is the sum of all the volumes subtended by each Gaussian cropped by its associated partition cell (cuboidal in shape, see Fig. 6.2). Unfortunately, the cumulative multivariate normal does not have a closed form solution. However, approximating its functional form is a well-researched problem and a number of good numerical approximations exist [148, 292].

---

[1] Better alternatives, perhaps incorporating priors, may be employed here.

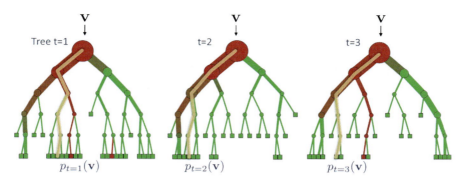

Fig. 6.3 Density forest: the ensemble model. A density forest is a collection of clustering trees trained on unlabeled data. The tree density is the Gaussian associated with the leaf reached by the input test point: $p_t(\mathbf{v})$. The forest density is the average of all tree densities

For more complex weak learners it may be easier to approximate Z_t by numerical integration over a regular grid, *i.e.*

$$Z_t \approx \Delta \cdot \sum_i \pi_{l(\mathbf{v}_i)} \, \mathcal{N}(\mathbf{v}_i; \, \boldsymbol{\mu}_{l(\mathbf{v}_i)}, \Lambda_{l(\mathbf{v}_i)}), \tag{6.9}$$

with the points $\mathbf{v}_i$ generated on a finite regular grid with spacing Δ (where Δ represents a length, area, volume *etc.* depending on the dimensionality of the domain). Also, in general smaller grid cells may yield more accurate approximations of the partition function at a greater computational cost. Recent, Monte Carlo-based techniques for approximating the partition function are also a possibility [263, 349]. Note that estimating the partition function is necessary only at training time. One may also think of using density forests with a predictor model other than Gaussian.

6.2.3 The Ensemble Model

Similar to classification and regression, the forest density is given by the average of all tree densities

$$p(\mathbf{v}) = \frac{1}{T} \sum_{t=1}^{T} p_t(\mathbf{v}), \tag{6.10}$$

with each tree density $p_t(\mathbf{v})$ defined in (6.6). An illustration is shown in Fig. 6.3.

6.2.4 Discussion

There are similarities and differences between the probabilistic density model defined above and a conventional Gaussian mixture model. For instance, both models are built upon Gaussian components. However, given a single tree, an input point $\mathbf{v}$ belongs *deterministically* to only one of its leaves, and thus only one domain-

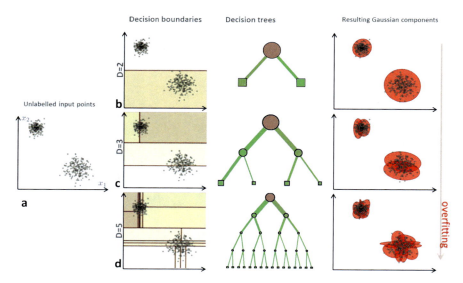

Fig. 6.4 The effect of tree depth on density. (**a**) Input unlabeled data points in a 2D feature space. (**b, c, d**) Individual trees out of three density forests trained on the same dataset, for different tree depths D. A forest with unnecessarily deep trees tends to fit to the training noise, thus producing very small, high-frequency artifacts in the estimated density

bounded Gaussian component. In a forest with T trees a point $\mathbf{v}$ belongs to T components, one per tree. The ensemble model (6.10) induces a uniform "mixing" across the different trees. The benefits of such forest-based mixture model will become clearer in the next section. The parameters of a GMM are typically learned via Expectation Maximization (EM). In contrast, the parameters of a density forest are learned via a greedy information gain maximization criterion. Both algorithms may suffer from local minima.

6.3 Effect of Model Parameters

This section studies the effect of the forest model parameters on the output density. We use many illustrative, synthetic examples, designed to bring to life different properties, advantages and disadvantages of density forests compared to alternative techniques. We begin by investigating the effect of two of the most important parameters: the tree depth D and the forest size T.

6.3.1 The Effect of Tree Depth

Figure 6.4 presents density forest results obtained on simple toy data. Figure 6.4a shows some unlabeled points used to train the forest. The points are randomly drawn from two well separated 2D Gaussian distributions.

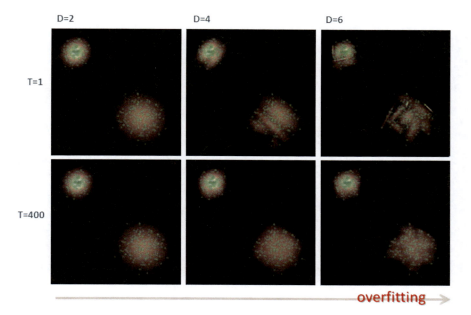

Fig. 6.5 The effect of forest size on density. Densities $p(\mathbf{v})$ for six density forests trained on the same unlabeled dataset for varying T and D. Increasing the forest size T always improves the smoothness of the density and the forest generalization, even for deep trees

Three different density forests have been trained on the same input set with $T = 200$ and varying tree depth D. In all cases the weak learner model was of the axis-aligned type. Trees of depth 2 (stumps) produce a binary partition of the training data which, in this simple example, produce perfect separation. As usual the trees are all slightly different from one another, corresponding to different decision boundaries (not shown in the figure). In all cases each leaf is associated with a bounded Gaussian distribution learned from the training points arriving at the leaf itself. We can observe that deeper trees (*e.g.* for $D = 5$) tend to create further splits and smaller Gaussians, leading to overfitting on this simple dataset. Deeper trees tend to "fit to the noise" of the training data, rather than capture the underlying nature of the data. In this simple example $D = 2$ (top row) produces the best visual results.

As illustrated in the accompanying "Sherwood" software library (see Chap. 22), the effect of tree depth on overfitting may be mitigated by careful use of Wishart priors when estimating the leaf Gaussians. Details are omitted here.

6.3.2 The Effect of Forest Size

Figure 6.5 shows the output of six density forests trained on the input data in Fig. 6.4a for two different values of T and three values of D. The images visualize

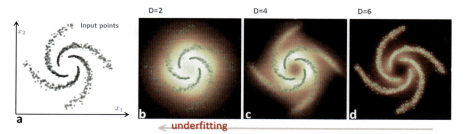

Fig. 6.6 Density forest applied to a spiral data distribution. (**a**) Input unlabeled data points in their 2D feature space. (**b, c, d**) Forest densities for different tree depths D. The original training points are overlaid in *green*. The complex distribution of input data points is captured nicely by a deeper forest, *e.g.* $D = 6$, while shallower trees produce under-fitted, overly smooth densities

the output density $p(\mathbf{v})$ computed for all points in a square subset of the feature space. Dark pixels indicate low values and bright pixels high values of density.

We observe that even if individual trees heavily over-fit (*e.g.* for $D = 6$), the addition of further trees tends to produce smoother densities. This is thanks to the randomness of each tree density estimation and reinforces the benefits of using an ensemble model. The tendency of larger forests to produce better generalization has been observed also for classification and regression and it is an important characteristic of forests. Since increasing T always produces better results (sometimes at an increased computational cost) in practical applications we can just set T to a "sufficiently large" value, without worrying too much about optimizing its value.

6.3.3 More Complex Examples

A more complex example is shown in Fig. 6.6. The noisy input data are organized in the shape of a four-arm spiral (Fig. 6.6a). Three density forests are trained on the same dataset with $T = 200$ and varying depth D. The corresponding densities are shown in Fig. 6.6b, c, d. Here, due to the greater complexity of the input data distribution shallower trees yield under-fitting, *i.e.* overly smooth and detail-lacking density estimates. In this example visually plausible results are obtained for $D = 6$ as the density nicely captures the individuality of the four spiral arms while avoiding fitting to high-frequency noise. Just like in classification and regression, the parameter D can be used to compromise between the output smoothness and the ability to capture structural details.

6.4 Comparison with Alternative Algorithms

So far we have described the density forest model and analyzed some of its properties on synthetic examples. This section presents some qualitative comparisons between density forests and alternative parametric and non-parametric techniques.

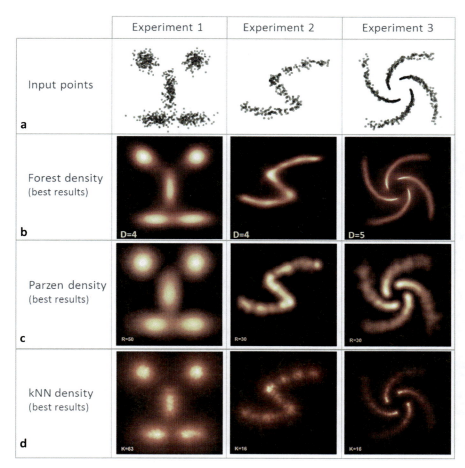

Fig. 6.7 Comparison between density forests and non-parametric estimators. (**a**) Input unlabeled points for three different experiments. (**b**) Forest-based densities. Forests were computed with $T = 200$ and varying depth D. (**c**) Parzen window densities (with Gaussian kernel). (**d**) K-nearest neighbor densities. For all algorithms, parameters were optimized to achieve visually smoothest results. The forest density (**b**) appears considerably smoother than both (**c**) and (**d**)

6.4.1 Comparison with Non-parametric Estimators

Figure 6.7 shows a visual comparison between forest density, Parzen window estimation and k-nearest neighbor density estimation. The comparison is run on the same three datasets of input points. In the first experiments points are randomly drawn from a five-Gaussian mixture. In the second they are arranged along an "S" shape and in the third they are arranged along four short spiral arms. Comparison between the forest densities in Fig. 6.7b and the corresponding non-parametric densities in Fig. 6.7c, d shows visually smoother results for the forest output. Both the Parzen and the nearest neighbor estimators produce artifacts due to hard choices of *e.g.* the Parzen window bandwidth or the number k of neighbors. Using heavily optimized single decision trees would also produce artifacts. However, the use of multiple trees in the forest yields the observed smoothness. In this experiment the parameters of the Parzen window and K-nearest neighbor approaches were optimized to produce the best results (visually). These are only qualitative results and a more rigorous, quantitative validation on standard datasets is necessary before drawing general conclusions. Next, we compare density forests with variants of the Gaussian mixture model.

6.4.2 Comparison with GMM EM

Figure 6.8 shows density estimates produced by forests in comparison to various GMM-based densities for the same input datasets as in Fig. 6.7a. Figure 6.8b shows the (visually) best results obtained with a GMM, using EM for its parameter estimation [28]. We can observe that on the simpler 5-component dataset (experiment 1) the two models seem to work equally well. However, the "S" and spiral-shaped examples show very distinct blob-like artifacts when using the GMM model. One may argue that this is due to the use of too few components. So we increased their number k and the corresponding densities are shown in Fig. 6.8c. Visual artifacts persist. Some of them are due to the fact that the greedy EM optimization gets stuck in local minima. So, a further alternative to improve the GMM results is to add randomness. In Fig. 6.8d, for each example we have trained 400 GMM-EM models (trained with 400 random initializations, a common way of injecting randomness in GMM training) and averaged together their output to produce a single density (as shown in the figure). The added randomness yields benefits in terms of smoothness, but the forest densities appear still slightly better, especially for the spiral dataset.

In summary, our synthetic experiments suggest that the use of randomness (either in a forest model or in a Gaussian mixture model) yields improved results. Possible issues with EM getting stuck in local minima produce artifacts which appear to be mitigated in the forest model. Let us now look at differences in terms of computational cost.

6.4.3 Comparing Computational Complexity

Given an input test point $\mathbf{v}$ evaluating $p(\mathbf{v})$ under a random-restart GMM model has cost

$$T \times K \times G, \tag{6.11}$$

with T the number of random restarts (the number of trained GMM models in the ensemble), K the number of Gaussian components and G the cost of evaluating $\mathbf{v}$ under each Gaussian.

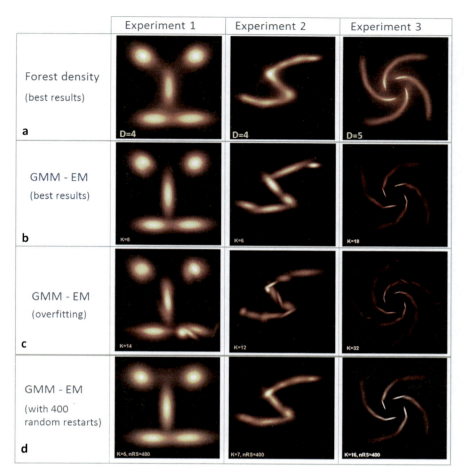

Fig. 6.8 Comparison with GMM-EM on the same input data as Fig. 6.7. (**a**) Forest-based densities. Forests were computed with $T = 200$ and optimized depth D. (**b**) GMM density with a relatively small number of Gaussian components. The model parameters are learned via EM. (**c**) GMM density with a larger number of Gaussian components. Increasing the components does not remove the blob-like artifacts. (**d**) GMM density with multiple (400) random re-initializations of EM. Adding randomness to the EM algorithm improves the smoothness of the output density considerably. However, the results in (**a**) still look smoother

Similarly, estimating $p(\mathbf{v})$ under a density forest with T trees of maximum depth D has cost

$$T \times (D \times B + G) \tag{6.12}$$

with B the cost of a binary test at a split node.

The cost in (6.12) is an upper bound because the average length of a generic root-leaf path is less than D nodes. Depending on the application, the binary tests can be

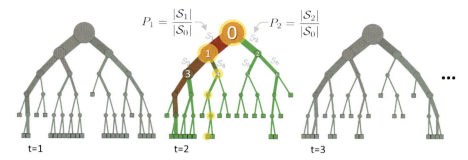

Fig. 6.9 Drawing random samples from the generative density model. Given a trained density forest we can generate random samples by: (i) randomly selecting one of the component trees, (ii) randomly traversing the tree down to a leaf and, (iii) drawing a sample from the associated Gaussian. The precise algorithmic steps are listed in Table 6.1

very efficient to compute.[2] Under these circumstances we may be able to ignore the term $D \times B$ in (6.12) and the cost of testing a density forest becomes comparable to that of a conventional, single GMM with T components.

Comparing training costs between the two models is a little harder because it involves the number of EM iterations (for the GMM model) and the value of ρ (in the forest). In practical applications (especially real-time ones) minimizing the testing time is usually more important than reducing the training time. Finally, testing of both GMMs as well as density forests can be easily parallelized.

6.5 Sampling from the Generative Model

The density distribution $p(\mathbf{v})$ we learn from the unlabeled input data represents a probabilistic *generative* model. In this section we describe an algorithm for the efficient sampling of random data under the learned model. The sampling algorithm uses the structure of the forest itself (for efficiency) and proceeds as described in Table 6.1. See also Fig. 6.9 for an accompanying illustration.

In this algorithm for each sample a random path from a tree root to one of its leaves is randomly generated and then a feature vector randomly generated from the associated Gaussian. Thus, drawing one random sample involves generating at most D random numbers from uniform distributions plus sampling a d-dimensional vector from a domain-bounded Gaussian.

An equivalent and slightly faster version of the sampling algorithm is obtained by compounding all the probabilities associated with individual edges at different levels together as probabilities associated with the leaves directly. Thus, the tree

---

[2] A split function is applied usually only to a small, selected subset of features $\boldsymbol{\phi}(\mathbf{v})$ and thus it can be computed efficiently, *i.e.* B is very small.

Table 6.1 Sampling from the density forest model

Given a density forest with T trees:

1. Draw uniformly a random tree index $t \in \{1, \dots, T\}$ to select a single tree in the forest.
2. Descend the tree:
    a. Starting at the root node, for each split node randomly generate the child index with probability proportional to the number of training points in the edge (proportional to the edge thickness in Fig. 6.9).
    b. Repeat step 2 until a terminal node is reached.
3. At the leaf draw a random sample from the *domain bounded* Gaussian stored at that leaf (*e.g.* using rejection-based sampling, *i.e.* discarding samples not lying within the cell).

Table 6.2 Sampling from a random-restart GMM

Given a set of T GMMs learned with random restarts:

1. Draw uniformly a GMM index $t \in \{1, \dots, T\}$ to select a single GMM in the set.
2. Select one Gaussian component by randomly drawing in proportion to the associated priors.
3. Draw a random sample from the selected Gaussian component.

traversal step (step 2 in the algorithm in Table 6.1) is replaced by direct random selection of one of the leaves.

6.5.1 Efficiency

The cost of randomly drawing N samples under the forest model is

$$N \times (2J + K) \tag{6.13}$$

with J the cost (almost negligible) of randomly generating a scalar number and K the cost of drawing a d-dimensional vector from a multivariate Gaussian distribution.

For comparison, sampling from a random-restart GMM is illustrated in the algorithm in Table 6.2. It turns out that the cost of drawing N samples under such a model is identical to (6.13). It is interesting to see how although the two algorithms are built upon different data structures, their steps are very similar. In summary, despite the added richness in the hierarchical structure of the density forest, its sampling complexity is very much comparable to that of a random-restart GMM.

6.5.2 Results

Figure 6.10 shows results of sampling $10{,}000$ random points from density forests trained on five different input point sets. The top row of the figure shows the learned

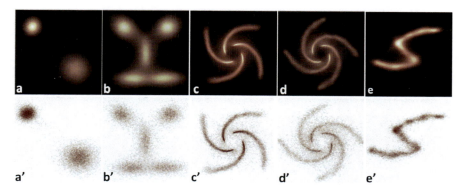

Fig. 6.10 Sampling results (*Top row*) Densities learned from hundreds of training points, via density forests. (*Bottom row*) Random points generated from the learned forests. We draw 10,000 random points per experiment (different experiments in different columns)

densities. The bottom row shows (with small red dots) random points drawn from the corresponding forests using the algorithm described in Table 6.1. Such a simple algorithm produces visually convincing results both for simpler Gaussian mixture distributions (Fig. 6.10a, b) as well as more complex densities like spirals and other convolved shapes (Fig. 6.10c, d, e).

6.6 Quantitative Analysis

This section attempts to analyze the accuracy of the density estimation algorithm with respect to ground truth.

Figure 6.11a shows a given ground truth probability density function. The density is represented non-parametrically as a normalized histogram defined over a 2D (x_1, x_2) domain. Using the multivariate inverse probability integral transform algorithm [91] we randomly sample $5,000$ points from the given density (see Fig. 6.11b). The goal now is as follows: Given the sampled points only, reconstruct a probability density function which is as close as possible to the initial, ground truth density.

Thus, a density forest is trained using the sampled points alone.[3] The trained forest is then tested on *all* points in a predefined domain (not just on the training points, Fig. 6.11c). Finally, a quantitative comparison between the estimated density $p(\mathbf{v})$ and the ground truth one $p_{gt}(\mathbf{v})$ can be carried out. The density reconstruction error is computed here as a sum of squared differences:

$$E = \sum_{\mathbf{v}} \big(p(\mathbf{v}) - p_{gt}(\mathbf{v})\big)^2. \tag{6.14}$$

---

[3]No use is made of the ground truth density in this stage.

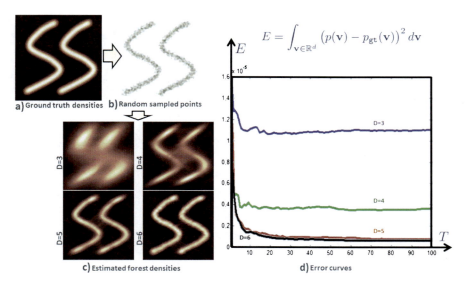

Fig. 6.11 Quantitative evaluation of forest density estimation. (**a**) An input ground truth density (non-Gaussian in this experiment). (**b**) Thousands of random points drawn randomly from the density. The points are used to train four density forests with different depths. (**c**) During testing the forests are used to estimate density values for all points in a square domain. (**d**) The reconstructed densities are compared with the ground truth and corresponding error curves plotted as a function of the forest size T. As expected, larger forests yield higher accuracy. In these experiments we have used four forests with $T = 100$ trees and $D \in \{3, 4, 5, 6\}$

Alternatively one may consider the technique in [362]. Note that due to probabilistic normalization the maximum value of the error in (6.14) is 4. The curves in Fig. 6.11d show how the reconstruction error diminishes with increasing forest size and depth. We notice that the reconstruction error decreases with the forest size. Additionally, in other experiments we have observed the overall error to start increasing again after an optimal value of D (suggesting overfitting for larger tree depths).

Figure 6.12 shows further quantitative results on more complex examples. In the bottom two examples some difficulties arise in the central part (where the spiral arms converge). This causes larger errors. Using different weak learners (*e.g.* curved surfaces) may produce better results in those troublesome areas. In Fig. 6.12 using larger and larger sets of sampled training points would produces lower and lower reconstruction errors. A more thorough analysis of the *consistency* of our forest-based density estimator is deferred to future work.[4]

---

[4]See "consistent estimator" in Wikipedia for a definition of consistency.

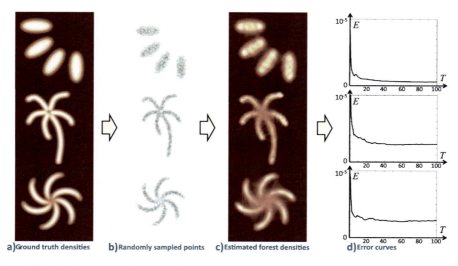

a) Ground truth densities   b) Randomly sampled points   c) Estimated forest densities   d) Error curves

Fig. 6.12 Further quantitative evaluation. (**a**) Input ground truth densities. (**b**) Thousands of points sampled randomly from the ground truth densities directly. (**c**) Densities corresponding to the learned density forests. Density values are computed for all points in the domain (not just the training points). (**d**) Error curves as a function of the forest size T. Larger forests yields better accuracy (lower error E). These results are obtained with $T = 100$ and $D = 5$. Different parameter values and using richer weak learners may improve the accuracy in troublesome regions (*e.g.* at the center of the spiral arms in the bottom row)

6.7 Summary

This chapter has taken the abstract decision forest model of Chap. 3 and specialized it for density estimation. Toy experiments have illustrated the effects of various parameters on the accuracy and confidence of the predicted output. The experiments are carried out on synthetic data to convey the main principles of density forests at an intuitive level. Therefore, this chapter cannot claim that density forests are always better than alternative techniques. However, it suggests the fact that forests can indeed also be used for density estimation. Many and more rigorous experiments on real data are necessary to validate quantitatively density forests in comparison with better established techniques. Additional details, experiments, animations and videos are available in [79] and in [80].

6.8 Exercises and Experiments

Here are a few exercises to allow the reader to gain familiarity with density forests. The Sherwood library necessary for the experiments may be downloaded from http://research.microsoft.com/projects/decisionforests, and is described in Chap. 22.

Exercise 6.1

To begin, type `sw density` in a command window to get a list of instructions.
Reproduce the results of Fig. 6.4 by running:

```
sw density exp1.txt /d 2 /t 3
```

- Try changing the tree depth D:
  ```
  sw density exp1.txt /d 1 /t 3
  sw density exp1.txt /d 3 /t 3
  sw density exp1.txt /d 4 /t 3
  sw density exp1.txt /d 5 /t 3
  ```
  What is the impact on under-, overfitting?
- Try changing the forest size T:
  ```
  sw density exp1.txt /d 4 /t 3
  sw density exp1.txt /d 4 /t 30
  sw density exp1.txt /d 4 /t 300
  ```
  and observe its effect.
- Try running the same experiments many times with less randomness (*e.g.* with `/f 50`).
  How does this affect the stability of the results?
  How does this affect possible overfitting?

Exercise 6.2

Reproduce the results of Fig. 6.8a ('Experiment 1') by running:

```
sw density exp3.txt /d 4 /t 300
```

- Try varying the values of D and T.
  What is the impact on the results?

Exercise 6.3

Reproduce the results of Fig. 6.8a ('Experiment 2') by running:

```
sw density exp7.txt /d 3 /t 300
```

How is this exercise different from Exercise 5.4?

- Please look at how the density changes as a function of D.
  ```
  sw density exp7.txt /d 1 /t 300
  sw density exp7.txt /d 2 /t 300
  sw density exp7.txt /d 4 /t 300
  sw density exp7.txt /d 5 /t 300
  ```
- Please look at how the density changes as a function of T.
  ```
  sw density exp7.txt /d 3 /t 3
  sw density exp7.txt /d 3 /t 30
  ```

You can refer to [80] for answers to some of these questions.

Exercise 6.4

Reproduce the results of Fig. 6.8a ('Experiment 3') by running:
```
sw density exp4.txt /d 4 /t 300
sw density exp4.txt /d 5 /t 300
```
Note that Fig. 6.8a was obtained using linear weak learners. Instead Sherwood is limited to using axis-aligned split functions for density estimation. This explains possible visual differences.

- Try varying *D* further:
```
sw density exp4.txt /d 2 /t 300
sw density exp4.txt /d 3 /t 300
sw density exp4.txt /d 7 /t 300
```
  What is the impact on the estimated density?
- As usual, also try changing the forest size and the amount of randomness.

Exercise 6.5

In the previous exercises, the parameters of the Gaussians at the leaves were obtained by maximum likelihood (ML) estimation. Here we highlight the effect of using maximum a-posteriori (MAP) parameter estimates instead. In the latter, the leaf Gaussians are conditioned on a prior model of the parameter values.

- Run the following commands and compare the results:
```
sw density exp4.txt /d 8 /t 1 /a 0
sw density exp4.txt /d 8 /t 1 /a 10
```
  Here the command line switches /a and /b allow specification of prior hyper-parameters *a* and *b*, where *a* is the number of 'effective' prior observations and *b* is their variance (default $b = 900$).
- Try varying *a* for example:
```
sw density exp4.txt /d 6 /t 300 /a 0
sw density exp4.txt /d 6 /t 300 /a 1
sw density exp4.txt /d 6 /t 300 /a 10
```
  Compare your results with those obtained in Exercise 6.4. What is the impact of using the prior on overfitting at larger tree depths?
- Finally, experiment with varying the amount of randomness and observe its effect.
```
sw density exp4.txt /d 6 /t 50 /f 5 /a 0
sw density exp4.txt /d 6 /t 50 /f 50 /a 0
sw density exp4.txt /d 6 /t 50 /f 5 /a 2
sw density exp4.txt /d 6 /t 50 /f 50 /a 2
```

Chapter 7
Manifold Forests

A. Criminisi and J. Shotton

The previous chapter discussed the use of decision forests for estimating the latent density of unlabeled data. This has led to a forest-based probabilistic generative model which captures efficiently the "intrinsic" structure of the data itself.

This chapter delves further into the issue of learning the structure of high-dimensional data as well as mapping it onto a lower dimensional space, while preserving spatial relationships between data points. This task goes under the name of manifold learning and is closely related to dimensionality reduction and embedding.

This task is important because real data is often characterized by a very large number of dimensions. However, a careful inspection often shows a much simpler, lower dimensional underlying distribution (*e.g.* on a hyperplane, or a curved surface). So, if we can automatically discover the underlying manifold and "unfold" it, this may lead to more direct visualization, easier data interpretation and perhaps more efficient algorithms for analyzing such data.

Here we show how decision forests can also be used for manifold learning. Properties of manifold forests include: (i) computational efficiency (*e.g.* due to the ease of parallelization of forest-based algorithms), (ii) automatic selection of discriminative features via information-based optimization, and (iii) all the other benefits inherited from our general forest model, such as code re-usability. After a brief literature survey, we discuss details of the manifold forest model, and then show its properties with examples and experiments.

7.1 Manifold Learning and Dimensionality Reduction in the Literature

Discovering the intrinsic structure of a dataset (namely manifold learning) and mapping it onto a lower dimensional representation (namely dimensionality reduction,

A. Criminisi (✉) · J. Shotton
Microsoft Research Ltd., 7 J.J. Thomson Avenue, Cambridge CB3 0FB, UK

A. Criminisi, J. Shotton (eds.), *Decision Forests for Computer Vision and Medical Image Analysis*, Advances in Computer Vision and Pattern Recognition, DOI 10.1007/978-1-4471-4929-3_7, © Springer-Verlag London 2013

or embedding) are related tasks which have been investigated at length in the literature. Perhaps one of the simplest and most common algorithms is principal component analysis (PCA) [175]. PCA is based on the computation of directions of maximum data spread. This is obtained by eigen-decomposition of the data covariance matrix computed in the original space. PCA is a linear model and as such has considerable limitations for more realistic problems where the data cannot be assumed to lie in a linear space. A popular, *non-linear* technique is isometric feature mapping (or IsoMap) [367] which estimates low-dimensional embeddings that tend to preserve geodesic distances between point pairs.

The task of manifold learning is related to that of estimating geodesic distances between point pairs in their intrinsic manifold. However, computing such distances for *all* possible point pairs may be intractable for high-dimensional or large datasets. Variants of decision forests have been used in the past for the efficient, approximate discovery of data neighborhoods and distance estimation [128, 142, 194, 236, 273, 335, 405]. In this scenario both supervised and unsupervised forests have been employed.

This chapter presents *manifold forests* as an instantiation of our abstract model of decision forests from Chap. 3. Here we make use of Laplacian eigenmaps [22, 23] which is a spectral technique for dimensionality reduction.[1] Laplacian eigenmaps try to preserve *local* pairwise point distances only, with a simple and efficient algorithm. This technique has very close connections with spectral clustering and the normalized cuts image segmentation algorithm in [336]. Recent probabilistic interpretation of spectral dimensionality reduction may be found in [87, 262]. A generative, probabilistic model for learning latent manifolds is discussed in [29].

Manifold learning has recently become popular in the medical image analysis community, *e.g.* for cardiac analysis [95, 415], registration [149] and brain image analysis [124, 142]. A more thorough exploration of the vast literature on manifold learning and dimensionality reduction is beyond the scope of this work. The interested reader is referred to some excellent surveys in [58, 61].

7.2 Specializing the Forest Model for Manifold Learning

The idea of using tree-based random space projections for manifold learning is not new [114, 160]. Here we show how a whole *ensemble* of randomized trees can be used for this purpose, and its advantages. We start by specializing the generic forest model (Chap. 3) for use in manifold learning.

Problem Statement   The manifold learning task is summarized here as follows:

---

[1] Multi-dimensional scaling (MDS) [73] or alternative techniques may also be considered.

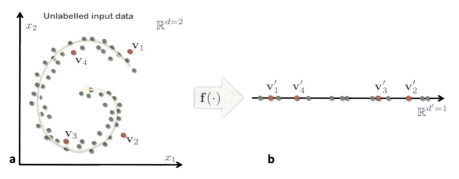

Fig. 7.1 Manifold learning and dimensionality reduction. (**a**) Input, unlabeled data points are denoted with *circles*. They live in a high-dimensional space (here $d = 2$ for illustration only). A *red* outline highlights some selected points of interest. (**b**) The target space is of much lower dimensionality (here $d' = 1$ for illustration). Geodesic distances and point ordering are preserved

> *Given a set of k unlabeled observations* $\{\mathbf{v}_1, \mathbf{v}_2, \ldots, \mathbf{v}_i, \ldots, \mathbf{v}_k\}$ *with* $\mathbf{v}_i \in$
> $\mathbb{R}^d$ *we wish to find a smooth mapping* $\mathbf{f} : \mathbb{R}^d \to \mathbb{R}^{d'}$ *with* $\mathbf{f}(\mathbf{v}_i) = \mathbf{v}'_i$ *that*
> *approximately preserves the observations' relative geodesic distances, with*
> $d' \ll d$.

As illustrated in Fig. 7.1 each input observation $\mathbf{v}$ (unlabeled) is represented as a multi-dimensional feature response vector $\mathbf{v} = (x_1, \ldots, x_d) \in \mathbb{R}^d$. The desired output is the mapping function $\mathbf{f}(\cdot)$.

In Fig. 7.1a input data points are denoted with circles. They live in a 2D space.[2] We wish to find a function $\mathbf{f}(\cdot)$ which maps those points to their corresponding locations in a lower dimensional space (in the figure $d' = 1$) such that Euclidean distances in the new space are as close as possible to the geodesic distances in the original space.

What Are Manifold Forests?   As mentioned, the problems of manifold learning and that of density estimation are closely related. This chapter builds upon density forests, with much of the mathematical modeling borrowed from Chap. 6. Manifold forests are also collections of clustering trees. However, unlike density forests, the manifold forest model requires extra components such as a model of *affinity* between data points, and an efficient algorithm for estimating the mapping $\mathbf{f}(\cdot)$. The high-level structure of the forest-based embedding algorithm presented here can be summarized as follows:

1. A decision forest is used to infer efficiently the $k \times k$ affinity matrix $\mathtt{W}$ between all pairs of input unlabeled data points;

---

[2]In practical applications the original space is usually of much higher dimensionality than 2D.

2. Given W, dimensionality reduction is performed by applying any known technique. As an example, here we employ Laplacian eigenmaps.

Details are presented next.

7.2.1 The Training Objective Function

Using randomized node optimization, forest training is achieved by maximizing a continuous information gain measure

$$\boldsymbol{\theta}_j = \arg\max_{\boldsymbol{\theta} \in \mathcal{T}_j} I(\mathcal{S}_j, \boldsymbol{\theta}), \tag{7.1}$$

with I defined as for density forests:

$$I(\mathcal{S}_j, \boldsymbol{\theta}) = \log(|\Lambda(\mathcal{S}_j)|) - \sum_{i \in \{L,R\}} \frac{|\mathcal{S}_j^i|}{|\mathcal{S}_j|} \log(|\Lambda(\mathcal{S}_j^i)|). \tag{7.2}$$

(These restate (3.13) and (6.4) for completeness.) The previous chapter has discussed properties and advantages of (7.2).

7.2.2 The Predictor Model

As for the density model, the statistics of all training points arriving at each leaf node are summarized with a single multivariate Gaussian:

$$p_t(\mathbf{v}) = \frac{\pi_{l(\mathbf{v})}}{Z_t} \mathcal{N}(\mathbf{v}; \boldsymbol{\mu}_{l(\mathbf{v})}, \Lambda_{l(\mathbf{v})}). \tag{7.3}$$

See Sect. 6.2.2 for more details.

7.2.3 The Affinity Model

Unlike other tasks, in manifold learning we need to estimate some measure of similarity, affinity, or distance between data points so that we can try and preserve those inter-point distances after the mapping. When working with complex data in high-dimensional spaces it is important for this affinity model to be as efficient as possible. Here we use decision forests to define data affinity in a simple and effective way.

As seen in the previous chapter, at its leaves a clustering tree t defines a partition of the input points

$$l(\mathbf{v}) : \mathbb{R}^d \to \mathcal{L} \subset \mathbb{N} \tag{7.4}$$

with l a leaf index and $\mathcal{L}$ the set of all leaves in a given tree (the tree index is not shown to avoid cluttering the notation). For a clustering tree t we can compute the $k \times k$ points' affinity matrix $\mathbf{W}^t$ with elements

$$\mathbf{W}_{ij}^t = e^{-Q^t(\mathbf{v}_i, \mathbf{v}_j)}. \tag{7.5}$$

The matrix $\mathbf{W}^t$ can be thought of as un-normalized transition probabilities in Markov random walks defined on a fully connected graph (where each data point corresponds to a node). The distance Q can be defined in different ways. For example:

Mahalanobis affinity

$$Q^t(\mathbf{v}_i, \mathbf{v}_j) = \begin{cases} \mathbf{d}_{ij}^\top (\Lambda_{l(\mathbf{v}_i)}^t)^{-1} \mathbf{d}_{ij} & \text{if } l(\mathbf{v}_i) = l(\mathbf{v}_j) \\ \infty & \text{otherwise} \end{cases} \tag{7.6}$$

Gaussian affinity

$$Q^t(\mathbf{v}_i, \mathbf{v}_j) = \begin{cases} \dfrac{\mathbf{d}_{ij}^\top \mathbf{d}_{ij}}{\varepsilon^2} & \text{if } l(\mathbf{v}_i) = l(\mathbf{v}_j) \\ \infty & \text{otherwise} \end{cases} \tag{7.7}$$

Binary affinity

$$Q^t(\mathbf{v}_i, \mathbf{v}_j) = \begin{cases} 0 & \text{if } l(\mathbf{v}_i) = l(\mathbf{v}_j) \\ \infty & \text{otherwise} \end{cases} \tag{7.8}$$

where $\mathbf{d}_{ij} = \mathbf{v}_i - \mathbf{v}_j$, and $\Lambda_{l(\mathbf{v}_i)}$ is the covariance matrix associated with the leaf reached by the point $\mathbf{v}_i$. Note that in contrast to density estimation, here it is not necessary to compute the partition function Z_t (*cf.* Chap. 6). More complex probabilistic models of affinity may also be used.

The simplest and perhaps most interesting model of affinity in the list above is the binary one [128, 142, 194, 335]. It can be thought of as a special case of the Gaussian model with the length parameter $\varepsilon \to \infty$ (thus the binary affinity model is parameter-free). It says that given a tree t and two points $\mathbf{v}_i$ and $\mathbf{v}_j$ we assign perfect affinity (affinity = 1, distance = 0) to the pair $(\mathbf{v}_i, \mathbf{v}_j)$ if those two points end up in the same cluster (leaf) and null affinity (infinite distance) otherwise.

One of the biggest problems in many existing manifold learning techniques is how to define appropriate data neighborhoods that yield good approximations of pairwise geodesic distances. In contrast, in manifold forests the maximization of an unsupervised information-theoretic objective function leads to a natural definition of point neighborhoods and pairwise similarities. In fact, the forest leaves automatically define pairwise relationships between input data points. The interested reader is also referred to the work in [223] for further reading on the relationship between forests and adaptive nearest neighbor approaches. In data-intensive applications, using an information gain objective may be more natural than having to hand-design pairwise distances between complex or high-dimensional data points (*e.g.* think of the problem of defining distances between images).

7.2.4 The Ensemble Model

A single randomly trained decision tree is not likely to produce affinities which are representative of the correct pairwise point similarities. This is true especially if the binary model (with hard 0 or 1 assignments) is employed. However, having a collection of random trees enables us to collect evidence from the entire ensemble. This has the effect of producing a smoother affinity matrix, even when the hard binary model is used. Once again, using a collection of randomly trained trees is key here. More formally, in a forest of T trees its affinity matrix is defined as

$$W = \frac{1}{T} \sum_{t=1}^{T} W^t. \tag{7.9}$$

In a given tree two points may not belong to the same cluster. In some other tree they do. The averaging operation in (7.9) has the effect of adding robustness to the pairwise affinities across the graph of all points.

Having discussed how to use forests for computing the data affinity matrix (*i.e.* building the graph), next we proceed with the actual estimation of the mapping function $\mathbf{f}(\cdot)$. This second step can be achieved with any existing non-linear dimensionality reduction technique. However, here we choose to work with the well known Laplacian eigenmaps for their simplicity [22, 262].

7.2.5 Estimating the Embedding Function

In Laplacian eigenmaps, given W, a low-dimensional embedding is found using straightforward linear algebra, as follows. Given a graph whose nodes are the input points, and its affinity matrix W, we first construct the $k \times k$ normalized graph-Laplacian matrix as

$$L = I - T^{-\frac{1}{2}} W T^{-\frac{1}{2}} \tag{7.10}$$

with the normalizing diagonal matrix T, such that $T_{ii} = \sum_j W_{ij}$. T is often called a "degree" matrix [61]. The mapping function $\mathbf{f}$ is found via eigen-decomposition of L. Let $\mathbf{e}_0, \mathbf{e}_1, \ldots, \mathbf{e}_{k-1}$ be the solutions of (7.10) in *increasing* order of eigenvalues

$$L\mathbf{e}_0 = \lambda_0 \mathbf{e}_0$$

$$L\mathbf{e}_1 = \lambda_1 \mathbf{e}_1$$

$$\cdots \tag{7.11}$$

$$L\mathbf{e}_{k-1} = \lambda_{k-1} \mathbf{e}_{k-1}$$

with

$$0 = \lambda_0 \leq \lambda_1 \leq \lambda_2 \leq \cdots \leq \lambda_{k-1}. \tag{7.12}$$

We ignore the first eigenvector $\mathbf{e}_0$ as it corresponds to a degenerate solution (global translation) and use the next $d' \ll d$ eigenvectors (from $\mathbf{e}_1$ to $\mathbf{e}_{d'}$) to construct the $k \times d'$ matrix E as follows:

$$E = \begin{pmatrix} | & | & | & | & | & | \\ \mathbf{e}_1 & \mathbf{e}_2 & \cdots & \mathbf{e}_j & \cdots & \mathbf{e}_{d'} \\ | & | & | & | & | & | \end{pmatrix} \tag{7.13}$$

with $j \in \{1, \ldots, d'\}$ indexing the eigenvectors represented as column vectors. Finally, mapping a point $\mathbf{v}_i \in \mathbb{R}^d$ onto its corresponding point $\mathbf{v}' \in \mathbb{R}^{d'}$ is done simply by reading the ith row of E:

$$\mathbf{v}'_i = \mathbf{f}(\mathbf{v}_i) = (E_{i1}, \ldots, E_{ij}, \ldots, E_{id'})^\top \tag{7.14}$$

where $i \in \{1, \ldots, k\}$ indexes the individual points. Note that d' must be $\leq k$ which is easy to achieve as we normally wish to have a small target dimensionality d'. In summary, the embedding function $\mathbf{f}$ remains implicitly defined by its k corresponding point pairs, through the eigenvector matrix E.

In contrast to existing techniques, here, we do not need to fine-tune a length parameter or a neighborhood size. In fact, when using the binary affinity model the point neighborhood remains defined automatically by the forest leaves. Of course, other parameters such as tree depth D are important, and these are discussed further below.

7.2.6 Mapping Previously Unseen Points

There may be applications where after having trained the forest on a given training set, further, previously unavailable data points become available. In order to map the new points to the corresponding lower dimensional space one may think of retraining the entire manifold forest from scratch. However, a more efficient, approximate technique consists of interpolating the point position given the already available embedding. More formally, given a previously unseen point $\mathbf{v}$ and an already trained manifold forest we wish to find the corresponding point $\mathbf{v}'$ in the low-dimensional space. The point $\mathbf{v}'$ may be computed as follows:

$$\mathbf{v}' = \frac{1}{T} \sum_t \frac{1}{\eta^t} \sum_i \left(e^{-Q^t(\mathbf{v},\mathbf{v}_i)} \mathbf{f}(\mathbf{v}_i)\right) \tag{7.15}$$

with $\eta^t = \sum_i e^{-Q^t(\mathbf{v},\mathbf{v}_i)}$ the normalizing constant and the distance $Q^t(\cdot,\cdot)$ computed by applying (testing) the existing tth tree on $\mathbf{v}$. This interpolation technique works well for points which are not too far from the original training set. More efficient alternatives are possible. For instance one may exploit the structure of the forest to quickly find nearest neighbors [194] and then use the only the retrieved neighbors for interpolation.

7.2.7 Properties and Advantages

Let us discuss briefly some properties of manifold forests.

7.2.7.1 Ensemble Clustering for Distance Estimation

When dealing with complex data (*e.g.* images), defining pairwise distances can be challenging. Here we mitigate that problem by directly using the pairwise affinities defined by the tree structure itself. In fact, given a set of training points and fixing some forest parameters such as the number of trees T, the maximum tree depth D, and the randomness parameter ρ allows us to train a forest and thus implicitly define the affinities $\mathtt{W}$. This is very different from hand-designing point distances as the optimal tree tests and features are automatically selected by minimizing a well defined energy. The effect of different choices of forest parameters are discussed later.

An Illustrative Example   As a toy example, imagine that we have a collection of holiday photos containing images of beaches, forests and cityscapes (see Fig. 7.2). Each image can be interpreted as a data point in a very high-dimensional space. When training a manifold forest we can imagine that *e.g.* some trees group all beach photos in a cluster, all forest photos in a different leaf and all cityscapes in yet another leaf. A different tree, using different features, may mix some of the forest photos with some of the beach ones (*e.g.* because of the many palm trees along the shore), but the cityscape photos are visually very distinct and might remain (mostly) in a separate cluster. So, forests and beach scenes are more likely to end up in the same leaf while building photos do not tend to mix with other classes (just as an example). Therefore, the matrix (7.9) will assign higher affinity (smaller distance) to a forest–beach image pair than to a beach–city pair. This shows how an ensemble of multiple hard clusterings can yield a soft distance measure.

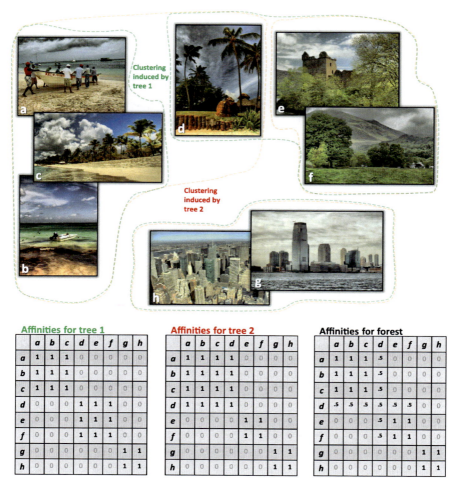

Fig. 7.2 Illustration of affinity smoothing via multiple tree-induced clusterings. Different trees induce different partitions of the input images. The *green partition* $\{\{a, b, c\}, \{d, e, f\}, \{g, h\}\}$ is induced by tree 1. The *red partition* $\{\{a, b, c, d\}, \{e, f\}, \{g, h\}\}$ is induced by tree 2. The corresponding affinity matrices (using the hard, binary model) are also shown. The overlap between clusters in different trees is captured by the fractional affinity values in the forest matrix W. Averaging affinity matrices across many trees tends to produce more stable and smooth affinities

7.2.7.2 Choosing the Feature Space

An issue with manifold learning is that often one needs to decide ahead of time how to represent each data point. For instance one has to decide what features and how many features to use. Thinking of the practical computer vision task of learning manifolds of images, the difficulty of this decision becomes apparent.

One potential advantage of manifold forests is that we do not need to manually specify the features to use. We can define the generic *family* of features (*e.g.* gradients, Haar wavelet, or the output of Gabor filter banks). Then the tree training process will automatically select discriminative features and corresponding parameters for each node of the forest, so as to (greedily) optimize the information gain measure. For instance, in the example in Fig. 7.2 as features we could use averages of pixel colors within rectangles placed within the image frame. Position and size of the rectangles would be automatically selected during training. This would allow the system to learn for example that brown-colored regions are expected towards the bottom of the image for beach scenes, or that vertical edges are expected in urban scenes.

7.2.7.3 Computational Efficiency

The bottleneck of this algorithm is the solution of the eigen-system (7.10), which could be slow for large numbers of input points k. However, in (7.14) only the $d' \ll k$ bottom eigenvectors are necessary. This, in conjunction with the fact that the matrix L is usually very sparse (especially for the binary affinity model) can yield efficient implementations. Please note that only one eigen-system needs be solved, independent from the forest size T. Additionally, all the individual tree-based affinity matrices W^t may be computed in parallel.

7.2.7.4 Estimating the Target Intrinsic Dimensionality

The algorithm above can be applied for any chosen dimensionality d' of the target space. If we do not know d' in advance (*e.g.* from application-specific knowledge) a sensible value can be chosen by: (i) looking at the profile of (ordered) eigenvalues λ_j, and (ii) selecting the minimum number of eigenvalues corresponding to a sharp elbow in such profile [22]. This will be illustrated with an experiment in Sect. 7.3.3. Being able to estimate the optimal manifold dimensionality is a property of spectral techniques in general, and is not unique to manifold forests.

7.3 Experiments and the Effect of Model Parameters

This section presents some experiments and studies the effect of the forest parameters on the output embedding.

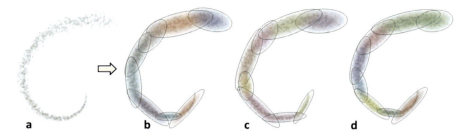

Fig. 7.3 Different clusterings induced by different trees. (**a**) The input data in 2D. (**b, c, d**) Different partitions learned by different random trees in the same manifold forest. Different colors indicate different Gaussian clusters, each associated with a different leaf node. A given pair of points will belong to the same cluster (leaf) in some trees and not in others

7.3.1 The Effect of the Forest Size

We begin by discussing the effect of the forest size. In a forest of size T each randomly trained clustering tree produces a different, disjoint partition of the data.[3] In the case of a binary affinity model the elements of the affinity matrices W^t are binary (either two points belong to the same leaf/cluster or they do not). A given pair of points will belong to the same cluster (leaf) in some trees and not in others (see Fig. 7.3). Via the ensemble model the *forest* affinity matrix W is much smoother since multiple trees enable different point pairs to exchange information about their relative position. Thus, even if we use the binary distance model, the forest affinity W is in general *not* binary. Large forests (large values of T) correspond to averaging many tree affinity matrices together, with positive effects in terms of robustness to noise.

Figure 7.4 shows two examples of non-linear dimensionality reduction. In each experiment we are given some noisy, unlabeled 2D points distributed according to an unknown underlying non-linear 1D manifold. We wish to discover the manifold and map those points onto a 1D real axis while preserving their relative geodesic distances. The figure shows that such a mapping does not work well when using a very small number of trees. This is illustrated *e.g.* in Fig. 7.4b-leftmost and in Fig. 7.4d-leftmost by the isolated red clusters. However, as the number of trees increases the affinity matrix W better approximates the true (unknown) pairwise graph affinity. Consequently the color coding (linearly going from dark blue to dark red) starts to follow correctly the smooth 1D evolution of the points.

---

[3]If the input points were reordered correctly for each tree we would obtain an affinity matrix W^t with a block-diagonal structure.

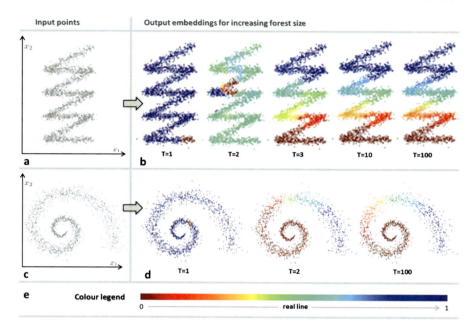

Fig. 7.4 Manifold forest and non-linear dimensionality reduction. The effect of T. (**a, c**) Input 2D points for two different synthetic experiments: a piece-wise linear point distribution (*top row*), and a noisy version of the popular "Swiss Roll" dataset (*bottom row*). (**b, d**) Non-linear mapping from the original 2D space to the target 1D real line is color coded, *from dark red to dark blue*. In both examples a small forest (small T) does not capture correctly the intrinsic 1D manifold. For larger values of T (*e.g.* $T = 100$) the accuracy of such a mapping increases and the ordering and position of mapped points is more correctly estimated. (**e**) The color legend. Different colors, *from red to blue*, denote the position of the mapped points in their target 1D space

7.3.2 Manifold Learning in Higher Dimensions

This section presents further results, on mapping points from a 3D space into a target 2D space. Here we are still dealing with relatively low dimensions because it is difficult to visualize high-dimensional data. However, the theory of manifold learning applies to any dimensionality.

In all experiments here we use a binary affinity model as we have observed little difference with respect to *e.g.* a Gaussian one. In [194] forests with binary affinity models were used to learn semantic similarities between images.

Figure 7.5 illustrates results on a set of points distributed according to a "Christmas tree" shape. The original, input points live within a 3D space, with their intrinsic manifold (unknown to our algorithm) being a 2D rectangle. A manifold forest of maximum depth $D = 4$ and $T = 100$ trees was trained and then used to map those points into their corresponding 2D positions. Using a 2D color legend (see figure) we then "painted" the 3D points according to their target 2D position. Figure 7.5b shows how the colors of the 3D points change smoothly along the underlying shape,

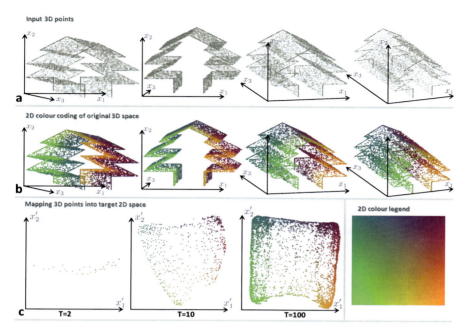

Fig. 7.5 Mapping from 3D to 2D. In this experiment we map 3D points into their intrinsic (and unknown) 2D manifold. (**a**) The input 3D points are randomly distributed along a tree-shaped surface. The data are viewed from four different viewpoints to aid understanding. The intrinsic manifold is a 2D rectangle. (**b**) The corresponding 2D manifold is computed and a 2D color map used to visualize the evolution of such surface directly in the original 3D space. (**c**) The original points mapped into their target 2D surface and color coded. As the forest size increases we obtain a more refined estimation of the rectangular shape of the intrinsic manifold. For this experiment we used a forest size of $T = 100$, with maximum trees depth $D = 4$, a binary affinity model, and oriented hyperplane (linear) weak learners

e.g. from orange to green etc. This suggests correct estimation of the underlying manifold.

Furthermore, Fig. 7.5c shows the points mapped into their target 2D space for increasing values of T. A small number of trees produces inaccurate mappings, but as T increases the output manifold becomes more rectangular, as expected. Notice that our model preserves local distances only. This is, in general, not sufficient to reproduce sharp 90-degree angles.

Figure 7.6a shows four views of a 3D variant of the popular "Swiss Roll" dataset. The automatically estimated underlying 2D manifold is again shown via a 2D color coding of the original points, in Fig. 7.6b. The smoothly varying distribution of colors confirms convincing results. Additionally, in similar experiments we have observed that the binary model converges (with T) a little more slowly than the Gaussian model, but with clear advantages in terms of computational and model complexity. In fact, in the Gaussian model the length parameter ε in (7.7) may be

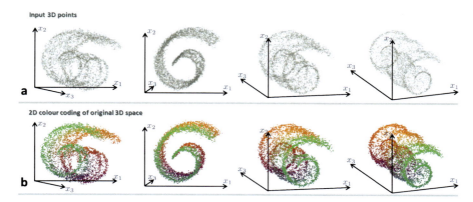

Fig. 7.6 Unfolding the "Swiss Roll". A further experiment mapping 3D points into their intrinsic (and unknown) 2D manifold. (**a**) The input 3D points are randomly distributed along a 3D "Swiss Roll" shaped surface. The data points are viewed from four different viewpoints to aid understanding. To add variability, the points position is modulated by a sinusoidal wave, function of x_3 (see *rightmost image*). The intrinsic manifold is a 2D rectangle. (**b**) The corresponding 2D manifold is computed and a 2D color map used to visualize the evolution of such surface directly in the original 3D space. For this experiment we used a forest size of $T = 100$, with maximum trees depth $D = 4$, a binary affinity model, and oriented hyperplane (linear) weak learners

difficult to set appropriately (because it has no immediate interpretation) for complex data. Therefore, a model which avoids this step is advantageous.

7.3.3 Discovering the Manifold Intrinsic Dimensionality

We conclude this chapter by discussing the issue of selecting the optimal dimensionality of the target space. In terms of accuracy it is easy to see that a value of d' identical to the dimensionality of the original space would produce the best results because there would be no loss of information. But one criterion for choosing d' is to drastically reduce the complexity of the target space. Thus we definitely wish to use small values of d'. As discussed in [22] the spectrum of eigenvalues of the normalized graph Laplacian presents sharp changes in some specific locations. This indicates that there are values of d' such that if we used $d' + 1$ we would not gain very much. These special loci can be used to define "good" values for the target dimensionality.

Figure 7.7 plots the eigenvalue spectra for the "Swiss Roll" dataset and the binary and Gaussian affinity models, respectively. As expected from theory $\lambda_0 = 0$ (corresponding to a translation component that we ignore). The sharp elbow in the curves, corresponding to λ_2 indicates an intrinsic dimensionality $d' = 2$ (correct) for this example. In our experiments we have observed that higher values of T produce a more prominent elbow in the spectrum and thus a clearer choice for the value of d'. Similarly, Gaussian affinities produce slightly sharper elbows than binary affinities.

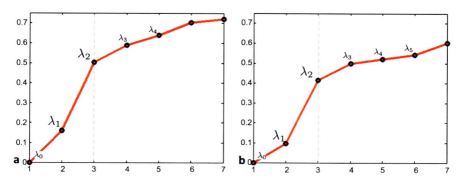

Fig. 7.7 Discovering the manifold intrinsic dimensionality. The sorted eigenvalues of the normalized graph Laplacian for the "Swiss Roll" 3D example, with (**a**) the binary affinity model, and (**b**) the Gaussian affinity model. In both curves there is a clear elbow in correspondence of λ_2 thus indicating an intrinsic dimensionality $d' = 2$. Here we used forest size $T = 100$, $D = 4$ and linear weak learners

7.4 Summary

This chapter has discussed how decision forests may be used to compute unsupervised affinities between data points and then use those for non-linear low-dimensional embedding. For example, we have seen that manifold forests can be efficient, avoid the need to predefine the features to be used, and can provide guidance with respect to the optimal dimensionality of the target space. On the flip side it is important to choose the forest depth D carefully, as this parameter influences the number of clusters in which the data are partitioned and, in turn, the smoothness of the recovered mapping. In contrast to existing techniques, we also need to choose a weak learner model to guide the way in which different clusters are separated. The forest size T is important, though increasing T should always result in higher test accuracy.

Just like in Chap. 6, the experiments here are just "proof of concepts". They are not sufficient to claim that manifold forests are superior to alternative techniques. However, they suggest that indeed, the same generic forest model can be effectively used for manifold learning, once again pointing at the flexibility of our general forest model. A more thorough experimental validation with real data is necessary to assess the accuracy of such model in a more rigorous, quantitative manner.

In the next chapter, we discuss a natural continuation of the supervised and unsupervised models discussed so far, and their use in semi-supervised learning.

Chapter 8
Semi-supervised Classification Forests

A. Criminisi and J. Shotton

Previous chapters have discussed the use of decision forests in supervised problems (regression and classification) as well as unsupervised ones (density and manifold estimation). This chapter puts the two things together to achieve *semi*-supervised learning. We focus here on semi-supervised *classification* but the approach can be extended to regression too.

In semi-supervised classification we have available a small set of labeled training data points and a large set of unlabeled ones. This is a typical situation in many practical scenarios. For instance, in medical image analysis, getting hold of numerous anonymized patients scans is relatively easy and cheap. However, labeling them with ground truth annotations requires experts' time and effort and thus it is very expensive. A key question then is whether we can exploit the existence of unlabeled data to improve classification.

Semi-supervised machine learning is interested in the problem of transferring existing ground truth labels to the unlabeled (and already available) data. When in order to solve this problem we make use of the underlying data distribution we talk of *transductive* learning. This is in contrast with the *inductive* learning already encountered in previous chapters (Chaps. 4 and 5), where the test data are *not* available at training time.

Intuitively, in transductive classification we wish to separate the data so as to: (i) keep different known class labels in different regions, and (ii) make sure that classification boundaries go through areas of low data density. This chapter discusses the use of decision forests for both: (i) transductive classification, and (ii) building an inductive classifier on top of a previously trained transductive one. We will borrow concepts from both supervised classification and density estimation.

After a brief literature survey, we show how to adapt the abstract forest model of Chap. 3 to achieve efficient semi-supervised classification. The use of decision forests for the related *active learning* task is also briefly discussed. Numerous illus-

A. Criminisi (✉) · J. Shotton
Microsoft Research Ltd., 7 J.J. Thomson Avenue, Cambridge CB3 0FB, UK

A. Criminisi, J. Shotton (eds.), *Decision Forests for Computer Vision and Medical Image Analysis*, Advances in Computer Vision and Pattern Recognition, DOI 10.1007/978-1-4471-4929-3_8, © Springer-Verlag London 2013

trative examples and experiments will show advantages and disadvantages of semi-supervised forests with respect to alternative algorithms.

8.1 Semi-supervised Learning in the Literature

Excellent, recent references for semi-supervised learning and active learning are [61, 68, 364, 425] which provide a nice structure to the vast amount of literature on these topics. A thorough literature survey is well beyond the scope of this chapter and here we focus on a few, key papers.

A popular technique for semi-supervised learning is transductive support vector machines [172, 395]. Transductive SVM (TSVM) is an extension of the popular support vector machine algorithm [380] which maximizes the separation of both labeled and unlabeled data. The experimental section of this chapter will present comparisons between forests and TSVM.

In [211] the authors discuss the use of decision forests for semi-supervised learning. They achieve this via an iterative, deterministic annealing optimization. Tree-based semi-supervised techniques for vision and medical applications are presented in [53, 60, 94]. Here we introduce a new, simple and efficient semi-supervised forest algorithm.

8.2 Specializing the Decision Forest Model for Semi-supervised Classification

This section specializes the generic forest model introduced in Chap. 3 for use in semi-supervised classification. This model can also be extended to semi-supervised regression though this is not discussed here.

Problem Statement   The transductive classification task may be summarized as follows:

> *Given a set of both labeled and unlabeled data points, we wish to associate a class label to all the already available unlabeled data points.*

Unlike inductive classification here all unlabeled "test" data are already available during training.

The desired output (and consequently the training labels) are of discrete, categorical type (unordered). More formally, given an input point $\mathbf{v}$ we wish to associate it with a discrete class label c. As usual the input is represented as a multi-dimensional feature response vector $\mathbf{v} = (x_1, \ldots, x_d) \in \mathbb{R}^d$.

We consider two types of input data: *labeled* $\mathbf{v}^l \in \mathcal{L}$ and *unlabeled* $\mathbf{v}^u \in \mathcal{U}$. This is illustrated in Fig. 8.1a, where data points are denoted with circles. Colored circles indicate labeled training points, with different colors denoting different labels. Unlabeled data are shown in gray. Figure 8.1b, c further illustrate the difference between transductive and inductive classification.

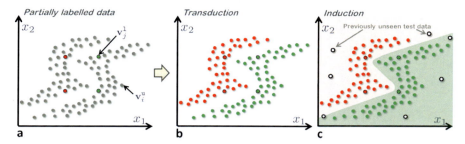

Fig. 8.1 Semi-supervised forest: transduction *vs.* induction. (**a**) Partially labeled input data points in their two-dimensional feature space. Different colors denote different class labels. Already available but unlabeled data are shown in *gray*. (**b**) In *transductive* learning we wish to propagate the existing ground truth labels to the many unlabeled data points available; and only to those. (**c**) In *inductive* learning we wish to learn (from all available training data) a generic function that can be applied to previously unavailable test points (denoted with *white circles*). Training a conventional classifier on the labeled data only would produce a sub-optimal classification surface (a vertical line in this case). Decision forests can effectively exploit partially labeled data and address both transduction and induction within the same efficient framework

What Are Semi-supervised Forests? A transductive forest is a collection of trees that have been trained on partially labeled data. Both labeled and unlabeled data are used to optimize an objective function with two components: a supervised component and an unsupervised component, as described next.

8.2.1 The Training Objective Function

As usual, forest training is achieved by optimizing the parameters of each internal node j via

$$\boldsymbol{\theta}_j = \arg\max_{\boldsymbol{\theta} \in \mathcal{T}_j} I(\mathcal{S}_j, \boldsymbol{\theta}). \tag{8.1}$$

Different trees are trained separately and independently. The main difference with respect to other forest types is that here the objective function I must encourage both: (i) separation of the labeled training data, as well as (ii) separating different high-density regions from one another. This may be achieved by maximizing the following mixed information gain:

$$I(\mathcal{S}_j, \boldsymbol{\theta}) = I^{\mathrm{u}}(\mathcal{S}_j, \boldsymbol{\theta}) + \alpha I^{\mathrm{s}}(\mathcal{S}_j, \boldsymbol{\theta}). \tag{8.2}$$

In the equation above I^{s} is a supervised term and depends on the labeled training data points only. In contrast, I^{u} is the unsupervised term and depends on all data points, both labeled and unlabeled. The scalar parameter α is user defined and specifies the relative weight between the two terms.

As in conventional classification, the term I^s is an information gain defined over discrete class distributions:

$$I^s(\mathcal{S}_j, \boldsymbol{\theta}) = H(\tilde{\mathcal{S}}_j) - \sum_{i \in \{L,R\}} \frac{|\tilde{\mathcal{S}}_j^i|}{|\tilde{\mathcal{S}}_j|} H(\tilde{\mathcal{S}}_j^i) \qquad (8.3)$$

with the entropy for the subset $\tilde{\mathcal{S}} = \mathcal{S} \cap \mathcal{L}$ of training points $H(\tilde{\mathcal{S}}) = -\sum_c p(c) \log p(c)$ with c the ground truth class labels of the points in $\tilde{\mathcal{S}}$.

Similarly, as in density estimation, the unsupervised gain term I^u is defined via the differential entropy of a multivariate Gaussian density. Therefore:

$$I^u(\mathcal{S}_j, \boldsymbol{\theta}) = \log|\Lambda(\mathcal{S}_j)| - \sum_{i \in \{L,R\}} \frac{|\mathcal{S}_j^i|}{|\mathcal{S}_j|} \log|\Lambda(\mathcal{S}_j^i)| \qquad (8.4)$$

for all points in $\mathcal{S}_j \subseteq (\mathcal{U} \cup \mathcal{L})$. Like in Chap. 6 we have made the working assumption of Gaussian node densities.

Having described the basic model components, the next two sections will describe both the transductive and inductive flavors of semi-supervised forests.

8.3 Transduction Trees for Classifying Already Available Data

This section presents tree-based transduction as a process of label propagation, from the annotated data points to the available un-annotated points. We are given a partially labeled dataset (as in Fig. 8.2a) which we use to train a transductive forest of size T and maximum depth D by maximizing the mixed information gain (8.2).

Different trees randomly produce different partitions of the feature space as shown in Figure 8.2b, c, d. The different colored regions represent different clusters (leaves) in each of the three partitions. If we use Gaussian models then each leaf stores a different Gaussian distribution (learned for example by maximum likelihood) for the points within. Label transduction from annotated data to un-annotated data can be achieved directly via the following minimization:

$$c(\mathbf{v}^u) \leftarrow c\left(\arg\min_{\mathbf{v}^l \in \mathcal{L}} Q(\mathbf{v}^u, \mathbf{v}^l)\right) \quad \forall \mathbf{v}^u \in \mathcal{U}. \qquad (8.5)$$

The function $c(\cdot)$ returns the class index associated with a point in $\mathcal{L}$. The generic geodesic distance $Q(\cdot, \cdot)$ is defined as

$$Q(\mathbf{v}^u, \mathbf{v}^l) = \min_{\Gamma \in \mathcal{G}} \sum_{i=0}^{|\Gamma|-1} d(\mathbf{s}_i, \mathbf{s}_{i+1}), \qquad (8.6)$$

with Γ a geodesic path (here represented as a discrete collection of points), $|\Gamma|$ the path's length, $\mathcal{G}$ the set of all possible geodesic paths and the initial and end points

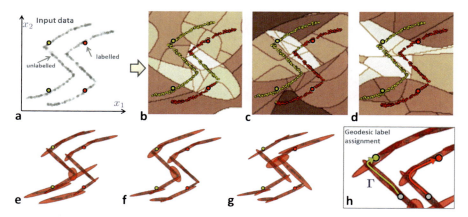

Fig. 8.2 Class label transduction in semi-supervised forests. (**a**) Input points, only four of which are labeled as belonging to two classes (*red* and *yellow*). (**b, c, d**) Different transductive trees produce different partitions of the feature space. Geodesic distance minimization enables assigning labels to the originally unlabeled points. Different regions of high data density tend to be separated by cluster boundaries. Points in the central region (away from original ground truth labels) tend to have less stable assignments. In the context of the entire forest this behavior captures uncertainty of transducted label assignments. (**e, f, g**) Different trees induce different Gaussian assignments at the leaves. (**h**) Label propagation via geodesic path assignment

$\mathbf{s}_0 = \mathbf{v}^u$, $\mathbf{s}_{|\Gamma|} = \mathbf{v}^l$, respectively. The local distances $d(\cdot, \cdot)$ are defined as symmetric Mahalanobis distances

$$d(\mathbf{s}_i, \mathbf{s}_j) = \frac{1}{2}\left(\mathbf{d}_{ij}{}^\top \Lambda_{l(\mathbf{v}_i)}^{-1}\mathbf{d}_{ij} + \mathbf{d}_{ij}{}^\top \Lambda_{l(\mathbf{v}_j)}^{-1}\mathbf{d}_{ij}\right) \tag{8.7}$$

with $\mathbf{d}_{ij} = \mathbf{s}_i - \mathbf{s}_j$ and $\Lambda_{l(\mathbf{v}_i)}$ the covariance associated with the leaf reached by the point $\mathbf{v}_i$ in the tth tree. Figure 8.2h shows an illustration. Using Mahalanobis local distances (as opposed to *e.g.* Euclidean ones) discourages paths from cutting across regions of low data density, a key requirement for transductive learning. In practice, we now have geodesics defined on the space of the automatically inferred probability density function.

Note that since all points in a leaf are associated with the same Gaussian, the label propagation algorithm can be implemented very efficiently (though approximately) by acting on each leaf cluster rather than on individual points. For instance, one can compute geodesic distances only between the cluster centroids and then assign the same label to all points within the same cluster. Very efficient geodesic distance transform algorithms exist [76].

Some example results of label propagation are shown in Fig. 8.2b, c, d. Figure 8.2e, f, g illustrate the corresponding Gaussian clusters associated with the leaves. Following label transduction (8.5) each unlabeled points remain associated with exactly one of the two labels for each tree (Fig. 8.2b, c, d). This label assignment process may be interpreted as *each individual tree* producing a distribution $p_t^u(c|\mathbf{v}^u)$ defined for the existing unlabeled data points in $\mathcal{U}$. The function $p_t^u(c|\mathbf{v}^u)$

is actually just a delta function centered at one of the class labels of interest, for each unlabeled input point $\mathbf{v}^u$. Thus $p_t^u(c = c_k|\mathbf{v}^u) \in \{0, 1\}$.

8.3.1 Transductive Ensemble

The transducted labels assigned to a point $\mathbf{v}^u$ are (in general) different for each tree, and they are more stable for points closer to the original supervised data points. Looking at this variability across the entire set of trees provides us with a means to estimate assignment confidence. In fact, by using the familiar averaging operation we have the following *transductive* forest posterior:

$$p^u(c|\mathbf{v}^u) = \frac{1}{T} \sum_t^T p_t^u(c|\mathbf{v}^u). \tag{8.8}$$

Thus, in contrast to some other transductive algorithms a semi-supervised forest may produce a soft, probabilistic output $p^u(c|\mathbf{v}^u)$.

8.4 Induction from Transduction

The previous section has described how to propagate class labels from annotated data points to already available but un-annotated ones. Here we describe how to infer a general probabilistic classification rule $p(c|\mathbf{v})$ that may be applied to previously unavailable test input ($\mathbf{v} \notin \mathcal{U} \cup \mathcal{L}$).

If we have already trained multiple transductive trees then they define multiple partitions of the entire input feature space (Fig. 8.2b, c, d). However, many cells (corresponding to tree leaves) in such partitions may contain no annotated data (while containing some un-annotated data). Therefore, trying to estimate empirical class posteriors directly (using only the annotated data) is not possible.

Usually, in the literature, once transduction has been achieved one may think of using the newly labeled data as ground truth and train a conventional inductive classifier from scratch. This could be expensive. We next show how one can avoid this second step and go directly from transduction to induction without further training.

We have two alternatives. First, we could apply the geodesic-based algorithm in (8.5) to every new test input point and propagate labels that way. However, this involves T shortest-path computations for each new point $\mathbf{v}$. A simpler alternative involves constructing an inductive posterior from the existing partitions of the feature space, as shown next.

After transduction forest training we are left with T trees and their corresponding partitions (Fig. 8.2b, c, d). After label propagation we have also attached a class label to *all* available data (with different trees possibly assigning different classes to the points in the set $\mathcal{U}$). Now, just like in supervised classification, counting the examples of each class arriving at each leaf defines the tree posteriors $p_t(c|\mathbf{v})$. These act upon the entire feature space in which a point $\mathbf{v}$ lives and not just the already available training points.

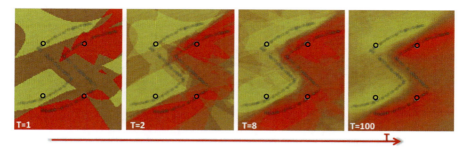

Fig. 8.3 Learning a generic, inductive classification rule from partially labeled data. Output classification posteriors, tested on all points in a rectangular section of the feature space. Labeled training points are indicated by *colored circles* (only four of those per image, here). Available unlabeled data are shown as *small gray squares*. A classifier trained only on the supervised data points would separate the left and right sides of the feature space with a *straight, vertical line*. In contrast here the separating surface is "S"-shaped because it has been correctly affected by the density of the unlabeled points. From left to right the number of trees in the forest increases from $T = 1$ to $T = 100$

8.4.1 Inductive Ensemble

Therefore, the *inductive* forest class posterior has the familiar form

$$p(c|\mathbf{v}) = \frac{1}{T} \sum_{t=1}^{T} p_t(c|\mathbf{v}). \tag{8.9}$$

The difference between this and a conventional classification forest (also inductive) is that training here has been achieved by maximizing a mixed information gain which takes into consideration both supervised *and* unsupervised, already available data. Building this form of inductive forest posterior is efficient as it does not require training a whole new classifier from scratch.

Figure 8.3 shows classification results on the same data as in Fig. 8.2. Now the inductive classification posterior is tested on *all* points within a rectangular section of the 2D feature space. As expected a larger forest size T produces much smoother posteriors. Note also how the inferred separating surface is "S"-shaped since it takes into account the unlabeled points (small gray squares). Finally, we observe that classification uncertainty is greater in the central region due to its increased distance from the four ground truth labeled points (yellow and red circles).

8.4.2 Discussion

In the above, we have shown how a relatively simple modification of the training objective function leads our generic forest model to deal with the task of semi-supervised classification. It turns out that semi-supervised classification can be used

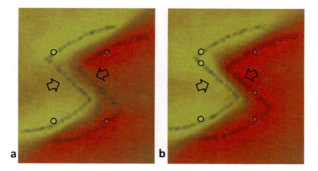

Fig. 8.4 Active learning. (**a**) Inductive posterior trained with only four annotated points and hundreds of unlabeled ones. The central region shows lower confidence (pointed at by *arrows*). (**b**) As before, but with two additional labeled points placed in regions of high uncertainty in (**a**). The confidence of the classifier increases in the central region, and the overall posterior appears sharper

effectively both for transduction and for building an inductive classifier out of existing transductive trees. The latter is achieved efficiently as it does not necessitate a further training procedure.

Finally, we should highlight that semi-supervised forests are very different from *e.g.* self-training techniques [312]. Self-training techniques work by: (i) training a supervised classifier, (ii) classifying the unlabeled data, (iii) using the newly classified data (or perhaps only the most confident subset) to train a new classifier, and then proceed iteratively. In contrast, semi-supervised forests are not iterative. Additionally, they are driven by a clear objective function, the maximization of which encourages the separating surface to go through regions of low data density, while respecting the few existing ground truth annotations.

8.5 Examples, Comparisons and Effect of Model Parameters

We now investigate the effect of the forest model parameters on the accuracy and generalization ability of our semi-supervised forests. The presented illustrative examples are designed to bring to life different properties of semi-supervised forests. Qualitative comparisons between semi-supervised forests and alternatives techniques are also presented.

Figure 8.3 has already shown how the (unknown) density of unlabeled data affects the classifier, and the effect of the forest size T. Next, we discuss the effect of increasing the amount of supervision (the number of labeled points).

8.5.1 The Effect of Additional Supervision, and Active Learning

In the experiment in Fig. 8.4a, the central region of the classification posterior shows higher uncertainty (dimmer, more orange pixels) than the rest. Thus, as typical of active learning [54] we might decide to collect and manually annotate additional

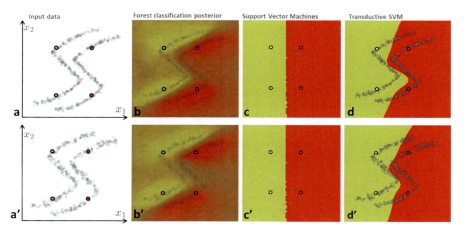

Fig. 8.5 Semi-supervised forests, SVMs and transductive SVMs. (**a**) Input partially labeled data points. (**b**) Semi-supervised forest classification posterior. Uncertainty is visualized through mixed, orange colors. (**c**) Unsurprisingly, conventional SVM produces a straight, vertical separating surface as it is not affected by the unlabeled set. (**d**) Transductive SVM tends to follow regions of low density. However, TSVM still does not model uncertainty. (**a′**) As in (**a**) but with larger noise in the point positions. (**b′**) The increased training noise is reflected in lower forest prediction confidence. (**c′**, **d′**) as (**c**) and (**d**), respectively, but run on the noisier training set (**a′**)

data precisely in those low-confidence regions. As illustrated in Fig. 8.4b, adding just two more annotated data points in the "right" place produces a much more confident posterior. By the same token, adding extra annotated data close to the existing supervised set would not make much of a difference.

The importance of having a probabilistic output and thus being able to reason about uncertainty should be clear here. In fact, it is the *confidence* of the prediction (and not the class prediction itself) which guides the selection of additional data to be annotated.

Next, we compare semi-supervised forests with alternative algorithms.

8.5.2 Comparison with Transductive SVMs

Figure 8.5 shows a comparison between semi-supervised forests, SVMs [380] and transductive SVMs [172, 395], on the same two input datasets.[1]

In the figure we observe a number of effects. First, unlike SVMs, the forest captures uncertainty. As expected, more noise in the input data (either in the labeled or unlabeled sets, or both) is reflected in lower prediction confidence. Second, while transductive SVMs manage to exploit the presence of available unlabeled data, they

---

[1] In this experiment the SVM and transductive SVM results were generated using the "SVM-light" Matlab toolbox in http://svmlight.joachims.org/. Parameters were chosen manually to try and produce the visually best results.

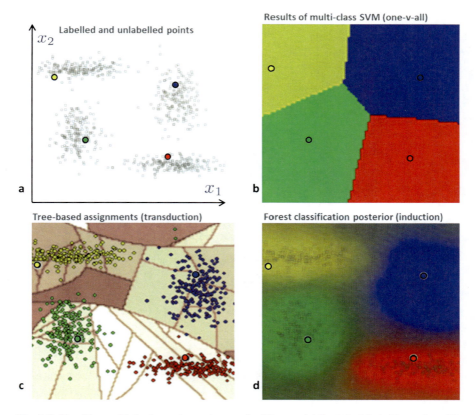

Fig. 8.6 Handling multiple classes in semi-supervised forests. (**a**) Partially labeled input data. We have only four labeled points, each annotated with a different class (different colors for different classes). (**b**) Classification results for one-vs.-all SVM. (**c**) Transduction results for a single decision tree. Originally unlabeled points are assigned a class via the tree-induced geodesic distances. (**d**) Inductive semi-supervised classification posterior. The density of all available data points contribute to the shape of the posterior. Regions of low prediction confidence nicely overlap regions of low data density

still produce a hard, binary classification; for instance, larger amounts of noise in the training data are not reflected in the TSVM separating surface.

8.5.3 Handling Multiple Classes

The hierarchical structure of semi-supervised forests allows them to handle both 2-class problems as well as multiple-class (>2) tasks effortlessly.

This is demonstrated in Fig. 8.6 with a four-class synthetic experiment. The input points are randomly drawn from four bi-variate Gaussians. Out of hundreds of points, only four are manually assigned to the four different classes (denoted by different colors). Conventional one-vs.-all SVM classification results in hard class

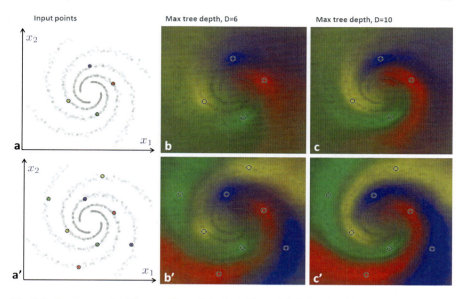

Fig. 8.7 Semi-supervised forest: effect of depth. (**a**) Input labeled and unlabeled points. We have four labeled points and four classes (*color coded*). (**a'**) As in (**a**) but with double the labeled data. (**b, b'**) Semi-supervised forest classification posterior for $D = 6$ tree levels. (**c, c'**) Semi-supervised forest classification posterior for $D = 10$ tree levels. The best results are obtained in (**c'**), with largest amount of labeled data and deepest trees

assignments (Fig. 8.6b). Tree-based transductive label propagation results are shown in Fig. 8.6c (for a single tree). Slightly different assignments are achieved for different trees (not shown). The forest-based inductive posterior (computed for $T = 100$) is shown in Fig. 8.6d. There, regions of low confidence in the inductive forest posterior are shown to be aligned with regions of low data density.

8.5.4 The Effect of Tree Depth

Figure 8.7 illustrates the effect of the depth parameter D. We have two four-class examples, with input data points distributed along four-arm spirals. In the top row we have only four labeled points (and hundreds of unlabeled ones). In the bottom row we have eight points manually annotated into the four classes. Unsurprisingly, increasing the depth D from 6 to 10 produces more accurate and confident results. So does increasing the amount of supervision. Adding further manually annotated points in the central region would produce better delineation of each individual spiral arm.

8.6 Summary

This chapter has taken the abstract decision forest model of Chap. 3 and specialized it for semi-supervised classification. We have also discussed the difference between transductive and inductive learning and shown how semi-supervised forests can achieve both in a unified way.

Toy experiments have illustrated the effects of various parameters on the accuracy and confidence of the predicted output. For examples we have analyzed the effect of additional supervision and its relation to active learning. Once again, here we have shown not more than proof of concepts. Further experiments on real data are necessary to assess the validity of this approach in practical applications. Many more examples, animations and demo videos are available in [79, 80].

8.7 Exercises and Experiments

This section presents exercises on semi-supervised forests. They can be run by using the now familiar Sherwood software library in http://research.microsoft.com/projects/decisionforests. As usual, please refer to Chap. 22 for instructions on how to build and use the library.

Exercise 8.1

To begin, type `sw ssclas` in a command window to get a list of instructions.
Reproduce the results of Fig. 8.4a by running:
```
sw ssclas exp1.txt /d 5 /t 100
```
- What happens if we decrease the forest size to $T = 1$?
  ```
  sw ssclas exp1.txt /d 5 /t 1
  ```
  Run the above command multiple times and observe changes.
  Explore further varying T.
- What happens when we vary the tree depth D?
  ```
  sw ssclas exp1.txt /d 2 /t 100
  sw ssclas exp1.txt /d 4 /t 100
  sw ssclas exp1.txt /d 6 /t 100
  sw ssclas exp1.txt /d 8 /t 100
  ```

Exercise 8.2

Compare the results of Fig. 8.4a and Fig. 8.4b by running the commands:
```
sw ssclas exp1.txt /d 5 /t 200 /split linear
sw ssclas exp4.txt /d 5 /t 200 /split linear
```
Which has more supervision? Which has higher prediction confidence?
Flip between the two output images to appreciate differences.

Exercise 8.3

Try experimenting with a noisier training set by running:
```
sw ssclas exp3.txt /d 5 /t 200 /split linear
```
and observe the confidence in the central region. As usual, experiment with modifying various other parameters.

Exercise 8.4

Reproduce the results of the multi-class classification problem in Fig. 8.6 by running:

```
sw ssclas exp5.txt /d 5 /t 20 /split linear
```

- Explore using a range of values for parameters T and D. E.g.
```
sw ssclas exp5.txt /d 5 /t 1 /split linear
sw ssclas exp5.txt /d 5 /t 200 /split linear
sw ssclas exp5.txt /d 2 /t 200 /split linear
sw ssclas exp5.txt /d 10 /t 200 /split linear
```
What are the effects on prediction confidence?

Exercise 8.5

Here is a more complex 4-class example:

```
sw ssclas exp9.txt /d 10 /t 200 /a 2 /split linear
```

- Compare the output of the above experiment with that of
```
sw ssclas exp10.txt /d 10 /t 200 /a 2 /split linear
```
What is the effect of the additional supervision?

As usual, analyze the effect of modifying various forest parameters for both sets of input data.

Part II
Applications in Computer Vision and Medical Image Analysis

Part II discusses the application of the general forest model of Part I to several concrete computer vision and medical image analysis tasks. The chapters in this part are contributed by various international researchers expert in decision forests and their variants.

Chapter 9
Keypoint Recognition Using Random Forests and Random Ferns

V. Lepetit and P. Fua

In many 3D object detection and pose estimation problems, run-time performance is of critical importance. However, there usually is time to train the system. We introduce an approach that takes advantage of this fact by formulating the wide-baseline matching of keypoints extracted from the input images to those found in the model images as a classification problem. This shifts much of the computational burden to a training phase and eliminates the need for expensive patch preprocessing, without sacrificing recognition performance. This makes our approach highly suitable for real-time operations on low-powered devices.

To this end, we developed two related methods. The first uses random forests that rely on simple binary tests on image intensities surrounding the keypoints. In the second, we flatten the trees to turn them into simple bit strings, which we will refer to as ferns, and combine their output in a Naïve Bayesian manner. Surprisingly, the ferns, while simpler, actually perform better than the trees. This is because the Naïve Bayesian approach benefits more from the thousands of synthetic training examples we can generate than output averaging as usually performed by decision forests. Furthermore, the more general partition that the trees allow does not appear to be of great use for our problem.

9.1 Introduction

In many 3D object detection and rigid object pose estimation problems ranging from augmented reality to visual servoing, run-time performance is of critical importance. However, there usually is time to train the system before actually using it. Furthermore 3D models, or multiple images from which such models can be built, tend to

Parts of this chapter are reprinted, with permission, from [214], © 2005 IEEE.

V. Lepetit (✉) · P. Fua
Ecole Polytechnique Fédérale de Lausanne, Lausanne, Switzerland

be available. As illustrated in Fig. 9.1, we describe here a technique designed to operate effectively in this context by shifting much of the computational burden to the training phase so that run-time detection becomes both fast and reliable. Our general approach, like many others, relies on matching interest points extracted from training images with those extracted from input images acquired at run-time, under potentially large perspective and scale variations. It turns out to be very simple to implement, and to perform as accurately as SIFT [225] while being faster.

Interest points are usually matched by building affine-invariant descriptors of the surrounding image patches and comparing them across images. This typically involves fine scale selection, rotation correction, and intensity normalization [225, 249]. It results in a high computational overhead and often requires handcrafting the descriptors to achieve insensitivity to specific kinds of distortion.

Instead, we turn this problem into a classification one. More specifically, we consider the set of all possible appearances of each individual object keypoint as a class, which we refer to as a *view set*. During training, given at least one image of the target object, we extract interest points and generate numerous synthetic views of their possible appearance under perspective distortion, which are then used to train a classifier. It is used at run-time to recognize the keypoints under perspective and scale variations by deciding to which view set, if any, their appearance belongs.

We first consider using classification forests [5], as described in Chap. 4, as the classification technique, because they naturally handle multi-class problems. Furthermore, they are robust and fast, while remaining reasonably easy to train. We then show that, for our application, the trees can be profitably replaced by non-hierarchical structures known as *ferns* to classify the patches. Each one consists of a small set of binary tests and returns the probability that a patch belongs to any one of the classes that have been learned during training. These responses are then combined in a Naïve Bayesian way. As before, we train our classifier by synthesizing many views of the keypoints extracted from a training image as they would appear under different perspective or scale. Thanks to the Naïve Bayesian approach, the ferns are more reliable than the trees, while being faster and simpler to implement. Neither of our approaches require *ad hoc* patch normalization, and allow for fast and incremental training.

9.2 Wide-Baseline Point Matching as a Classification Problem

Our approach to object detection and pose estimation relies on matching keypoints found in an input image against those on a target object $\mathcal{O}$. Once potential correspondences have been established, we apply standard techniques to estimate the 3D pose. Therefore, the critical step in achieving results such as those depicted in Fig. 9.1 is the fast and robust wide-baseline matching that handling large perspective and scale changes implies. We formulate this below as a classification problem.

During training, we first select a set $\mathcal{K}$ of K prominent keypoints lying on the object model. At run-time, given an input patch $\mathbf{v}$ centered at a keypoint extracted

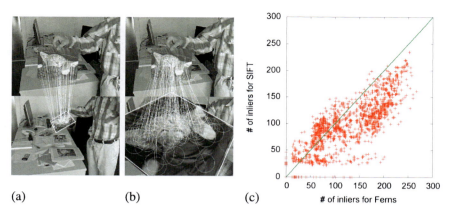

Fig. 9.1 Matching a mouse pad in a 1074-frame sequence against a reference image. (**a, b**) Matches obtained using ferns in a few frames. The reference image appears at the *top* and the input image from the video sequence at the *bottom*. (**c**) Scatter plot showing the number of inliers for each frame. The values on the x- and y-axes give the number of inliers for the ferns and SIFT, respectively. Most of the time, the ferns match at least as many points as SIFT and often even more, as can be seen from the fact that most of the points lie below the diagonal

from the input image, we want to decide whether or not its appearance matches that one of the K keypoints in $\mathcal{K}$. In other words, we want to find for $\mathbf{v}$ its class label $c(\mathbf{v}) \in \mathcal{C} = \{-1, 1, 2, \ldots, K\}$, where the -1 label denotes all the points that do not belong to $\mathcal{K}$.

In other tasks, such as face detection or character recognition, large training sets of labeled data are usually available. However, for automated pose estimation, it is expensive to require a very large number of real sample images. Instead, to achieve robustness with respect to pose and complex illumination changes, we use a small number of reference images and synthesize many new views of the object using simple rendering techniques. For each keypoint, this gives us a sampling of its view set, the set of all its possible appearances under different viewing conditions. These samplings are virtually infinite training sets. Figure 9.2 depicts such a sampling for several keypoints.

9.3 Keypoint Recognition with Classification Forests

Several classification algorithms, such as K-nearest neighbor, support vector machines or neural networks could have been chosen to implement the classifier Y introduced in Sect. 9.2. Among those, we have found decision forests [5] to be eminently suitable because they naturally handle multi-class problems, and are robust and fast, while remaining reasonably easy to train. We describe in this section their application to our specific problem. In the next section, we will show how they can be further simplified into another classifier we call ferns, while improving the performance.

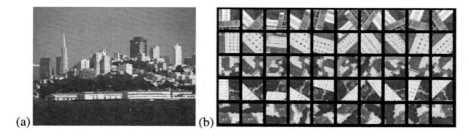

(a)   (b)

Fig. 9.2 (**a**) One of our reference images used in the evaluations. (**b**) Warped patches obtained by applying affine deformations to this image. In each line, the left most patch is the original one and the others are deformed versions of it. They are used to train our algorithms after the addition of noise

9.3.1 Random Classification Forests

We briefly recall here how decision forests can be used for classification. Each internal node of a tree contains a simple test that splits the space of data to be classified, in our case the space of image patches. Each leaf contains an estimate based on training data of the posterior distribution over the classes. A new patch is classified by dropping it down the tree and performing an elementary test at each node that sends it to one side or the other. When it reaches a leaf, it is assigned probabilities of belonging to a class depending on the distribution stored in the leaf. Since the numbers of classes, training examples and possible tests are large in our case, building the optimal tree quickly becomes intractable. Instead, multiple trees are grown so that each tree yields a different partition of the space of image patches.

Once the trees indexed by $t \in \{1, \dots, T\}$ are built, their responses are combined during classification to achieve a better recognition rate than that of a single tree. More formally, the tree leaves store posterior probabilities $p(c \mid l(t, \mathbf{v})) = p_t(c \mid \mathbf{v})$, where c is a label in $\mathcal{C}$ and $l(t, \mathbf{v})$ is the leaf of tree t reached by patch $\mathbf{v}$. Such probabilities are evaluated during training as the ratio of the number of patches of class c in the training set that reach l to the total number of patches that reach l. Patch $\mathbf{v}$ is classified by considering the average of the probabilities $p(c \mid l(t, \mathbf{v}))$:

$$\hat{Y}(\mathbf{v}) = \arg\max_c \sum_{t=1\dots T} p\big(c \mid l(t, \mathbf{v})\big). \tag{9.1}$$

A drawback of classification forests is their greedy use of memory. Their size in memory increases exponentially with the depth, and linearly with the number of trees. For example, a single tree of depth 15 uses about 32 MB for a 200 class problem. Therefore, the chosen number of trees and their depth are a trade-off between the computer memory dedicated to store them and the recognition rate. In Sect. 9.5, we study the influence of these parameters on the recognition rate.

9.3.2 Node Tests

In our implementation, the tests performed at the nodes are simple binary tests based on the difference of intensities of two pixels at position $\mathbf{p}_1$ and $\mathbf{p}_2$ taken in the neighborhood of the keypoint. We write these tests as

$$h_i\left(\mathbf{v}, \left(\mathbf{p}_1^i, \mathbf{p}_2^i\right)\right) = \left[J\left(\mathbf{v}, \mathbf{p}_1^i\right) \le J\left(\mathbf{v}, \mathbf{p}_2^i\right)\right] \qquad (9.2)$$

where $J(\mathbf{v}, \mathbf{p})$ is the intensity of patch $\mathbf{v}$ at pixel location $\mathbf{p}$, after Gaussian smoothing to reduce influence of noise. Such a test can be seen as a test on the polarity between the two locations $\mathbf{p}_1^i$ and $\mathbf{p}_2^i$. In all our experiments, the patches are of size 32×32, so that the total number of possible h tests is 2^{19}. Fortunately, since real-world images exhibit spatial coherence, only a very small subset of such candidate tests is required to yield good recognition rates.

As shown below, a few hundred of these simple tests are usually enough to classify a patch. This involves only a few hundreds intensity comparisons and additions per patch, and is therefore very fast. Furthermore, because they only depend on the order of the pixel intensities between neighbors, they tend to be fairly insensitive to illumination changes other than those caused by a moving shadow. In other words, to achieve the robustness to illumination effects demonstrated in Fig. 9.1, our technique, unlike many others, does *not* require us to normalize the pixel intensities, for example by setting the L_2 norm of the intensities to one.

9.3.3 Building the Trees

To improve the recognition rate, we use multiple trees that should partition the patch space in different manners. We experimented with two different methods for building such trees.

The first method is the one described in Chap. 4: the trees are constructed in the classical, top-down manner, where the tests are chosen by a greedy algorithm to best separate the given examples. The expected gain in information is used to evaluate the separation efficiency.

The second method is much faster and simpler: Instead of picking questions according to a criterion, we simply pick a random set, as also done in the extremely randomized trees [128] approach discussed in Chap. 10. This can be seen as an extreme simplification of the first method. The two locations $\mathbf{p}_1^i$ and $\mathbf{p}_2^i$ for each node are picked at random within the patch, independently of the training samples that fall into the node and of the tests performed further up in the tree.

To compare the two tree-building methods we have introduced, we used them both on a set of 200 keypoints. This resulted in two sets of trees whose depth was limited to the same value.

When using the entropy minimizing approach, we first synthesized 100 new views different for each tree to grow. We then recursively built the trees by trying

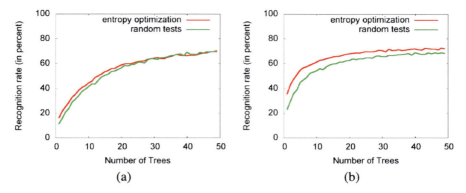

Fig. 9.3 Comparing the classification rates obtained using trees grown in two different manners, as a function of the number of trees. (**a**) Without and (**b**) with patch orientation normalization. The *red curves* depict results obtained by selecting tests that maximize the information gain. The *green curves* depict results obtained by randomly chosen tests, which result in a small loss of reliability but considerably reduces the training time. Note that in all cases the normalization lets us achieve better results with fewer trees. However, when enough trees are used, it does not improve the rates anymore

ρ different tests at each node and keeping the best one according to the information gain. For the root node, we chose $\rho = 10$, a very small number, to reduce the correlation between the resulting trees. For all other nodes, we used $\rho = 100d$, where d is the depth of the node.

In the case of the completely random approach to building trees, $\mathbf{p}_1^i$ and $\mathbf{p}_2^i$ were simply chosen uniformly at random. For the two sets, the tree depth is limited to a given maximum depth, and the posterior probabilities are estimated from 1000 new random views per keypoint.

For this experiment, we used trees with a depth limited to $D = 12$, which was found to be a good trade-off between the memory requirements and recognition rate. After having grown the trees, the posterior probabilities in the terminal nodes were estimated using 5000 new training images. We then measured the recognition rate R of the two sets of trees by generating new images under random poses, as the ratio of the number of correctly recognized patches and the total number of generated patches. The evolution of R for the two sets of trees with respect to the number of trees is depicted Fig. 9.3a. Taking the tests at random usually results in a small loss of reliability at least when the number of trees is not large enough but considerably reduces the learning time. The time dedicated to growing the trees drops from tens of minutes to a few seconds on a 2.8 GHz machine.

We also experimented with normalizing the **v** patches' orientations both during training and at run-time to achieve higher recognition rates for a given number of trees. As in [225] we attribute a 2D orientation to the keypoints that is estimated from the histogram of gradient directions in a patch centered at the keypoint. Note that in contrast with [225], we do not require a particularly repeatable method. We just want it to be reliable enough to reduce variation within classes. Once the orientation of an extracted keypoint is estimated, its neighborhood is rectified. Figure 9.3b compares the recognition rates with this normalization step for the two different methods of selecting the tests. Taking the tests at random results in a slightly larger but still small loss of reliability. More importantly, the normalization gives us significantly improved rates when using only a small number of trees. However, when using a large number of trees, the recognition rates are similar with and without the normalization.

We draw two practical conclusions from these experiments. First, using random tests is sufficient and keeps the learning time reasonable for practical applications. Second, the orientation normalization step is not required, but lets us reduce the number of trees. Therefore the choice of using such a normalization becomes a trade-off between the amount of time required to normalize and to classify, which is proportional to the number of trees. However, in the next section, we discuss an approach closely related to trees that reaches, without normalization, performances similar to the trees when normalization is used, for an equal amount of computation.

9.4 Keypoint Recognition with Random Ferns

In this section, we will argue that, when the tests are chosen randomly, the power of our general approach derives not from the tree structure itself but from the fact that combining groups of binary tests yields improved classification rates. To this end, we drop the hierarchical structure of the trees and group the tests into a flat structure that we call a fern. We first show that our ferns fit nicely into a Naïve Bayesian framework and yield better results and scalability in terms of number of classes. As a result, we can combine many more features, which is key to increasing performance.

9.4.1 Random Ferns

Our general approach is still similar to the one taken with the randomized trees in the previous section: given the patch surrounding a keypoint detected in an image, our task is to assign it to the most likely class. Let $h_j = h_j(\mathbf{v}, (\mathbf{p}_1^j, \mathbf{p}_2^j))$, $j = 1, \ldots, N$ be the set of binary features that will be calculated over the patch $\mathbf{v}$ we are trying to classify. Formally, we are looking for

$$\hat{Y}(\mathbf{v}) = \arg\max_c p(c \mid h_1, h_2, \ldots, h_N), \tag{9.3}$$

where c is a random variable that represents the class. Bayes' rule yields

$$p(c \mid h_1, h_2, \ldots, h_N) = \frac{p(h_1, h_2, \ldots, h_N \mid c) p(c)}{p(h_1, h_2, \ldots, h_N)}. \tag{9.4}$$

Assuming a uniform prior $p(c)$, since the denominator is simply a scale factor that is independent from the class, our problem reduces to finding

$$\arg\max_c p(h_1, h_2, \ldots, h_N \mid c). \tag{9.5}$$

Since the h_j features are very simple, we require many ($N \approx 300$) for accurate classification. Therefore a complete representation of the joint probability in (9.5) is not feasible since it would require estimating and storing 2^N entries for each class. One way to compress the representation is to assume independence between features. An extreme version is to assume complete independence, that is,

$$p(h_1, h_2, \ldots, h_N \mid c) = \prod_{j=1}^{N} p(h_j \mid c). \tag{9.6}$$

However, this completely ignores the correlation between features. To make the problem tractable while accounting for these dependencies, a good compromise is to partition our features into F groups of size $S = \frac{N}{F}$. These groups are what we define as *ferns* and we compute the joint probability for features in each fern. The conditional probability becomes

$$p(h_1, h_2, \ldots, h_N \mid c) = \prod_{f=1}^{F} p(\mathsf{F}_k \mid c), \tag{9.7}$$

where $\mathsf{F}_f = \{h_{\sigma(f,1)}, h_{\sigma(f,2)}, \ldots, h_{\sigma(f,S)}\}$, $f = 1, \ldots, F$ represents the fth fern and $\sigma(f, j)$ is a random permutation function with range $1, \ldots, N$. Hence, we follow a Semi-Naïve Bayesian [418] approach by modeling only some of the dependencies between features. The viability of such an approach has been shown by [168] in the context of image retrieval applications. In this new method, patch $\mathbf{v}$ is therefore classified using:

$$\hat{Y}(\mathbf{v}) = \arg\max_c \prod_{f=1}^{F} p(\mathsf{F}_f \mid c). \tag{9.8}$$

This formulation yields a tractable problem that involves $F \times 2^S$ parameters, with F between 30–50. In practice, as will be shown in Sect. 9.5, $S = 11$ yields good results. $F \times 2^S$ is therefore in the order of 80,000, which is much smaller than 2^N with $N \approx 450$ that the full joint probability representation would require. Our formulation is also flexible since performance/memory trade-offs can be made by changing the number of ferns and their sizes.

Note that we use randomization both in feature selection and also in grouping. An alternative approach would involve selecting feature groups to be as independent from each other as possible. This is routinely done by Semi-Naïve Bayesian classifiers based on a criteria such as the mutual information between features. However, in practice, we have not found this to be necessary to achieve good performance.

We have therefore chosen not to use such a strategy that preserves the simplicity and efficiency of our training scheme and that allows for incremental training.

9.4.2 Training the Ferns

The training phase estimates the class conditional probabilities $p(F_f \mid c)$ for each fern F_f and class c, as described in (9.7). For each fern F_f we write these terms as

$$p_{k,c} = p(F_f = k \mid c), \tag{9.9}$$

where we simplify our notations by considering F_f to be equal to k if the base 2 number formed by the binary features of F_f taken in sequence is equal to k. With this convention, each fern can take $K = 2^S$ values and we need to estimate the $p_{k,c}, k = 1, 2, \ldots, K$ under the constraint that their sums over k should be equal to 1. The simplest approach would be to assign the maximum likelihood estimate to these parameters from the training samples. For parameter $p_{k,c}$ it is

$$p_{k,c} = \frac{N_{k,c}}{N_c}, \tag{9.10}$$

where $N_{k,c}$ is the number of training samples of class c that evaluates to fern value k and N_c is the total number of samples for class c. These parameters can therefore be estimated for each fern independently.

In practice however, this simple scheme yields poor results because if no training sample for class c evaluates to k, which can easily happen when the number of samples is not infinitely large, both $N_{k,c}$ and $p_{k,c}$ will be zero. Since we multiply the $p_{k,c}$ for all ferns, it implies that, if the fern evaluates to k, the corresponding patch can *never* be associated to class c, no matter the response of the other ferns. This would make the ferns far too selective because the fact that $p_{k,c} = 0$ may simply be an artifact of the necessarily limited size of the training set. To overcome this problem we take $p_{k,c}$ to be

$$p_{k,c} = \frac{N_{k,c} + N_r}{N_c + K \times N_r}, \tag{9.11}$$

where N_r represents a regularization term, which behaves as a uniform Dirichlet prior [28] over feature values. If a sample with a specific fern value is not encountered during training, this scheme will still assign a non-zero value to the corresponding probability. We have found our estimator to be insensitive to the exact value of N_r and we use $N_r = 1$ in all our experiments. However, having N_r be strictly greater than zero is essential. This tallies with the observation that combining classifiers in a Naïve Bayesian fashion can be unreliable if improperly done.

In effect, our training scheme marginalizes over the pose space since the class conditional probabilities $P(F_f \mid c)$ depend on the camera poses relative to the

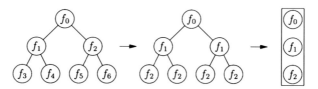

Fig. 9.4 Ferns *vs.* trees. A tree can be transformed into a fern by performing the following steps. First, we constrain the tree to systematically perform the same test across any given hierarchy level, which results in the same feature being evaluated independently of the path taken to get to a particular node. Second, we do away with the hierarchical structure and simply store the feature values at each level. This means applying a sequence of tests to the patch, which is what ferns do

object. By densely sampling the pose space and summing over all samples, we marginalize over these pose parameters. Hence at run-time, the statistics can be used in a pose independent manner, which is key to real-time performance. Furthermore, the training algorithm itself is very efficient since it only requires storing the $N_{k,c}$ counts for each fern while discarding the training samples immediately after use, which means that we can use arbitrarily many if needs be.

9.5 Comparing Random Forests, Random Ferns, and SIFT

9.5.1 Empirical Comparisons of Trees and Ferns

Ferns differ from trees in two important respects: as shown in Fig. 9.4, ferns can be considered as simplified trees. Also, as can be easily seen by comparing (9.1) and (9.8), the trees average posteriors while the ferns rely on products of conditional probabilities. Whether or not the differences degrade the classification performance hinges on whether our randomly chosen binary features are still appropriate in this context. In this section, we will show that they are indeed. In fact, because our Naïve Bayesian scheme outperforms the averaging of posteriors, the ferns are both simpler and more powerful.

To compare randomized trees and ferns, we experiment with three reference images including the one shown in Fig. 9.2. We extracted stable keypoints from these images and assigned a unique class id to each of them. The classification is done using patches that are 32×32 pixels in size. To disentangle the influence of the differences between trees and ferns, we consider four different scenarios:

1. Using randomized trees and averaging of class posterior distributions.
2. Using randomized trees and combining class conditional distributions in a Naïve-Bayesian way.
3. Using ferns and averaging of class posterior distributions.
4. Using ferns and combining class conditional distributions in a Naïve-Bayesian way.

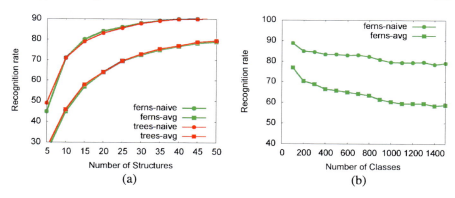

Fig. 9.5 Average percentage of correctly classified image patches over many trials (recognition rate) for randomized trees of depth 11 and random ferns with 11 features each. (**a**) Recognition rate as a function of the number of trees or ferns. Using the Naïve Bayesian assumption gives much better rates at reduced number of structures, while the fern and tree structures are interchangeable. (**b**) Recognition rate as a function of the number of classes. While the naïve combination produces a very slow decrease in performance, posterior averaging exhibits a much sharper drop

Also the number of features evaluated per patch by the two classifiers is equal in all cases. As explained in Sect. 9.2, the training and testing sets are obtained from the reference images. We randomly deform these images with affine deformations that can arbitrarily rotate the images, skew and scale them over a large range, and add Gaussian noise. More details on this experimental setup can be found in [280].

In Fig. 9.5a, we plot the results as a function of the number of trees or ferns being used. We first note that using either flat fern or hierarchical tree structures does not affect the recognition rate, which was to be expected as the features are taken completely at random. In contrast, the Naïve-Bayesian combination strategy outperforms the averaging of posteriors and achieves a higher recognition rate even when using relatively few structures.

Figure 9.5b shows that the performance of the Naïve-Bayesian combination does not degrade rapidly with the number of classes, and scales much better than averaging posteriors. For both methods, the required amounts of memory and computation increase linearly with the number of classes, since we assign a separate class for each keypoint.

Increasing the fern size S or the tree depth by one doubles the number of parameters hence the memory required to store the distributions. It also implies that more training samples should be used to estimate the increased number of parameters. It has, however, negligible effect on the run-time speed and larger ferns or trees can therefore handle more variation at the cost of training time and memory but without much of a slow-down.

In contrast, adding more ferns or trees to the classifier requires only a linear increase in memory and computation time. Since the training samples for other ferns or trees can be reused, it only has a negligible effect on training time. As shown in Fig. 9.6, for a given amount of memory the best recognition rate is obtained by using many relatively small ferns. However, this comes at the expense of run-time

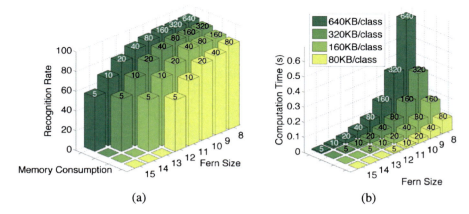

Fig. 9.6 Recognition rate (**a**) and computation time in seconds (**b**) as a function of the amount of memory available and the size of the ferns being used. The number of ferns used is indicated on the top of each bar and the y-axis shows the fern size. The color of the bar represents the required memory amount, when using single precision floating numbers. Note that while using many small ferns achieves higher recognition rates, it also entails a higher computational cost

speed and when sufficient memory is available, a fern size of $S = 11$ (used in our experiments) represents a good compromise.

9.5.2 Empirical Comparisons Between SIFT and Ferns

We used the 1074-frame video depicted in Fig. 9.1 to compare ferns against SIFT for planar object detection. It shows a mouse pad undergoing motions involving a large range of rotations, scalings, and perspective deformations against a cluttered background. The graph on the right shows that the ferns can match as many points as SIFT and sometimes even more.

It is difficult to perform a completely fair speed comparison between our ferns and SIFT for several reasons. SIFT reuses intermediate data from the keypoint extraction to compute canonical scale and orientations and the descriptors, while ferns can rely on a low-cost keypoint extraction. On the other hand, the distributed SIFT C code is not optimized, and the Best-Bin-First KD-tree of [21] is not used to speed up the nearest-neighbor search. However, it is relatively easy to see that performing the individual tests of Sect. 9.3.2 requires very little time and most of the time is spent computing the sums of the posterior probabilities. Computing the SIFT descriptors, which is the most difficult part to optimize, takes about 1 ms on a laptop without including the time required to convolve the image. In contrast, ferns take 13.5×10^{-3} milliseconds to classify one keypoint into 200 classes on the same machine. Of course, the ability to classify keypoints fast comes at the cost of requiring a training stage, which is usually off-line. In contrast, SIFT does not require training and for some applications such as matching of arbitrary images, this is still clearly an advantage.

9.6 Discussion

The key conclusion of our work is that, in our specific context, the Naïve-Bayesian combination of classifiers as done by the ferns clearly outperforms the averaging of probabilities, as in the case of random forests. While we do not know of a clear theoretical argument explaining the superiority of Naïve-Bayesian techniques for our purposes, there are pragmatic reasons for choosing them. First, the product models can represent much sharper distributions [163] (see also Chap. 3). Indeed, when averaging is used to combine distributions, the resulting mixture has higher variance than the individual components. More intuitively, if a single fern strongly rejects a keypoint class, it can counter the combined effect of all the other ferns that gives a weak positive response. This increases the necessity of larger amounts of training data and the help of a prior regularization term as discussed in Sect. 9.2. Second, the classification task, which just picks a single class, will not be adversely affected by the approximation errors in the joint distribution as long as the maximum probability is assigned to the correct class [92, 116]. We have shown that such a naïve combination strategy is a worthwhile alternative when the specific problem is not overly sensitive to the implied independence assumptions.

9.7 Application Example

We briefly present in this section an application of our approach to real-time image annotation. With the recent proliferation of ultra mobile platforms with higher processing power, there has been a surge of interest in building real-world applications that can automatically annotate the photos and provide useful information about places of interest. These applications test keypoint matching algorithms to their limits under constantly changing lighting conditions and with changes in the scene texture that reduces the number of reliable keypoints. We have tested the ferns on such an application that annotates parts of a historical building with 3D structure. It runs smoothly at frame rate using a standard laptop and an off-the-shelf web camera.

Annotating a 3D object requires training using multiple images from different viewpoints. Thanks to the ferns approach, we can easily integrate the information from several images. We then obtain a 3D model for the object using standard structure from motion algorithms to register the training images followed by dense reconstruction [357]. The resulting fine mesh was too detailed and we approximated it by a coarser one. Despite its rough structure, this 3D model allows annotation of important parts of the object and the correct reprojection of this information onto the image plane under change in viewpoint as depicted by Fig. 9.7.

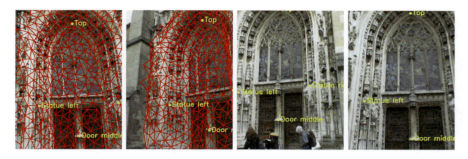

Fig. 9.7 Annotation of a cathedral door using a 3D model. The first two images also show the 3D model that is used to estimate the camera position which allows us to reproject the annotation correctly

9.8 Conclusion

We have presented a simple yet powerful approach for image patch recognition that performs well even in the presence of severe perspective distortion. The ferns prove to be particularly adapted, as their "semi-naïve" approach yields a scalable, simple, fast, and powerful implementation.

Chapter 10
Extremely Randomized Trees and Random Subwindows for Image Classification, Annotation, and Retrieval

R. Marée, L. Wehenkel, and P. Geurts

We present a unified framework involving the extraction of random subwindows within images and the induction of ensembles of extremely randomized trees. We discuss the specialization of this framework for solving several general problems in computer vision, ranging from image classification and segmentation to content-based image retrieval and interest point detection. The methods are illustrated on various applications and datasets from the biomedical domain.

10.1 Introduction

With the advent of digital imaging technologies (*e.g.* digital cameras, microscopes, telescopes), large numbers of images are acquired daily and these could hardly be processed by human visual inspection. Computer vision techniques are thus highly desirable in order to automatically search, organize, and annotate large sets of images acquired in various domains. Depending on the application, user needs, and available annotations, these tasks could be translated in terms of distinct computer vision tasks, such as content-based image retrieval (or visual image search), image classification (or categorization), image annotation (or labeled segmentation), and interest point detection. In image retrieval, given a training set of images without any labeling, one may want to retrieve images similar to a new query image. In supervised image classification, given a set of training images labeled into a finite number of classes, the goal is to build a model that will be able to predict accurately the class (among a set of predefined classes) of new, previously unseen images. In image annotation, given a training set of images with pixel-wise labeling (*i.e.* every pixel is labeled with one class among a finite set of predefined classes), the goal is to build a model that will be able to predict accurately the class of every pixel of any new, unseen image. In interest point detection, given annotated images where

R. Marée (✉) · L. Wehenkel · P. Geurts
University of Liège, Liège, Belgium

A. Criminisi, J. Shotton (eds.), *Decision Forests for Computer Vision and Medical Image Analysis*, Advances in Computer Vision and Pattern Recognition, DOI 10.1007/978-1-4471-4929-3_10, © Springer-Verlag London 2013

interest points coordinates have been localized by experts, the goal is to train models able to localize those interest points in new, unseen images.

In the early days of computer vision practice, when a researcher approached a new particular computer vision task, he or she developed a dedicated program to implement human prior knowledge as a sequence of specific operations (a 'hand-crafted approach'), and that often involves the design and calculation of tailored filters and features capturing expected image characteristics. Although this approach has proven effective, the design choices were rarely straightforward. Therefore such a strategy requires a lot of research and development efforts for each specific problem. In some fields, such as life science research and medical imaging, this engineering approach does not scale well as there are potentially thousands of species, tissues, organs, and cell phenotypes whose images can be acquired using tens of sample preparation techniques and imaging modalities.

Motivated by these challenges, we seek to develop generic methods for the exploitation of various types of image without relying on overly strong assumptions about the types of pattern to recognize and about the acquisition conditions. In this chapter, we summarize our work [96, 233–235, 237, 239, 240, 356] and illustrate the application of our methods on specific problems in life sciences and biomedical imaging where efficient machine learning and computer vision techniques are expected to play more and more of an active role in the future [85, 259, 332].

10.2 Random Subwindow-Based Image Analysis

We want to address the general supervised learning problem instantiated for images, which can be stated as follows:

From a training set $\{\langle J_i, Y_i \rangle | i = 1, \ldots, N\}$ of N images $J_i \in \mathcal{J}$ each with an output $Y_i \in \mathcal{Y}$, we want to construct a function $\hat{y} : \mathcal{J} \to \mathcal{Y}$ from the space of images $\mathcal{J}$ to the space of labels $\mathcal{Y}$ that predicts as well as possible the output label for any new (test) image $J_{\text{test}} \in \mathcal{J}$.

This general problem formulation includes for example image classification (where $\mathcal{Y}$ is a finite set of discrete classes), regression on images (where $\mathcal{Y} = \mathbb{R}^n$), and image annotation or segmentation (where the output associates a label to each pixel of an image). It also encompasses many typical computer vision tasks such as scene or object category recognition, facial feature detection, and age estimation.

The application of standard supervised learning (SL) methods to solve this problem is not straightforward. First, SL methods typically require that each training set instance is described by a feature vector of fixed size, while most image datasets gather images of various sizes. While this can be solved by rescaling all training images to a common fixed size and then describing them by raw image pixels, standard SL method are not equipped to explicitly account for dependencies between features, such as those that arise from the 2D spatial arrangement of image pixels. One common way to address these issues is to compute a (fixed) number of features from the training images before applying a standard SL algorithm. However, the choice of these features is very application dependent. The choice thus requires the

Training stage

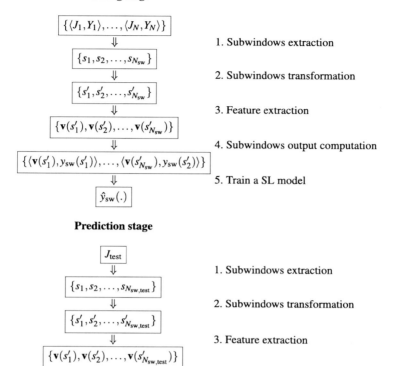

Fig. 10.1 Generic training and prediction stages. The notation is explained in the text

practitioner either to exploit some particular prior knowledge about the problem, or to construct a huge set of features that will hopefully contain good ones for the predictive task at hand.

The alternative generic approach that we have developed consists of: (i) extracting a large number of random subwindows from the training images, transforming them and then describing them by a fixed number of features; (ii) training a predictive model operating on the subwindows; and (iii) computing the output prediction for a new image by combining the predictions of its constituent subwindows obtained from the trained model. The main steps of our generic algorithm are depicted in Fig. 10.1. Each step (and our notation) is detailed below separately for the training and prediction stages.

10.2.1 Training Stage

Training consists of five main steps (see the left part of Fig. 10.1):

- **Subwindows extraction:** The first step is the extraction, in a randomized way, of a large number N_{sw} of possibly overlapping subwindows (or patches) $s_i \in J$, $i = 1, \ldots, N_{sw}$, within the training images, *i.e.* subimages of smaller sizes than the original parent image. This extraction is controlled by several parameters:
  - The subwindows sampling distribution: in the simplest case, each subwindow s_i is drawn uniformly in the training set of images, *i.e.* by first randomly selecting an image and then a subwindow position within this image. Departure from uniform sampling allows for example to take into account class imbalance (by extracting the same number of subwindows from images of each class) or to select subwindows around some interest points (see Sect. 10.4.3).
  - The number of subwindows N_{sw}: typically, the higher the number of extracted subwindows, the better the accuracy (as it increases the subwindows training sample in a subsequent step). The value of this parameter is therefore set according to computational constraints rather than according to predictive accuracy.
  - The subwindows sizes: we typically extract square subwindows whose sizes can be either fixed a priori or chosen randomly in a given size range.
- **Subwindows transformations:** Several image transformations/normalizations can then be applied to these subwindows with the goal of rendering the subwindow model invariant with respect to corresponding sources of variations. This step results in a new set of subwindows $\{s'_1, s'_2, \ldots, s'_{N_{sw}}\}$, where $s'_i \in J$ is a transformed version of subwindow s_i.
- **Feature extraction:** A vector of features $\mathbf{v}(s) = (x_1(s), x_2(s), \ldots, x_d(s)) \in \mathcal{F}$ of fixed size d is computed to describe each subwindow s.
- **Output computation:** An output $y_{sw}(s)$ is associated to each subwindow s which is derived from the output of its parent image. Its nature is of course dependent on the supervised learning problem one wants to address.
- **Training:** Any supervised learning method is then applied on the training sample of subwindows to get a prediction model $\hat{y}_{sw}(\cdot)$ defined on the feature space, which constitutes the final output of the training stage.

10.2.2 Prediction Stage

Making output predictions for a new image using the subwindow predictive model follows essentially the same steps as for training (see the right part of Fig. 10.1):

- **Subwindows extraction, transformation and feature extraction:** Subwindows are extracted from the test image, they are transformed and then turned into a feature vector. For the subwindows prediction model to be applicable, these three steps should mimic the corresponding steps applied during the training stage (*i.e.*

the same subwindows size selection, transformations, and feature extraction). In terms of prediction accuracy, the optimal choice is to extract a maximal number of subwindows from the test image, within the available computational budget. We denote this number by $N_{sw,test}$.

- **Per-subwindow output computation:** an output prediction $\hat{y}_{sw}(\mathbf{v}(s))$ is obtained for each subwindow s by applying the learnt SL model on the feature vector $\mathbf{v}(s)$ of this subwindow.
- **Output aggregation over subwindows:** the predictions by the learnt SL model over all subwindows of a given test image J_{test} are aggregated in order to obtain a final prediction for this test image, denoted $\hat{y}_{aggr}(J_{test})$ ($\in \mathcal{Y}$). Again, the aggregation procedure is highly dependent on the nature of the targeted prediction task, and could range from a simple averaging or voting based on the individual subwindows' predictions to much more complex post-processing schemes.

10.2.3 Discussion

Output computation and aggregation depend on the kind of problem we want to address and will be discussed in Sect. 10.4 in the context of the different types of target task. We discuss in this section in further detail the other remaining degrees of freedom of the proposed generic framework, relating to subwindows extraction, transformation, and feature representation. The description, motivation and discussion of the SL method applied on the subwindows training sample is postponed to Sect. 10.3.1.

10.2.3.1 Subwindows Extraction

One key step of our generic algorithm is the extraction of subwindows. This extraction transforms the original prediction problem over images into a similar problem on smaller images (the subwindows), thus inducing a reduction of the dimensionality. In addition, since many subwindows can typically be extracted from a given image, the resulting subwindows training sample is typically much larger than the original training sample of images by several orders of magnitude ($N \ll N_{sw}$). The subwindows SL problem is thus typically much better statistically conditioned than the original problem. In addition, since the final prediction is obtained by combining the predictions obtained for several overlapping subwindows in the test image, there is an averaging effect induced by this combination, which can further improve predictive accuracy by reducing variance.

The subwindow size is an important parameter of the method: small subwindows focus on local characteristics within the images, while larger subwindows capture more global characteristics. In our applications, we have considered two ways to set this parameter: (i) using a cross-validation wrapper to identify an optimal (fixed) size from the training data and (ii) randomizing subwindows sizes during the extraction. The second approach is typically followed by a rescaling of the subwindows to a common size (*e.g.* 16×16 pixels) and therefore introduces invariance with respect to scaling into the resulting predictive model. Whether or not this is an advantage is of course application dependent.

10.2.3.2 Subwindows Transformation

The second key ingredient of our approach is subwindows transformation. The main goal of this step is to inject invariance (or robustness) into the model with respect to some image alterations. This can be done in essentially two ways. The first one is to perform some normalization of the subwindows. For example, rescaling variable size subwindows to a common fixed size is a way to introduce scaling invariance. The second approach consists of adding to the training sample randomly altered versions of the original subwindows. This is implemented in our framework by defining a transformation operator $O(s, \lambda)$ that depends on some parameter λ and to apply this operator with a random value of λ to each subwindow. For example, $O(s, \lambda)$ could rotate the subwindows by some angle λ to introduce rotation invariance, or $O(s, \lambda)$ could randomly mask some parts of the subwindows to introduce invariance with respect to occlusions.

10.2.3.3 Feature Extraction

Features used to describe the subwindows can in principle be any visual features that can be computed on the subwindows [218] or even any global features derived from the parent image of the subwindows. However, good accuracy is often already obtained by simply describing subwindows by raw pixel values, leaving the task of determining how to combine these pixels to make good predictions entirely to the responsibility of the base learner. Using the HSV color space (instead of the RBG one) is usually preferable as it improves robustness to illumination changes. Using raw pixels as features has several advantages: the resulting representation is very fast to compute, it does not discard any informational content (all other visual features are based on this representation), and it is also not application specific.

10.3 Extremely Randomized Trees

While any supervised learning method can be used to train the subwindow predictor, decision forests are especially appealing in this context because of their non-parametric nature, their state-of-the-art predictive accuracy, their low computational costs, and their flexibility that allow them to tackle various kinds of SL (and even unsupervised) problems. They furthermore often obtain state-of-the-art accuracy among all SL methods [56].

We describe in Sect. 10.3.1 a particular decision forests algorithm called *extremely randomized trees* (Extra-Trees) that we have used extensively in the context of the proposed framework. Section 10.3.2 is dedicated to extensions of this method to handle more complex output spaces, and Sect. 10.3.3 explains how to derive a similarity measure, in the form of a kernel, from an ensemble of trees.

10.3.1 Extremely and Totally Randomized Trees

The *extremely randomized trees* algorithm [128] is a form of decision forest algorithm [44]. It was introduced with the idea of further increasing the randomization when splitting decision tree nodes, in order to improve accuracy by reducing further variance and also to reduce training times. Adopting the terminology and notation of Part I of this book, the algorithm has the following distinct features:

- A forests of T randomized trees is grown, where each tree is built independently of the other trees in the ensemble from the totality of the training data (*i.e.* without any form of training data sampling).
- Split functions considered at tree internal nodes are limited to standard CART-like axis-aligned splits [45], *i.e.* binary split functions of the form[1]

$$h\big(\mathbf{v}, (i, \tau)\big) = [x_i < \tau]. \qquad (10.1)$$

These are parameterized by an attribute number i ($1 \le i \le d$) and a discretization threshold $\tau \in \mathbb{R}$.
- Split function optimization at each tree node j is carried out by first selecting a set of random candidate splits $\mathcal{T}_j$ and then identifying the best one among them according to the current objective function (see below). The set of candidate splits $\mathcal{T}_j = \{(i_1, \tau_1), \ldots, (i_\rho, \tau_\rho)\}$ is obtained at each node j by randomly selecting ρ pairs of features and discretization thresholds, where the features i_l are sampled uniformly and without replacement from the set of all d features (*i.e.*, $i_l \neq i_m, \forall 1 \le l < m \le \rho$) and the discretization thresholds τ_l are not optimized but are uniformly drawn between the minimal and maximal values of the features i_l in the training instances that have reached this node. This additional threshold randomization, compared to *e.g.* random forests [44], was initially motivated by the high variance resulting from threshold optimization in the original CART method, as experimentally observed in [127], and is shown to improve further accuracy by decreasing variance [128].
- We stop growing a tree branch as soon as the output or the feature vector is constant in the node, or the number of instances that reach a node is (strictly) lower than some parameter $n_{\min}$.

---

[1] We restrict our discussion here to numerical features and refer the interested reader to [128] for the treatment of discrete features.

Any objective function can be used within the Extra-Tree algorithm to optimize splits at tree interior nodes. In classification, we use a particular normalized version of the information gain [128] and in regression, we use output variance reduction as used in CART [45]. In classification, we attach to each leaf conditional class probabilities. In regression, we attach to each leaf the average output value among training points reaching this leaf. Both kinds of predictions are averaged over the T individual tree predictions when testing a new example with the ensemble.

The main parameters of the algorithm are the number of trees T, the number of inputs randomly selected at each node ρ, and the stopping criterion parameter n_{min}. Since the larger the value of T, the better the resulting forest accuracy, T is usually chosen based on computational considerations only. Because of the averaging effect related to the extraction of subwindows, the number of trees required to reach convergence within our framework is typically much smaller than in standard classification or regression settings. Typical default values of ρ are $\rho = \sqrt{d}$ where d is the feature vector dimensionality, and $\rho = d$, respectively for classification and regression. We also advise setting n_{min} to its minimal value in classification (i.e., $n_{min} = 2$, corresponding to no pruning), while using slightly greater value of n_{min} might help on some noisy regression problems (e.g. $n_{min} \in [5, 10]$).

When ρ is set to 1, only one random split is considered at each tree node and the tree structure is therefore totally independent of the output values in the training sample. We call such trees *totally randomized trees* as their randomization is pushed further than *extremely randomized trees*. These trees are, for most SL problems, not as good as extremely randomized trees, because they lack robustness with respect to noisy features. However, they are very fast to construct and they can be exploited to derive a similarity measure for content-based image retrieval even in the absence of an output (see Sect. 10.4.1).

10.3.2 Multiple Output Trees

The basic classification and regression tree models can be extended to handle the prediction of multiple outputs simultaneously, i.e., a vectorial output $\mathbf{y} \in \mathbb{R}^n$ in the case of regression, or $\mathbf{y} \in \mathcal{C}^n$, where $\mathcal{C} = \{c_1, c_2, \ldots, c_{|\mathcal{C}|}\}$ is the finite set of all possible classes, in the case of classification. The extension only modifies the objective function used to evaluate splits and the way predictions are computed at tree leaves. The former is simply taken as the sum of the individual objective functions for each individual output. Predictions at leaf nodes in regression and classification are, respectively, vectors in $\mathbb{R}^n$ or n conditional class probability distributions, each corresponding to one of the n outputs. Both are estimated from the output of the training examples that reach the leaf (see e.g. [32, 130] for a treatment of multiple output trees). Within the general image analysis framework, this extension allows for example to address image annotation problems, where the output associates a class label to each pixel of the input image (or subwindows).

10.3.3 Kernel View of Tree-Based Ensembles

In addition to providing output predictions, an ensemble of trees can be used to define a similarity metric between input feature vectors [128, 142, 194, 236, 238] (see also Chap. 7). Denoting by N_L the number of training examples of the training sample that are located at a certain leaf L of the tth tree of the ensemble, this tree defines the following similarity between any two input feature vectors $\mathbf{v}$ and $\mathbf{v}'$ [128, 236, 238]:

$$k_t\left(\mathbf{v}, \mathbf{v}'\right) = \begin{cases} \frac{1}{N_L} & \text{if } \mathbf{v} \text{ and } \mathbf{v}' \text{ reach the same leaf } L \text{ in } t \\ 0 & \text{otherwise.} \end{cases} \tag{10.2}$$

This expression amounts to considering that two examples are *very similar* if they fall in a same leaf that contains a *very small* subset of training examples.[2]

The similarity induced by an *ensemble* of T trees is furthermore defined by

$$k_{\text{ens}}\left(\mathbf{v}, \mathbf{v}'\right) = \frac{1}{T} \sum_{t=1}^{T} k_t\left(\mathbf{v}, \mathbf{v}'\right). \tag{10.3}$$

This expression amounts to considering that two examples are similar if they are considered similar by a large proportion of the trees. The spread of the similarity measure is controlled by the parameter $n_{\min}$: when $n_{\min}$ increases, training examples tend to fall more often in the same leaf which yields a higher similarity according to (10.3). On the other hand, the number of trees controls the smoothness of the similarity. With only one tree, the similarity (10.2) is very discrete as it can take only two values when one of the examples is fixed. The combination of several trees provides a finer-grained similarity measure.

When tree ensembles are considered at the last step of our generic subwindow-based framework, similarity (10.3) defines a similarity measure between subwindows and it can furthermore be used to derive a similarity between two images J and J' as follows (see also [194]):

$$k\left(J, J'\right) = \frac{1}{|\mathcal{S}(J)||\mathcal{S}(J')|} \sum_{s \in \mathcal{S}(J), s' \in \mathcal{S}(J')} k_{\text{ens}}\left(\mathbf{v}(s), \mathbf{v}(s')\right), \tag{10.4}$$

where $\mathcal{S}(J)$ and $\mathcal{S}(J')$ are the sets of (transformed) subwindows that have been extracted from J and J', respectively. The similarity between two images is thus the average similarity between all pairs of their subwindows (described by their features).

Since (10.3) defines a positive kernel [128] (among subwindows), (10.4) actually defines a positive (convolution) kernel among images [334]. This means that this

---

[2]Intuitively, as it is less likely a priori that two examples will fall together in a small leaf, it is natural to consider them very similar when they actually do.

similarity measure has several nice mathematical properties. For example, it can be used to define a distance metric and it can be directly exploited in the context of kernel methods [334]. We will exploit it in Sect. 10.4.1 for content-based image retrieval and in Sect. 10.4.2 to train an SVM-based classifier as a post-processing of the decision forests model.

10.4 Applications

This section presents several illustrations of the general framework introduced here for various computer vision applications. We present problems in the order of increasing amounts of available ground truth, starting with unsupervised content-based image retrieval, then supervised image classification, interest point detection, and ending with fully labeled supervised image segmentation.

10.4.1 Content-Based Image Retrieval

Content-based image retrieval, or visual image search, aims at retrieving a ranked list of images similar to a given query image, based on the visual content of these images.

10.4.1.1 Method

We proposed in [236, 238] to exploit the similarity measure and indexing structure of totally randomized tree ensembles induced from a set of subwindows randomly extracted from unlabeled samples of images, as described in Sect. 10.3.3. In [240], we adapted the approach for the more realistic setting where images are distributed across multiple cooperating servers and added in an incremental fashion, using fully data-independent, randomized indexing structures (vectors of random tests somehow similar to random ferns or randomized lists [279, 401]) instead of totally randomized trees, but still using the similarity measure of Sect. 10.3.3. In this approach, random subwindows are propagated into visual words using vectors of predefined, random tests on raw pixel values shared between all distributed servers. In contrast with our approach, traditional bag-of-words approaches (such as k-means and random forests) are not so well suited in a distributed and incremental context, since their mapping structures are dataset-dependent and consequently the image similarities inferred by a given local server using these latter methods are not directly comparable to the similarities computed by other servers, and not equivalent to the case where all data are available at a single point. Furthermore, these local data-driven structures are not designed with the possibility to be easily updated, as the structure of their visual dictionary (*e.g.* the number of clusters) is fixed a priori.

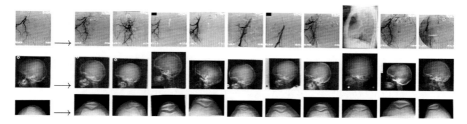

Fig. 10.2 Three query images (*left*) and the retrieval results (*right*) ranked according to their similarity, using the distributed, incremental approach [240] on the IRMA-2005 database ($N = 9000$ classified into 57 categories). Overall results are significantly better than baselines *e.g.* using nearest neighbors with Euclidian distance computed on downscaled 32×32 images [240]

10.4.1.2 Illustration

Our experiments in [240] showed that the simpler approach with vectors of random tests yields interesting results on real-world, varied images, while being straightforward to implement. Although the recognition results were slightly inferior to those obtained by supervised classification or retrieval using extremely randomized trees [240], these results were practically relevant as illustrated for example in Fig. 10.2. Moreover, we believe that the incremental and distributed capabilities of this method make it a good candidate for very large image retrieval studies at the web scale, or within distributed networks of specialized image repositories (*e.g.* hospitals). We recently implemented this algorithm as a web service within a rich internet application in order to provide biomedical experts with instantaneous, automatic, ontology term suggestions thanks to automatic learning from annotations made previously by other experts and incorporated into the image repository. It allowed users to speed-up and consolidate annotations of various tissues and cells in high-resolution microscopy images [241].

10.4.2 Image Classification

In image classification, given a set of training images labeled into a finite number of classes, the goal is to build a model that will be able to predict accurately the class (among a set of predefined classes) of new, unseen images.

10.4.2.1 Method

The general framework presented in Sect. 10.2 was initially motivated by image classification problems, first in [233] then in subsequent works [234, 235, 237]. For these applications, the output associated to each subwindow is the class of its parent image and the final class prediction for an image is obtained by voting the class predictions of its subwindows, obtained by the extremely randomized tree model. Moosman *et al.* [254] proposed an alternative aggregation scheme that first uses extremely randomized trees to build a global "bag-of-visual words" representation of the training images, and then trains a linear SVM model over this global image representation to perform the final image classification. In the bag-of-visual words representation, images are represented by a (large) feature vector, where each component corresponds to a tree leaf of the ensemble (corresponding to a "visual word") and is equal to the proportion of image subwindows falling into that leaf (or a 0/1 binarization of this proportion). This approach is actually equivalent to exploiting the image kernel (10.4) within an SVM model.

10.4.2.2 Illustration

In our previous work, this approach was applied on various image types including identification of man-made objects, buildings, faces, handwritten digits, *etc.* Here we illustrate the approach on a dozen datasets from the biomedical domain. These datasets are summarized in Table 10.1 and illustrated in Fig. 10.3. They are related to the classification of:

- tissue types in cancer research (BREASTCANCER, LYMPHOMA) and aging studies (AGEMAP-FAGING);
- cell phenotypes related to diseases such as cancer (SEROUS), acute lymphoblastic leukemia (ALL-IDB2) autoimmune diseases (HEP2) or protein subcellular patterns (CHO, SUBCELLULAR); and
- human body parts using X-rays (IRMA2005) or other imaging modalities (MMODALITY).

Parameters were set as follows in our evaluation. We extracted $N_{sw} = 10^6$ training subwindows of random sizes that were all rescaled into 16×16 patches and described by raw pixel values (HSV). Other parameters were only weakly optimized. In particular, we first optimized the ranges of original subwindow sizes by cross-validation, then a few values for other parameters were evaluated (number of trees from $T = 1$ to $T = 40$, minimum node sample size from $n_{min} = 1$ (unpruned trees) to 50000, node test filtering parameter ρ from 1 (totally randomized trees) to the maximum values). For the variant using an SVM as a post-processing, we considered both binary or frequency visual word counts. In Table 10.1, we only report the best result for each dataset (detailed results, including a comparison with other methods, are included in [232]). One can observe that low error rates are achieved on a wide variety of problems without the need to design manually specific features, neither to precompute large sets of image transforms and statistical features, as done in other approaches (*e.g.* [278]). Our experiments also show that the range of original subwindow sizes has a strong influence on the accuracy; some problems (such as tissue recognition) require subwindows of small random sizes, while larger subwindows close to the original image sizes are better for other tasks (such as cell recognition).

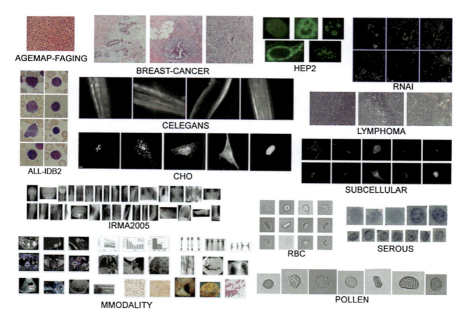

Fig. 10.3 We consider the generic problem of supervised image classification without any preconception about image classes as illustrated by the variability of biomedical classification datasets tackled in our experiments

10.4.3 Interest Point Detection

In interest point detection, given annotated images where interest points coordinates have been localized by experts, the goal is to train models able to localize those interest points in new, previously unseen images. Examples of application include the detection of facial features (*e.g.* eyes) in face recognition, or point matching for object tracking [213] (see also Chap. 9).

10.4.3.1 Method

We exploit manually annotated images where interest points coordinates have been localized by experts. While other works have formulated point matching as a single-output classification problem [213], we considered in [356] various approaches that first extract subwindows around points of interest and at other randomly chosen positions within images, describe these patches with visual features, and then build either a classification or a regression model, with single or multiple outputs. In the classification scheme, the output of each subwindow is a binary class stating whether the central pixel of the subwindow is (close to) the interest point or not. In the regression scheme, the subwindows output is the distance between the central pixel of the subwindows and the interest point. The predicted position of the interest point

Table 10.1 Summary of classification dataset characteristics and our classification results

Datasets	# Images	# Classes	Short description	Our error rate
AGEMAP-FAGING	850	4	Mouse liver tissues at different development stages [331]	**3.62 %**
ALL-IDB2	260	2	Normal and lymphoblast cells [93]	**0.19 %**
BINUCLEATE	40	2	DAPI images of binucleate and regular cells [331]	**0.25 %**
BREAST-CANCER	361	3	Biopsies of breast cancer (H&E straining) [46]	**6.39 %**
C.ELEGANS	237	4	C.elegans muscles at different ages [331]	**25.47 %**
CHO	327	5	Subcellular localizations [34]	**2.31 %**
HEP2	721	6	Cells in indirect immunofluorescence [288]	**2.64 %**
IRMA 2005	10000	57	Human body radiographs [90]	**11.3 %**
LYMPHOMA	374	3	Biopsies of lymphoma (H&E staining) [331]	**4.05 %**
MMODALITY	5010	8	Biomedical imaging modalities [285]	**20.95 %**
POLLEN	6039	7	Pollen grains [331]	**3.10 %**
RBC	5062	3	Red-blood cells [181]	**29.14 %**
RNAI	200	10	Cell populations following RNA interference [331]	**11.0 %**
SEROUS	3652	11	Cells from serous effusion cytology [216]	**24.04 %**
SUBCELLULAR	948	10	Subcellular localizations [33]	**11.63 %**
TERMINALBULB	970	7	DIC of pharynx terminal bulb [331]	**53.04 %**

within a new test image is then taken as the median point of all subwindows central pixels that are predicted to be the interest point with the highest probability by the classification model or that are predicted to be the closest to the interest point by the regression model. When several interest points need to be detected, we proposed either to build a model separately for each interest point or to exploit multiple output trees (see Sect. 10.3.2) to predict jointly all interest points. The latter typically gives better results.

10.4.3.2 Illustration

We proposed in [356] to apply our method to automatically detect specific interest points in microscopy images with the aim of performing automatic morphometric measurements in the context of development research studies using the Zebrafish model. The Zebrafish is a well-known model organism increasingly used for biological studies on development, gene function, toxicology, and pharmacology, and whose skeleton can be easily observed at different stages of development

Fig. 10.4 Images of Zebrafish embryos (*left*: ventral view of cartilaginous structures highlighted by alcian blue staining, *middle*: mineralized bone revealed by alizarin red staining, *right*: bright-field image of a larva). *Colored dots* represent automatically predicted interest points corresponding to the position of distinct cartilaginous/bone elements. The multiple output regression approach was applied using the same parameter settings for all three imaging modalities [356]

using staining agents. From these images, one seeks to perform morphometric measurements of the cartilage skeleton to describe the effects of different experimental conditions such as chemical treatments or gene knock-downs (see Fig. 10.4 for example images). Our study [356] showed that all detection schemes give good results provided that parameters are well chosen. In particular, we found that the parameter which has the strongest influence is the subwindow sizes, and that the multiple output setting is less sensitive to parameter choices than the single-output setting.

10.4.4 Image Segmentation

In image semantic segmentation, given a training set of images with pixel-wise labeling (*i.e.* every pixel is labeled with one class among a finite set of predefined classes), the goal is to build a model that will be able to predict accurately the class of every pixel of any new, previously unseen image.

10.4.4.1 Method

In [96], we proposed two methods to address pixel-wise image labeling following the random subwindows framework of Sect. 10.2. In both cases, random subwindows of fixed sizes are sampled densely in training images and represented by raw pixel values. In the first approach, the output associated to each subwindow is the class of its central pixel. The labels of all pixels of a test image are then obtained by exhaustively extracting and classifying all subwindows within the test image. In the second approach, the output of a subwindow consists of the classes of all subwindow pixels that are predicted jointly by using a multiple output model (see Sect. 10.3.2). At prediction time, all subwindows of the test images are extracted and tested by the multiple output model and a class prediction is obtained for each image pixel by averaging the predictions for all subwindows that contain that pixel. The latter variant therefore introduces an averaging effect at prediction time, which is in general very beneficial.

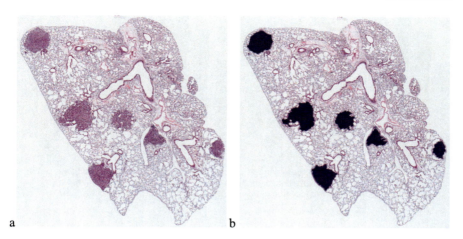

a   b

Fig. 10.5 (**a**) Histology image of a whole mouse lung. (**b**) Binary prediction of tumoral tissues using the multiple output classification approach

10.4.4.2 Illustration

We evaluated the approach on several benchmarks in [96] with images of natural scenes, roads, and cells, and in [239] on thermal infra red hyperspectral imagery to detect gaseous traces. In both cases, the multiple output approach yields better, smoother, results than the single, central pixel, approach. In Fig. 10.5 we illustrate the multiple output method for the recognition of tumoral tissues in whole-slide histology images in the context of lung cancer studies where the final objective is to assess the effects of novel treatments on tumor sizes. From the computer vision point of view, this application involves the segmentation of different classes of tissues (tumors, bronchus, blood vessels, cartilage, *etc.*) and their quantification within high-resolution images (typical image sizes are tens or hundreds thousands of pixels wide by tens or hundreds thousands of pixels tall). Manual annotations were created using our collaborative web-based annotation platform [241] and then ensembles of trees were built to detect tumoral tissues (binary problem), hence derive surface measurements. Given the high-throughput acquisition procedure (a single, high-resolution, image can be acquired in less than five minutes using modern scanning microscopes), fast processing is a strong requirement and therefore we only used raw pixel values in HSV colorspace to describe subwindows.

10.5 Conclusions and Future Works

This chapter has presented a generic framework for the analysis of images based on random subwindow extraction and the use of extremely randomized trees. Building on the flexibility of tree-based ensemble methods, this framework can be used to solve various computer vision tasks ranging from content-based image retrieval and image classification to interest point detection and image segmentation. The framework was illustrated on a variety of biomedical problems.

All possible instances of the proposed general framework have not been explored yet, and given its generality, there exist many possible directions for further work. Among these, we believe that it would be worth exploring more sophisticated aggregation schemes, in order to extend further the range of applications covered by the approach or to improve its accuracy for some tasks. In our framework, the sub-window SL model is trained to predict as accurately as possible subwindow outputs independently from the way these outputs will be aggregated in the final prediction. Coupling more tightly the subwindow model training and the aggregation step could improve accuracy significantly for some tasks. Multiple output trees are a key component of our image segmentation solution. In [130], we have proposed an extension of multiple output trees to handle kernelized output spaces, *i.e.* any output space over which a kernel can be defined. The exploitation of these output kernelized trees within our framework could further extend its applicability to image analysis tasks. Finally, in our previous work [129], we proposed a generic segment-and-combine approach for the classification of topologically structured data such as images, time-series, and texts. The present chapter extends the segment-and-combine idea far beyond supervised classification but focuses on the analysis of images. The application of similar ideas to structured data such as time-series and text documents is straightforward and certainly worth being investigated as future work.

Acknowledgements   R.M. is supported by the CYTOMINE research grant (number 1017072) of the Wallonia (DGO6) and by the GIGA center with the help of the Wallonia and the European Regional Development Fund (ERDF). P.G. is a research associate of the FNRS, Belgium.

Chapter 11
Class-Specific Hough Forests for Object Detection

J. Gall and V. Lempitsky

We present a method for the detection of instances of an object class, such as cars or pedestrians, in natural images. Similarly to some previous work, this is accomplished via the generalized Hough transform, where the detections of individual object parts cast probabilistic votes for possible locations of the centroid of the whole object; the detection hypotheses then correspond to the maxima of the Hough image that accumulates the votes from all parts. However, whereas previous methods detect object parts using generative codebooks of part appearances, we take a more discriminative approach to object part detection. Towards this end, we train a class-specific *Hough forest*, which is a decision forest that directly maps the image patch appearance to the probabilistic vote about the possible location of the object centroid. We demonstrate that Hough forests improve the results of the Hough-transform object detection significantly and achieve state-of-the-art performance for several classes and datasets.

11.1 Introduction

The appearance of objects of the same class such as cars or pedestrians in natural images vary greatly due to intra-class differences, changes in illuminations, and imaging conditions, as well as object articulations. Therefore, to ease the detection (localization) most of the methods take a bottom-up, part-based approach, where the detections of individual object parts (features) are further integrated to reason about the positioning of the entire object.

This chapter is based on the CVPR'09 conference paper [118].
Parts of this chapter are reprinted, with permission, from [118], © 2012 IEEE.

J. Gall (✉)
Max Planck Institute for Intelligent Systems, Tübingen, Germany

V. Lempitsky
Skolkovo Institute of Science and Technology, Moscow, Russia

A. Criminisi, J. Shotton (eds.), *Decision Forests for Computer Vision and Medical Image Analysis*, Advances in Computer Vision and Pattern Recognition, DOI 10.1007/978-1-4471-4929-3_11, © Springer-Verlag London 2013

Toward this end, the Hough-transform-based method of Leibe *et al.* [208, 210] learns the class-specific *implicit shape model* (*ISM*), which is essentially a codebook of interest point descriptors typical for a given class. After the codebook is created, each entry is assigned a set of offsets with respect to the object centroid that are observed on the training data. At runtime, the interest point descriptors in the image are matched against the codebook and the matches cast probabilistic votes about possible positions of the object in the scale-space. These votes are summed up into a Hough image, the peaks of it being considered as detection hypotheses. The whole detection process can thus be described as a generalized class-specific Hough transform [15].

Implicit shape models can integrate information from a large number of parts. They also demonstrate good generalization as they are free to combine parts observed on different training examples. Furthermore, the additive nature of the Hough transform makes the approach robust to partial occlusions and atypical part appearances. However, such codebook-based Hough transform comes at a significant computational price. Firstly, a large generative codebook is required to achieve good discrimination. Secondly, the construction of large codebooks involves solving difficult, large-scale clustering problems. Finally, matching with the constructed codebook is time-consuming, as it is typically linear in the number of entries.

In this chapter, we develop a new Hough-transform-based detection method, which takes a more discriminative approach to part detection. Rather than using an explicit codebook of part appearances, we learn a direct mapping between the appearance of an image patch and its Hough vote. We demonstrate that such a mapping can be efficiently accomplished within the decision forest framework. Thus, given a dataset of training images with the bounding box annotated samples of the class instances, we learn a class-specific forest that is able to map an image patch to a probabilistic vote about the position of an object centroid. At runtime, such a class-specific *Hough forest* is applied to the patches in the test image and the resulting votes are accumulated in the Hough image, where the maxima are sought. The approach is illustrated in Fig. 11.1.

Related to our work, the idea of replacing generative codebooks with random forests has been investigated in the context of image classification (Chap. 10) and semantic segmentation (Chap. 15) in [235, 253, 324, 341]. For instance, Marée *et al.* [235] sample a random set of various sized patches from an image and use random forests for classifying the patches. The class confidences of all patches are then accumulated to classify the entire image. Within the prior work, most similar to Hough forests are the classification random forests used to obtain the unary potentials within the LayoutCRF method [403].

While Hough forests are in many aspects similar to other random forests in computer vision, they possess several interesting specific properties, motivated by their use within the generalized Hough transform framework:

- The set of leaf nodes of each tree in the Hough-forest can be regarded as a discriminative codebook. Each leaf node makes a probabilistic decision whether a patch corresponds to a part of the object or to the background, and casts a probabilistic vote about the centroid position with respect to the patch center.

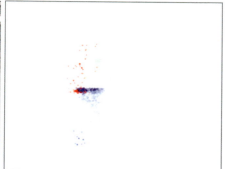

(a) – Original image with three sample patches emphasized

(b) – Votes assigned to these patches by the Hough forest

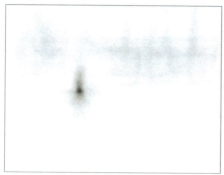

(c) – Hough image aggregating votes from all patches

(d) – The detection hypothesis corresponding to the peak in (c)

Fig. 11.1 For each of the three patches highlighted in (**a**), the pedestrian class-specific Hough forest casts a vote about the possible location of a pedestrian centroid (**b**) (each color channel corresponds to the vote of a sample patch). Note the weakness of the vote from the background patch (*green*). After the votes from all patches are aggregated into a Hough image (**c**), the pedestrian can be detected as a peak in this image. The enclosing bounding box (**d**) can be estimated by taking the average bounding box for pedestrians centered at the detection peak

- The trees in a Hough forest are built directly to optimize their voting performance. In other words, the training process builds each tree so that the leaves produce probabilistic votes with small uncertainty.
- Each tree is built based on the collection of patches drawn from the training data. Importantly, the building process employs all the supervision available for the training data: namely, whether a patch comes from a background or an object, and, in the latter case, which part of the object it comes from.

Our method also benefits from the advantages typical of other random-forest applications. Thus:

- Decision forests can be trained on large, very high-dimensional datasets without significant overfitting and within a reasonable amount of time (hours). For our method, this permits the use of a discriminative, high-dimensional (up to 8192D) patch appearance descriptor and large training datasets.

- Decision forests are very efficient at runtime, since matching a sample against a tree is logarithmic in the number of leaves. Therefore, rather than restricting our attention to the interest points as in [208, 210], our method is able to sample patches densely, while maintaining similar or better computational performance.
- Decision forests can tolerate a significant amount of labeling noise and errors in the training data. Therefore, our method permits the use of bounding box annotated training data as opposed to pixel-accurate segmentations used by previous Hough-based methods [208, 210].

11.2 Related Work

The set of leaves of each tree in a Hough forest can be regarded as a discriminative Hough voting codebook. Importantly, while generative codebooks for ISMs [208, 210] are constructed via *unsupervised* clustering of appearances, each tree in a Hough forest is constructed in a supervised way. Such a supervision allows to optimize the codebook entries to produce more reliable votes in Hough space.

Opelt *et al.* [277] also investigated the use of the supervised construction of Hough voting codebooks with the emphasis on contour shape features. Their generative codebook is constructed by picking the exemplars that tend to produce more reliable votes at train time. They further increase the discriminative power of their model by picking the small ensemble of original entries and combining them within the boosting framework. Our approach, therefore, shares the idea of supervision for the voting codebook construction with [277], but does this within a discriminative random forest framework.

Similarly to our approach, Marée *et al.* [235] and Moosmann *et al.* [253] as well as Shotton *et al.* [341] and Schroff *et al.* [324] train random forests on image patches in order to use them as discriminative codebooks. Those codebooks, however, are employed for image categorization or semantic segmentation rather than Hough-based object detection. As such, no geometric information but only class labels are stored at leaves and are used as a supervision for trees construction, as opposed to our method.

Winn and Shotton [403] build decision forests in order to distinguish between the patches from different parts of the object as well as from background (with a similar purpose to Hough forests). However, they consider a pure classification problem by splitting the object into a predefined number of parts treated as independent classes. This is because the output of their forests is used on a later stage as unary terms for a discrete-labeled conditional random field. Instead, as Hough forests are used for voting, their output are essentially the votes in the continuous domain. Thus, unlike [403], we avoid splitting objects into discrete parts.

Simultaneously with our work, Okada [275] has suggested a very similar framework for object detection and hand tracking. Following our work, Hough forests and similar approaches have been extended to the tasks of tracking [120, 135] (Chap. 12), action recognition [120, 409], head and body pose estimation [102, 131] (Chap. 12), among others.

11.3 Building Hough Forests

Following the notation of Chap. 3, decision forests can be used for predicting discrete class labels c or regressing continuous labels $\mathbf{y}$. Object detection, however, involves both classifying patches belonging to an object and using them to regress the location of the object as illustrated in Fig. 11.1. The Hough forests are therefore trained to satisfy both objectives and the leaf statistics capture $p(c|\mathbf{v})$ and $p(\mathbf{y}|c, \mathbf{v})$, where the continuous label $\mathbf{y}$ depends on the discrete label c.

In the context of object detection, $\mathbf{v}$ is the appearance vector of a patch (Fig. 11.1(a)), c is the *class label* of the patch, and $\mathbf{y}$ is the *offset* vector of the patch to the centroid of the object. The leaf statistics capture the probability of an object c being at the relative location $\mathbf{y}$ of a patch with appearance $\mathbf{v}$ (Fig. 11.1(b)):

$$p(\mathbf{y}, c|\mathbf{v}) = p(\mathbf{y}|c, \mathbf{v})p(c|\mathbf{v}). \tag{11.1}$$

The probabilities from all patches are then collected to get evidence for the absolute position of an object (Fig. 11.1(c)). This can be performed by Hough voting and the forests are therefore called *Hough forests*, but the forests can also be regarded as a combination of regression and classification forests (see also [131, 134]).

11.3.1 Training Data and Leaf Information

For Hough forests, each tree is constructed based on a set of training patches $\mathcal{S}_0 = \{(\mathbf{v}, c, \mathbf{y})\}$. The patches are sampled from the training collection of images, some of them containing examples of the class of interest with known bounding boxes. The patches sampled from the background (*background patches*) are assigned the *class label* $c = 0$, while the patches sampled from the interior of the object bounding boxes (*object patches*) are assigned $c = 1$. Each object patch is also assigned a 2D *offset vector* $\mathbf{y}$ equal to the offset from the centroid of the bounding box to the center of the patch. For a background patch, $\mathbf{y}$ is undefined. In our current implementation, scale invariance is not introduced during training, and therefore the object patches are sampled from the pre-scaled object images to have approximately the same size. However, patches with various sizes and orientations as in Marée *et al.* [235] (Chap. 10) could also be used. To achieve the scale invariance at runtime, we apply Hough forests at several scales as described in Sect. 11.4.

For each leaf node l in the constructed tree, the information about the patches that have reached this node (denoted with $\mathcal{S}_l$) at training time is stored. Thus, we store the proportion $c_l = p(c = 1|l)$ of the object patches (*e.g.* $c_l = 1$ means that only object patches have reached the leaf) and the list $\mathcal{D}_l = \{\mathbf{y} \in \mathcal{S}_l\}$ of the offset vectors

(a) – Training data for the car side class (UIUC car dataset): sample background images (blue) and sample object bounding boxes (red).

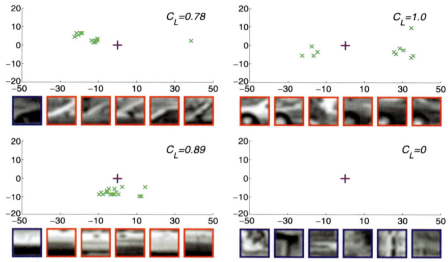

(b) – Sample leaves in the Hough forest: at the top, green crosses correspond to the offset vectors in D_l; the object proportion c_l is also given; at the bottom, sample patches that fall inside each of the leaves above during training are shown (red corresponds to object patches).

Fig. 11.2 For the set of training images shown in (**a**), we visualize the data recorded in some of the leaves of the constructed class-specific Hough forest in (**b**). These data consist of the object patch proportion $c_l = p(c = 1|l)$ and the list of the offset vectors for object patches D_l. Note that the leaves of the Hough forest form a discriminative class-specific codebook: the training examples falling inside each of the first three leaves can be associated with different parts of a car

corresponding to the object patches. The leaves of the tree thus form a discriminative codebook with the assigned information about possible locations of the centroid (Fig. 11.2). At runtime, this information is used to cast the probabilistic Hough votes about the existence of the object at different positions (Sect. 11.4).

11.3.2 Patch Appearance and Binary Tests

During training, each non-leaf node in each tree is assigned a binary test applicable to the appearance of a patch **v**. At both train and test time, the patches have a fixed size, *e.g.* 16-by-16 pixels, and the appearance is defined by the extracted feature channels, which may correspond to raw intensities, derivative filter responses, *etc.*

Thus, the appearance of a patch can be written as $\mathbf{v} = (J^1, J^2, \ldots, J^f)$, where each J^j is a 16-by-16 image and f is the number of channels.

The binary tests on a patch appearance $h(\mathbf{v}) \to \{0, 1\}$ can be defined in any of the ways discussed in Chap. 3 (*e.g.* coordinate splits, linear splits, *etc.*). In our experiments, we have chosen pairwise-comparison tests. Such a test is defined by a channel $a \in \{1, 2, \ldots, f\}$, two positions (p, q) and (r, s) in the 16-by-16 image, and a real handicap value τ. The test $h(\mathbf{v}; \boldsymbol{\theta})$, where $\boldsymbol{\theta} = (a, p, q, r, s, \tau)$ is then defined as

$$h(\mathbf{v}; \boldsymbol{\theta}) = \begin{cases} 0, & \text{if } J^a(p, q) - J^a(r, s) < \tau \\ 1, & \text{otherwise.} \end{cases} \tag{11.2}$$

Such a test simply compares the values of a pair of pixels in the same channel with some handicap.

11.3.3 Tree Construction

Below, for clarity and with a slight abuse of notation, we treat the sets of patches as multi-sets of patch class labels as well as the sets of patch displacements. In general, the tree construction for Hough forests follows the popular decision forest framework. Each tree is constructed recursively starting from the root. During construction, each node receives a subset S of training patches. If the depth of the node is equal to the maximal one ($D = 15$) or the number of patches is small ($|S| \leq 20$), the constructed node is declared a leaf and the leaf vote information ($c_l, \mathcal{D}_l$) is accumulated and stored. Otherwise, a split node is created and an optimal binary test $h(\cdot; \boldsymbol{\theta}^*)$ is chosen from a large pool of randomly generated binary tests $\mathcal{T}$. The training patch set that has arrived to the node is then split according to the chosen test into two subsets S^{L} and S^{R} that are passed to the two newly created children nodes; after that the recursion proceeds.

Since Hough forests perform classification and regression, both objectives need to be optimized during training [134]. Therefore, prior to choosing a binary test for a non-leaf node, we choose between the two objectives. The classification objective (see Chap. 4) maximizes the information gain using Shannon entropy:

$$H(S) = - \sum_{c \in \{0, 1\}} p(c) \log(p(c)). \tag{11.3}$$

The regression objective (see Chap. 5) looks at the distribution of the displacement vectors $\mathbf{y}$ of the object patches and ignores the background patches. In our implementation, we look at the variance of the displacement:

$$H(S) = \sum_{\substack{(\mathbf{v}, c, \mathbf{y}) \in S \\ c=1}} \|\mathbf{y} - \bar{\mathbf{y}}\|^2, \tag{11.4}$$

where $\bar{\mathbf{y}}$ is the mean displacement over the object patches. This objective is proportional to the differential entropy, when displacements are modeled using an isotropic

Gaussian parametric model (see Chap. 5). While the parametric measure is not the optimal regression objective for object detection as depicted in Fig. 11.2, it was preferred for computational efficiency reasons.

Given the two criteria, the binary test is chosen as follows. Given a training set of patches S reaching the non-leaf node, we first generate a pool of pixel tests by sampling a, p, q, r, and s uniformly. The handicap value τ for each test is chosen uniformly at random from the range of differences observed on the data. Then, the randomized decision is made whether the split should optimize the classification objective in (11.3) or the regression objective in (11.4). In general, we choose this with equal probability unless the number of negative patches is small (<5 %), in which case the node is chosen to minimize the regression objective (11.4).

By interleaving the objective functions, we obtain leaves that both classify patches belonging to an object and regress the location of the object with low uncertainty, as depicted in Fig. 11.2.

11.4 Object Detection with Hough Forests

Class-specific Hough forests can be used to localize (detect) the bounding boxes of the instances of a class in a test image using the Hough transform. Let us first assume that the size of the object bounding boxes is fixed to $W \times H$ during both training and testing. Under this assumption, the only parameter defining an object bounding box is the centroid.

Consider a patch $(\mathbf{v}(\mathbf{p}), c(\mathbf{p}), \mathbf{y}(\mathbf{p}))$ centered at the position $\mathbf{p}$ in the test image. Here, $\mathbf{v}(\mathbf{p})$ is the observed appearance of the patch, $c(\mathbf{p})$ is the hidden class label (whether $\mathbf{p}$ lies inside the object bounding box or not), and $\mathbf{y}(\mathbf{p})$ is the hidden offset vector from the center of the object bounding box to $\mathbf{p}$ (meaningful only in the case $c(\mathbf{p}) = 1$). Furthermore, $E(\mathbf{q})$ denotes the random event corresponding to the existence of the object centered at the location $\mathbf{q}$ in the image.

We are now interested in computing the probabilistic evidence $p(E(\mathbf{q}) \mid \mathbf{v}(\mathbf{p}))$ that the appearance $\mathbf{v}(\mathbf{p})$ of the patch brings about the availability $E(\mathbf{q})$ at different positions $\mathbf{q}$ in the image. We will distinguish between the two cases: whether $\mathbf{p}$ belongs to the bounding box $B(\mathbf{q})$ centered at $\mathbf{q}$ or not. If $\mathbf{p} \notin B(\mathbf{q})$, then we assume that $\mathbf{v}(\mathbf{p})$ is not informative about $E(\mathbf{q})$, putting $p(E(\mathbf{q}) \mid \mathbf{v}(\mathbf{p})) = p(E(\mathbf{q}))$. This is, of course, a simplifying assumption, and such "long-range" *context* information has been proven useful for object recognition [369]. In fact, it has even been exploited for semantic segmentation in random forest-based methods [324, 341] (Chap. 15) and it can be incorporated in our system in a similar way.

Here, however, we consider the evidence coming from the patches within the bounding box only and thus focus on the second case when $\mathbf{p} \in B(\mathbf{q})$. Here, the existence of an object centered at $\mathbf{q}$ inevitably implies $c(\mathbf{p}) = 1$ by our definition of the class label. As a result, one gets

$$
\begin{aligned}
p\big(E(\mathbf{q}) \mid \mathbf{v}(\mathbf{p})\big) &= p\big(E(\mathbf{q}), c(\mathbf{p}) = 1 \mid \mathbf{v}(\mathbf{p})\big) \\
&= p\big(E(\mathbf{q}) \mid c(\mathbf{p}) = 1, \mathbf{v}(\mathbf{p})\big) \cdot p\big(c(\mathbf{p}) = 1 \mid \mathbf{v}(\mathbf{p})\big) \\
&= p\big(\mathbf{y}(\mathbf{p}) = \mathbf{p} - \mathbf{q} \mid c(\mathbf{p}) = 1, \mathbf{v}(\mathbf{p})\big) \cdot p\big(c(\mathbf{p}) = 1 \mid \mathbf{v}(\mathbf{p})\big). \quad (11.5)
\end{aligned}
$$

Both factors in (11.5) can be estimated by passing the patch appearance $\mathbf{v}(\mathbf{p})$ through the trees in the class-specific Hough forest of T trees. Let us assume that for a tth tree the patch appearance ends up in a leaf l. The first factor can then be approximated using the Parzen-window estimate based on the offset vectors $\mathcal{D}_l$ collected in the leaf at train time, while the second factor can be straightforwardly estimated as the proportion c_l of object patches at train time. For a single tree t, the probability estimate can be written as

$$p_t\big(E(\mathbf{q}) \mid \mathbf{v}(\mathbf{p})\big) = \left[\frac{1}{|D_l|} \sum_{\mathbf{y} \in \mathcal{D}_l} \frac{1}{2\pi\sigma^2} \exp\left(-\frac{\|(\mathbf{p} - \mathbf{q}) - \mathbf{y}\|^2}{2\sigma^2}\right)\right] \cdot c_l \qquad (11.6)$$

where $\sigma^2 I_{2 \times 2}$ is the covariance of the Gaussian Parzen window. For the entire forest, we then simply average the probabilities (11.6) coming from different trees [6, 44], getting the forest-based estimate:

$$p\big(E(\mathbf{q}) \mid \mathbf{v}(\mathbf{p})\big) = \frac{1}{T} \sum_{t=1}^{T} p_t\big(E(\mathbf{q}) \mid \mathbf{v}(\mathbf{p})\big). \qquad (11.7)$$

Equations (11.6) and (11.7) define the probabilistic vote cast by a single patch about the existence of the objects in nearby locations. To integrate the votes coming from different patches, we accumulate them in an (admittedly non-probabilistic) additive way into a 2D Hough image $V(\mathbf{q})$, which for each pixel location $\mathbf{q}$ sums up the votes (11.7) coming from the nearby patches:

$$V(\mathbf{q}) = \sum_{\mathbf{p} \in B(\mathbf{q})} p\big(E(\mathbf{q}) \mid \mathbf{v}(\mathbf{p})\big). \qquad (11.8)$$

The detection procedure simply computes the Hough image V and returns the set of its maxima locations and values $\{\hat{\mathbf{q}}, V(\hat{\mathbf{q}})\}$ as the detection hypotheses. The $V(\hat{\mathbf{q}})$ values serve as the confidence measures for each hypothesis. A more principled approach to generalized Hough transform that avoids non-probabilistic addition and non-maxima suppression for Hough forests has been investigated in [16, 17].

The computation of the Hough image using the order of operations as suggested by Eqs. (11.6)–(11.8) would be inefficient. Instead, the same image (up to a constant multiplicative factor and minor pixel discretization issues) can be computed by going through each pixel location $\mathbf{p}$, passing the patch appearance $\mathbf{v}(\mathbf{p})$ through every tree in the Hough forest, and adding the value $\frac{c_l}{|\mathcal{D}_l|}$ to all pixels $\{\mathbf{p} - \mathbf{y} \mid \mathbf{y} \in \mathcal{D}_l\}$. The Hough image $V(\mathbf{q})$ is then obtained by Gaussian filtering the vote counts accumulated in each pixel. An alternative way to find the maxima of the Hough image would be to use the mean-shift procedure as it is done in other Hough voting-based frameworks [208, 210, 277].

11.4.1 Handling Variable Scales and Aspect Ratios

To handle scale variations, we resize a test image by a set of scale factors $s_1, s_2, \ldots, s_S$. The Hough images $V^1, V^2, \ldots, V^S$ are then computed independently at each scale. After that, the images are stacked in a 3D scale-space frustum, the Gaussian filtering is performed across the third (scale) dimension, and the maxima of the resulting function are localized in 3D. The resulting detection hypotheses have the form $(\hat{\mathbf{q}}, \hat{s}, V^{\hat{s}}(\hat{\mathbf{q}}))$. The hypothesized bounding box in the original image is then centered at the point $\frac{\hat{\mathbf{q}}}{\hat{s}}$, has the size $\frac{W}{\hat{s}} \times \frac{H}{\hat{s}}$, and the detection confidence $V^{\hat{s}}(\hat{\mathbf{q}})$. Similar ideas can be applied if significant variations of the aspect ratio are expected as is briefly discussed in Sect. 11.5. Due to the quantization of the scales and aspect ratios, the accuracy of the hypothesized bounding box is limited. A more precise estimate of the bounding box can be obtained by projecting the hypothesis back to the image domain and taking the tightest bounding box encompassing the image patches that voted for the hypothesis [306].

11.4.2 Leaf Pruning

To speed up the detection, we prune leaves with a low class confidence ($c_l < 0.5$). In our experiments, we observed that this threshold corresponding to 50 % object probability did not reduce the detection performance in contrast to higher threshold values. Since the object bounding boxes also contain background patches as shown in Fig. 11.2, most of the pruned leaves actually model the background of object bounding boxes.

11.5 Experiments

We evaluated the Hough forests on several challenging datasets (Fig. 11.3), where we provide a performance comparison with the related detection methods as well as with the best (as far as we know) results published prior to our initial work [118]. The performance curves were generated by changing the acceptance threshold on the hypotheses vote strength $V(\hat{\mathbf{q}})$. We adhered to the experimental protocols and detection correctness criteria established for each of the datasets in previous work. When generating recall-precision curves, we rejected the detection hypotheses with centroids inside the bounding boxes detected with higher confidence in order to avoid multiple detections of the same instance.

The training settings were as follows. During training, the positive examples were rescaled to the same height, chosen so that the larger bounding box dimension (width or height) was equal to 100 pixels on average over a dataset. 20,000 random binary tests were considered for each node. Each tree was trained on 25,000 positive and 25,000 negative patches.

Fig. 11.3 The results of our detector at equal recall-precision rates on challenging images from TUD pedestrian, UIUC-Scale, and Weizmann Horse datasets (*green* = correct, *red* = false positive, *cyan* = missed detection)

To bias our training to work better on hard examples, we used the following heuristic procedure, which can be regarded as a compromise between boosting and bagging of trees, and allowed us to achieve good accuracy with few ($T = 15$) trees. For the first five trees, the training patches were sampled with uniform probabilities from all available positive and negative examples. Then the constructed random forest was applied to the training data and the positive and negative instances that were harder to classify were acquired. These were used to construct the next five trees added to the previous 5. We applied this procedure once more, ending up with the forest having 15 trees.

For detection, we used a Parzen window with $\sigma^2 = 9$. In a multi-scale setting, the additional third dimension was filtered with $\sigma^2 = 1$. Typically, 4–5 scales with equal spacing were used to handle the variety of scales in the test data.

11.5.1 UIUC Cars

The UIUC car dataset [1] contains images of side views of cars. The test data are split into the set of 170 images with 210 cars of approximately same scale (*UIUC-Single*) and the set of 108 images containing 139 cars at multiple scales (*UIUC-Multi*). The sets include partially occluded cars, cars with low contrast, images with multiple car instances, cluttered backgrounds, and challenging illumination. The shape of the objects remains, however, mostly rigid, which makes the detection task easier.

On the available 550 positive and 450 negative training images, we trained a class-specific Hough forest. For patch appearance, three channels were used (intensity, absolute value of x- and y-derivatives). Applying this forest for the detection achieved an impressive 98.5 % EER for UIUC-Single and 98.6 % for UIUC-Multi, thus exactly matching the state-of-the-art performance reported recently in [200] (Table 11.1).

Table 11.1 Performance of different methods on the two UIUC car datasets at recall-precision equal error rate (EER). Hough Forest outperforms the previous Hough-based and random forest-based methods and achieves state-of-the-art results

Methods	UIUC-Single	UIUC-Multi
Hough-based methods		
Implicit Shape Model [210]	91 %	–
ISM + verification [210]	97.5 %	95 %
Boundary Shape Model [277]	85 %	–
Random forest-based method		
LayoutCRF [403]	93 %	–
State-of-the-art		
Mutch and Lowe CVPR'06 [261]	99.9 %	90.6 %
Lampert *et al.* CVPR'08 [200]	98.5 %	98.6 %
Our approach		
Hough Forest	98.5 %	98.6 %
HF-Weaker supervision	94.4 %	–

Importantly, the Hough forest outperformed considerably the Hough-based implicit shape model [210] (even with its additional MDL verification step) and boundary-shape model [277] approaches, as well as the random forest-based LayoutCRF method [403]. It has to be mentioned, at the same time, that these related methods used smaller subsets of the provided training data. In the case of the ISM and the LayoutCRF, this is due to the necessity of obtaining pixel-accurate annotations. Additionally, in the case of ISM and the Boundary-Shape Model [277] this might be due to the computational burden of constructing and processing generative codebooks. As Hough Forests are not limited by these factors, we used the provided training data completely, possibly accounting for some part of the improvement.

Another distinguishing factor is that our method samples patches densely, while ISM methods instead consider sparse interest points, which is likely to give our method a significant advantage [267]. We therefore investigated the performance of our method on the single scale dataset as the density of patch sampling is decreased. The graceful degradation of the performance in Fig. 11.4, as the number of patches is decreased down to 1/256 of the original, suggests that the relative accuracy of the Hough forest detection is not only due to a very large number of patch votes, but also has to do with the discriminative training of the codebook.

11.5.2 TUD Pedestrians, INRIA Pedestrians, Weizmann Horses

To assess the performance of our method for more challenging, articulated classes we evaluated it on two pedestrian datasets: a recent one from TU Darmstadt introduced in [7] containing mostly side views, and a more established dataset from INRIA [83] containing mostly front and back views. Both datasets contain partial

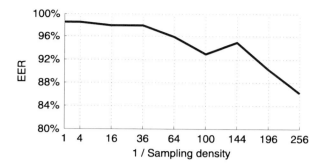

Fig. 11.4 As the sampling density is decreased, the recall-precision equal error rate (EER) of our method on UIUC-Single degrades gracefully

occlusions and variations in scales, poses, clothing styles, illumination, and weather conditions.

For the TUD dataset 400 training images with pedestrians are provided and, as the diversities of the backgrounds were low, we augment it with training background images from the INRIA dataset. Otherwise, we followed the experimental protocol of [7] and tested it on 250 images with 311 pedestrians in it. For the INRIA dataset, we used the provided training data of 614 images with pedestrians and 1218 background images. According to [83], we applied our method as a classifier on 288 cropped, pre-scaled images with pedestrians and 453 images without them.

We have also considered the Weizmann Horses dataset [35] containing the near-side views of horses in natural environments under varying scale and strongly varying poses. We used the training-test split (100 horse images and 100 background image for training, 228 horse images and 228 background images for testing) as suggested in [340].

For all three datasets we used the same color channels. We have considered the following 16 feature channels: three color channels of the *Lab* color space, the absolute values of the first-order derivatives $\frac{\partial}{\partial x}$, $\frac{\partial}{\partial y}$, the absolute values of the two second-order derivatives $\frac{\partial^2}{\partial x^2}$, $\frac{\partial^2}{\partial y^2}$, and the nine HOG-like [83] channels. Each HOG-like channel was obtained as the soft bin count of gradient orientations in a 5-by-5 neighborhood around a pixel. To increase the invariance under noise and articulations of individual parts, we further processed the above-introduced 16 channels by applying min and max filters with 5-by-5 filter size, yielding $C = 32$ feature channels (16 for the min filter and 16 for the max filter).

The performance of different methods including ours is shown in Fig. 11.5. For TUD pedestrians our method (recall-precision EER = 86.5 %, AUC = 0.87, recall at 90 % precision = 85 %) performed on a par with the state-of-the-art method [7] and significantly better than the implicit shape model-based method [327] (reproduced from [7]). Furthermore, it should be noticed that both competitors require additional annotation for training (the ISM-based approach, however, was again trained on a smaller training set).

For an image from the TUD dataset, our system requires 6 seconds where each of the four operations, namely feature extraction, passing patches through the trees, casting the votes, and processing the Hough images, takes around a quarter of the

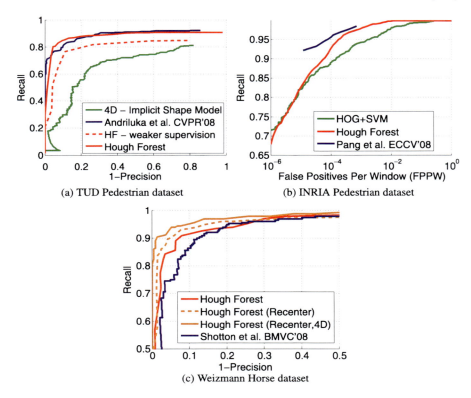

Fig. 11.5 Hough forests (*red* and *orange curves*) demonstrate a competitive performance with respect to the previous state-of-the-art methods (*blue curves*) on several challenging datasets. See text for a more detailed discussion

computation time. These timings are for a 720×576 pixel resolution with four scales (0.3, 0.4, 0.5, 0.6) and running on a modern CPU.

For the INRIA dataset, the Hough forest performance (recall = 93 % at FFPW = 10^{-4}) was not as good as that of the state-of-the-art method [281]. Yet it is still quite competitive and, in particular, performs better than the SVM-based detection for similar features (HOG) [83]. It may be also argued that the non-standard testing protocol for this dataset favors sliding-window approaches to some extent. We also used the dataset to measure the impact of the min and max filtration of the original channels, where we got a decrease of around 10 % recall at 10^{-4} FPPW when working with the 16 unfiltered channels. This suggests that the min and max filtering is needed to make the response of pixel-based comparison tests (11.2) more stable, at least when working with such deformable classes as pedestrians.

Finally, for the Weizmann Horse dataset the performance of the Hough forest was clearly better than the previous state-of-the-art [339]. Nevertheless, we have tried two more improvements addressing the two challenges of this dataset. Firstly, the position of bounding box centroids are not stable with respect to the horse bodies, which leads to a certain smearing of votes. To address this, we ran our detector on the positive training images and recentered the bounding boxes to the peaks of the response. After that the forest was retrained. Secondly, the aspect ratios of the boxes varied considerably due to the articulations and variations in the viewpoint. To address this, we performed voting in 4D Hough space, where the fourth dimension corresponded to the aspect ratio multiplier (the number of patch-against-tree matching operations was not increased though, as the votes were reused between different ratios). As can be seen from Fig. 11.5(c), both improvements increased the performance considerably (recall-precision EER went from 91 % to 93.9 %, AUC from 0.96 to 0.98, recall at 90 % precision from 91.5 % to 95.1 %) obtaining a substantial margin over the previous state-of-the-art.

11.5.3 Does Offset Supervision Matter?

Quite a few previous approaches have used random forests as discriminative code-books [214, 235, 253, 324, 341]. Hough forests differ from them as they store the patch offsets at leaves and use them at runtime to perform voting. Furthermore, the offset information is used as supervision during training of Hough forests since half of the binary tests are chosen to minimize the offset uncertainty (11.4). We therefore addressed the question whether such additional supervision matters. Thus, for the datasets UIUC-Single and TUD, we built forests where all binary splits were chosen to minimize the class uncertainty (11.3) (a similar criterion drove forest constructions in the above-mentioned work). The leaf information and the detection procedure remained as before.

The performance of the new forests is shown in Table 11.1 and Fig. 11.5(a), in the entries denoted *'HF-weaker supervision'*. A considerable drop in performance compared to fully supervised Hough forests is observed, suggesting that indeed offset vector supervision is a valuable addition.

11.6 Discussion

We have introduced the *Hough forests* approach for object detection. Hough forests build discriminative class-specific part appearance codebooks based on decision forests that are able to cast probabilistic votes within the Hough transform framework. Such forests can be efficiently used to detect instances of classes in natural images, with the accuracy that is not only superior to previous methods using related techniques but also improves the state-of-the-art for several datasets. Apart from the accuracy, the use of random forests potentially allows a very time-efficient implementation. While our current unoptimized CPU version takes several seconds per image, the speed-up factors reported for the GPU implementation of random forests in [333] suggest that near real-time performance is attainable.

Chapter 12
Hough-Based Tracking of Deformable Objects

M. Godec, P.M. Roth, and H. Bischof

Online learning has shown to be successful in tracking-by-detection of previously unknown objects. However, most approaches are limited to a bounding box representation with fixed aspect ratio and cannot handle highly non-rigid and articulated objects. Moreover, they provide only a limited foreground/background separation, which in turn, increases the amount of noise introduced during online self-training. To overcome this limitation, we present a tracking-by-detection approach based on the generalized Hough transform. We extend the idea of Hough forests (Chap. 11) to the online domain, and couple the voting-based detection and back-projection with a rough GrabCut segmentation [315]. This significantly reduces the amount of noisy training samples during online learning and thus effectively prevents the tracker from drifting. To show these benefits, we demonstrate our method for tracking a variety of previously unknown objects, even under heavy non-rigid transformations, partial occlusions, scale changes and rotations. Moreover, we compare our tracker to state-of-the-art methods including both bounding box-based and part-based trackers.

12.1 Introduction

Visual object tracking is a major component of a wide range of computer vision applications such as surveillance, driving assistant systems, interactive games, or augmented reality. If the task is well defined and the object-of-interest is known in advance, prior knowledge can be used to learn an efficient model. However, there are numerous applications such as collision avoidance, video re-targeting, or image stabilization, where no information is available beforehand.

A popular way to address this lack of knowledge has been to apply online learning to train a discriminative object detector during tracking and to adapt the detector

M. Godec (✉) · P.M. Roth · H. Bischof
Graz University of Technology, Graz, Austria

A. Criminisi, J. Shotton (eds.), *Decision Forests for Computer Vision and Medical Image Analysis*, Advances in Computer Vision and Pattern Recognition,
DOI 10.1007/978-1-4471-4929-3_12, © Springer-Verlag London 2013

to changes of the object over time (*e.g.* [10, 12, 139]). These approaches formulate tracking as alternation between object detection and online learning, where the current prediction is used to update the classifier. In this setting, a detector for an arbitrary object—not restricted to specific classes or categories—can be trained from scratch, only requiring the initial bounding box containing the object-of-interest. In this way, a discriminative object model is estimated which can be adapted online over time via self-learning, *i.e.* the model generates the update on its own.

Thus, we have to distinguish between allowed transformations (*e.g.* non-rigid deformations, rotations, appearance changes) and invalid ones (*e.g.* occlusions, drifting). This problem is well-known as the *template update problem* [242] or the *stability–plasticity dilemma* [145] and has been addressed by using, *e.g.*, more robust learning algorithms [317], different learning paradigms [12, 140], multiple classifiers [182, 318], or coupling a conservative learning framework to a very adaptive tracking approach [178].

However, most of these approaches are limited to a bounding box representation of the object. Therefore, they have to cope with a rather inaccurate object description (*e.g.* parts of the bounding box may consist of background). To avoid this problem, non-rigid or articulated objects can be represented by a part-based representation such as the Deformable Parts Model [105] or models obtained via the generalized Hough transform [117, 228, 275]. However, such approaches need a large amount of labeled training data. This is not a problem for detection/tracking tasks where the object classes are known in advance (*e.g.* pedestrians [119]), but makes them infeasible for tracking unknown objects.

In this chapter, we address two major limitations of previous approaches in the tracking-by-detection domain. First, we get rid of holistic bounding box description by using a parts-based model. In particular, we transfer the Hough-based classification idea to the online domain by introducing totally randomized Hough ferns using simple pixel comparisons on different feature channels as splitting tests (*cf.* Chap. 9 and Chap. 10). This allows us to robustly detect deformable objects. Second, we use back-projections to locate the support of our detection, which gives a fine-grained detection of object parts that have a valid geometric relation. This support guides a segmentation process (using GrabCut [315] in our case), which roughly separates the object from the background pixel-wise. Having such a segmentation has two advantages. First, since tracking-by-detection approaches directly use this annotation to update themselves, the amount of noise (*i.e.* pixels that do not belong to the object) introduced to the learning process can be reduced. Second, this allows for tracking objects with changing aspect ratio, scale, and orientation.

Thus, as illustrated in Fig. 12.1, the intended tracking scenario is to start from a bounding box initialization and then to continuously train a Hough-based detector with the current object appearance and to guide the segmentation process. The approach, denoted *HoughTrack* (HT), allows robust tracking of unknown objects under non-rigid transformations, appearance changes and partial occlusions.

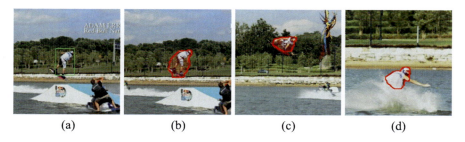

      (a)   (b)   (c)   (d)

Fig. 12.1 Tracking deformable objects: (**a**) manual bounding box initialization (*green*) in the first frame; and (**b–d**) continuous tracking and segmentation of the object (*red*). The images are cropped for better visibility

12.2 Related Work

Javed *et al.* [171] and Avidan [10] have been the first to use online learning for object detection and tracking. While Javed *et al.* [171] use online AdaBoost and holistic (PCA-based) features, Avidan [10] already performs pixel-wise classification and uses Mean-Shift to find the current object position. Additionally, to overcome the bounding box limitation, he incorporates a rejection scheme for pixels that are *too hard* to classify. From that time, there has been a reasonable interest in online learning within the visual tracking domain. Grabner *et al.* [139] defined tracking as an unsupervised online learning problem and transferred *Boosting for Feature Selection* [388] to the online domain. They apply a patch-based detector based on Haar-like features which is trained from frame-to-frame via online AdaBoost.

To overcome drifting, Grabner *et al.* later extended this approach to the semi-supervised learning (SSL) domain [140]. Thus, only the training samples given in the very first frame are considered as correctly labeled, while all samples generated by the classifier during runtime are considered as unlabeled. Similarly, Babenko *et al.* [12] define tracking as a multiple-instance learning (MIL) problem, where the current tracking position is considered uncertain and several positive samples are selected close to the current object position. Both concepts, SSL and MIL, shift the problem of sample selection from the tracking application towards the learning algorithm.

In contrast, Saffari *et al.* [317] transform the more robust random forests algorithm to the online learning domain and apply it to tracking. They use a tree-growing scheme to establish the ensemble of decision trees during runtime. Learning a stable object detector during tracking is the main goal of the approach of Kalal *et al.* [178]. They combine an adaptive Lukas–Kanade tracker and several restrictive learning constraints to establish an incremental tree-like classifier while avoiding drifting over time. This results in quite a robust object detector.

To avoid the limitations of bounding box trackers, Nejhum *et al.* [264] propose a tracker for articulated objects. They use blocks of appearance histograms and shape descriptions and assume stationary foreground appearance. Additionally, they use a rough segmentation to find the object's outline and re-arrange the blocks to maximize the overlap and similarity to the current object appearance and shape. Kwon and Lee [197] define a fixed number of object parts that are automatically renewed during tracking and track the geometric relations of these parts over time. Additionally, to reduce the computational complexity, they apply Basin Hopping Monte Carlo sampling. Bibby and Reid [27] describe the tracking problem within a probabilistic framework. Using pixel-wise posteriors they model the foreground and background appearance and the object contour jointly. Since such a theoretic framework is complex and computationally infeasible, they separate the tracking of deformable objects into registration, level-set segmentation, and online appearance learning for continuous refinement of both the object and the background model.

Another branch of research is the development of segmentation-based trackers. Such methods, however, either need prior knowledge (*e.g.* [75]), use only very simple object appearance models (*e.g.* color histograms [27, 307]), require an offline processing of the sequence (*e.g.* [146, 373]), or are computationally too complex for real-time applications (*e.g.* [255, 412]). Fan *et al.* [101] proposed a tracking approach, where salient points within and outside the object region are tracked and used to generate so called *scribbles* (*i.e.* foreground/background markings with high probability). Subsequently, these scribbles are used for image matting, which results in a high-quality object segmentation. Cehovin *et al.* [59] proposed a coupled-layer visual model for tracking deformable objects. They combine a local layer for tracking single patches and their geometric relations and a global layer describing holistic object properties.

In the domain of generic object detection, part-based representations have become very popular, since they provide excellent generalization while handling intra-class variations very well. One prominent approach is the *deformable parts model* [105], which allows to reliably detect objects even under heavy non-rigid transformations and partial occlusions. Using a latent support vector machine (SVM), a discriminative part-based object detector is trained which can handle a small number of parts selected automatically during the training phase. However, due to its complexity the approach is infeasible for real-time applications and has not, so far, been adapted for use in an online framework.

An alternative approach is the *Generalized Hough Transform* [15, 209], which was successfully applied to object detection [117, 228, 275], action recognition [409] and tracking [119]. In addition to the object's localization (see Chap. 11), the Hough-based classification framework also provides the support of a detectors decision (*i.e.* the local image positions that voted for the possible object center). This has in particular been addressed by Razavi *et al.* [306] and is also of high interest for our approach. However, in the case of tracking, only objects from a known class can be recognized using a pre-trained classifier. During tracking, only specific instances are distinguished from each other by an additional probability that is estimated online.

12.3 Online Hough Ferns

In the following, we first give a short review on decision forests [44], random ferns [280], and their application to Hough-voting-based classification. Subsequently, we introduce a new incremental leaf node statistics that allows for online adaptation, and define the sample generation process used for updating the classifier during tracking.

Let $\mathbf{v}$ be a rectangular image patch of size $n \times n$ and (assuming a binary classification) $\mathcal{C} = \{1, 0\}$ be the label space describing the object and the background class, respectively. In decision forests, each tree node j splits the training samples $\mathcal{S}_j$ into two subsets according to the splitting function

$$h(\mathbf{v}, \boldsymbol{\theta}_j) \in \{0, 1\}, \tag{12.1}$$

where the triple $\boldsymbol{\theta} = (\boldsymbol{\phi}, \boldsymbol{\psi}, \tau)$ defines the parameters of the splitting function.

The resulting subsets of training samples are passed to the left and to the right child node, respectively, and splitting is performed recursively until the subsets are internally consistent (*i.e.* belonging to the same class c) or a maximum tree depth D has been reached. The internal consistency of the resulting training sample subsets is measured using, *e.g.* the Gini-Index or entropy and the binary tests $h(\mathbf{v}, \boldsymbol{\theta})$ are selected to optimize the information gain. Since optimizing over the entire feature space is infeasible, the feature dimensions are sub-sampled randomly. Geurts *et al.* [128] proposed to additionally reduce the number of thresholds used per feature dimension and to randomly sample these thresholds from the feature range (see Chap. 10). In our concrete implementation, the splitting functions are defined as

$$h(\mathbf{v}, \boldsymbol{\theta}) = \left[\boldsymbol{\phi}(\mathbf{v}) \cdot \boldsymbol{\psi} > \tau \right], \tag{12.2}$$

where $\boldsymbol{\phi}(\mathbf{v})$ randomly selects two individual entries from $\mathbf{v}$, $\boldsymbol{\psi} = (1 \; -1)^\top$, and τ is a random threshold. These tests calculate the difference of two feature values in $\mathbf{v}$ and compare them to a threshold τ.

During evaluation, a sample $\mathbf{v}$ is sent down the tree according to the result of the node tests until it reaches a leaf node l. Within each leaf node, the object probability $p(c = 1|l)$ is stored. Finally, the overall probability $p(c|\mathbf{v})$ of the whole ensemble is determined by averaging the individual leaf probabilities $p(c = 1|l)$ of each tree. The actual class prediction of a sample $\mathbf{v}$ is computed as

$$c(\mathbf{v}) = \arg \max_c \sum_{t=1}^{T} p_t(c|\mathbf{v}). \tag{12.3}$$

Because of the tree-like classifier structure, the training can be done recursively and the evaluation is very fast due to the logarithmic dependency of the complexity of the classifier with respect to the number of nodes.

Showing several benefits, random forests also have a few limitations in the context of object tracking. First, a substantial training set is required to establish the classifier structure. Especially when tracking unknown objects, the amount of available training data is very limited. Second, streaming data sources and incremental learning are not supported. Even though online random forests [317] and online Hough forests [325] have been proposed, both use a tree-growing scheme to establish the classifier's structure during runtime, but the node tests are still optimized to fit the object's appearance at training time and cannot be adjusted afterwards. Third, the node tests are sequentially/hierarchically dependent on each other which introduces conditional jumps into the execution pipeline. For these reasons, we decided to completely randomize all test parameters θ referred to as *totally randomized trees* [235] and use random ferns, which results in completely independent tests.

12.3.1 Random Ferns

Random ferns [280] are ensemble classifiers which are highly related to random forests. However, instead of tree-like structures random ferns use flat node test structures making the tests independent from each other, which allows to evaluate them in parallel. For more details, see Chap. 9.

In contrast to random forests, ferns are usually used with completely randomized tests [280, 387], which are not optimized using training data. In particular, for tracking of unknown objects, node optimization is not necessary for two reasons. First, since only the very first frame is labeled, there is only a limited amount of data available to optimize the fern structure. Second, using only the appearance from the very first frame for optimizing may result in very tailored node tests, so that these tests may not be able to cover the changing appearance of the object over time.

12.3.2 Hough Voting

While the leaf nodes of random forests and ferns only store the probability $p(c|l)$ of a sample $\mathbf{v}$ ending up in node l being of class c, a Hough forest additionally stores displacement vectors $\mathbf{d} \in \mathbb{R}^2$ that point toward the expected object center. Thus, a positive (*i.e.* $c = 1$) training sample for a Hough forest consists of the triplet $(\mathbf{v}, c, \mathbf{d})$, where $\mathbf{d}$ is the displacement vector to the object's center position in the training data. Negative training samples (*i.e.* $c = 0$) do not contain a displacement vector since there is no relation towards the object center. The distribution of these vectors within each leaf node is modeled by a sum of Dirac measures according to the set of displacement vectors $\mathcal{D}_l$ from all samples $(\mathbf{v}, 1, \mathbf{d})$ that ended up in leaf node l. While training a tree node of a Hough forest, either the class consistency or the uncertainty of the displacement vectors for the given training set is optimized, as proposed in [117]. See Chap. 11 for more details.

During evaluation, a voting map is generated by accumulating the displacement vectors $\mathcal{D}_l$, weighted by the foreground probability $p(c = 1|l)$ of the corresponding leaf node l. This is done for all possible locations in the image.

12.3.3 Incremental Leaf Node Statistics

To establish a Hough-based classifier, we have to model (a) the foreground probability $p(c = 1|l)$ of the leaf node and (b) the corresponding displacement vectors

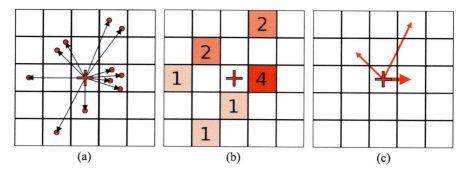

Fig. 12.2 Displacement map M_l: (**a**) training / input vectors; (**b**) weighted displacement cells; and (**c**) weighted output vectors for $\kappa = 3$

$\mathcal{D}_l$ during online training. The foreground probability is modeled incrementally by counting positive and negative samples arriving at leaf node l during runtime. To simulate an equal amount of positive and negative data, we additionally count the amount of positive and negative samples per fern.

Since the splitting tests used are not optimized to cluster similar voting directions, the set of displacement vectors $\mathcal{D}_l$ may be diverse. Therefore, we discretize the voting space into small rectangular displacement cells. We further weight each cell according to the number of samples that share the corresponding displacement vectors. This can be done incrementally. When the classifier is applied at a certain image position, we retrieve the corresponding leaf node l and collect a subset of displacement vectors from the displacement map M_l with respect to the weight of the cells. This is done by picking κ displacement cells with the largest weights ω_{cell}, setting their vote strength to

$$\omega_{\text{vote}} = p(c = 1|l) \cdot \omega_{\text{cell}} \tag{12.4}$$

and returning a displacement vector to the center of the cell (see Fig. 12.2).

12.3.4 Online Adaptation

Using only incremental statistics within the leaf nodes would limit the adaptivity of the classifier due to saturation effects. Therefore, we apply an *infinite impulse response*-like forgetting function

$$\omega_l(c = 1) = \sum_{q=-\infty}^{q_0} \left| \mathcal{S}_l^q(c = 1) \right| \cdot f^{q_0 - q}, \tag{12.5}$$

where $\omega_l(c = 1)$ is the current weight of the positive class in leaf node l and $|\mathcal{S}_l^q(c = 1)|$ is the number of positive samples in leaf node l at time q, respectively. q_0 denotes the current time and $f \in (0, 1]$ is the forgetting factor. The same function is applied to weight the negative class $\omega_l(c = 0)$ and all individual cells of the displacement map M_l, respectively. Thus, we determine the current foreground probability of a leaf node l as

$$p(c = 1|l) = \frac{\omega_l(c = 1)}{\sum_{i \in C_k} \omega_l(c = i)}. \qquad (12.6)$$

The described adaptations allow for online training of Hough forests using the current frame and for detection of the object in subsequent frames. Therefore, we apply the random fern classifier in a sliding window scheme and accumulate the retrieved displacement vectors. To suppress noise and effects from the displacement vector discretization, we perform Gaussian smoothing. The value of the voting map on a specific position corresponds to the probability of an object being centered there.

12.3.5 Support

Besides the detection capabilities, the voting mechanism of Hough ferns can also be applied in the reverse direction to localize the *support* S of a specific center position. Given an image position $\mathbf{p}$, the support $\mathcal{S}(\mathbf{p}, r)$ is defined as the sample set containing all image positions (*i.e.* samples $\mathbf{v}$) that have voted to the center position $\mathbf{p}$ with maximum Euclidean distance r. Using the corresponding set of displacement vectors $\mathcal{D}_l$ of samples $\mathbf{v}$, the voting origins can be back-projected onto the image space. Thus, we obtain a sparse point-set of positions belonging to the object that voted for the position $\mathbf{p}$ (*i.e.* the maximum of the voting map).

12.4 Closing the Tracking Loop

Additionally to online learning, the second crucial part is to close the tracking loop by *online training sample selection*. Selecting the right update strategy is important for online tracking-by-detection and heavily influences the overall performance. The major problem is that the correctness of the tracking result is not guaranteed (due to misalignments, occlusions or cluttered background) but the learning algorithm has to generate training samples including as little noise as possible itself.

Therefore, we propose to roughly segment the object, using the support $\mathcal{S}(\mathbf{p}, r)$ of the detected object with center $\mathbf{p}$ as an initialization. This segmentation is subsequently used to accurately update the classifier, which allows learning of highly non-rigid object deformations during tracking. Figure 12.3 illustrates the application flow of our tracking system.

Using the support $\mathcal{S}(\mathbf{p}, r)$ of the detected object position (*i.e.* the parts that share a stable geometric relation to the object center $\mathbf{p}$), we guide a segmentation process that extracts the object. Even if this segmentation is not very precise, compared to a bounding box approach this lowers the amount of noise introduced to the online up-

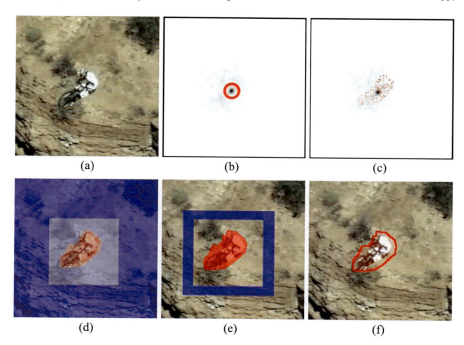

Fig. 12.3 The tracking loop: (**a**) current image; (**b**) Hough-based object detection; (**c**) back-projection and supporting image positions; (**d**) guided segmentation; (**e**) robust updating; and (**f**) tracking result. (*Red*: foreground support, segmentation and updates; *blue*: background segmentation and updates)

date steps. To establish the segmentation, we apply the well-known *GrabCut* [315] algorithm.[1] We use the support of the maximum of the likelihood map as foreground and a maximum-object-sized rectangle as background to initialize the tri-map, consisting of foreground, background, and unknown pixels. The segmentation labels the pixels marked as unknown and returns a binary separation of the image. Since the segmentation is not expected to be precise (due to, *e.g.*, missing parts or over-segmentations), we omit a region in-between the foreground and background segment during training.

To enforce adaptivity to geometric reconfiguration of the object, we shift the object's center position (*i.e.* the basis to calculate the displacement vectors **d** of the training samples) to the current center-of-mass of the foreground segment. Thereby, the detected object center represents only the center of the currently visible part of the tracked object, because there is no discrimination between occlusions and geometric reconfiguration of the object. However, this simple but efficient strategy delivers accurate training data which are used to update the classifier during tracking. If the segmentation fails (*i.e.* reporting the maximum-object-sized rectangle),

---

[1] Implementation from http://opencv.willowgarage.com.

the tracker acts like a traditional bounding box-based tracker. However, randomized ensemble methods such as random ferns are known to be more robust to a large number of incorrectly labeled samples.

12.5 Experimental Evaluation

To demonstrate the performance of our tracking approach, denoted as *HoughTrack* (HT), we run two different experiments. First, we give a comparison to two state-of-the-art trackers on a dataset widely used for evaluation of bounding box-based approaches, where we show competitive results. Second, we compare our approach to a recent part-based tracking approach. For this comparison, we collected a set of very diverse and challenging sequences including highly non-rigid object transformations. We additionally include the sequences used for evaluation of the compared approach. Moreover, to justify the additional effort of segmentation, we give a comparison of the approach with and without the segmentation step.

The settings of our tracker are fixed for all sequences: the classifier pool consists of 20 ferns and $T = 10$ ferns with the highest population are selected for detection. The used ferns have a group size of $S = 8$, with $M = 1$ groups (see Chap. 9). We use Lab-color space (3 channels), first and second derivatives in the x and y directions (4 channels) and a 9-bin histogram of gradients (9 channels) to form the feature vector $\mathbf{v}$. Please note that the group size S corresponds to the tree depth D and that we use single-group ferns ($M = 1$) as we embed them into an ensemble of size T. The used patch size of the training samples $\mathbf{v}$ is 12×12 and $\kappa = 10$ strong votes are returned per leaf node l. The forgetting constant f is set to 0.9 and the maximum support deviation r is 0.5 pixels.

12.5.1 Bounding Box Dataset

For quantitative analysis, we use the publicly available tracking dataset by Babenko *et al.* [12], consisting of eight sequences collected from several different publications and having an overall size of more than 5000 frames. For comparison, the original results of *MILTrack* (MIL) [12] using 50 weak classifiers and *Online Random Forests* (ORF) [317] using 50 trees are denoted. Both trackers deliver state-of-the-art performance on this dataset. To deliver similar results as the compared trackers, the results of *HoughTrack* (HT) are transformed to bounding boxes of original size, centered at the center-of-mass of the segmentation. Table 12.1 clearly shows that the proposed approach delivers competitive results, even not considering partial or full occlusions in the evaluation due to the lack of annotations.

Based on the ground truth annotation included in the dataset of [12], which is represented by a simple bounding box of the same size as the initialization, we cannot fairly compare our approach to other bound-box-based trackers because object occlusions are completely ignored in the ground truth annotation. To alleviate the influence of occlusions to the overall performance, we measure the tracking accu-

Table 12.1 Results on
Babenko sequences.
Percentage of correctly
tracked frames for individual
sequences, and average across
sequences

Sequence	**HT**	MIL [12]	ORF [317]
David	**100**	84	95
Sylvester	**99**	93	71
Girl	86	85	**99**
Face Occlusion 1	**100**	91	**100**
Face Occlusion 2	**100**	94	70
Coke	24	**46**	17
Tiger 1	45	78	27
Tiger 2	71	**78**	21
Average	78	81	63

racy using the Agarwal criterion [1], which is defined as score $= \frac{R_T \cap R_{GT}}{R_T}$, where R_T is the tracking rectangle and R_{GT} the ground truth. We report the number of successfully tracked frames (score > 0.5). In Fig. 12.4, we show some selected frames from the dataset and demonstrate that the raw accuracy values from Table 12.1 fail to demonstrate the true performance of the proposed tracking approach.

12.5.2 Tracking Deformable Objects

Since the intended purpose of our approach is tracking deformable objects, we additionally demonstrate the performance on several challenging sequences showing different ranges of complexity and non-rigid deformations. Therefore, we collected a set of seven videos consisting of about 2500 frames. We compare to *Basin Hopping Monte Carlo Tracking* (BHMC) [197]. This tracker is also designed to track deformable objects in a part-based manner. We also include the sequences provided by the authors of [197] to give a fair comparison (see Table 12.2). Although tracking non-rigid objects, BHMC does not report a segmentation of the object but a bounding box.

Table 12.2 depicts the tracking results of the selected approaches evaluated on the test sequences. The percentage of frames for each sequence until the tracking approach fails has been determined by visual inspection because the kind of output of the compared approaches is very different. As a bounding box baseline, we also state the results of *Online Random Forests* (ORF) [317], but this tracker cannot cope well with the amount of transformation presented in this videos, and the estimated object position is less accurate than using the two other approaches. Figure 12.5 shows some selected frames of the sequences and the tracking results of *HoughTrack* (HT).

12.5.3 Bounding Box vs. Segmentation-Based Tracking

The major remaining question of the presented approach is whether the effort of an additional segmentation is justified. Therefore, we performed a simple experiment

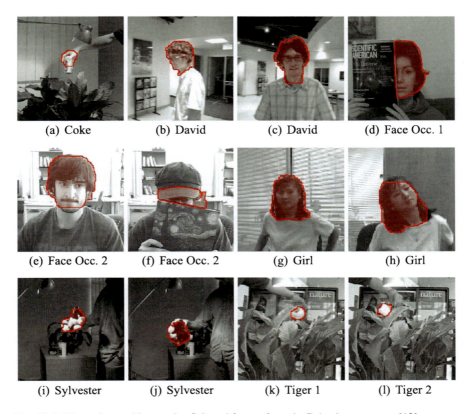

(a) Coke	(b) David	(c) David	(d) Face Occ. 1
(e) Face Occ. 2	(f) Face Occ. 2	(g) Girl	(h) Girl
(i) Sylvester	(j) Sylvester	(k) Tiger 1	(l) Tiger 2

Fig. 12.4 Illustrative tracking results. Selected frames from the Babenko sequences [12]

comparing *HoughTrack* with and without the subsequent segmentation step. Thus, the only difference between the compared methods is the set of update patches that is used to update the classifier.

We use a subset of the sequences from Sects. 12.5.1 and 12.5.2, which have different grades of deformation and occlusion. For simplicity, we use the same criteria to measure the tracking quality per dataset as stated above. The first block of Table 12.3 shows the comparison for standard sequences taken from the Babenko [12] dataset. The target objects in this sequences are only slightly deformed, which does not affect the bounding box version of our approach too much. However, significant occlusions decrease the tracking performance and the tracker starts to drift because the occluding object is not removed from the update region as it is the case if segmentation is performed. Also out-of-plane rotations of the appearance of the tracked object decrease the performance because the proposed shift to the center of the segmentation helps to stick to the original object if the appearance differs from the background.

Comparing both versions on more challenging sequences including highly non-rigid transformations of the target object reveals the positive influence of the seg-

Fig. 12.5 Illustrative tracking results. Manual initialization (*first row*) and selected frames (*row 2 to 6*) from several sequences. (*Green*: initialization rectangle; *red*: tracking result)

Table 12.2 Tracking
deformable objects.
Percentage of frames
correctly tracked until failure

Sequence	HT	BHMC [197]	ORF [317]
Cliff-dive 1	100	100	100
Motocross 1	100	5	15
Skiing	100	0	5
Mountain-bike	100	50	100
Cliff-dive 2	100	30	50
Volleyball	100	60	45
Motocross 2	100	25	10
Transformer	100	100	100
Diving	75	100	30
High Jump	100	100	5
Gymnastics	100	100	65
Average	92	55	36

Table 12.3 Bounding box *vs.*
segmentation-based tracking.
Percentage of correctly
tracked frames for selected
sequences and average

Sequence	with Seg.	without Seg.
Sylvester	99	90
Girl	86	84
Face Occlusion 2	100	91
Coke	24	10
Motocross 1	100	5
Volleyball	100	42
Transformer	100	30
High Jump	100	14
Average	89	46

mentation. This effect can be recognized in the second block of Table 12.3, where rotations, non-rigid transformations and fast motion are present in the sequences. Overall, the results obtained using segmentation are far better than those without segmentation, which experimentally justifies the additional effort of back-projection and segmentation of the target object in our approach.

12.5.4 Discussion and Implementation Details

Since we use a rectangular initialization of our tracker in the first frame, the support of our detection in the subsequent frames may also include background positions. Since they have also been included in the initial training set, they may confuse the classifier. However, these votes disappear as soon as the object moves and the associated votes do not match the support criterion any more. Only if the majority of the support originates from the near background of the object, the recognized object center will be supported by the background and the tracker is not able to follow the object any longer. This effect may occur when there is very cluttered background (*Diving* sequence) or the segmentation algorithm fails due to similar colors in the background (*Gymnastics* sequence).

We have defined a maximum object size that is used for background initialization of our segmentation algorithm. If the segmentation fails, it is not allowed to grow beyond this maximum scale. This prevents some leakage of the object segmentation. In *Cliff-dive 2* sequence (3rd column in Fig. 12.5), this effect is clearly visible. However, the segmentation improves over time and the effect disappears if the set of supporting pixels is large enough.

To overcome changing aspect ratios of the object, we reshape the maximum object size to a square box, which can be switched off if there is prior knowledge on the stability of the aspect ratio. These last bounding box limitations could be avoided easily by using a narrow-band segmentation scheme, which would also prevent extremely fast changes of the shape of the segmentation and make the visual result even more appealing. For comparison to future approaches, our reference implementation and the used sequences are available online.[2]

12.6 Conclusion

In this chapter, we have presented an object tracking approach which is able to handle non-rigid object transformations as well as partial- and self-occlusions. By combining a Hough-voting-based classification framework, online learning techniques and a segmentation algorithm, we are able to track various objects in several challenging sequences. We use the classification framework for both detection of objects and identification of the support of the currently estimated object position. The segmentation is guided by the support and gives a per-pixel separation for object and background, which enables a more robust online training during runtime.

In future work, we plan to investigate the robustness of our learner and the appropriate integration of prior information (*e.g.* a pedestrian model). To further enhance the tracking, the incorporation of a motion model and a more advanced occlusion handling that also supports re-detection of the object would be beneficial. To further speed up the approach, we can easily parallelize all modules. This, in particular allows the usage of a General Purpose Graphics Processing Unit (GP-GPU). That would also allow the application of more complex segmentation algorithms, which could further improve the overall performance of our approach.

Acknowledgements   The work was supported by the Austrian Research Promotion Agency (FFG) projects MobiTrick (8258408) in the FIT-IT program and SHARE (831717) in the IV2Splus program, and by the Austrian Science Foundation (FWF) project Advanced Learning for Tracking and Detection in Medical Workflow Analysis (I535-N23).

---

[2]http://lrs.icg.tugraz.at/research/houghtrack/.

Chapter 13
Efficient Human Pose Estimation from Single Depth Images

J. Shotton, R. Girshick, A. Fitzgibbon, T. Sharp, M. Cook, M. Finocchio, R. Moore, P. Kohli, A. Criminisi, A. Kipman, and A. Blake

We describe two new approaches to human pose estimation. Both can quickly and accurately predict the 3D positions of body joints from a single depth image, without using any temporal information. The key to both approaches is the use of a large, realistic, and highly varied synthetic set of training images. This allows us to learn models that are largely invariant to factors such as pose, body shape, and field-of-view cropping. Our first approach employs an intermediate body parts representation, designed so that an accurate per-pixel classification of the parts will localize the joints of the body. The second approach instead directly regresses the positions of body joints. By using simple depth pixel comparison features, and parallelizable decision forests, both approaches can run super-realtime on consumer hardware. Our evaluation investigates many aspects of our methods, and compares the approaches to each other and to the state of the art.

13.1 Introduction

The fast and reliable estimation of the pose of the human body from images has been a goal of computer vision for decades. Robust interactive pose estimation has

This work was undertaken at Microsoft Research, Cambridge, in collaboration with Xbox. See http://research.microsoft.com/vision/. Ross Girshick is currently a postdoctoral fellow at UC Berkeley.

Parts of this chapter are reprinted, with permission, from [343], © 2011 IEEE.

J. Shotton (✉) · A. Fitzgibbon · T. Sharp · M. Cook · P. Kohli · A. Criminisi · A. Blake
Microsoft Research Ltd., 7 J.J. Thomson Avenue, Cambridge CB3 0FB, UK

R. Girshick
University of California, Berkeley, CA, USA

M. Finocchio · A. Kipman
Microsoft Corporation, Redmond, WA, USA

R. Moore
ST-Ericsson, Redmond, WA, USA

A. Criminisi, J. Shotton (eds.), *Decision Forests for Computer Vision and Medical Image Analysis*, Advances in Computer Vision and Pattern Recognition, DOI 10.1007/978-1-4471-4929-3_13, © Springer-Verlag London 2013

applications including gaming, human-computer interaction, security, telepresence, and even health-care. The recent availability of high-speed depth sensors has greatly simplified the task [121, 144, 186, 293, 345, 423]. However, until the launch of the Microsoft Kinect camera and gaming platform [247] in November 2010, even the best systems exhibited failures when faced with unusual poses, occlusion, sensor noise, and the constraints of super-realtime operation.

This paper describes two related approaches for estimating human pose from Kinect depth images, illustrated in Fig. 13.1. We will refer to these as *body part classification* (BPC) and *offset joint regression* (OJR). Both were designed with the goals of computational efficiency and robustness in mind: our aim was to build systems that could run in super-realtime and for hours at a time without failing catastrophically. The algorithms output high-quality shortlists of confidence-weighted proposals for the 3D locations of the skeletal body joints. These proposals are computed at each frame and for each joint independently. Our original design was for these proposals to provide initialization and per-frame recovery to complement any appropriate tracking algorithm [41, 50, 121, 144, 346, 396]. These infer a complete skeleton by exploiting kinematic constraints and can achieve high frame rates by using temporal coherence from frame-to-frame. However, without regular re-initialization, tracking algorithms are prone to catastrophic loss of track. Our experiments below will demonstrate that even without temporal or kinematic information, our per-frame, per-joint proposals are remarkably accurate, and might even be usable without a tracking algorithm.

Both BPC and OJR use an efficient decision forest that is applied at each pixel in the image. Evaluating each pixel separately avoids any combinatorial search over body joints. The forest uses simple yet discriminative depth comparison image features that give 3D translation invariance while maintaining high computational efficiency. In an optimized implementation, these features and the classifier itself can be evaluated in parallel across each pixel on a GPU [333] or multi-core CPU. Both algorithms can run at super-realtime rates on consumer hardware, leaving sufficient computational resources to allow complex game logic and graphics to run in parallel. Indeed, the BPC algorithm forms a core component of the skeletal tracking pipeline that ships in the Kinect gaming platform [247].

Using depth images as input gives several advantages for human pose estimation. Depth cameras work in low light conditions (even in the dark), help remove ambiguity in scale, are largely color and texture invariant, and resolve silhouette ambiguities. They also greatly simplify the task of background subtraction which we assume in this work as a pre-processing step. Most importantly for our approaches, since variations in color and texture are not imaged, it is relatively easy to synthesize realistic depth images of people.

The two methods can thus share the use of a very large, realistic, synthetic training corpus, generated by rendering depth images of humans. Each render is assigned randomly sampled parameters including body shape, size, pose, scene position, *etc.* We can thus quickly and cheaply generate hundreds of thousands of varied images *with associated ground truth* (the body part label images and the set of 3D body joint positions). The availability of large amounts of training data allows us to train

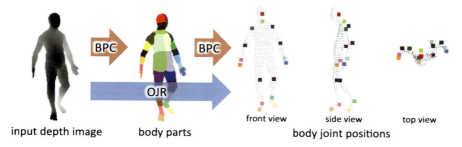

Fig. 13.1 Method overview on ground truth example. Body part classification (BPC) first predicts a (color-coded) body part label at each pixel, and then uses these inferred labels to localize the body joints. Offset joint regression (OJR) instead directly regresses the joint positions. The input depth point cloud is shown overlaid on the body joint positions for reference

deep forests, without the risk of overfitting, that can naturally handle a full range of human body shapes undergoing general body motions [378], self-occlusions, and poses cropped by the image frame.

Body part classification, originally published in [343], was inspired by recent object recognition work that divides objects into parts (*e.g.* [37, 107, 293, 403]). BPC uses a *classification* forest (Chap. 4) to densely predict discrete body part labels across the image. The pattern of these labels is designed such that the parts are spatially localized near skeletal joints of interest. Given the depth image and the known calibration of the depth camera, the inferred per-pixel label probabilities can be reprojected to define a density over 3D world space. Offset joint regression [131] instead employs a randomized *regression* forest to directly cast a set of 3D offset votes from each pixel to the body joints. These votes are used to again define a world space density. Modes of these density functions can be found using mean shift [69] to give the final set of 3D body joint proposals. Optimized implementations of our algorithms can run at around 200 frames per second on consumer hardware, at least one order of magnitude faster than alternative approaches.

To validate our algorithms, we evaluate on both real and synthetic depth images, containing challenging poses of a varied set of subjects. Even without exploiting temporal or kinematic constraints, the 3D body joint proposals are both accurate and stable. We investigate the effect of several training parameters and show a substantial improvement over the state of the art.

Our main contributions are as follows.

- We demonstrate that using efficient machine learning approaches, trained with a large-scale, highly varied, synthetic training set, allows one to accurately predict the positions of the human body joints in super-realtime.
- We show how a carefully designed pattern of body parts can transform the hard problem of pose estimation into an easier problem of per-pixel semantic segmentation.
- We examine both classification and regression objective functions for training the decision forests, and obtain slightly surprising results that suggest a limitation of the standard regression objective.

Fig. 13.2 Synthetic *vs.* real data. Pairs of depth images and corresponding color-coded ground truth body part label images. The 3D body joint positions are also known (but not shown). Note the wide variety in pose, shape, clothing, and crop. The synthetic images look remarkably similar to the real images, lacking primarily just the high-frequency texture

- We employ regression models that compactly summarize the pixel-to-joint offset distributions at leaf nodes. We show that these make our method both faster and more accurate than Hough Forests [117]. We will refer to this as 'vote compression'.

This chapter builds on our earlier publications [131, 343], and summarizes [344]. It unifies the notation, explains the approaches in more detail, and shows how they naturally stem from the generic forest model presented in Chap. 3.

13.2 Data

Hundreds of thousands of labeled depth images are generated using a motion capture system and a 3D rendering software as explained in detail in [344]. A major advantage of using synthetic training images is that the ground truth labels can be generated almost for free (see Fig. 13.2), allowing one to scale up supervised learning to very large scales. The complete rendering pipeline allows us to rapidly sample hundreds of thousands of unique images of people.

The particular tasks we address in this work, BPC and OJR, require different types of label, described next.

Body Part Classification Labels Our first algorithm, BPC, aims to predict a discrete body part label at each pixel. At training time, these labels are required for all pixels, and we thus represent the labels as a color-coded body part label image that accompanies each depth image (see Figs. 13.1 and 13.2). The use of an intermediate body part representation that can localize 3D body joints is a key contribution of this work. It transforms the pose estimation problem into one that can readily be solved by efficient classification algorithms. The particular pattern of body parts used was designed by hand to aid accurate joint localization in 3D.

The parts definition can be specified in a texture map and retargetted to the various 3D base character meshes for rendering. For our experiments, we define 31 body parts: LU/RU/LW/RW head, neck, L/R shoulder, LU/RU/LW/RW arm, L/R elbow, L/R wrist, L/R hand, LU/RU/LW/RW torso, LU/RU/LW/RW leg, L/R knee, L/R ankle, and L/R foot (Left, Right, Upper, lower). Distinct parts for left and right allow the classifier to learn to disambiguate the left and right sides of the body. The precise definition of these parts might be changed to suit a particular application. For example, in an upper body tracking scenario, all the lower body parts could be merged into a single part.

Offset Joint Regression Labels   Our second algorithm, OJR, instead aims to estimate the 3D joint positions more directly. As such, the ground truth labels it requires are simply the 3D joint positions. These are trivially recorded during the standard mesh skinning process. In our experiments, we use 16 body joints: head, neck, L/R shoulder, L/R elbow, L/R wrist, L/R hand, L/R knee, L/R ankle, and L/R foot. This selection allows us to directly compare the BPC and OJR approaches on a common set of predicted joints.

13.3 Method

Our algorithms cast votes for the position of the body joints by evaluating a decision forest at each pixel in the input image. These votes are then aggregated to infer reliable 3D body joint position proposals. In this section we describe: (1) the features we employ to extract discriminative information from the image; (2) the structure of a random forest, and how it combines multiple such features to achieve an accurate set of votes; (3) the different leaf node prediction models used for BPC and OJR; (4) how the pixel votes are aggregated into a set of joint position predictions at test time; and (5) how the forests are learned.

13.3.1 Depth Image Features

We employ simple depth comparison features, inspired by those in [214]. Individually, these features provide only a weak discriminative signal, but combined in a decision forest they prove sufficient to accurately disambiguate different appearances and regions of the body. Using the notation in Chap. 3, at a given *reference* pixel position $\mathbf{u} = (u_x, u_y)$, the feature response vector is computed as

$$\mathbf{v}(\mathbf{u}) = \big(z(\mathbf{q}_1), \dots, z(\mathbf{q}_i), \dots, z(\mathbf{q}_d)\big) \qquad (13.1)$$

with

$$\mathbf{q}_i = \mathbf{u} + \frac{\delta_i}{z(\mathbf{u})} \qquad (13.2)$$

denoting the position of a *probe* pixel, where the parameter δ denotes a 2D offset with respect to the reference position $\mathbf{u}$. The function $z(\cdot)$ looks up the depth at a given position in a particular image.

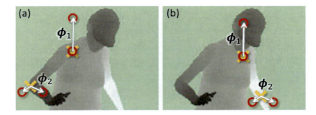

Fig. 13.3 Depth image features. The *yellow crosses* indicate the reference image pixel **u** being classified. The *red circles* indicate the offset pixels as defined in (13.3). In (**a**), the two example features give a large depth difference response, *i.e.* $|f(\mathbf{u}; \boldsymbol{\phi}, \boldsymbol{\psi})|$ is large. In (**b**), the same two features at new image locations give a much smaller response. In practice, many such features combined in a decision forest provide a strong discriminative signal

In this application the split tests employed at internal nodes are simple differences between two chosen coordinates of the vector **v**. In our general notation this corresponds to defining the selector function as $\boldsymbol{\phi}(\mathbf{v}) = (v_i, v_j)$ (with $i, j \in \{1, \ldots, d\}$), and defining $\boldsymbol{\psi} = (1, -1)$, fixed for all split nodes. Therefore, depths at two probes offset from the reference **u** are subtracted from one another via

$$f(\mathbf{u}; \boldsymbol{\phi}, \boldsymbol{\psi}) = \boldsymbol{\phi}(\mathbf{v}(\mathbf{u})) \cdot \boldsymbol{\psi}. \qquad (13.3)$$

For efficiency, only the required elements of the whole feature vector **v(u)** are computed.

If a probe pixel **q** lies on the background or outside the bounds of the image, the depth probe $z(\mathbf{q})$ is assigned a large positive constant value. The normalization of the offsets by $1/z(\mathbf{u})$ ensures that the feature response is depth invariant: at a given point on the body, a fixed world space offset will result whether the depth pixel is close or far from the camera. The features are thus 3D translation invariant, modulo perspective effects.

During training of the tree structure, offsets $\boldsymbol{\delta}$ are sampled at random within a box of fixed size. We further set $\boldsymbol{\delta}_2 = \mathbf{0}$ with probability $1/2$. This means that roughly half the features evaluated are 'unary' (look at only one offset pixel) and half are 'binary' (look at two offset pixels).

Figure 13.3 illustrates two different features. The unary feature with parameters $\boldsymbol{\phi}_1$ looks upwards: (13.3) will give a large positive response for pixels **u** near the top of the body, but a value close to zero for pixels **u** lower down the body. By similar reasoning, the binary feature ($\boldsymbol{\phi}_2$) may be seen instead to help find thin vertical structures such as the arm.

The design of these features was strongly motivated by their computational efficiency: no pre-processing is needed; each feature need only read at most three image pixels and perform at most five arithmetic operations. Further, these features can be straightforwardly implemented on the GPU. Given a larger computational budget, one could employ potentially more powerful features based on, for example, depth integrals over regions, curvature, or more complex local descriptors such as shape contexts [24].

13.3.2 Weak Learners

A forest is an ensemble of T decision trees, each consisting of split and leaf nodes. We will use n to denote any node in the tree, and l to denote a leaf node specifically. Each split node contains a 'weak learner' represented by its parameters $\theta = (\phi, \psi, \tau)$. In this application the parameters ϕ and ψ have already been defined in the previous section. The symbol τ denotes a scalar threshold. To make a prediction for pixel $\mathbf{u}$ in a particular image, one starts at the root and traverses a path to a leaf by repeated evaluating the following weak learner function at each split node n:

$$h(\mathbf{u}; \theta_n) = \left[f(\mathbf{u}; \phi_n, \psi) \geq \tau_n \right], \tag{13.4}$$

where $[\cdot]$ is the 0–1 indicator. If $h(\mathbf{u}; \theta_n)$ evaluates to 0, the path branches to the left child of n, otherwise it branches to the right child. This repeats until a leaf node l is reached. We will use $l(\mathbf{u})$ to indicate the particular leaf node reached for pixel $\mathbf{u}$. The same algorithm is applied at each pixel for each tree t, resulting in the set of leaf nodes reached $\mathcal{L}(\mathbf{u}) = \{l_t(\mathbf{u})\}_{t=1}^{T}$.

13.3.3 Leaf Node Prediction Models

At each leaf node l in each tree is stored a learned *prediction* model. In this work we use two types of prediction model. For BPC, where a classification forest is used, the prediction model is a probability mass function $p_l(c)$ over body parts c. For OJR, where a regression forest is used, the prediction model is instead a set of weighted relative votes V_{lj} for each joint j. In this section we describe these two models, and show how both algorithms can be viewed as casting a set of weighted world space *votes* for the 3D positions of the each joint in the body. Section 13.3.4 will then show how these votes are aggregated in an efficient smoothing and clustering step based on mean shift to produce the final 3D body joint proposals.

Body Part Classification (BPC) BPC predicts a discrete body part label at each pixel as an intermediate step towards predicting joint positions. The classification forest approach achieves this by storing a distribution $p_l(c)$ over the discrete body parts c at each leaf l. For a given input pixel $\mathbf{u}$, the tree is descended to reach leaf $l = l(\mathbf{u})$ and the distribution $p_l(c)$ is retrieved. The distributions are averaged together for all trees in the forest to give the final classification as

$$p(c|\mathbf{u}) = \frac{1}{T} \sum_{l \in \mathcal{L}(\mathbf{u})} p_l(c). \tag{13.5}$$

One can visualize the most likely body part inferred at each pixel as an image, and examples of this are given in Fig. 13.6. One might consider smoothing this signal in the image domain. For example, one might use probabilities $p(c|\mathbf{u})$ as the unary

Algorithm 13.1 Body part classification voting

 1: initialize $\mathcal{X}_j^{\mathrm{BPC}} = \emptyset$ for all joints j
 2: **for all** foreground pixels **u** in the test image **do**
 3:     evaluate forest to reach leaf nodes $\mathcal{L}(\mathbf{u})$
 4:     evaluate distribution $p(c|\mathbf{u})$ using (13.5)
 5:     compute 3D pixel position $\mathbf{x}(\mathbf{u}) = (x(\mathbf{u}), y(\mathbf{u}), z(\mathbf{u}))^\top$
 6:     **for all** joints j **do**
 7:         compute pushed-back position $\mathbf{x}_j(\mathbf{u}) = \mathbf{x}(\mathbf{u}) + \boldsymbol{\zeta}_j$
 8:         lookup relevant body part $c(j)$
 9:         compute weight w as $p(c = c(j)|\mathbf{u}) \cdot z^2(\mathbf{u})$
10:         add vote $(\mathbf{x}_j(\mathbf{u}), w)$ to set $\mathcal{X}_j^{\mathrm{BPC}}$
11: **return** set of votes $\mathcal{X}_j^{\mathrm{BPC}}$ for each joint j

---

term in a conditional random field with a pairwise smoothness prior [338]. However, since the per-pixel signal is already very strong and such smoothing would likely be expensive to compute, we do not use such a prior.

The image space predictions are next reprojected into world space. We denote the reprojection function as $\mathbf{x}(\mathbf{u}) = (x(\mathbf{u}), y(\mathbf{u}), z(\mathbf{u}))^\top$. Here x, y, z denote point coordinates in 3D. Conveniently, the known $z(\mathbf{u})$ from the calibrated depth camera allows us to compute $x(\mathbf{u})$ and $y(\mathbf{u})$ straightforwardly.

Next, we must decide how to map from surface body *parts* to interior body *joints*. In Sect. 13.2 we defined many, though not all, body part labels c to spatially align with the body joints j, and, conversely, most joints j have a specific part label c. We will thus use $c(j)$ to denote the body part associated with joint j.

Now, no matter how well aligned in the x and y directions, the body parts inherently lie on the surface of the body. They thus cannot align in the z direction with the *interior* body joint position we are after (see Fig. 13.1). We therefore use a learned per-joint vector $\boldsymbol{\zeta}_j = (0, 0, \zeta_j)^\top$ that pushes the reprojected pixel surface positions back into the world to better align with the interior joint position: $\mathbf{x}_j(\mathbf{u}) = \mathbf{x}(\mathbf{u}) + \boldsymbol{\zeta}_j$. This simple approach implicitly assumes each joint is spherical, but works well and efficiently in practice. As a rough indication, the mean across the different joints of the learned push-backs ζ is 0.04 m.

We finally create the set $\mathcal{X}_j^{\mathrm{BPC}}$ of weighted world space votes using Algorithm 13.1. These votes will be used in the aggregation step below. As you see, the position of each vote is given by the pushed-back world space pixel position $\mathbf{x}_j(\mathbf{u})$. The vote weight w is given by the probability mass for a particular body part, multiplied by the squared pixel depth. This depth-weighting compensates for observing fewer pixels when imaging a person standing further from the camera, and ensures the aggregation step is depth invariant. In practice this gave a small but consistent improvement in joint prediction accuracy.

Note that each pixel produces exactly one vote for each body joint, and these votes all share the same world space position. In practice many of the votes will have zero probability mass and can be ignored. This contrasts with the OJR prediction model, described next, where each pixel can cast several votes for each joint.

Offset Joint Regression (OJR)   The OJR approach aims to predict the set of weighted votes directly, without going through an intermediate representation. The forest used here is a regression forest [78, 80] since the leaves make continuous predictions (see also Chap. 5). At each leaf node l we store a distribution over the *relative* 3D offset from the reprojected pixel coordinate $\mathbf{x}(\mathbf{u})$ to each body joint j of interest. Each pixel can thus potentially cast votes to all joints in the body, and unlike BPC, these votes may differ in all three coordinate dimensions and thus directly predict interior rather than surface positions.

Ideally, one would like to make use of a *distribution* of such offsets. Even for fairly deep trees, we have observed highly multi-modal empirical offset distributions at the leaves. Thus for many nodes and joints, approximating the distribution over offsets as a Gaussian would be inappropriate. One alternative, Hough forests [117], represents the distribution non-parametrically as the set of *all* offsets seen at training time (see also Chap. 11). However, Hough forests trained on our large training sets would require vast amounts of memory and be prohibitively slow for a realtime system.

We therefore, in contrast to [117, 210], represent the distribution using a *small* set of 3D *relative vote* vectors $\boldsymbol{\Delta}_{ljk} \in \mathbb{R}^3$. The subscript l denotes the tree leaf node (as before), j denotes a body joint, and $k \in \{1, \ldots, K\}$ denotes a cluster index.[1] We have found $K = 1$ or 2 has given good results, and while the main reason for keeping K small is efficiency, we also empirically observed that increasing K beyond 1 gives only a very small increase in accuracy. As described below, the relative votes $\boldsymbol{\Delta}_{ljk}$ are obtained by clustering an unbiased sample of all offsets seen at training time using mean shift (see Sect. 13.3.5.2). Unlike [257], a corresponding confidence weight w_{ljk} is assigned to each vote, given by the size of its cluster. We will refer below to the *set* of relative votes for joint j at node l as $\mathcal{V}_{lj} = \{(\boldsymbol{\Delta}_{ljk}, w_{ljk})\}_{k=1}^{K}$.

We detail the test-time voting approach for OJR in Algorithm 13.2, whereby the set $\mathcal{X}_j^{OJR}$ of *absolute* votes cast by all pixels for each body joint j is collected. As with BPC, the vote weights are multiplied by the squared depth to compensate for differing surface areas of pixels. Optionally, the set $\mathcal{X}_j^{OJR}$ can be sub-sampled by taking either the top N_{sub} weighted votes or instead N_{sub} randomly sampled votes. Our results show that this can dramatically improve speed while maintaining high accuracy.

Compared to BPC, OJR more directly predicts joints that lie behind the depth surface, and can cope with joints that are occluded or outside the image frame. Figure 13.4 illustrates the voting process for OJR.

13.3.4 Aggregating Predictions

We have seen above how, at test time, both BPC and OJR can be seen as casting a set of weighted votes in world space for the location of the body joints. These votes

---

[1] We use K to indicate the *maximum* number of relative votes allowed. In practice we allow some leaf nodes to store fewer than K votes for some joints.

Algorithm 13.2 Offset joint regression voting

1: initialize $\mathcal{X}_j^{\text{OJR}} = \emptyset$ for all joints j
2: **for all** foreground pixels $\mathbf{u}$ in the test image **do**
3:     evaluate forest to reach leaf nodes $\mathcal{L}(\mathbf{u})$
4:     compute 3D pixel position $\mathbf{x}(\mathbf{u}) = (x(\mathbf{u}), y(\mathbf{u}), z(\mathbf{u}))^{\top}$
5:     **for all** leaves $l \in \mathcal{L}(\mathbf{u})$ **do**
6:         **for all** joints j **do**
7:             lookup weighted *relative* vote set $\mathcal{V}_{lj}$
8:             **for all** $(\boldsymbol{\Delta}_{ljk}, w_{ljk}) \in \mathcal{V}_{lj}$ **do**
9:                 compute *absolute* position $\mathbf{x} = \mathbf{x}(\mathbf{u}) + \boldsymbol{\Delta}_{ljk}$
10:                compute weight w as $w_{ljk} \cdot z^2(\mathbf{u})$
11:                add vote $(\mathbf{x}, w)$ to set $\mathcal{X}_j^{\text{OJR}}$
12: sub-sample $\mathcal{X}_j^{\text{OJR}}$ to contain at most N_{sub} votes
13: **return** sub-sampled vote set $\mathcal{X}_j^{\text{OJR}}$ for each joint j

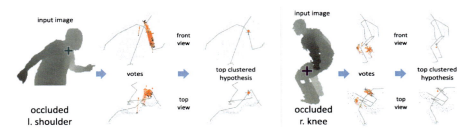

Fig. 13.4 Offset joint regression voting at test time. Each pixel (*black square*) casts a 3D vote (*orange line*) for each joint. Mean shift is used to aggregate these votes and produce a final set of 3D predictions for each joint. The highest confidence prediction for each joint is shown. Note accurate prediction of internal body joints even when occluded

must now be aggregated to generate reliable proposals for the positions of the 3D skeletal joints, the final output of our algorithm. As we will see in our experiments, these proposals can accurately localize the positions of body joints from a single image. By producing multiple proposals for each joint we can capture some of the inherent uncertainty in the data. Given a whole sequence, these proposals could also be used by a tracking algorithm to self-initialize and recover from failure.

A simple option for aggregating the votes might be to accumulate the global centroid of the votes for each joint. However, the votes are typically highly multimodal, and so such a global estimate is inappropriate. Instead we employ a local mode finding approach based on mean shift [69].

We first define a Gaussian Parzen density estimator per joint j as

$$p_j^m(\mathbf{x}') \propto \sum_{(\mathbf{x}, w) \in \mathcal{X}_j^m} w \cdot \exp\left(-\left\|\frac{\mathbf{x}' - \mathbf{x}}{b_j^m}\right\|^2\right), \tag{13.6}$$

where $\mathbf{x}'$ is a coordinate in 3D world space, $m \in \{\text{BPC}, \text{OJR}\}$ indicates the approach, and b_j^m is a learned per-joint bandwidth.

Mean shift is then used to find modes in this density efficiently. The algorithm starts at a subset $\hat{\mathcal{X}}_j^m \subseteq \mathcal{X}_j^m$ of the votes, and iteratively walks up the density by computing the mean shift vector [69] until convergence. Votes that converge to the same 3D position within some tolerance are grouped together, and each group forms a body joint proposal, the final output of our system. A confidence weight is assigned to each proposal as the sum of the weights w of the votes in the corresponding group. For both BPC and OJR this proved considerably more reliable than taking the modal density estimate (*i.e.* the value $p_j(\mathbf{x}')$). For BPC the starting point subset $\hat{\mathcal{X}}_j^{\text{BPC}}$ is defined as all votes for which the original body part probability was above a learned probability threshold $\alpha_{c(j)}$. For OJR, all votes are used as starting points, *i.e.* $\hat{\mathcal{X}}_j^{\text{OJR}} = \mathcal{X}_j^{\text{OJR}}$.

13.3.5 Training

Each tree in the decision forest is trained on a set of images randomly synthesized as described in Sect. 13.2. Each image is fully labeled: for BPC there is one body part label c per foreground pixel $\mathbf{u}$, and for OJR there is instead one pose $P = (\mathbf{p}_1, \ldots, \mathbf{p}_J)$ of 3D joint position vectors $\mathbf{p}_j$ per training image. For notational simplicity, we will assume that $\mathbf{u}$ uniquely encodes a 2D pixel location in a *particular* image, and thus can range across all pixels in all training images. A random subset of $N_{\text{ex}} = 2000$ example pixels from each image is used. Using a subset of pixels reduces training time and ensures a roughly even contribution from each training image.

The following sections describe training the structure of the trees, the leaf node prediction models, and the hyper-parameters.

13.3.5.1 Tree Structure Training

To train the tree structure, and thereby the weak learner parameters used at the split nodes, we use the standard greedy decision tree training algorithm. At each split node n, a set $\mathcal{T}_n \subseteq \mathcal{T}$ of many candidate weak learner parameters is sampled. Each candidate parameter $\boldsymbol{\theta} \in \mathcal{T}_n$ is then evaluated against an objective function H (these $\boldsymbol{\theta}$ parameters are those used in (13.4)). Each sampled $\boldsymbol{\theta}$ induces a partition of the input set $\mathcal{S}_n$ of all training pixels that reached the node n, into left $\mathcal{S}_n^{\text{L}}(\mathcal{S}_n, \boldsymbol{\theta})$ and right $\mathcal{S}_n^{\text{R}}(\mathcal{S}_n, \boldsymbol{\theta})$ subsets, according to the evaluation of the weak learner function (13.4). The best $\boldsymbol{\theta}$ is selected by maximizing a measure of information gain, or equivalently by minimizing the following:

$$\boldsymbol{\theta}_n = \arg\min_{\boldsymbol{\theta} \in \mathcal{T}_n} \sum_{i \in \{\text{L}, \text{R}\}} \frac{|\mathcal{S}_n^i|}{|\mathcal{S}_n|} H\big(\mathcal{S}_n^i(\mathcal{S}_n, \boldsymbol{\theta})\big). \tag{13.7}$$

Minimizing the above objective function minimizes the objective H while balancing the sizes of the left and right partitions. If the tree is not too deep, the algorithm recurses on the example sets $S_n^{\mathrm{L}}(S_n, \theta_n)$ and $S_n^{\mathrm{R}}(S_n, \theta_n)$ for the left and right child nodes, respectively. In this chapter we investigate both classification and regression specialization of the generic objective function H.

Training the tree structure is by far the most expensive part of the training process, since many candidate parameters must be tried at an exponentially growing number of tree nodes as the depth increases. To keep the training times practical we employ a distributed implementation. At the high end of our experiments, training three trees to depth 20 from 1 million images takes about a day on a 1000 core cluster. (GPU-based implementations are also possible and might be considerably faster.) The resulting trees each have roughly 500K nodes, suggesting fairly balanced trees. We next describe the two objective functions investigated in this work.

Classification The standard classification objective $H^{\mathrm{cls}}(S)$ is the Shannon entropy of the distribution of the known ground truth labels corresponding to the pixels in S. Entropy is computed as

$$H^{\mathrm{cls}}(S) = -\sum_c p(c|S) \log p(c|S), \tag{13.8}$$

where $p(c|S)$ is the normalized histogram of the set of body part labels $c(\mathbf{u})$ for all $\mathbf{u} \in S$.

Regression Here, the objective is to partition the examples to give nodes with minimal uncertainty in the joint offset distributions at the leaves [117, 155]. In our problem, the offset distribution for a given tree node is likely to be highly multimodal (see examples in Fig. 13.5). One approach might be to fit a Gaussian mixture model (GMM) to the offsets and use the negative log likelihood of the offsets under this model as the objective. However, GMM fitting would need to be repeated at each node for thousands of candidate weak learners, making this prohibitively expensive. Following existing work [117], we employ the much cheaper sum-of-squared-differences objective:

$$H^{\mathrm{reg}}(S) = \sum_j \sum_{\mathbf{u} \in S_j} \|\Delta_{\mathbf{u} \to j} - \mu_j\|_2^2, \tag{13.9}$$

where offset vector $\Delta_{\mathbf{u} \to j} = \mathbf{p}_j - \mathbf{x}(\mathbf{u})$, and

$$\mu_j = \frac{1}{|S_j|} \sum_{\mathbf{u} \in S_j} \Delta_{\mathbf{u} \to j}, \tag{13.10}$$

$$S_j = \{\mathbf{u} \in S \mid \|\Delta_{\mathbf{u} \to j}\|_2 < \rho\}. \tag{13.11}$$

Unlike [117], we introduce an offset vector length threshold ρ to remove offsets that are large and thus likely to be outliers. While this model implicitly assumes a uni-modal Gaussian, which we know to be unrealistic, this assumption is tractable for learning the tree structure and can still produce satisfactory results.

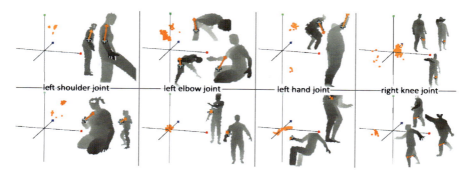

Fig. 13.5 Empirical offset distributions for offset joint regression. We visualize the set R_{lj} of 3D relative offset vectors $\boldsymbol{\Delta}_{\mathbf{u}\rightarrow j}$. Each set of axis represents a different leaf node, and the *orange squares* denote the vectors $\boldsymbol{\Delta}_{\mathbf{u}\rightarrow j} \in R_{lj}$ at that leaf. (The *red, green,* and *blue squares* indicate, respectively, the positive x, y, and z axes; each half-axis represents 0.5m in world space.) We also show training images for each node illustrating the pixel that reached the leaf node as a *cyan cross*, and the offset vector as an *orange arrow*. Note how the decision trees tend to cluster pixels with similar local appearance at the leaves, but the inherent remaining ambiguity results in multi-modal offset distributions. The OJR algorithm compresses these distributions to a very small number of modes while maintaining high test accuracy

Discussion Recall that the two objective functions above are used for training the tree *structure*. We are then at liberty to fit the leaf prediction models in a different fashion (see next section). Perhaps counter-intuitively, we observed in our experiments that optimizing with the classification objective H^{cls} works well for the OJR task. Training for classification will result in image patches reaching the leaf nodes that tend to have both similar appearances and local body joint configurations. This means that for nearby joints, the leaf node offsets are likely to be small and tightly clustered. The classification objective further avoids the assumption of the offset vectors being Gaussian distributed. See [344] for more discussion.

We did investigate further node splitting objectives, including various forms of mixing body part classification and regression (as used in [117]), as well as variants such as separate regression forests for each joint. However, for our application, none proved better than either the standard classification or regression objectives defined above.

13.3.5.2 Leaf Node Prediction Models

Given the learned tree structure, we must now train the prediction models at the leaf nodes. For the BPC task, we simply take $p_l(c) = p(c|\mathcal{S})$, the normalized histogram of the set of body part labels $c(\mathbf{u})$ for all pixels $\mathbf{u} \in \mathcal{S}$ that reached leaf node l.

For OJR, we must instead build the weighted relative vote sets

$$\mathcal{V}_{lj} = \left\{ (\boldsymbol{\Delta}_{ljk}, w_{ljk}) \right\}_{k=1}^{K} \tag{13.12}$$

Algorithm 13.3 Learning relative votes

1: // *Collect relative offsets*
2: initialize $\mathcal{R}_{lj} = \emptyset$ for all leaf nodes l and joints j
3: **for all** training pixels $\mathbf{u} \in \mathcal{S}$ **do**
4:     descend tree to reach leaf node $l = l(\mathbf{u})$
5:     compute 3D pixel position $\mathbf{x}(\mathbf{u})$
6:     **for all** joints j **do**
7:         lookup ground truth joint positions $P = \{\mathbf{p}_j\}$
8:         compute relative offset $\boldsymbol{\Delta}_{\mathbf{u} \to j} = \mathbf{p}_j - \mathbf{x}(\mathbf{u})$
9:         store $\boldsymbol{\Delta}_{\mathbf{u} \to j}$ in $\mathcal{R}_{lj}$ with reservoir sampling
10: // *Cluster*
11: **for all** leaf nodes l and joints j **do**
12:     cluster offsets $\mathcal{R}_{lj}$ using mean shift
13:     discard modes for which $\|\boldsymbol{\Delta}_{ljk}\|_2 >$ threshold λ_j
14:     take top K weighted modes as $\mathcal{V}_{lj}$
15: **return** relative votes $\mathcal{V}_{lj}$ for all nodes and joints

---

for each leaf and joint. To do this, we employ a clustering step using mean shift, detailed in Algorithm 13.3. This algorithm describes how each training pixel induces a relative offset to all ground truth joint positions,[2] and once aggregated across all training images, these are clustered using mean shift. To maintain practical training times and keep memory consumption reasonable we use reservoir sampling [392] to maintain a fixed-size unbiased sample of N_{res} offsets.

Mean shift mode detection is again used for clustering, this time on the following density:

$$p_{lj}(\boldsymbol{\Delta}') \propto \sum_{\boldsymbol{\Delta} \in \mathcal{R}_{lj}} \exp\left(-\left\|\frac{\boldsymbol{\Delta}' - \boldsymbol{\Delta}}{b^\star}\right\|^2\right). \tag{13.13}$$

This is similar to (13.6), though now defined over *relative* offsets, without weighting, and using a shared bandwidth $b^\star$. Figure 13.5 visualizes a few examples sets $\mathcal{R}_{lj}$ that are clustered. The positions of the modes form the relative votes $\boldsymbol{\Delta}_{ljk}$ and the numbers of offsets that reached each mode form the vote weights w_{ljk}. To prune out long range predictions which are unlikely to be reliable, only those relative votes that fulfil a per joint distance threshold λ_j are stored.[3] We found that there is little or no benefit in storing more than $K = 2$ relative votes per leaf.

In our unoptimized implementation, learning these relative votes for 16 joints in three trees trained with 10k images took approximately 45 minutes on a single 8-core machine. The vast majority of that time is spent traversing the tree; the use of reservoir sampling ensures the time spent running mean shift totals only about 2 minutes.

---

[2]Recall that for notational simplicity we are assuming $\mathbf{u}$ defines a pixel 2D position in a particular image; the ground truth joint positions P will therefore correspond for each particular image.

[3]This threshold could equivalently be applied at test time though would waste memory in the tree.

13.4 Experiments

This section briefly evaluates the two proposed algorithms with respect to one another and in comparison with state of the art. A more thorough evaluation and description of the metrics may be found in [344].

13.4.1 Test Data

We use both synthetic and real depth images to evaluate our approach. For the synthetic test set ('MSRC-5000'), we synthesize 5000 test depth images, together with the ground truth body part labels and body joint positions, as described in Sect. 13.2. However, to ensure a fair and distinct test set, the original mocap poses used to generate these test images are held out from the training data. We also evaluate on the real test depth data from [121]. Interestingly, our synthetic test set appears to be far 'harder' than the real test set due to its extreme variability in pose and body shape.

13.4.2 Qualitative Results

Figure 13.6 shows example inferences for both the BPC and OJR algorithms. Note high accuracy of both classification and joint prediction, across large variations in body and camera pose, depth in scene, cropping, and body size and shape (*e.g.* small child *vs.* heavy adult). Note that no temporal or kinematic constraints (other than those implicitly encoded in the training data) are used for any of our results. When tested on video sequences (not shown), most joints can be accurately predicted in most frames with remarkably little jitter.

A few failure modes are evident: (i) difficulty in distinguishing subtle changes in depth such as the crossed arms; (ii) for BPC, the most likely inferred part may be incorrect, although often there is still sufficient correct probability mass in distribution $p(c|\mathbf{u})$ that an accurate proposal can still result during clustering; and (iii) failure to generalize well to poses not present in training. However, the inferred confidence values can be used to gate bad proposals, maintaining high precision at the expense of recall.

In these and other results below, unless otherwise specified, the following training parameters were used. We trained three trees in the forest. Each was trained to depth 20, on 300K images per tree, using $N_{ex} = 2000$ training example pixels per image. At each node we tested 2000 candidate offset pairs δ and 50 candidate thresholds τ per offset pair, *i.e.* $|\mathcal{T}_n| = 2000 \times 50$ fixed for all split nodes.

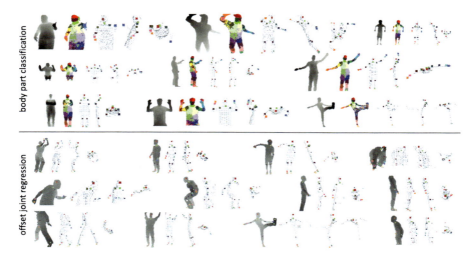

Fig. 13.6 Example inferences on both synthetic and real test images. In each example we see the input depth image, the inferred most likely body part labels (for BPC only), and the inferred body joint proposals shown as front, right, and top views overlaid on a depth point cloud. Only the most confident proposal for each joint above a fixed, shared threshold is shown, though the algorithms predict multiple proposals per joint. Both algorithms achieve accurate prediction of body joints for varied body sizes, poses, and clothing. We show failure modes in the bottom rows of the two panels. There is little qualitatively to tell between the two algorithms, though the middle row of the OJR results shows accurate prediction of even occluded joints (not possible with BPC), and further results in Sect. 13.4.3 compare quantitatively

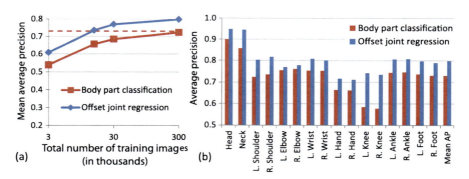

Fig. 13.7 Comparing body part classification (BPC) with offset joint regression (OJR). (**a**) Effect of total number of training images. (**b**) Average precision on each of the 16 test body joints

13.4.3 Comparison Between BPC and OJR

Figure 13.7(a) compares mean average precision of joint location for different training set sizes. In all cases we observe OJR performing more accurately than BPC. In Fig. 13.7(b) we show a per-joint breakdown of these results, using the best results

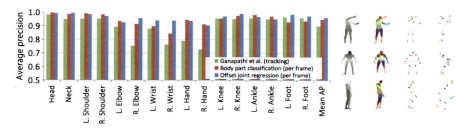

Fig. 13.8 Comparison with [121]. Even without the kinematic and temporal constraints exploited by [121], both our approaches are able to more accurately localize body joints

obtained for each method (900k and 300k training images for BPC and OJR, respectively).[4] An optimized implementation of both approaches can run at around 200 frames per second.

There are several possible reasons for OJR giving a more accurate result than BPC. One possibility is that OJR can directly regress the positions of joints *inside* the body. The joints showing the most substantial improvements (head, neck, shoulders, and knees) are also those where surface body parts cover a large area and are furthest from the joint center. Another ability of OJR is predicting occluded joints. When the mean average precision (mAP) metric is changed to penalize failure to predict occluded joints, the improvement of OJR over BPC is even more apparent: 0.663 *vs.* 0.560 mAP (both methods trained with 30k images). Example inferences showing localization of occluded joints are presented in Fig. 13.6 (OJR panel, middle row).

13.4.4 Comparison to Ganapathi et al. [121]

The authors of [121] kindly provided their test data and results for direct comparison. Their algorithm uses sparse body part proposals from [293] and further tracks the skeleton with kinematic and temporal information. Their real data come from a time-of-flight depth camera with very different noise characteristics to our structured light sensor. Without any changes to our training data or algorithm, Fig. 13.8(a) shows considerably improved joint prediction average precision for both BPC and OJR. Our algorithms also run at least 10 times faster. Further experimental details, results, and comparisons are available in [344].

13.5 Conclusions

We have presented two algorithms, body part classification and offset joint regression. The two algorithms have much in common. They both use decision forests and

---

[4]The results for OJR at 300k images were so compelling we chose not to expend the considerable energy in training a directly comparable 900k forest.

simple depth-invariant image features. Both methods exploit a large, highly varied, synthetic training set, allowing us to train very deep trees. We have shown that the forests can learn invariance to both pose and shape while avoiding overfitting. The BPC approach introduces a set of surface body parts that a classification forest tries to infer. These body parts are aligned with the joints of interest, so that an accurate classification will localize the joints of the body. The OJR approach instead casts votes that try to directly predict the positions of interior body joints. In both methods, mean shift is used to aggregate votes to produce a final set of confidence-weighted 3D body joint proposals.

Our experiments have demonstrated that both algorithms can accurately predict the 3D locations of body joints in super-realtime from single depth images. We have further shown state of the art accuracy and speed against a competing approach.

Of our two approaches, which should you use? The numerical results show that OJR will give considerably higher accuracy than BPC. OJR also seems intuitively a 'cleaner' solution: it does not need the intermediate definition of body parts, and the offsets vote directly for interior joint positions. This also means that OJR is capable of predicting occluded joints, while BPC will instead give no proposals for an occluded joint. However, OJR proved considerably more complex: the obvious regression objective does not work well, and many hyper-parameters had to be optimized against a validation set. A promising direction for future work is to investigate alternative tree structure learning objectives that handle multi-modal problems effectively.

Chapter 14
Anatomy Detection and Localization in 3D Medical Images

A. Criminisi, D. Robertson, O. Pauly, B. Glocker, E. Konukoglu, J. Shotton,
D. Mateus, A. Martinez Möller, S.G. Nekolla, and N. Navab

This chapter discusses the use of regression forests for the automatic detection and simultaneous localization of multiple anatomical regions within computed tomography (CT) and magnetic resonance (MR) three-dimensional images. Important applications include: organ-specific tracking of radiation dose over time; selective retrieval of patient images from radiological database systems; semantic visual navigation; and the initialization of organ-specific image processing operations. We present a continuous parametrization of the anatomy localization problem, which allows it to be addressed effectively by multivariate random regression forests (Chap. 5). A single pass of our probabilistic algorithm enables the direct mapping from voxels to organ location and size, with training focusing on maximizing the confidence of output predictions. As a by-product, our method produces *salient anatomical landmarks*, *i.e.* automatically selected "anchor" regions which help localize organs of interest with high confidence. This chapter builds upon the work in [78, 286] and demonstrates the flexibility of forests in dealing with both CT and multi-channel MR scans. Quantitative validation is performed on two ground truth labeled datasets: (i) a database of 400 highly variable CT scans, and (ii) a database of 33 full-body, multi-channel MR scans. In both cases localization errors

A. Criminisi (✉) · B. Glocker · E. Konukoglu · J. Shotton
Microsoft Research Ltd., 7 J.J. Thomson Avenue, Cambridge, UK

D. Robertson
Redimension Ltd., Cambridge, UK

O. Pauly · D. Mateus
Institute of Biomathematics and Biometry, Helmholtz Zentrum München, München, Germany

A. Martinez Möller · S.G. Nekolla
Nuklearmedizin, Klinikum rechts der Isar, Technische Universität München, München, Germany

O. Pauly · D. Mateus · N. Navab
Computer Aided Medical Procedures, Technische Universität München, München, Germany

A. Criminisi, J. Shotton (eds.), *Decision Forests for Computer Vision and Medical Image Analysis*, Advances in Computer Vision and Pattern Recognition, DOI 10.1007/978-1-4471-4929-3_14, © Springer-Verlag London 2013

are reduced and results are more stable than those from more conventional atlas-based registration approaches. The simplicity of the regressor's context-rich visual features yield typical run-times of only 4 seconds per scan on a standard desktop. This anatomy recognition algorithm has now received FDA approval and is part of Caradigm's Amalga (www.caradigm.com).

14.1 Introduction

This chapter presents a new algorithm for the efficient detection and localization of anatomical structures ('organs') in CT and MR 3D images. A possible application is the automatic estimation of cumulative radiation dose being absorbed by the patient's individual organs during their lifetime, an important topic in modern radiology. Another application is the efficient retrieval of selected portions of patients' scans from radiological databases (PACS systems). When a physician wishes to inspect a particular organ, the ability to determine its position and extent automatically means it is not necessary to retrieve the entire scan (which could comprise gigabytes of data) but only a small region of interest, thus making economical use of the limited bandwidth. Other applications include single-click semantic navigation, automatic hyper-linking of textual radiological reports to the corresponding image regions, and the initialization of organ-specific image processing operations.

The main contribution of this work is a new parametrization of the anatomy localization task as a continuous multivariate parameter estimation problem. This is addressed effectively via non-linear regression, in the form of regression forests (see Chap. 5 and our previous work in [78, 286]). Our approach is fully probabilistic and, unlike previous techniques (*e.g.* [106, 422]), maximizes the confidence of output predictions. As a by-product, our method yields *salient anatomical landmarks, i.e.* automatically selected "anchor" regions that help localize organs of interest with high confidence. Our algorithm can localize both macroscopic anatomical regions[1] (*e.g.* abdomen, thorax, trunk, *etc.*) and smaller scale structures (*e.g.* heart, left adrenal gland, femoral neck, *etc.*) using a single model (*cf.* [108]).

The focus of our approach is both on accuracy of prediction and speed of execution, as we wish to achieve anatomy localization in seconds.

Regression Approach   Regression algorithms [152] estimate functions which map input variables to *continuous* outputs.[2] The regression paradigm fits the anatomy localization task well. In fact, its goal is to learn the non-linear mapping from voxels *directly* to organ position and size. The work in [421] presents a thorough overview of regression techniques and demonstrate the superiority of boosted regression [115] with respect to *e.g.* kernel regression [380]. In contrast to

---

[1]DICOM tags for the anatomical region are often erroneous [147].

[2]As opposed to *classification* where the predicted variables are categorical.

the boosted regression approach, maximizing confidence of output prediction is integral to our forest approach. An empirical comparison between boosting, forests and cascades is found in [413].

Comparison with Classification-Based Approaches   In [414] organ detection is achieved via a confidence maximizing sequential scheduling of multiple, organ-specific *classifiers*. In contrast, our single, tree-based regressor allows us to deal naturally with *multiple* anatomical structures simultaneously. As shown in the machine learning literature [371] this encourages feature sharing and, in turn better generalization. In [328] a sequence of PBT classifiers (first for salient slices, then for landmarks) are used. In contrast, our single forest regressor maps directly from voxels to organ locations and extents; latent, salient landmark regions are extracted as a by-product. In [77] the authors achieve localization of organ *centers* but fail to estimate the organ extent (similar to [117]). Here we present a more direct, continuous model which estimates the position of the walls of the bounding box containing each organ thus achieving simultaneous organ localization and extent estimation.

Comparison with Registration-Based Approaches   Although atlas-based methods have enjoyed much popularity [106, 337, 408], their conceptual simplicity belies the technical difficulty inherent in achieving robust, inter-subject registration. Robustness may be improved by using multi-atlas techniques [170] but only at the expense of multiple registrations and hence increased computation time. Our algorithm incorporates atlas information implicitly, within a tree-based model. As shown in the results section, such model is more efficient than keeping around multiple atlases and can achieve anatomy localization in only a few seconds. Comparisons with global affine atlas registration methods (somewhat similar to ours in computational cost) show that our algorithm produces lower errors and more stable localization results. Next we describe details of our approach.

14.2 Organ Localization as Regression Task

This section presents mathematical notation, our parametrization of organ locations within a medical scan, and the formulation of the localization problem as a regression task.

Following the notation set out in Chap. 3, vectors are represented in boldface (*e.g.* **p**), matrices as teletype capitals (*e.g.* Λ), and sets in calligraphic style (*e.g.* $\mathcal{S}$). The position of a voxel in a volumetric image is denoted as a 3-vector $\mathbf{p} = (p_x, p_y, p_z)$. A voxel at position **p** is associated with a d-dimensional vector of feature responses which is denoted as $\mathbf{v}(\mathbf{p}) = (v_1, \ldots, v_i, \ldots, v_d) \in \mathbb{R}^d$.

14.2.1 Parametrization and Regression Formulation

A 3D patient scan is represented by the intensity function $J : \Omega \to \mathbb{R}$, where $\Omega \subset \mathbb{N}^3$ is the image domain. Given a set $\mathcal{C}$ of organs of interest, we propose

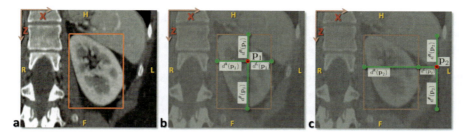

Fig. 14.1 Problem parametrization. (**a**) A 2D (coronal) view of a left kidney within a 3D CT scan, and the associated ground truth bounding box (*in orange*). (**b, c**) *Every* voxel $\mathbf{p}_i$ in the volume votes for the position of the six walls of each organ's 3D bounding box via six relative, offset displacements $d^k(\mathbf{p}_i)$ in the three canonical directions x, y and z

to model their absolute positions within the patient scan by a set of 3D bounding boxes. Each bounding box $\mathbf{b}_c$ contains one organ $c \in \mathcal{C}$ and is parametrized as a 6-dimensional vector $\mathbf{b}_c = (b_c^L, b_c^R, b_c^A, b_c^P, b_c^H, b_c^F)$. Each vector element represents the absolute position (in mm) of one axis-aligned face.[3] The goal of multiple organ localization is to estimate simultaneously the parameters of the different bounding boxes containing the organs of interest. Thus, the desired output is one six-dimensional vector $\mathbf{b}_c$ per organ, a total of $6 \times |\mathcal{C}|$ continuous parameters. In a probabilistic fashion, we aim at modeling the probability distribution $p(\mathbf{b}_c|\mathbf{v})$ for all $c \in \mathcal{C}$, so that given a previously unseen image and all per-voxel features $\{\mathbf{v}\}$, we can predict the location of all visible organs by estimating

$$\mathbf{b}_c^* = \arg\max_{\mathbf{b}_c} p(\mathbf{b}_c|\mathcal{V}) \quad \text{with } \mathcal{V} = \left\{\mathbf{v}(\mathbf{p}) \mid \mathbf{p} \in \Omega\right\}. \tag{14.1}$$

More generally, one could also define the regression over a single distribution $p(\mathbf{b}|\mathbf{v})$ with $\mathbf{b} = (\mathbf{b}_1, \ldots, \mathbf{b}_c, \ldots, \mathbf{b}_{|C|}) \in \mathbb{R}^{6|C|}$. This would allow to model inter-organ location dependencies.

Key to our algorithm is the idea that *all* voxels in a test image contribute with varying degrees of confidence to the estimates of the positions of *all* organs. Formally, we propose a probabilistic regression strategy in which each voxel $\mathbf{p} \in \Omega$ votes for the *relative offsets* to all organs' bounding boxes. Thus, each voxel $\mathbf{p}$ in a medical scan is associated with an offset with respect to the bounding box, $\mathbf{b}_c$ for each organ $c \in \mathcal{C}$ (see Fig. 14.1b, c). Such offset is a function of both $\mathbf{p}$ and c as follows: $\mathbf{d}(\mathbf{p}; c) = \hat{\mathbf{p}} - \mathbf{b}_c$, with $\hat{\mathbf{p}} = (p_x, p_x, p_y, p_y, p_z, p_z)$. Therefore $\mathbf{d}(\mathbf{p}; c) \in \mathbb{R}^6$. Given a database of annotated scans, our goal becomes then to learn the conditional distribution of 3D displacements $p(\mathbf{d}|c, \mathbf{v})$ for each organ $c \in \mathcal{C}$.

Intuitively, some distinct voxel clusters (*e.g.* tips of ribs, or vertebrae) may predict the position of an organ (*e.g.* the heart) with high confidence. Ideally, at detection time those clusters would be automatically detected and used as landmarks for the localization of those organs. In contrast, clusters of voxels in larger regions

---

[3]Superscripts follow standard radiological orientation convention: L = left, R = right, A = anterior, P = posterior, H = head, F = foot.

of texture-less tissue or even air should contribute little to the estimation of organ positions because of their higher prediction uncertainty. Therefore, our aim is to learn to cluster voxels based on their appearance, their spatial context and, above all, their confidence in predicting the position and size of all organs of interest. Note that this is different from the task of assigning a categorical label to each voxel (*i.e.* the classification approach in [77]). Here we wish to produce confident predictions of a small number of continuous localization parameters. The *latent* voxel clusters (think of them as some sort of predictive landmarks) are discovered automatically.

To tackle the simultaneous feature selection and parameter regression task, we use a multivariate random regression forest (Chap. 5); *i.e.* an ensemble of regression trees trained to predict the location and size of all organs simultaneously. Next we describe the details of our approach.

14.3 Regression Forests for Organ Localization

This section presents how to solve the organ localization problem using multivariate regression forests. First, we start by detailing the type of feature response we employ in order to capture the visual appearance and contextual information of each voxel within a medical scan. The feature responses form the input of the regression forest, while the absolute organ locations are the output.

14.3.1 Feature Responses for Application in CT and MR

Medical images are acquired using different physical principles (*e.g.* based on X-rays or magnetic resonance), and thus the images have very different visual appearance. Intensity values correspond to different physical properties, and image analysis applications need to be tailored with respect to a specific imaging modality. Motivated by the underlying imaging technique, we employ distinct visual features for the two cases of CT and MR images.

The feature vector $\mathbf{v}(\mathbf{p}) = (v_1, \ldots, v_i, \ldots, v_d) \in \mathbb{R}^d$ for a reference 3D voxel location $\mathbf{p}$ is a collection of mean intensity values over (possibly) displaced feature boxes, *i.e.*

$$v_i = \frac{1}{|\mathbf{F}_{\mathbf{p};i}|} \sum_{\mathbf{q} \in \mathbf{F}_{\mathbf{p};i}} J(\mathbf{q}) \qquad (14.2)$$

where $J(\mathbf{q})$ denotes the image intensity at position $\mathbf{q}$ in the image, and $\mathbf{q} \in \mathbf{F}_{\mathbf{p};i}$ are the image points within the feature box. The box $\mathbf{F}_{\mathbf{p};i}$ is displaced relative to the reference point $\mathbf{p}$ (see Fig. 14.2). In theory, for each reference point we can determine an infinite number of such features. In practice we will randomly generate thousands of such features during the training phase, which is part of the feature selection process of decision forests. The types of feature used here are similar to those in [77, 117, 342], *i.e.* mean intensities over displaced, asymmetric cuboidal

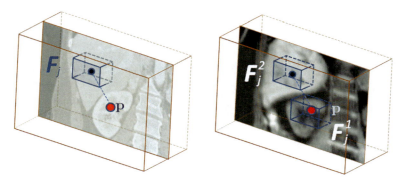

Fig. 14.2 Visual features. As shown *on the left*, voxel features in CT images are computed as the mean intensity over a 3D cuboid displaced with respect to the reference voxel position. *On the right*, voxel features in MR images are binary numbers encoding the difference between the mean intensity computed over two 3D cuboids

regions within the volume. These features are efficient to compute via integral images/volumes [389] and are able to capture spatial context.

Similar to Chap. 13 we define a selector function

$$\boldsymbol{\phi}(\mathbf{v}) = (v_i, v_j) \quad \text{with } i, j \in \{1, \ldots, d\} \tag{14.3}$$

thus, the tests applied by internal nodes will act upon scalar values computed as

$$f(\mathbf{p}; \boldsymbol{\phi}, \boldsymbol{\psi}) = \boldsymbol{\phi}(\mathbf{v}(\mathbf{p})) \cdot \boldsymbol{\psi}. \tag{14.4}$$

Visual Features in CT Computed tomography images are characterized by the fact that the intensity values directly indicate the tissue density (in Hounsfield units) at a particular location. So, it makes sense to use absolute intensity values to construct visual features. This is achieved readily by fixing $\boldsymbol{\psi} = (1, 0)$ for all split nodes.

Visual Features in MR In magnetic resonance images, we cannot rely on the absolute intensity values since there is no calibration between different scans. However, the relative intensity changes between different regions within the same scan can provide important visual cues. In the case of MR it makes sense to construct visual features which are invariant to global additive intensity biases and take into consideration image gradients. This is achieved here by fixing $\boldsymbol{\psi} = (1, -1)$ for all split nodes. This corresponds to taking the difference of mean intensities in two image regions. As detailed in [286], the feature boxes can also be chosen by using a predefined 3D pattern, and can be seen as a multi-scale 3D version of local binary patterns [274].

The set of feature vectors is a crucial component of the regression function, whose aim is to determine a functional mapping from the input feature space to the output space of organ bounding boxes. We will now describe how this mapping is learned.

14.3.2 Regression Forest Learning

Weak Learners   The training process constructs each regression tree and decides at each node how to best split the incoming voxels. We are given a subset of all labeled volumes (the training set), and the associated ground truth organ bounding box positions (Fig. 14.1a). A subset of voxels in the training volumes is used for forest training. These training voxels are sampled on a regular grid within ± 10 cm of the center of each axial slice in the training volume. The size of the forest T is fixed and all trees are trained in parallel.

Each training voxel $\mathbf{p}$ is sent down each of the trees starting at the root. The jth split node applies an axis-aligned weak learner test $h(\mathbf{p}, \boldsymbol{\theta}_j)$ and based on the result sends the voxel to the left or right child node. The parameters $\boldsymbol{\theta}_j = (\boldsymbol{\phi}_j, \boldsymbol{\psi}, \tau_j)$ characterize the weak learners associated with the jth node. The corresponding weak learner is

$$h(\mathbf{p}, \boldsymbol{\theta}_j) = \left[f(\mathbf{p}; \boldsymbol{\phi}_j, \boldsymbol{\psi}) > \tau_j \right]. \tag{14.5}$$

For application in CT, τ is a learned scalar parameter. Instead, in MR we usually set $\tau = 0$. As usual the voxel $\mathbf{p}$ is sent to the right child node if h is true and to the left child node otherwise.

Objective Function   Node optimization is driven by maximizing a *continuous* information gain measure, defined in general terms as

$$I(\mathcal{S}, \boldsymbol{\theta}) = H(\mathcal{S}) - \sum_{i=\{\mathrm{L},\mathrm{R}\}} \omega_i H\left(\mathcal{S}^i\right) \tag{14.6}$$

where H denotes entropy, $\mathcal{S}$ is the set of training points reaching a node, L and R denote the left and right sets generated from $\mathcal{S}$ through the split defined by parameters $\boldsymbol{\theta}$, and finally $\omega_i = |\mathcal{S}^i|/|\mathcal{S}|$.

For a given organ c we model the continuous conditional distribution of the 3D displacement $\mathbf{d}(\mathbf{p}; c)$ at each node as a multivariate Gaussian; *i.e.*

$$p(\mathbf{d} \mid c, \mathcal{S}) = \frac{1}{(2\pi)^{\frac{N}{2}} |\Lambda_c(\mathcal{S})|} e^{-\frac{1}{2}((\mathbf{d}-\overline{\mathbf{d}}_c(\mathcal{S}))^\top \Lambda_c(\mathcal{S})^{-1}(\mathbf{d}-\overline{\mathbf{d}}_c(\mathcal{S})))}, \tag{14.7}$$

with $N = 6$ and $\int_{\mathbb{R}^6} p(\mathbf{d}|c, \mathcal{S}) \, d\mathbf{d} = 1$. The vector $\overline{\mathbf{d}}_c$ indicates the mean displacement and Λ_c the 6×6 covariance matrix of $\mathbf{d}$ for all points in the set $\mathcal{S}$.

In the context of organ localization, we incorporate an organ visibility prior in the objective function. In fact, due to surgery or image cropping a given organ may not be present or visible in a scan. For the set $\mathcal{S}$ this prior is defined as

$$p(c|\mathcal{S}) = n_c(\mathcal{S})/Z, \tag{14.8}$$

where $n_c(\mathcal{S})$ is the number of training voxels in the set $\mathcal{S}$ for which it is possible to compute the displacement $\mathbf{d}(\mathbf{p}; c)$; *i.e.* the training points in the set that come from training volumes for which the organ c is present. Z is a normalization constant which ensures that $\sum_c p(c|S) = 1$. Thus we can estimate the joint distribution for displacement and organ class as

$$p(\mathbf{d}, c|S) = p(\mathbf{d}|c, S)p(c|S). \tag{14.9}$$

Now, using the definition of the differential entropy of a Gaussian density and after some algebraic manipulation we obtain the following joint entropy for the node:

$$H(\mathbf{d}, c; S) = H(c; S) + \sum_c p(c|S)\left(\frac{1}{2}\log\big((2\pi e)^N |\Lambda_c(S)|\big)\right). \tag{14.10}$$

The joint information gain is

$$I(S, \boldsymbol{\theta}) = H(\mathbf{d}, c; S) - \sum_{i \in \{L,R\}} \omega_i H\big(\mathbf{d}, c; S^i\big), \tag{14.11}$$

which after some manipulation can be rewritten as

$$I(S, \boldsymbol{\theta}) = I^{\mathrm{reg}}(S, \boldsymbol{\theta}) + I^{\mathrm{cls}}(S, \boldsymbol{\theta}) \tag{14.12}$$

where

$$I^{\mathrm{reg}}(S, \boldsymbol{\theta}) = \frac{1}{2}\left(\sum_c p(c|S)\log|\Lambda_c(S)| - \sum_{i \in \{L,R\}} \omega_i \sum_c p\big(c|S^i\big)\log|\Lambda_c\big(S^i\big)|\right) \tag{14.13}$$

with $\omega_i = |S^i|/|S|$, and

$$I^{\mathrm{cls}}(S, \boldsymbol{\theta}) = H(c; S) - \sum_{i \in \{L,R\}} \omega_i H\big(c; S^i\big), \tag{14.14}$$

with $H(c; S)$ the standard Shannon entropy for categorical distributions.

We remember from Chap. 3 that optimizing the node parameters implies maximizing the information gain. Here nodes are trained via "randomized node optimization", as

$$\boldsymbol{\theta}_j = \arg\max_{\boldsymbol{\theta} \in \mathcal{T}_j} I(S, \boldsymbol{\theta}). \tag{14.15}$$

But maximizing (14.12) corresponds to minimizing the determinants of the 6×6 covariance matrices Λ_c (covariances defined over displacement random variables) associated with the $|\mathcal{C}|$ organs, where each organ's contribution is weighted by the associated prior probability for its visibility. This decreases the uncertainty in the probabilistic vote cast by each cluster of voxels on each organ pose. In our experiments we have found that this prior-driven organ weighting produces more balanced trees and has a noticeable effect on the accuracy of the results. In practice, the visibility prior favors a clustering of points of both similar locations but also corresponding to images with similar field-of-views.

Stopping Criterion Branching stops when the number of points reaching the node is smaller than a threshold n_{min}, or a maximum tree depth D has been reached. After training, the jth split node remains associated with the parameters $\boldsymbol{\theta}_j$. At each leaf node we store the learned means $\bar{\mathbf{d}}_c$ and covariance matrices Λ_c, and the class priors $p(c)$.

This framework may be reformulated using non-parametric distributions, with pros and cons in terms of regularization and storage. We have found our parametric assumption not to be restrictive since the multi-modality of the input space is captured by our hierarchical piece-wise Gaussian model. However, under the simplifying assumption that bounding box face positions are uncorrelated (*i.e.* diagonal Λ_c), it is convenient to store at each leaf node learned 1D histograms over face offsets $p(\mathbf{d}|c; \mathcal{S})$.

Discussion Equation (14.12) is an information-theoretical way of maximizing the confidence of the desired continuous output *for all* organs, without going through intermediate voxel classification (as in [77] where positive and negative examples of organ centers are needed). Furthermore, this gain formulation enables testing different context models, for example imposing a *full* covariance Λ_c would allow correlations between all walls in each organ. One could also think of enabling correlations between different organs. Taken to the extreme, this might have undesirable overfitting consequences. On the other hand, assuming *diagonal* Λ_c matrices can lead to uncorrelated output predictions. Interesting models live in the middle ground, where some but not all correlations are enabled to capture *e.g.* class hierarchies or other forms of spatial context.

14.3.3 Regression Forest Prediction

Forest Testing Given a previously unseen image volume J, test voxels are sampled in the same manner as at training time. Each test voxel $\mathbf{p}$ is pushed through each tree starting at the root and the corresponding sequence of weak learners applied. The voxel stops when it reaches its leaf node $l(\mathbf{v}(\mathbf{p}))$, with l indexing leaves across the whole forest. The stored distribution $p(\mathbf{d}_c|\mathbf{v}, l)$ over *relative* displacements for class c also defines the posterior for the *absolute* bounding box position: $p(\mathbf{b}_c|\mathbf{v}, l)$ since $\bar{\mathbf{b}}_c(\mathbf{p}) = \hat{\mathbf{p}} - \bar{\mathbf{d}}_c(\mathbf{p})$. Thus $p(\mathbf{b}_c|\mathbf{v}, l)$ is also a multivariate Gaussian. The forest posterior for $\mathbf{b}_c$ is now given by

$$p(\mathbf{b}_c|\mathbf{v}) = \sum_{t=0}^{T} \sum_{l \in \tilde{\mathcal{L}}_t} p(\mathbf{b}_c|\mathbf{v}, l) p(l). \qquad (14.16)$$

$\tilde{\mathcal{L}}_t$ is a subset of the leaves of tree t. We select $\tilde{\mathcal{L}}_t$ as the set of leaves corresponding to the 75 % of all test voxels which have the highest confidence (for each class c). Finally $p(l)$ is simply the proportion of samples arriving at leaf l. Note that here the leaf prediction model is a multivariate, probabilistic-*constant* model rather than the more flexible probabilistic-*linear* one used in Chap. 5.

Organ Localization   The final prediction $\mathbf{b}_c^*$ for the absolute position of the cth organ is given by

$$\mathbf{b}_c^* = \arg\max_{\mathbf{b}_c} p(\mathbf{b}_c|\mathbf{v}). \qquad (14.17)$$

Under the assumption of uncorrelated output predictions for bounding box faces, it is convenient to represent the posterior probability $p(\mathbf{b}_c|\mathbf{v})$ as six 1D histograms, one per face. We aggregate evidence into these histograms from the leaf distributions $p(\mathbf{b}_c|\mathbf{v}, l)$. Then $\mathbf{b}_c^*$ is determined by finding the histogram maximum. Furthermore, we can derive a measure of the confidence of this prediction by fitting a 6D Gaussian with diagonal covariance matrix Λ^* to the histograms in the vicinity of $\mathbf{b}_c^*$. A useful measure of the confidence of the prediction is then given by $|\Lambda^*|^{-1/2}$.

Organ Detection   The organ c is declared present in the scan if the prediction confidence is greater than a manually chosen value β. The parameter β is tuned to achieve the desired trade-off between the relative proportions of false positive and false negative detections.

14.4 Results, Comparisons and Validation

This section assesses the proposed algorithm for anatomy localization within 3D computed tomography and magnetic resonance scans in terms of accuracy, runtime speed and memory efficiency, and compares it to state of the art techniques.

14.4.1 Anatomy Localization in Computed Tomography Scans

The Labeled CT Database   We wish to recognize the following 26 anatomical structures $\mathcal{C} = \{$abdomen, l./r. adrenal gland, l./r. clavicle, l./r. femoral neck, gall bladder, head of l./r. femur, heart, l./r. atrium of heart, l./r. ventricle of heart, l./r. kidney, liver, l./r. lung, l./r. scapula, spleen, stomach, thorax, thyroid gland$\}$. We are given a database of 400 scans which have been manually annotated with 3D bounding boxes tightly drawn around the structures of interest (see Fig. 14.1a).

The database comprises patients with a wide variety of medical conditions and body shapes and the scans exhibit large differences in image cropping, resolution, scanner type, and use of contrast agents (Fig. 14.3). Voxel sizes are $\sim$0.5–1.0 mm along x and y, and $\sim$1.0–5.0 mm along z. The images were not pre-registered.

A regression forest was trained using 318 volumes selected randomly from our 400-volume dataset. Organ localization accuracy was measured using the remaining 82 volumes, which contained a total of 1504 annotated organs of which 907 were fully visible within the scan. Only organs that are entirely contained in the volumes are used for training and test. Training and test volumes were downsampled using nearest neighbor interpolation. Integer downsampling factors were chosen so that

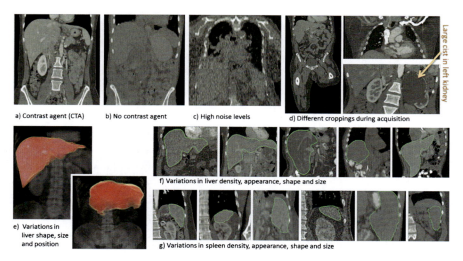

Fig. 14.3 Variability in our labeled CT database. (**a, b, c**) Variability in appearance due to presence of contrast agent, or noise. (**d**) Difference in image geometry due to acquisition parameters and possible anomalies. (**e**) Volumetric renderings of liver and spine to illustrate large changes in their relative position and in the liver shape. (**f, g**) Mid-coronal views of liver and spleen across different scans in our database to illustrate their shape variability. (The organ outlines, drawn by hand, are highlighted in *green*). All CT scans are natively calibrated, both metrically and photometrically

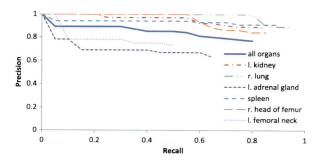

Fig. 14.4 Precision-recall curves for some representative organ classes and for all organ classes. The *curves* show how precision and recall change as the detection confidence threshold β is varied, both for all organs and for a representative group of individual organs (several organ classes are omitted to avoid clutter)

the resulting voxel pitch was as near as possible to 3 mm per voxel in the x, y, and z directions. Downsampling to this resolution reduces memory usage without noticeable reduction in accuracy.

Quantitative Evaluation   To characterize the performance of the algorithm, *precision-recall* curves are plotted (Fig. 14.4). In this context *precision* refers to the proportion of organs that were correctly detected, and *recall* to the proportion of reported detections that were correct. Here, a correct detection is considered to be a detection for which the centroid of the predicted organ bounding box is contained by the ground truth bounding box.[4] The plot shows how precision and recall vary as the detection confidence β is varied.

In the figure the average precision remains high until recall reaches approximately 80 %. Accuracy is best for larger organs; those with smaller size or greater positional variability are more challenging.

Table 14.1 shows mean localization errors, *i.e.* the absolute difference between predicted and ground truth bounding box face positions. Errors are averaged over all faces of the bounding boxes. Despite the large variability in our test data we obtain a mean error of only 13.5 mm, easily sufficient for our intended applications. Errors in the axial (z) direction are approximately the same as those in x and y despite significantly more crop variability in this direction. Consistently good results are obtained for different choices of training set as well as different training runs.

Computational Efficiency   With our C# software running in a single thread, organ detection for a typical $30 \times 30 \times 60$ cm volume requires approximately 4 s of CPU time for a typical four-tree forest. Most of the time is spent aggregating offset distributions (which are represented as histograms) over salient leaves. However, significant speed-up could be achieved with relatively simple code optimizations, *e.g.* by using several cores in parallel for tree evaluation and histogram aggregation.

Comparison with Affine, Atlas-Based Registration   An alternative strategy for anatomy localization is to align the input volume with a suitable *atlas*, *i.e.* a reference scan for which organ bounding box positions are known. Approximate bounding box positions in the input volume are then determined by using the computed atlas alignment transformation to map bounding box locations from the atlas into the input image.

Non-linear atlas registration (via non-rigid registration algorithms) can, in theory, provide the most accurate localization results. In practice, however, this approach is not robust to bad initialization and requires significantly greater computation times than the approach we describe here. Since speed is an important aspect of our work, here we chose to compare our results with those from comparably fast atlas-based algorithms, *i.e.* those based on global affine registration. This is a rather approximate approach because accuracy is limited by inter- and intra-subject variability in organ location and size. However, it is robust and its computation times are close to those of our method.

Instead of using a single atlas we use a multi-atlas approach due to its higher accuracy [170]. From the training set, five scans were selected to be used as atlases. The selected scans included three abdominal-thorax scans (one female, one male and one slightly overweight male), one thorax scan, and one whole body scan. This

---

[4]This metric is appropriate in light of our intended data retrieval and semantic navigation applications because the bounding box centroid would typically be used to select which coronal, axial, and sagittal slices to display to the user. If the ground truth bounding box contains the centroid of the predicted bounding box, then the selected slices will intersect the organ of interest.

Table 14.1 Regression forest results for CT. Bounding box localization errors in mm and associated standard deviations. The table compares results for our method with those for the Elastix and Simplex methods. Lowest errors for each class of organ are shown in bold. Our method gives lower errors for *all* organ classes

organ	Our method		Elastix		Simplex	
	mean	std	mean	std	mean	std
abdomen	**14.4**	13.4	34.6	74.2	27.6	36.5
l. adrenal gland	**11.7**	9.6	20.5	42.4	15.5	20.9
r. adrenal gland	**12.1**	9.9	22.2	45.0	18.2	29.6
l. clavicle	**19.1**	17.4	34.3	20.5	31.1	16.3
r. clavicle	**14.9**	11.6	39.0	44.3	24.1	13.9
l. femoral neck	**9.7**	7.5	38.3	78.5	16.1	15.4
r. femoral neck	**10.8**	8.3	38.4	82.3	17.3	17.7
gall bladder	**18.0**	15.0	28.1	54.5	23.2	26.6
l. head of femur	**10.6**	14.4	38.8	80.8	19.4	26.6
r. head of femur	**11.0**	15.7	39.6	84.9	19.1	28.4
heart	**13.4**	10.5	34.4	52.0	16.9	15.8
l. heart atrium	**11.5**	9.2	30.7	50.5	15.4	15.4
r. heart atrium	**12.6**	10.0	33.0	51.9	15.2	15.5
l. heart ventricle	**14.1**	12.3	35.9	51.7	18.1	16.7
r. heart ventricle	**14.9**	12.1	35.4	52.8	17.2	16.8
l. kidney	**13.6**	12.5	22.1	46.1	18.7	25.6
r. kidney	**16.1**	15.5	25.3	49.8	21.1	27.0
liver	**15.7**	14.5	26.9	53.3	23.2	30.4
l. lung	**12.9**	12.0	24.5	29.2	16.9	23.4
r. lung	**10.1**	10.1	25.0	27.2	16.0	21.7
l. scapula	**16.7**	15.7	50.9	54.1	33.1	20.1
r. scapula	**15.7**	12.0	44.4	41.2	22.7	12.4
spleen	**15.5**	14.7	29.0	46.6	23.0	22.8
stomach	**18.6**	15.8	27.6	48.9	22.8	23.4
thorax	**12.5**	11.5	36.5	37.4	25.3	35.1
thyroid gland	**11.6**	8.4	13.3	10.3	12.9	10.2
all organs	**13.5**	13.0	28.9	52.4	19.4	24.7

selection was representative of the overall distribution of image types in the dataset. All five atlases were registered to all the scans in the test set. For each test scan, the atlas that yielded the smallest registration cost was selected as the best one to represent that particular test scan. Registration was achieved using two different global affine registration algorithms. The first algorithm ('Elastix') is that implemented by the popular *Elastix* toolbox [184] and works by maximizing mutual information using stochastic gradient descent. The second algorithm ('Simplex') is our own implementation and works by maximizing correlation-coefficient between the aligned images using the simplex method as the optimizer [265]. In each case parameters were optimized for best accuracy.

Resulting errors (computed on the same test set) are reported in Table 14.1. The atlas registration techniques give larger mean errors and error standard deviation (nearly double in the case of Elastix) compared to our approach. Furthermore, atlas registration requires between 90 s and 180 s per scan (*cf.* our algorithm runtime is $\sim$4 s for $T = 4$ trees, on a single CPU core).

Figure 14.5 further illustrates the difference in accuracy between the three approaches. For the atlas registration algorithms, the error distribution's larger tails suggest a less robust behavior. This is reflected in larger values of the error mean and standard deviation and is consistent with our visual inspection of the registrations. In fact, in about 30 % of cases the registration process got trapped in local minima and produced grossly inaccurate alignment. In those cases, results tend not to be improved by using a non-linear registration step (which tends not to help the registration algorithm to escape bad local minima, whilst increasing the runtime considerably).

Automatic Landmark Detection   Figure 14.6 visualises the anatomical landmark regions that were automatically selected for organ localization. Given a trained regression tree and an input volume, we select one or two leaf nodes with high prediction confidence for a chosen organ class (*e.g.* left kidney). Then, for each sample arriving at the selected leaf nodes, we shade in green the cuboidal feature boxes used during weak learner evaluation. Those green regions represent some of the anatomical locations that were automatically selected and used to predict the location of the chosen organ. In this example, the bottom of the left lung and the top of the left pelvis are used to predict the position of the left kidney. Similarly, the bottom of the right lung is chosen to localize the right kidney. Such regions correspond to meaningful, visually distinct, anatomical landmarks that have been discovered in a completely unsupervised manner.

14.4.2 Anatomy Localization in Magnetic Resonance Scans

The Labeled MR Database   As described in [286] we also have a database of 33 patients. For each patient we have available labeled MR Dixon 3D images [226]. This means that for each patient we have two image channels, a "water" channel J^w and a "fat" channel J^f. As these two channels are captured simultaneously, they are aligned to each other. In this application, we propose to use both J^w and J^f, *i.e.* to extract features in both channels. Just like in the CT database, an expert has annotated different anatomical structures with axis-aligned bounding boxes. Here we have annotated the following five anatomical structures: head, heart, l. lung, r. lung and liver.

Fig. 14.5 Comparison with atlas-based registration. Distributions of bounding box localization errors for our algorithm ('Forest') and two atlas-based techniques ('Elastix' and 'Simplex'). Error distributions are shown separately for (**a**) left and right, (**b**) anterior and posterior, and (**c**) head and foot faces of the detected bounding boxes, and (**d**) averaged over all bounding box faces for each organ. The error distributions for the atlas techniques (particularly in plots (**c**) and (**d**)), have more probability mass in the tails, which is reflected by larger mean errors and error standard deviations

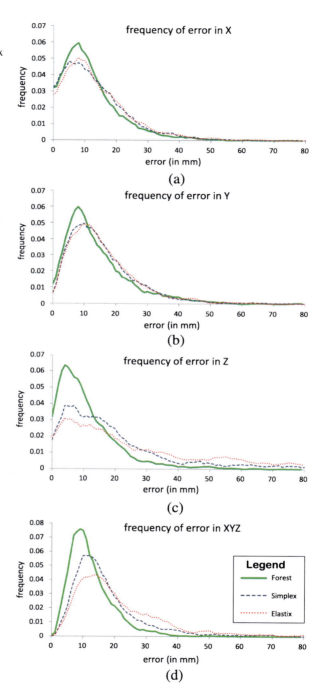

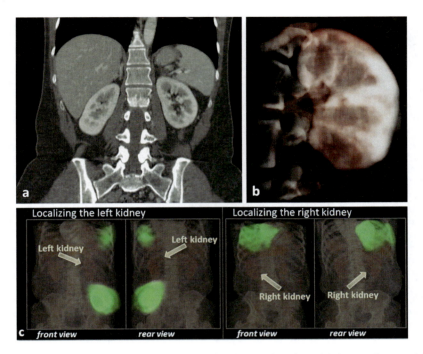

Fig. 14.6 Automatic discovery of salient anatomical landmark regions. (**a**) A test volume and (**b**) a 3D volume rendering of the left kidney's bounding box, as detected by our algorithm. (**c**) The highlighted *green regions* correspond to regions of the volume that were automatically selected as salient predictors of the position of the kidneys

Comparative Experiments   When dealing with MR images we chose to implement both random forests and their special case, random ferns (see Chap. 9). Both are compared quantitatively with an atlas-based registration approach and the results shown in Table 14.2. The reported lower and upper bounds correspond to the best and worst results across different atlases. Of course, in practice, it is not possible to know which atlas yields best results for a specific test image, so we report the mean error achieved when averaging over the different atlas results. For further reading on the relationship between forests and ferns please refer to Chap. 9 and [80].

The table shows that both regression forests and regression ferns achieve an accuracy which is better than the best case atlas accuracy, while providing increased robustness (smaller standard deviation of errors). Taking a look at the localization error per organ, one can notice that the lowest error for our approach is achieved for the localization of the head, which is due to the fact that the head is surrounded by a lot of air which makes it easier to localize. While the heart shows the second lowest error, lungs and liver were more difficult to localize. This is mainly due to the high inter-patient variability of the shape of these organs. The best results were obtained with 14 ferns and six nodes for random ferns, six trees of depth 8 for regression forests. On a 64 Core Duo 2.4 GHz laptop running MATLAB the training/testing time on 20/13 patients is only 0.7/0.5 s for random ferns. Decision forests need

Table 14.2 Regression forest results for MR bounding box localization errors in mm and associated standard deviations. The table compares results for our method using random forest, random ferns and multi-atlas registration

organ	Random ferns		Random forests		Atlas lower bound		Atlas upper bound		Atlas mean	
	mean	std	mean	std	mean	std	mean	std	mean	std
head	**9.82**	8.07	10.02	8.15	18.00	14.45	70.25	34.23	35.10	13.17
l. lung	14.95	11.35	**14.78**	11.72	14.94	11.54	60.78	29.47	30.41	11.39
r. lung	**16.12**	11.73	16.20	12.14	15.02	13.69	63.95	30.13	29.85	12.62
liver	**18.69**	13.77	18.99	13.88	18.13	16.26	70.59	32.88	31.74	13.49
heart	**15.17**	11.70	15.28	11.89	13.31	11.03	60.38	28.90	29.82	12.23
all organs	**14.95**	11.33	15.06	11.55	15.88	13.40	65.19	31.12	31.38	12.58

25/1 s. Concerning atlas registration, each single affine registration needs 12.5 s. See [286] for more details.

14.5 Conclusion

Anatomy localization has been cast here as a non-linear regression problem where *all* voxel samples vote for the position of all anatomical structures. Location estimates are obtained by a multivariate regression forest algorithm that is shown to be more accurate and efficient than competing registration-based techniques. At the core of the algorithm is a new information-theoretic metric for regression tree learning which works by maximizing the confidence of the predictions over the position of all organs of interest, simultaneously. Such strategy produces accurate predictions as well as meaningful anatomical landmark regions.

Accuracy and efficiency have been assessed on a database of 400 diverse CT studies as well as on a database of 33 2-channel MR Dixon sequences. Our algorithm for anatomy detection and localization in 3D CT scans has now been validated by the FDA and has been approved for commercial use.

In more academic settings, the usefulness of our algorithm has been demonstrated in the context of systems for efficient visual navigation of 3D CT studies [283] and robust linear registration [193]. Another application where regression forests have been used is automatic vertebrae localization in arbitrary field-of-view CT scans [133]. Here, the regression part is used to provide robust initialization for a subsequent localization refinement stage based on a shape and appearance model. Similarly, one could employ the organ localization as a first step in an organ segmentation approach. Organ-specific algorithms could then be applied at the predicted organ location, removing the often necessary step of manual interaction.

Chapter 15
Semantic Texton Forests for Image Categorization and Segmentation

M. Johnson, J. Shotton, and R. Cipolla

Semantic texton forests (STFs) are a form of random decision forest that can be employed to produce powerful low-level codewords for computer vision. Each decision tree acts directly on image pixels, resulting in a codebook that bypasses the expensive computation of filter-bank responses or local descriptors. Further, STFs are extremely fast to both train and test, especially when compared with k-means clustering and nearest-neighbor assignment of feature descriptors. The nodes in the STFs provide both an implicit hierarchical clustering into semantic textons, and also an explicit pixel-wise local classification estimate. In this chapter we (i) investigate STFs as learned visual dictionaries; (ii) show how STFs can be used for both image categorization and semantic segmentation by aggregating hierarchical *bags of semantic textons*; (iii) demonstrate that STFs allow us to exploit semantic context in segmentation; and (iv) show how a global image-level categorization can be used as a prior to improve the accuracy of semantic segmentation. We also see that the efficient tree structures of STFs allow at least a five-fold increase in execution speed over competing techniques.

This work was undertaken while the first two authors were at the University of Cambridge and Toshiba Corporate Research and Development Center respectively.

M. Johnson (✉)
Unicorn Media, Temple, USA

J. Shotton
Microsoft Research, Cambridge, UK

R. Cipolla
University of Cambridge, Cambridge, UK

A. Criminisi, J. Shotton (eds.), *Decision Forests for Computer Vision and Medical Image Analysis*, Advances in Computer Vision and Pattern Recognition, DOI 10.1007/978-1-4471-4929-3_15, © Springer-Verlag London 2013

  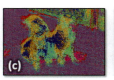 

Fig. 15.1 Semantic texton forests. (**a**) Test image, with ground truth in-set. Semantic texton forests very efficiently compute (**b**) a set of semantic textons per pixel and (**c**) a rough per-pixel classification (a prior for the subsequent segmentation). Our algorithm uses both the textons and priors as features to give coherent semantic segmentation (**d**). Colors show texton indices in (**b**), but categories corresponding to the ground truth in (**c**) and (**d**)

15.1 Introduction

This chapter discusses *semantic texton forests*, and demonstrates their use for image categorization and semantic segmentation; see Fig. 15.1. Our aim is to show that one can build powerful texton codebooks *without* computing expensive filter-banks or descriptors, and *without* performing costly k-means clustering and nearest-neighbor assignment. Semantic texton forests (STFs) achieve both these goals. STFs are randomized decision forests that use only simple pixel comparisons on local image patches, and output both an implicit hierarchical clustering into semantic textons and an explicit local classification of the patch category.

We look at two applications of STFs: image categorization (inferring the object categories present in an image) and semantic segmentation (dividing the image into coherent regions and simultaneously categorizing each region). To these ends, we propose the *bag of semantic textons* (BOST). The BOST is computed over a given image region, and extends the bag of words model [81] by combining a histogram of the hierarchical semantic textons with a region prior category distribution. For categorization, we obtain a highly discriminative descriptor by considering the image as a whole. For segmentation, we use many local rectangular regions and build a second randomized decision forest that achieves efficient and accurate segmentation.

Inferring the correct segmentation depends on local image information that can often be ambiguous. The global statistics of the image, however, are more discriminative and may be sufficient to accurately estimate the image categorization. We therefore investigate how an SVM-based image categorization can act as an *image-level prior* to improve segmentation: the classification output of the SVM is used as a prior to emphasizing the categories most likely to be present given the global appearance of the image.

To summarize, the main topics in this chapter are: (i) semantic texton forests which efficiently provide both a hierarchical clustering into semantic textons and a local classification; (ii) the bag of semantic textons model, and its applications in categorization and segmentation; (iii) how STFs allow us to exploit semantic context for segmentation; and (iv) the use of the image-level prior to improve segmentation accuracy.

15.1.1 Related Work

Textons [176, 229, 381] and visual words [348] have proven powerful discrete image representations for categorization and segmentation [81, 342, 404, 416]. Filterbank responses (derivatives of Gaussians, wavelets, *etc.*) or invariant descriptors (*e.g.* SIFT [225]) are computed across a training set, either at sparse interest points (*e.g.* [248]) or more densely; results in [267] suggest that densely sampling visual words improves categorization accuracy. The collection of descriptors are then clustered to produce a codebook of visual words, typically with the simple but effective k-means, followed by nearest-neighbor assignment. Unfortunately, this three stage process is extremely slow and often the most time consuming part of the whole system, even with optimizations such as kd-trees, the triangle inequality [97], or hierarchical clusters [266, 321].

The work of Moosmann *et al.* [253] proposed a more efficient alternative, in which training examples are recursively divided using a randomized decision forest [5, 44, 128] and where the splits in the decision trees are comparisons of a descriptor dimension to a threshold. With semantic texton forests, we extend [253] in three ways: (i) we learn a codebook that acts directly on image pixels, bypassing the expensive step of computing image descriptors; (ii) while [253] use the learned decision forest only for clustering, we also use it as a classifier, which enables us to use semantic context for image segmentation; and (iii) in addition to the leaf nodes used in [253], we include the split nodes as hierarchical clusters. A related method, the pyramid match kernel (PMK) [141], exploits a hierarchy in descriptor space, though the PMK requires the computation of feature descriptors and is primarily applicable only to kernel-based classifiers. The pixel-based features we use are similar to those in [214], but our forests are trained to recognize object categories, not to match particular feature points.

Other work has also looked at alternatives to k-means. The work of [376] quantized feature space into a hyper-grid, but required descriptor computation and can result in very large visual word codebooks. Winder and Brown [402] learned the parameters of generic image descriptors for 3D matching, though did not address visual word clustering. Jurie and Triggs [177] proposed building codebooks using mean shift, but did not incorporate semantic supervision in the codebook generation.

15.2 Randomized Decision Forests

We begin with a brief review of randomized classification forests [5, 128]. We follow the notation and terminology introduced in Chaps. 3 and 4 as closely as possible. A decision forest is an ensemble of T decision trees. Associated with each node j in the tree is a learned class distribution $p_j(c)$. A decision tree works by recursively branching left or right down the tree according to a series of learned binary functions computed at 2D pixel position $\mathbf{u} = (u_x, u_y)$, until a leaf node l is reached. The whole forest achieves an accurate and robust classification by averaging the class distributions over the leaf nodes $\mathcal{L}(\mathbf{u}) = \{l_t(\mathbf{u})\}_{t=1}^T$ reached for all T trees:

$$p(c|\mathbf{u}) = \frac{1}{T} \sum_{l \in \mathcal{L}(\mathbf{u})} p_l(c). \tag{15.1}$$

Existing work has shown the power of decision forests as either classifiers [36, 214] or a fast means of clustering descriptors [253]. In this chapter we show how to simultaneously exploit *both* classification and clustering. Furthermore, we generalize [253] to use the tree hierarchies as hierarchical clusters.

We use the standard randomized learning algorithm described in Chap. 4 to learn binary forests. Each tree is trained separately on a small random subset $\mathcal{S}' \subseteq \mathcal{S}$ of the training data $\mathcal{S}$ (here we employ the bagging randomness model). We will denote the weak learner decision function as

$$h(\mathbf{u}; \boldsymbol{\theta}_j) = \left[f(\mathbf{u}; \boldsymbol{\phi}_j) \geq \tau_j \right] \tag{15.2}$$

which is governed by node-specific parameters $\boldsymbol{\theta}_j = (\boldsymbol{\phi}_j, \tau_j)$ consisting of offset parameters $\boldsymbol{\phi}$ (see below) and a threshold τ. Learning proceeds as described in Chap. 4, using the standard entropy-based information gain objective. The training continues to a maximum depth D or until no further information gain is possible. The class distributions $p_j(c)$ are estimated empirically as a histogram of the class labels $c(\mathbf{u})$ of the training examples $\mathbf{u} \in \mathcal{S}_j$ that reached node j.

The amount of training data may be significantly biased towards certain classes in some datasets. A classifier learned on these data will have a corresponding prior preference for those classes. We weight each training example by the inverse class frequency as $w(\mathbf{u}) = \xi_{c(\mathbf{u})}$ with $\xi_c = (\sum_{\mathbf{u} \in \mathcal{S}} [c = c(\mathbf{u})])^{-1}$. This weight is applied to each example when accumulating the histograms used to compute the information gain. The classifiers trained using this weighting tend to give a better class average accuracy.

Using ensembles of trees trained on only small random subsets of the data helps to speed up training time and reduce over-fitting [5]. The trees are fast to learn and extremely fast to evaluate since only a small portion of the tree is traversed for each data point. After training, an improved estimate of the class distributions is obtained using *all* pixels in the training data $\mathbf{u} \in \mathcal{S}$, not just the subset $\mathcal{S}'$. We found this to improve the generalization of the classifiers slightly, especially for classes with few training examples.

15.3 Semantic Texton Forests

Semantic texton forests (STFs) are a specific form of randomized decision forests that can be used for both clustering and classification. The features $f(\mathbf{u}; \boldsymbol{\phi})$ in STFs act on small image patches centered at pixel $\mathbf{u}$ of size $\Delta \times \Delta$ pixels, as illustrated in Fig. 15.2(a). The feature parameters $\boldsymbol{\phi}$ denote one of the following functions:

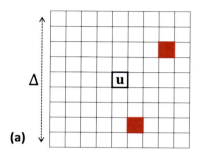

Fig. 15.2 (**a**) Semantic texton forests features. The split nodes in semantic texton forests use simple functions of raw image pixels within a $\Delta \times \Delta$ patch: either the raw value of a single pixel, or the sum, difference, or absolute difference of a pair of pixels (*red*). (**b**) Semantic textons. A visualization of leaf nodes from one tree (distance $\Delta = 21$ pixels). Each patch is the average of all patches in the training images assigned to a particular leaf node l. We can observe distinct patterns of color, horizontal, vertical, and diagonal edges, blobs, ridges, and corners. This visualization also allows a simple image reconstruction; see Fig. 15.8. Note that also associated with each semantic texton is a learned distribution $p_l(c)$ (not shown) which is used as the rough local segmentation of Fig. 15.1(c)

(i) the value $v(\mathbf{u} + \boldsymbol{\delta}, b)$ of a single pixel at $\mathbf{u} + \boldsymbol{\delta}$ in color channel b; (ii) the sum $v(\mathbf{u} + \boldsymbol{\delta}_1, b_1) + v(\mathbf{u} + \boldsymbol{\delta}_2, b_2)$; (iii) the difference $v(\mathbf{u} + \boldsymbol{\delta}_1, b_1) - v(\mathbf{u} + \boldsymbol{\delta}_2, b_2)$; or (iv) the absolute difference $|v(\mathbf{u} + \boldsymbol{\delta}_1, b_1) - v(\mathbf{u} + \boldsymbol{\delta}_2, b_2)|$. Here, function v denotes a look-up into the image pixel colors. The color channels b_1 and b_2 need not be the same.

To textonize an image, the $\Delta \times \Delta$ patch centered at each pixel $\mathbf{u}$ is passed down the STF resulting in semantic texton leaf nodes $\mathcal{L} = \{l_t\}_{t=1}^{T}$ and the averaged class distribution $p(c|\mathbf{u})$. Examples are shown in Fig. 15.1 and Fig. 15.3(b). A pixel-level classification based on the local distributions $P(c|\mathcal{L})$ gives poor but still surprisingly good accuracy (see Sect. 15.6.1). We will shortly describe in Sect. 15.3.3 how the *bag of semantic textons* can pool the statistics of semantic textons $\mathcal{L}$ and distributions $P(c|\mathcal{L})$ over an image region to form a much more powerful feature for image categorization and semantic segmentation.

Examples of the appearance clusters learned in STFs are given in Fig. 15.2(b).

15.3.1 Learning Invariances

Although using raw pixels as features is much faster than first computing descriptors or filter-bank responses, one risks losing their inherent invariances. To avoid this loss, we augment the training data with image copies that are artificially transformed geometrically and photometrically [214]. This augmentation allows one to *learn* the right degree of invariance required by suitably designing these transformations for a particular problem. In our experiments we explored small rotations and scalings, and left-right flipping as geometric transformations, and affine photometric transformations.

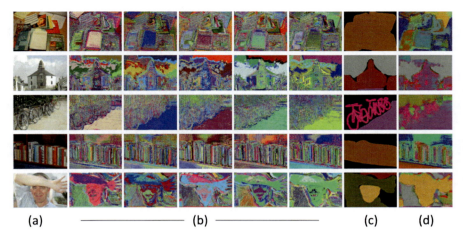

(a) ——————————— (b) ——————————— (c)   (d)

Fig. 15.3 Example semantic textonizations. (**a**) Test image. (**b**) One texton map per tree in the STF. Colors represent tree leaf nodes. (**c**) Ground truth classification. (**d**) Inferred rough local segmentation, showing the most likely class per pixel. Colors in (**c**) and (**d**) represent category labels. Both the textons and the rough segmentation are used as features for whole image categorization and higher-level segmentation. A further example is given in Fig. 15.1

15.3.2 *Implementation Details*

As discussed in Part I of this book, forests can be trained both in a supervised or unsupervised manner. Similarly, an STF can be trained using (i) pixel-level supervision, (ii) weak supervision, in which the members of the set of classes present in the whole image are used as training labels for all pixels, or (iii) no supervision, where the split function that most evenly divides the data is used. In the unsupervised case, the STF forest acts only as a hierarchical clusterer, not a classifier, similar to the density forests of Chap. 6. We examine the effect of different levels of supervision in Sect. 15.6.

We found the CIELab color space to generalize better than RGB, and it is used in all experiments. Training example pixels are taken on a regular grid (every 5×5 pixels) in the training images, excluding a narrow band of $\frac{\Delta}{2}$ pixels around the image border to avoid artifacts; at test time, the image is extended to ensure a smooth estimate of the semantic textons near the border.

15.3.3 *Bags of Semantic Textons*

A popular and powerful method for categorizing images and detecting objects is the bag of words model [81, 348, 416]. A histogram of visual words is created over the whole image or a region of interest [67], either discarding spatial layout or using a spatial hierarchy [204]. The histogram is used as input to a classifier

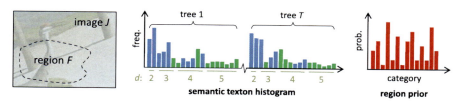

Fig. 15.4 Bags of semantic textons. Within a region F of image J we generate the semantic texton histogram and region prior. The histogram incorporates the implicit hierarchy of clusters in the STF, containing both STF leaf nodes (*green*) and split nodes (*blue*). The depth d of the nodes in the STF is shown. The STFs need not be to full depth, and empty bins in the histogram are not shown as the histogram is stored sparsely. The region prior is computed as the average of the individual leaf node class distributions $p_l(c)$

to recognize object categories. We propose the localized bag of semantic textons (BOST), illustrated in Fig. 15.4. This extends the bag of words to be hierarchical and to include low-level semantic information, as follows.

Given the leaf nodes $\mathcal{L}(\mathbf{u}) = \{l_t\}_{t=1}^{T}$ and the inferred class distribution $p(c|\mathbf{u})$ for each pixel $\mathbf{u}$, one can compute the following over an image region F: (i) a non-normalized histogram $G_F(j)$ that concatenates the occurrences of tree nodes j across the different trees [253]; and (ii) a prior over the region given by the average class distribution $p(c|F) = \sum_{\mathbf{u} \in F} p(c|\mathbf{u})$. In contrast to [253], we include both leaf nodes l and split nodes j in the histogram, noting that $G_F(j) = \sum_{j' \in \text{child}(j)} G_F(j')$. The histogram therefore uses the hierarchy of clusters implicit in each tree. Each $p(c|\mathbf{u})$ is already averaged across trees, and hence there is a single region prior $p(c|F)$ for the whole forest.

Our results in Sect. 15.6 show that the histograms and region priors are complementary, and that the hierarchical clusters are better than the leaf node clusters alone. For categorization (Sect. 15.4), we use BOSTs where the region is the whole image. For segmentation (Sect. 15.5), we use a combination of BOSTs over many local rectangular regions to model layout and context.

Implementation Details   The counts of tree *root* nodes hold no useful information and are not included in the histograms. The histograms are sparse near the leaves, and can be stored efficiently since the histogram counts at the parent split node can be quickly computed on-the-fly. If the region F is rectangular, the histograms and class distributions can be calculated very efficiently using integral histograms [295, 342].

15.4 Image Categorization

The task of image categorization is to determine those categories (*e.g.* dog images, beach images, indoor images) to which an image belongs. For our purposes, every image belongs to those categories for which there exists a pixel in the image that has been labeled with that category. Thus, an image with a sheep eating grass will belong to both the 'grass' and 'sheep' categories. Example previous approaches have used global image information [276], bags of words [104] or textons [404].

We propose an image categorization algorithm that exploits the hierarchy of semantic textons and the node prior distributions $p_j(c)$. This algorithm uses a nonlinear support vector machine (SVM), though of course decision forests could also be used instead. The SVM depends on a kernel function K that defines the similarity measure between images. To take advantage of the hierarchy in the STF, we adapt the pyramid match kernel [141] to act on a pair of BoST histograms computed across the whole image.

Consider first the BoST histogram computed for just one tree in the STF. The kernel function (based on [141]) is then

$$K(P, Q) = \frac{1}{\sqrt{Z}} \tilde{K}(P, Q), \tag{15.3}$$

where Z is a normalization term for images of different sizes computed as

$$Z = \tilde{K}(P, P)\tilde{K}(Q, Q). \tag{15.4}$$

Here, $\tilde{K}$ is the actual matching function, computed over levels of the tree as

$$\tilde{K}(P, Q) = \sum_{d=1}^{D} \frac{1}{2^{D-d+1}}(\mathcal{G}_d - \mathcal{G}_{d+1}), \tag{15.5}$$

using the histogram intersection $\mathcal{G}$

$$\mathcal{G}_d = \sum_{j} \min(P_d[j], Q_d[j]). \tag{15.6}$$

In the above, D is the maximum depth of the tree, P and Q are the hierarchical histograms, and P_d and Q_d are the portions of the histograms at depth d, with j indexing over all nodes at depth d. There are no nodes at depth $D + 1$, hence $\mathcal{G}_{D+1} = 0$. If the tree is not full depth, missing nodes j are simply assigned $P_d[j] = Q_d[j] = 0$.

The kernel over all trees in the STF is calculated as $K = \sum_t \gamma_t K_t$ with mixture weights γ_t. Similarly to [416], we found $\gamma_t = \frac{1}{T}$ to result in the best categorization results. While effective, this kernel can be improved by using the learned 'prior' distributions $p_j(c)$ from the STF. We build a 1-vs.-all SVM kernel K_c per category, in which the count for node j in the BoST histogram is weighted by the value $p_j(c)$.[1] This weighting helps balance the categories, by selectively down-weighting those that cover large image areas (e.g. grass, water) and thus have inappropriately strong

---

[1] At training time, we compute and store the distributions $p_j(c)$ for all nodes j in the tree, not just for leaf nodes.

influence on the pyramid match, masking the signal of smaller classes (*e.g.* cat, bird).

In Sect. 15.6.2, we show the improvement that the pyramid match kernel on the hierarchy of semantic textons gives over a radial basis function on histograms of just leaf nodes. We also obtain an improvement using the per-category kernels K_c instead of a global kernel K. Finally, we show how this categorization can act as an image-level prior for segmentation in Sect. 15.5.1.

15.5 Semantic Segmentation

To demonstrate the power of the BOSTs as features for segmentation, we adapt the TextonBoost algorithm [342]. The goal is to segment an image into coherent regions and simultaneously infer the class label of each region (see Sect. 15.6.3.1).

Appearance Context *vs.* Semantic Context   In [342], a boosting algorithm selected features based on localized counts of textons to model patterns of texture, layout, and context. The context modeled in [342] was appearance-based, for example: sheep often stand on something green. We adapt the rectangle count features of [342] to act on both the semantic texton histograms and the BOST region priors. The addition of region priors allows us to model context based on *semantics* [303], not just texture. Continuing the example, our model can capture the notion that sheep often stand on *grass*. This concept of basing the output of one classifier as the input to another was proposed concurrently by [341] (the original version of this chapter) and [375]. The related idea of entanglement is explored in Chap. 19.

The segmentation algorithm works as follows. For speed we use a second classification forest in place of the boosting classifier used by [342]. We train this forest to act at image pixels **u**, using pixels on a regular grid as training examples. At test time, the segmentation forest is applied at each pixel **u** densely or, for more speed, on a grid. The most likely class in the averaged category distribution (15.1) gives the final segmentation for each pixel. The split node functions f now compute either the count $G_{F+\mathbf{u}}(j)$ of semantic texton j, or the probability $p(c \mid F + \mathbf{u})$ of class c, within rectangle F translated relative to pixel **u**. By translating rectangle F relative to the pixel **u** being classified, and uniformly sampling rectangles F within a box offset from **u** by up to half the image size, such features can exploit texture, layout and context information (see [342] for more details). Our extension to these features exploits semantic context by using the region prior probabilities $p(c|F + \mathbf{u})$ inferred by the semantic textons. We show the benefit this brings in Sect. 15.6.3.

15.5.1 Image-Level Prior

We could embed the above segmentation forest in a conditional random field model to achieve more coherent results or to refine the grid segmentation to a per-pixel segmentation [157, 342]. Instead, we decided to investigate a simpler and more efficient approach using the image categorizer we built in Sect. 15.4. For each test image we separately run the categorization and segmentation algorithms. This gives an image-level prior (ILP) distribution $p(c)$ and a per-pixel segmentation distribution $p(c|\mathbf{u})$ respectively. We use the ILP to emphasize the likely categories and discourage unlikely categories, by multiplying the somewhat independent distributions as $p'(c|\mathbf{u}) = p(c|\mathbf{u})p(c)^{\alpha}$, using parameter α to soften the prior. We show in Sect. 15.6.3 and Sect. 15.6.3.1 how the addition of the ILP gives a considerable improvement to the resulting segmentations. Li and Fei-Fei [219] proposed a related idea that uses scene categorization as priors for object detection.

15.6 Experiments

We performed experiments on the following two datasets:

	# classes	# training images	# test images
MSRC [342]	21	276	256
VOC 2007 (Seg) [99]	21	422	210

We use the standard train/test splits where available, and the hand-labeled ground truth to train the classifiers. Image categorization accuracy is measured as mean average precision [99]. Segmentation accuracy is measured as the category average accuracy (the average proportion of pixels correct in each category). We also report the global accuracy (total proportion of pixels correct), but note that the category average is fairer and more rigorous as it normalizes for category bias in the test set. Training and test times are reported using an unoptimized C# implementation on a single 2.7 GHz core.

15.6.1 Learning the Semantic Texton Forest Vocabulary

Before presenting in-depth results for categorization and segmentation, let us look briefly at the STFs themselves. In Figs. 15.1 and 15.3 we visualize the inferred leaf nodes $\mathcal{L}(\mathbf{u})$ for each pixel $\mathbf{u}$ and the most likely category $c^{\star}(\mathbf{u}) = \arg\max_c p(c|\mathbf{u})$. Observe that the textons in each tree capture different aspects of the underlying texture and that even at such a low level the distribution $p(c|\mathbf{u})$ contains significant semantic information. Table 15.1 gives a naïve segmentation baseline on the MSRC dataset by comparing $c^{\star}(\mathbf{u})$ to the ground truth, with either fully or weakly supervised training pixels (see Sect. 15.3.2).

Clearly, this segmentation is poor, especially when trained in a weakly supervised manner, since only very local appearance (and no context) is used. Even so, the signal is remarkably strong for such simple features (random chance is un-

Table 15.1 Naïve
segmentation baseline
on MSRC

	Global	Average
supervised	49.7 %	34.5 %
weakly supervised	14.8 %	24.1 %

Table 15.2 Image
categorization results.
(Mean AP)

	Global kernel K	Per-category kernel K_c
RBF	49.9	52.5
PMK	76.3	**78.3**

der 5 %). We show below how using semantic textons as features in higher-level classifiers greatly improves these numbers, even with weakly supervised or unsupervised STFs.

Except where otherwise stated, we used STFs with the following parameters, hand-optimized on the MSRC validation set: distance $\Delta = 21$, $T = 5$ trees, maximum depth $D = 10$, 500 feature tests and 10 threshold tests per split node, and bagging using $\frac{1}{4}$ of the data per tree, resulting in approximately 500 leaves per tree. Training the STF on the MSRC dataset took only 15 minutes.

15.6.2 Image Categorization

We performed an experiment on the MSRC data to investigate our SVM categorization algorithm. The mean average precisions (AP) in Table 15.2 compare our modified pyramid match kernel (PMK) to a radial basis function (RBF) kernel, and compare the global kernel K to the per-category kernels K_c. In the baseline results with the RBF kernel, only the leaf nodes of the STF are used, separately per tree, using term frequency/inverse document ('tf/idf', from standard information retrieval) frequency to normalize the histogram. The PMK results use the entire BOST which for the per-category kernels K_c are weighted by the prior node distributions $p_j(c)$. As can be seen, the pyramid match kernel considerably improves on the RBF kernel. By training a per-category kernel, a small but noticeable improvement is obtained. For the image-level prior for segmentation, we thus use the PMK with per-category kernels. In Fig. 15.5 we plot the global kernel accuracy against the number T of STF trees, and see that categorization accuracy increases with more trees though it eventually levels out.

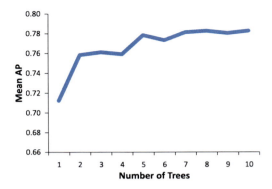

Fig. 15.5 Categorization accuracy *vs.* number of STF trees

Further categorization experiments are provided in Tables 15.3 and 15.4.

15.6.3 Semantic Segmentation

15.6.3.1 Experiments on the MSRC Dataset [342]

We first examine the influence of different aspects of our system on segmentation accuracy. We trained segmentation forests using (a) the histogram $G_F(l)$ of just leaf nodes l; (b) the histogram $G_F(j)$ of *all* tree nodes j; (c) just the region priors $p(c|F)$; (d) the full model using all nodes and region priors; (e) the full model trained without random geometric/photometric transformations; (f) all nodes using an unsupervised STF (no region priors are available); and (g) all nodes using a weakly supervised STF (only image labels). The category average accuracies are given in Table 15.5 with and without the image-level prior (ILP).

There are several conclusions to draw. (1) In all cases the ILP improves results. (2) The hierarchy of clusters in the STF gives a noticeable improvement. (3) The region priors alone perform remarkably well. Comparing to the segmentation result using only the STF leaf distributions (34.5 %) this shows the power of the localized BOSTs that exploit semantic context. (4) Each aspect of the BOST adds to the model. While, without the ILP, score (b) is slightly better than the full model (d),

Table 15.3 MSRC categorization results. The values shown are the average precision (AP) and the area under the ROC curve (AuC) for the MSRC21 dataset

	building	grass	tree	cow	sheep	sky	airplane	water	face	car	bicycle	flower	sign	bird	book	chair	road	cat	dog	body	boat	**Mean**
AP	71	92	81	91	97	95	97	86	83	87	79	85	47	43	89	61	77	62	60	85	76	**78**
AuC	85	96	94	99	100	98	100	94	95	99	98	99	88	86	99	93	92	95	94	97	94	**95**

Table 15.4 VOC2007 categorization results. The values shown are the average precision (AP) and the area under the ROC curve (AuC) for the VOC2007 segmentation dataset

	aeroplane	bicycle	bird	boat	bottle	bus	car	cat	chair	cow	table	dog	horse	motorbike	person	plant	sheep	sofa	train	tv/monitor	**Mean**
AP	69	15	11	26	11	24	35	12	15	18	22	15	33	40	67	29	19	10	55	16	**27**
AuC	93	67	70	68	71	73	79	72	77	66	80	72	88	83	72	78	80	79	92	75	**77**

Table 15.5 Comparative segmentation results on MSRC

	Without ILP	With ILP
(a) only leaves	61.3 %	64.1 %
(b) all nodes	**63.5 %**	65.5 %
(c) only region priors	62.1 %	66.1 %
(d) **full model**	63.4 %	**66.9 %**
(e) no transformations	60.4 %	64.4 %
(f) unsupervised STF	59.5 %	64.2 %
(g) weakly supervised STF	61.6 %	64.6 %

adding in the ILP shows how the region priors and textons work together.[2] (5) Random transformations of the training images improve accuracy by adding invariance. (6) Accuracy increases with more supervision, but even unsupervised STFs allow good segmentations.

Given this insight, we compare against [342] and [384]. We use the same train/test split as [342] (though not [384]). The results are summarized in Fig. 15.6 with further examples given in Fig. 15.9. Across the whole challenging dataset, using the full model with ILP achieved a class average accuracy of 66.9 %, a considerable improvement on both the 57.7 % of [342] and the 64 % of [384]. The global accuracy also improves slightly on [342]. The image-level prior improves accuracy for all but three classes, but even without it, results are still highly competitive with respect to other methods. Our use of balanced training has resulted in more consistent accuracy across classes, and significant improvements for certain difficult classes: cow, sheep, bird, chair, and cat. We do not use a Markov or conditional random field, which would likely further improve our accuracy [342].

These results used our learned and extremely fast STFs, without needing any hand-designed filter-banks or descriptors that are potentially slow to compute. Extracting the semantic textons at every pixel takes an average of only 275 millisec-

---

[2]This effect may be due to segmentation forest (b) being over-confident: looking at the five most likely classes inferred for each pixel, (b) achieves 87.6 % while (d) achieves a better 88.0 %.

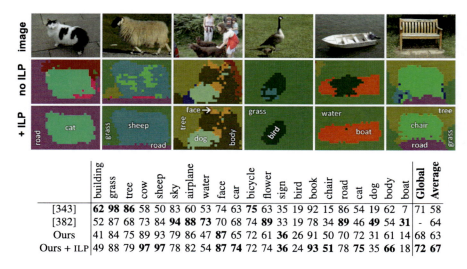

	building	grass	tree	cow	sheep	sky	airplane	water	face	car	bicycle	flower	sign	bird	book	chair	road	cat	dog	body	boat	Global	Average
[343]	**62**	**98**	**86**	58	50	83	60	53	74	63	**75**	63	35	19	**92**	15	86	54	19	62	7	71	58
[382]	52	87	68	73	84	**94**	**88**	73	70	68	74	**89**	33	19	78	34	**89**	46	**49**	54	**31**	-	64
Ours	41	84	75	89	93	79	86	47	**87**	65	72	61	**36**	26	91	50	70	72	31	61	14	68	63
Ours + ILP	49	88	79	**97**	**97**	78	82	54	**87**	**74**	72	74	**36**	24	**93**	**51**	78	**75**	35	**66**	18	**72**	**67**

Fig. 15.6 MSRC segmentation results. *Above*: Segmentations on test images using semantic texton forests. Note how the good but somewhat noisy segmentations are cleaned up using our image-level prior (ILP) that emphasizes the categories likely to be present. Further examples, including failure cases, in Fig. 15.9. (Note we do not use a Markov or conditional random field which could clean up the segmentations to precisely follow image edges [342]). *Below*: Segmentation accuracies (percent) over the whole dataset, without and with the ILP. Our highly efficient semantic textons achieve a significant improvement on previous work

onds per image, categorization takes 190 ms, and evaluating the segmentation forest only 140 ms. For comparison [342] took over 6 seconds per test image, and [384] took an average of over 2 seconds per image for feature extraction and between 0.3 to 2 seconds for estimating the segmentation. Our algorithm is well over 5 times faster *and* improves quantitative results. Minor optimizations have subsequently led to a real-time system that runs at over 8 frames per second.

15.6.3.2 Experiments on the VOC 2007 Segmentation Dataset [99]

This dataset contains 21 challenging categories including background. We trained a STF, a segmentation forest, and an ILP on these data, using the 'trainval' split and keeping parameters as for MSRC. The results in Fig. 15.7 compare with [99]. Our algorithm performs over twice as well as the only segmentation entry (Brookes), and the addition of the ILP further improves accuracy by 4 %. The actual winner of the segmentation challenge, the TKK algorithm, used segmentation by detection that fills in the detected object bounding boxes by category. To see if our algorithm could use a *detection*-level prior DLP (identical to the ILP but using the detected bounding boxes and varying with image position) we took the TKK entry output as the DLP. Our algorithm gave a 12 % improvement over the TKK segmentation by detection, highlighting the power of STFs as features for segmentation.

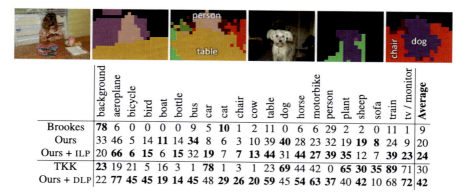

	background	aeroplane	bicycle	bird	boat	bottle	bus	car	cat	chair	cow	table	dog	horse	motorbike	person	plant	sheep	sofa	train	tv / monitor	Average
Brookes	78	6	0	0	0	0	9	5	10	1	2	11	0	6	6	29	2	2	0	11	1	9
Ours	33	46	5	14	11	14	34	8	6	3	10	39	40	28	23	32	19	19	8	24	9	20
Ours + ILP	20	66	6	15	6	15	32	19	7	7	13	44	31	44	27	39	35	12	7	39	23	24
TKK	23	19	21	5	16	3	1	78	1	3	1	23	69	44	42	0	65	30	35	89	71	30
Ours + DLP	22	77	45	45	19	14	45	48	29	26	20	59	45	54	63	37	40	42	10	68	72	42

Fig. 15.7 VOC 2007 segmentation results. *Above*: Test images with ground truth and our inferred segmentations using the ILP (not the DLP). *Below*: Segmentation accuracies (percent) over the whole dataset. The top three results compare our method to the Brookes segmentation entry [99], and show that our method is over twice as accurate. The lower two results compare the best automatic segmentation-by-detection entry (see text) [99] with our algorithm using the TKK results as a detection-level prior (DLP). Our algorithm improves the accuracy of segmentation by detection by over 10 percentage points

Fig. 15.8 Reconstruction from texton maps. By simply averaging the patches in Fig. 15.2(b) according to the texton maps in Fig. 15.3 one gets a blurry reconstruction of the original images. These reconstructions show that our semantic textons discretely capture significant image texture

Since the original publication of this work [341], there has been considerable progress in the field. Please see the latest PASCAL VOC challenge for the state of the art.

Fig. 15.9 A random selection of results on the MSRC dataset, including successes and failures. *Left*: Test image. *Middle*: Ground truth. *Right*: Our result. Image-level prior is used. Black pixels in the ground truth are 'void' and not used for evaluation

15.7 Conclusions

This chapter presented semantic texton forests as an efficient method for encoding textons. STFs do not depend on local descriptors or expensive k-means clustering, and when supervised during training they can infer a distribution over categories at each pixel. We showed how bags of semantic textons enabled state-of-the-art accuracy on challenging datasets for image categorization and semantic segmentation, and how the use of an inferred image-level prior significantly improves segmentation results. The substantial gains of our method over traditional textons are training and testing efficiency and improved quantitative performance.

The main limitation of our system is the large dimensionality of the bag of semantic textons, which necessitates a trade-off between the memory usage of the semantic texton integral images and the training time if they are computed at runtime. However, using just the region priors is more memory efficient.

As future work, it would be interesting to investigate how STFs might be used for image reconstruction. A few examples of a simple experiment are given in Fig. 15.8.

Acknowledgements We would like to thank J. Winn, B. Wenger, O. Yamaguchi, and V. Viitaniemi for helpful conversations and insights contributing to the work in this paper.

Chapter 16
Semi-supervised Video Segmentation Using Decision Forests

V. Badrinarayanan, I. Budvytis, and R. Cipolla

We present a novel semi-supervised video segmentation algorithm which delivers pixel labels along with their uncertainty estimates. The underlying probabilistic model is a temporal tree-structured Markov Random Field. Our algorithm takes as input user labeled key frame(s) of a video sequence. We then infer the marginal class posteriors of the unlabeled pixels. These posteriors are used to learn pixel unaries by training a decision forest in a semi-supervised manner. We term this the soft label Random Forest (slRF), in which the pixel posterior is treated as its vector label at training time. This allows us to use the standard Shannon entropy-based information gain as objective function, in an iterative, self-training semi-supervised framework. This is in contrast to the transductive forest of Chap. 8 which uses separate entropy measures for labeled and unlabeled data, respectively. We demonstrate the efficacy of our approach in foreground/background segmentation problems, based on quantitative studies on the challenging SegTrack dataset. We envisage our results to have wide applicability, including harvesting labeled video data for several applications such as action recognition, shape learning and developing priors for video segmentation.

16.1 Introduction

Semi-supervised video segmentation has a number of interesting applications, including video editing, harvesting labeled video data for training classifiers and learning shape and actions [203], as well as developing priors for unsupervised video segmentation [359]. In the past, several heuristic systems for semi-automatic video segmentation have been proposed [14, 220] which process a few frames at each step. But unlike semi-supervised image segmentation [315, 386], rigorous video modeling and inference for semi-supervised video segmentation have rarely been

V. Badrinarayanan (✉) · I. Budvytis · R. Cipolla
University of Cambridge, Cambridge, UK

A. Criminisi, J. Shotton (eds.), *Decision Forests for Computer Vision and
Medical Image Analysis*, Advances in Computer Vision and Pattern Recognition,
DOI 10.1007/978-1-4471-4929-3_16, © Springer-Verlag London 2013

explored. This can perhaps be attributed to high cost of inference and limited availability of computational power. In this work, we propose a probabilistic graphical model and an efficient inference method dedicated to semi-supervised video segmentation. Closely associated with the inference strategy is the learning of class unaries for segmentation using classification forests. In particular, we exploit the flexibility of training forests with soft or probabilistic labels, *i.e.* using pixel posteriors as labels at training time. This allows us to use both labeled and unlabeled data to learn class likelihoods in a seamless fashion for foreground/background video object segmentation problems. The additional advantage in using random forests is the low training and testing time.

Recently, unsupervised video segmentation has gained much attention [207, 215, 382], especially as extensions of image super-pixelization to space-time super-pixels. The aim of these methods is to group pixels which are photometrically and motion-wise consistent. In simple cases, where there is a clear distinction between foreground and background, the grouping may appear to be semantically meaningful. However, in more complex videos, the result is, in general, an over-segmentation, and requires additional knowledge (through user interaction for example) to achieve any object level segmentation. In contrast, in this work, we develop a probabilistic framework which jointly models both appearance and semantic labels, with a view to perform semi-supervised video segmentation. A second distinction of our algorithm is that it performs probabilistic inference, as opposed to the more commonly used point-wise maximum a posteriori (MAP) inference. This is to enable semi-supervised learning of pixel unaries (class likelihoods), for a given video sequence, from both labeled and unlabeled data. These unaries are then used to further improve the quality of segmentation.

One or two notable instances [38, 188] have tried to extend their image segmentation algorithms directly for n-D sequences/videos, though have met only limited success. A few others [103, 373] have tackled the problem of joint tracking and segmentation using unaries learnt at the start frame. We demonstrate via quantitative studies on such problems that our algorithm can achieve better or comparative results without using heuristics such as fixing the labels at each frame successively.

In this work, the semantic objects of interest are defined by the user labeled key frame(s) of the video sequence (see Fig. 16.2). It is also possible to input only a few user mouse strokes in some frames. Our proposed segmentation algorithm uses this input to label each pixel in the video data into one of the user defined categories and infers their confidence estimates. The resulting *soft labels* can then be used for learning pixel unaries using a classification forest [44] in a semi-supervised manner to further improve the segmentation (see Sect. 16.3.3 for details).

As we perform probabilistic inference as opposed to MAP inference, a family of labelings at various confidence levels are available to the user as output. The user can then select one of these labelings at one or more frames, fix or clamp them, and re-infer the labeling over the whole video. This is similar to the self-training flavor of semi-supervised learning [103], as opposed to transductive learning of Chap. 8. Probabilistic inference is also an important component for active learning methods [103, 330, 407, 424].

To summarize, we make the following contributions:

1. A patch-based probabilistic graphical model for semi-supervised video segmentation, which employs a novel temporal tree structure to link patches between frames.
2. An efficient structured variational inference scheme which infers pixel-wise labels and their confidences.
3. The use of decision forests, trained in a semi-supervised manner, to incorporate both labeled and unlabeled data to learn pixel unaries for segmentation.

16.2 Literature Review

We review some of the related state of the art in unsupervised, classification based, semi-supervised and work-flow-based video segmentation.

16.2.1 Unsupervised Video Segmentation

The rectangular patch-based Epitome model [63, 174] and the pixel-based Jigsaw model [179] learn a compact latent representation of an image or a sequence of images. For a video sequence, this translates to learning correlations between pixels in both successive and non-successive frames. However, there is a model selection step (number of clusters, size of Epitomes or Jigsaws) which is usually hand-crafted. In our proposed algorithm, we employ an epitomic model to learn correlations between successive frames which circumvents the aperture problem afflicting optical flow. However, we avoid costly learning of compact latent representations for the video to establish correlations between non-successive frames, and instead choose a simpler alternative in the form of a decision forest [44] to achieve the same goal.

Video super-pixelization methods such as [49, 146, 207, 215, 382] rely on grouping pixels in space and time using appearance and motion cues. Unfortunately, often this results in over fragmentation, and pixel clusters which cannot be easily interpreted as semantically meaningful regions. However, consistent video super-pixelization can reduce the input dimension for structured discriminative models.

16.2.2 Classification-Based Segmentation

We broadly divide methods in this category into unstructured and structured classification methods.

Unstructured Classification Unstructured classifiers predict class labels independently for each pixel without incorporating any neighborhood constraints. Decision forests [44], an example of unstructured classifiers, have recently gained popularity in image and video segmentation [48, 53, 341, 343]. In this work, we train a decision forest in a semi-supervised manner to learn pixel unaries and demonstrate that this learning can often help improve the quality of video segmentation.

Structured Classification Structured classifiers incorporate neighborhood constraints, such as spatial or temporal smoothness, to perform pixel class prediction. Conditional random field (CRF) models [38, 196] are an example of widely applied structured classifiers which have led the way in image segmentation problems. In practice, their main attraction arises from the ability to perform global optimization or in finding a strong local minimum of a particular class (sub-modular) of CRFs at interactive speeds [39]. There are one or two notable instances which have tried to extend their image segmentation algorithms directly for videos by propagating MAP estimates sequentially [188] or for N-D sequences [38]. As pointed out by [14], performing MAP inference on large 3D volumes results in an uncontrollable work flow. Multi label MAP inference on the full video volume is extremely expensive [373]. More recent work has concentrated on using random forests to learn the potentials of CRF models as opposed to hand setting them [271]. The use of forests for structured labeling tasks has also been explored in [192].

16.2.3 Semi-supervised Video Segmentation

In our earlier work [13], we jointly modeled appearance and semantic labels using a coupled-HMM model. The key idea was to influence the learning of frame to frame patch correlations as a function of both appearance and class labels. We extended this method in [53] to include correlations between non-successive frames using a classification forest. In this new chapter, we follow these in jointly modeling appearance and semantic labels. The significant difference is that we use an undirected model which lends itself more naturally to fusion of classifiers and temporal modeling. In contrast, the directed models in our earlier work introduced competition (the 'explaining away' effect [164]) between classifiers and temporal models, which is not always desirable.

Tsai *et al.* [373] jointly optimize for temporal motion and semantic labels in an energy minimization framework. In this interesting framework, a sliding window approach is used to process overlapping n-frame grids for the sake of reducing computational burden. The result of one n-frame grid is employed as a hard constraint in the next grid and so on. Such an approach is also used in [397]. In contrast, we treat the whole video volume at once, inferring both temporal correlations and label uncertainties. Fathi *et al.* [103] use semi-supervised and active learning for video segmentation. Each unlabeled pixel is provided a confidence measure based on its distance in a neighborhood graph to a labeled point. These confidences are used to recommend frames in which more interaction is desired. In our approach, inference directly leads to confidences and active learning can also be pursued.

16.2.4 Work-Flow-Based Video Segmentation

The VideoSnapCut algorithm of [14] is an example of a work-flow-based system which relies on a heuristic combination of low level cues for video segmentation. This technique is motivated by the fact that methods based on global optimization [220] often results in an uncontrollable work flow. To avoid this issue, they employ spatially local classifiers and propagate their predictions over time using optical flow. The main drawbacks are the heuristic nature of cue integration, use of unreliable flow measurements and small time window processing.

16.3 Video Model for Semi-supervised Segmentation

We introduce a patch-based undirected graphical model for semi-supervised video segmentation which jointly models both the observed sequence of images (appearance layer) and their corresponding labels (label layer). See Fig. 16.1(d) for an illustration. In conjunction with this generative model for the video time-series we also introduce the soft label Random Forest (slRF). The slRF is trained in a semi-supervised manner using both labeled and unlabeled video data and its predictions are used as class unaries. The learnt unaries are particularly useful when the foreground object undergoes fast motion and self-occlusion is present.

Our segmentation method has three steps. First, is to perform label inference using the generative video time-series model and with the unaries set to uniform distribution. Second, is to use the inferred labels to learn class unaries by training a random forest in a semi-supervised manner. Finally, in the third step these unaries are injected back in a second iteration of label inference to improve the overall segmentation quality. The model construction and label inference scheme are described below.

16.3.1 Model Construction

Figure 16.1 illustrates a step-by-step construction of our model. We begin with the image epitome [174], a compact version of the image with no spatial structure, as shown in Fig. 16.1(a). In this image generative model, the original frame/image J_k is assumed to be given as a set of patches $Z_k = \{Z_{k,m}\}_{m=1}^{M}$, each containing pixels from a subset of image coordinates $C_{k,m}$. The patches are taken to be square in shape and it is assumed that their coordinate sets can overlap. For each patch, a latent variable $S_{k,m}$ maps coordinates $C_{k,m}$ to coordinates in the epitome $\mathbf{e}$. A square

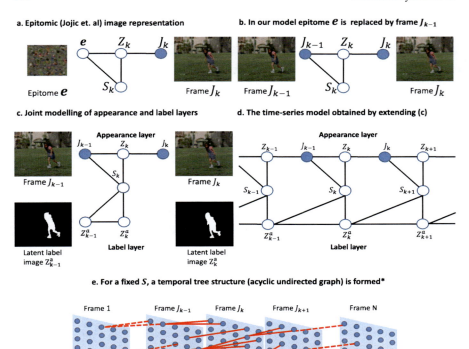

Fig. 16.1 Step-wise build up of our proposed model for semi-supervised video segmentation. In (**a**) we show the underlying graphical model for the epitomic generative model of a frame J_k. In (**b**) we replace the epitome of frame J_k by the previous frame in the image sequence. This avoids the computationally expensive learning of the epitome. In (**c**) we extend (**b**) to jointly model both frame appearance and corresponding labels. We show in (**d**) the full generative model for the entire video sequence obtained by repeating the basic model in (**c**) over time. For a single instance of the mapping variables $S_{1:n}$ we obtain a temporal tree structure as shown in (**e**). We use the term tree structure to denote the undirected acyclic graphical model. The tree is rarely a spanning tree and most often is a *forest of sub-trees* as shown in (**e**). Note that for clarity we do not show connections for all the nodes in (**e**)

patch is mapped to a square patch in the epitome through $S_{k,m}$. At pixel coordinate n in the epitome, a mean and variance μ_n, ϕ_n is stored. Given $\mathbf{e} = (\boldsymbol{\mu}, \boldsymbol{\phi})$, the patch $Z_{k,m}$ is obtained by copying the epitome mean and adding Gaussian noise to a level prescribed by the variance map:

$$p(Z_{k,m}|\mathbf{e}, S_{k,m}) = \prod_{i \in C_{k,m}} \mathcal{N}(z_{k,m,i}; \mu_{S_{k,m}(i)}, \phi_{S_{k,m}(i)}). \tag{16.1}$$

Note that coordinate i is defined on the input image J_k and $z_{k,m,i}$ is the intensity or color of pixel i in patch m. In practice, the number of possible mappings $S_{k,m}$ is restricted to coordinates within a rectangular window centered around patch m in the epitome (like when patch cross-correlation is performed). So the prior over $S_{k,m}$ is set to uniform over the corresponding window.

Treating the patches to be independent, the *generative model for the set of patches* is as follows:

$$p\left(\{Z_{k,m}\}_{m=1}^M, \mathbf{e}, \{S_{k,m}\}_{m=1}^M\right)$$

$$= p(\mathbf{e}) \prod_{m=1:M} p(S_{k,m}) \prod_{i \in C_{k,m}} \mathcal{N}(z_{k,m,i}; \mu_{S_{k,m}(i)}, \phi_{S_{k,m}(i)}). \qquad (16.2)$$

The prior on the patch mapping variables is usually assumed flat. From this patch generative model, the *image generation* is defined using patch averaging as follows:

$$p\left(J_{k,i} | \{Z_{k,m}\}_{m=1}^M\right) = \mathcal{N}\left(J_{k,i}; \frac{1}{N_{k,i}} \sum_{m, i \in C_{k,m}} z_{k,m,i}; \psi_{k,i}\right), \qquad (16.3)$$

where $N_{k,i}$ is the number of patches which overlap pixel i. Therefore, the entire epitome model is

$$p\left(J_k, \{Z_{k,m}, S_{k,m}\}_{m=1}^M, \mathbf{e}\right) = p\left(\{Z_{k,m}, S_{k,m}\}_{m=1}^M, \mathbf{e}\right) \prod_i p\left(J_{k,i} | \{Z_{k,m}\}_{m=1}^M\right).$$

$$(16.4)$$

So far in this model, the patches $\{Z_{k,m}\}_{m=1}^M$ have been treated independently, even though their coordinates overlap, for the sake of tractable inference. This is unrealistic, and therefore during inference of the latent patches, the solution space is constrained to those in which overlapping coordinates share the same intensity. This is ensured by estimating a single point posterior distribution at each coordinate. We discuss this part in Sect. 16.3.2.

Learning an epitome is computationally expensive and the quality of the generated image depends strongly on the size of the epitome. These problems are more severe with video epitomes [63]. Therefore, we avoid learning epitomes and substitute frame J_{k-1} as an epitome for J_k (see Fig. 16.1(b)). The similarity between frames J_k and J_{k-1} makes J_{k-1} a natural source of patches used to generate J_k. With these changes, (16.2) is transformed to

$$p\left(\{Z_{k,m}\}_{m=1}^M, J_{k-1}, \{S_{k,m}\}_{m=1}^M\right) = p(J_{k-1}) \prod_{m=1:M} p(S_{k,m})$$

$$\times \prod_{i \in C_{k,m}} \mathcal{N}(z_{k,m,i}; J_{k-1,S_{k,m}(i)}, \phi_{S_{k,m}(i)}).$$

$$(16.5)$$

Latent variable Z_k^a in the *label layer* is the counterpart of latent variable Z_k in the appearance layer (see Fig. 16.1(c)). $Z_k^a = \{Z_{k,m}^a\}_{m=1}^M$ is seen as a set of labeled patches, each containing labeled pixels from a subset of image coordinates $C_{k,m}$.

The common mapping variable $S_{k,j}$ maps coordinates $C_{k,m}$ to coordinates (patches) in Z_{k-1}^a. The clique is then defined as

$$\Psi\left(Z_{k,m}^a, Z_{k-1,S_{k,m}}^a; \lambda\right) = \prod_{i \in C_{k,m}} \Psi\left(Z_{k,m,i}^a, Z_{k-1,S_{k,m}(i)}^a; \lambda\right), \qquad (16.6)$$

where

$$\Psi\left(Z_{k,m,i}^a = l, Z_{k-1,S_{k,m}(i)}^a = v; \lambda\right) = \begin{cases} \lambda & \text{if } l = v, \\ 1 - \lambda & \text{otherwise,} \end{cases} \qquad (16.7)$$

and $l, v \in \mathcal{L}$, with $\mathcal{L}$ denoting the label set. Notice that in this layer again we have avoided the issue of overlapping coordinates as in the appearance layer for sake of tractable inference. However, unlike the appearance layer, we do not explicitly enforce overlapping coordinates to share the same label by computing a single point posterior. This is because we wish to evaluate the full posterior distribution to estimate label confidences at each image coordinate. Therefore, we average the marginal posteriors of the latent variables which share the same coordinate (see Sect. 16.3.2) and consider this average distribution as the label posterior at that coordinate.

The entire time-series model for the video sequence is now obtained by extending the basic model in Fig. 16.1(c). This is shown in Fig. 16.1(d). In this model, for any single state of the mapping variables $S_k = \{S_{k,m}\}_{m=1}^M$, the label layer patches are connected in a *tree structure* as shown in Fig. 16.1(e). Therefore, the time-series model is a *mixture of trees* graphical model. In this work, we approximate this mixture by its most probable component to arrive at a *tree-structured graphical model* for video sequences (see Sect. 16.3.2). Note that this temporally tree-structured model must not be confused with the decision trees which are also used in this work to learn the class unaries.

The full probabilistic joint appearance and label model for video sequences is as given here:

$$p\left(J_{0:n}, Z_{1:n}, Z_{0:n}^a, S_{1:n} | \psi, \phi, \lambda\right) \propto \prod_{k=1:n} p(J_k | Z_k; \psi) p(Z_k | S_k, J_{k-1}; \phi)$$

$$\times \Psi\left(Z_k^a, Z_{k-1,S_k}^a; \lambda\right) \Psi_u\left(Z_k^a\right) \Psi_u\left(Z_0^a\right) p(S_k), \qquad (16.8)$$

with Eqs. (16.3), (16.5), and (16.6) defining the first three terms of the right hand side. The unary terms are defined as follows:

$$\Psi_u\left(Z_k^a\right) = \prod_{m=1:M} \prod_{i \in C_{k,m}} \Psi_u\left(Z_{k,m,i}^a\right). \qquad (16.9)$$

The prior on the mapping variable $p(S_{k,m})$ is set to a uniform distribution within a rectangular window in frame $k - 1$ around the center coordinate of patch $Z_{k,m}$.

16.3.2 Inference

It is clear from (16.8) that the proportionality constant cannot be computed due to the combinatorial sum involved on the right hand side. Therefore, we resort to approximate inference as discussed below. The log probability of the observed data V (images, labeled start frame) can be lower bounded as follows:

$$\log p\big(V|\Upsilon = \{\psi, \phi, \lambda\}\big) \geq \int_{\Xi} q(\Xi) \log \frac{p(V, \Xi|\Upsilon)}{q(\Xi)}, \tag{16.10}$$

where $q(\Xi)$ is a variational posterior over the latent variables in the model. We choose

$$q(\Xi) = q_1(\mathcal{S})q_2(\Theta), \tag{16.11}$$

where $\Theta = \{Z_{1:n}, Z_{1:n}^a\}$, $\mathcal{S} = S_{1:n}$, and

$$q_1(\mathcal{S}) \triangleq \prod_{k=1}^{n} \prod_{m=1}^{M} q_1(S_{k,m}),$$

$$q_2(\Theta) \triangleq \prod_{k=1}^{n} \prod_{m=1}^{M} \prod_{i \in m} \delta_{Z_{k,m,i}^*}(Z_{k,m,i})\tilde{q}_2(\Theta_{\backslash Z_{1:n}}). \tag{16.12}$$

Notice from the above equation that the variational posterior does not factorize into independent terms (over the latent variables Θ) as in a mean-field approximation [28]. Therefore, our approximation is a *structured variational posterior*, which leads to better approximate inference [319]. Secondly, notice the single point posterior approximation over the latent variables $Z_{1:n}$. This ensures that overlapped coordinates have the same value.

We now apply the calculus of variations [28] to maximize the lower bound w.r.t. q_1, q_2 and arrive at

$$q_1(S_{k,m}) \propto \exp\Bigg\{ \int_{Z_{k,m}, Z_{k,m}^a, Z_{k-1, S_{k,m}}^a} \tilde{q}_2\big(Z_{k,m}^a, Z_{k-1, S_{k,m}}^a\big)$$

$$\times \log\big[\Psi\big(Z_{k,m}^*, J_{k-1, S_{k,m}}; \phi\big)\Psi\big(Z_{k,m}^a, Z_{k-1, S_{k,m}}^a; \lambda\big)\big] \Bigg\} p(S_{k,m}), \tag{16.13}$$

$$\tilde{q}_2(\Theta_{\backslash Z_{1:n}}) = \exp \int_{\mathcal{S}} q_1(\mathcal{S}) \log p(\Theta_{\backslash Z_{1:n}}|V, \mathcal{S}; \Upsilon). \tag{16.14}$$

The second of the above fixed point equations is computationally intensive as it involves marginalizing over all the mapping variables. For this reason, we approximate it by

$$\tilde{q}_2(\Theta_{\backslash Z_{1:n}}) \approx \exp \int_{\mathcal{S}} \delta_{\mathcal{S}^*}(\mathcal{S}) \log p(\Theta_{\backslash Z_{1:n}} | V, \mathcal{S}; \Upsilon),$$

$$= p(\Theta_{\backslash Z_{1:n}} | V, \mathcal{S}^*; \Upsilon), \tag{16.15}$$

where $\mathcal{S}^* = \arg\max_{\mathcal{S}} q_1(\mathcal{S})$. A second motivation for this approximation is that $p(\Theta_{\backslash Z_{1:n}} | V, \mathcal{S}^*; \Upsilon)$ is *temporally tree structured*. From a variational inference viewpoint, $\mathcal{T}^*$ represents the best (MAP) tree-structured component of the mixture model. We exploit this temporal tree structure to perform efficient and *exact inference* of the latent variables in the set $\Theta_{\backslash Z_{1:n}}$. Notice that $\tilde{q}_2(\Theta_{\backslash Z_{1:n}})$ is a joint distribution over the MAP tree and thus the exact marginal posteriors are easily computed using standard sum-product belief propagation [28].

We also emphasize that the tree structure need not be a spanning tree. Indeed, we employ the term tree structured to mean an undirected acyclic graph on which exact inference can be performed. In practice, there can be several disjoint trees in the model or a forest of non-spanning trees (see Fig. 16.1).

16.3.2.1 From Patches to Pixel Posteriors

So far in the inference, we have exploited the best tree structure to compute the marginal posteriors of variables $z_{k,m,i}^a$, where i is the image coordinate. As mentioned in Sect. 16.3.1, since patches share coordinates (overlap), we average the marginal posteriors of all latent variables which share the same coordinate. For example

$$\hat{q}_2(z_{k,i}^a) \approx \frac{1}{N_{k,i}} \sum_{m,i \in C_{k,m}} \tilde{q}_2(z_{k,m,i}^a), \tag{16.16}$$

where $\hat{q}_2(z_{k,i}^a)$ is the averaged posterior. Notice that the patch index is now removed on the left hand side.

16.3.2.2 Forward and Backward Trees

From Fig. 16.1(e), we see that the tree has its root in the start frame and leaves at the end frame. We denote this as the forward tree. This directionality in the temporal structure can sometimes lead to a labeling bias. For example, the user provided root frame labels can have a stronger influence than the leaf (end) frame labels on the remaining latent variables. To correct for this bias, we compute the best tree in the reverse direction (backward tree with root at the end frame) and perform inference on it. Finally, we average the label posteriors from the two trees, at each coordinate, to obtain the approximate posterior at each pixel.

Algorithm 16.1 Semi-supervised video segmentation using decision forests

Input: $J_{0:n}$ (video) and hand labeled key frame(s)
Output: Pixel label probabilities

Initialization
Set Z_0^a to user provided labels and $Z_k^* = J_k$, $k \in 1 : n$
Set the initial values of λ, ψ, ϕ to the values given in Sect. 16.4
Set the pixel unaries to uniform distributions
Set the prior on the mapping variables to uniform distributions

Inference
1. Compute the forward and backward trees using (16.13) (Sect. 16.3.2.2)
2. For each tree separately:
– **a.** Perform exact inference to obtain pixel marginals (Sect. 16.3.2)
– **b.** Obtain the coordinate-wise approximate marginals by averaging
  (Sect. 16.3.2.3)
3. Optionally smooth the pixel labels in each frame using loopy BP (Sect. 16.3.2.3)
4. Average the posteriors at each coordinate from both the trees

Learning unaries
5. Learn unaries using a random forest trained with the label posteriors (Sect. 16.3.3)

Bootstrapped inference
6. Repeat steps 1–3 using the learned unaries (an example of typical results at each step is shown in Fig. 16.2)

It can be argued that since our model is undirected (no temporal directionality is intended), the forward and backward tree could be combined into a single undirected model. However, this model would have a loopy temporal structure and lose the desirable property of performing efficient and exact inference of pixel labels.

16.3.2.3 Intra-frame Smoothing of Pixel Labels

We can *optionally* obtain a smooth, yet edge sensitive, labeling in each frame by using the pixel posteriors computed thus far as pixel unaries and applying loopy BP [28] on a standard 8-neighborhood grid. We use contrast sensitive edge potentials as in [315], and 50 iterations of message passing. The resulting marginals provide us with label confidences (see Fig. 16.2(c)). The drawback of performing smoothing is that the marginals tend to be over confident (see Fig. 16.2(d)). This is sometimes undesirable, for example in long sequences, in which new objects/categories appear, the inference should ideally assign low confidence to them to reduce false positive labeling. Therefore, we avoid smoothing in long sequences (see Sect. 16.4).

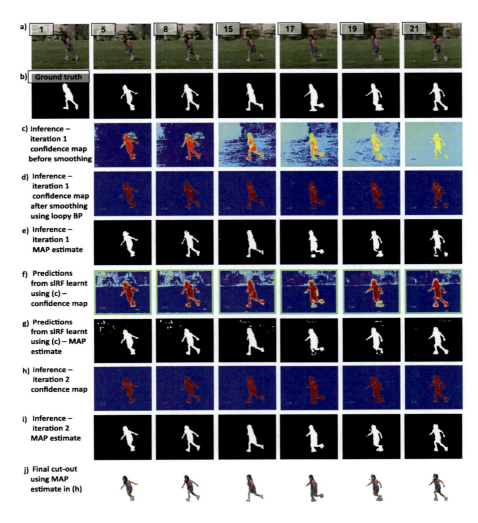

Fig. 16.2 The first two rows show the image sequence and ground truth from the SegTrack dataset [373]. The camera is moving in this sequence. The segmentation algorithm in this sequence has to cope with fast shape changes, motion blur and overlap between foreground and background appearance models. Inferred marginals of $Z^a_{1:n-1}$ before smoothing are shown in row (**c**). Note how the confidence decreases from the labeled first frame. The marginals after smoothing are shown in row (**d**). Observe the increased confidence due to smoothing. The MAP estimates of these marginals are shown in row (**e**). Note that some part of the girl's hands and leg are missing. The unaries learnt using the marginals in row (**c**) are shown in row (**f**) and its MAP estimate is shown in row (**g**). We see from (**h**) that the legs and hands are labeled correctly along with some false positive background labels. Bootstrapping this prediction and performing inference once again results in the confidences shown in row (**g**). The corresponding MAP estimate in row (**i**) shows almost no background false positives, and the missing legs and hand in row (**d**) are recovered. The cut-out in row (**j**) has sharp edges and is clean

16.3.3 Learning Pixel Unaries Using a Random Forest

In the first iteration of inference, we set the unaries to uniform distributions and use our proposed inference technique to estimate the pixel label posteriors. We then train a decision forest [44] using these posteriors as soft pixel labels, *i.e.* each pixel has a vector label instead of a scalar class label. We term this forest trained in a *semi-supervised* manner, the soft label Random Forest (slRF). In practice, we adopt the standard information gain evaluation criterion (see Chap. 4) to train our slRF, as it is directly suited to training by taking into account the entropy of soft labels. We use simple but computationally efficient pixel intensity difference features at each split node as in [341].

Our semi-supervised training of the forest is different from the transductive forest described in Chap. 8. In the transductive forests, labeled and unlabeled data are treated separately and a new information gain criterion is introduced to combine label and appearance-based entropies. In contrast, we first assign each unlabeled data point a soft label obtained from the label inference step. At training time, we compute a histogram of soft labels at each node and use the conventional information gain criterion to evaluate the split function.

Some interesting contrast can be drawn with the auto-context work of [375] and related ideas in [341], where the confidence maps from a classifier output (soft labels) are used as the basis of features for training a subsequent classifier that can then learn higher level context. These iterative approaches demonstrate that the classification accuracy improves by using soft labels as *features*. However, the auto-context learning is fully supervised, unlike the semi-supervised training of the slRF which uses posterior marginals as *labels*.

In the second iteration of inference, we use the predictions from the slRF as pixel unaries and perform label inference. These unaries, learnt in a semi-supervised manner can help improve segmentation accuracy, as shown in Fig. 16.2(g, h). Unlike traditional tracking algorithms were the unaries are learnt using the first frame labels, we use the entire set of video data and the corresponding inferred labels to learn the unaries.

In some approaches to segmentation [103], labels are propagated to the adjacent frame and their MAP estimate is used to update the unary parameters. This is sub-optimal, given that the entire video volume is not used to update the unary. In contrast, our efficient inference method allows us to pool in the entire set of video data and the label posteriors to learn the unaries. The whole approach is summarized in Algorithm 16.1.

16.4 Experiments and Results

We evaluated the performance of our approach in a tracking and segmentation setting using the challenging SegTrack [373] dataset. This dataset, annotated with ground truth, consists of six sequences with clutter, self-occlusion, small sized objects and deformable shape. The sequences are captured with a moving camera in

Table 16.1 Quantitative evaluation on the SegTrack tracking and segmentation dataset [373]. In all these experiments only the start frame of the video sequence is user labeled. We used a single set of model parameters to obtain these results. The score is the average label mismatch per frame. Our score is better or only marginally worse in five out of the six sequences as compared to the state of the art methods. Note how the score improves between the first and second pass of inference. In the Penguin sequence, inference without unaries outperforms the other methods. However, poor unary accuracy results in performance degradation after bootstrapping the learnt unary for a second round of inference. We used label smoothing for this dataset. See Fig. 16.3 for qualitative results

Sequence	Chockalingam et al. [66]	Tsai et al. [373]	Fathi et al. [103]	Our method		
				Inference	Learnt unary	Inference with learnt unary
Parachute	502	**235**	251	405	1294	**258**
Girl	1755	1304	**1206**	1232	2236	**820**
Monkey-dog	683	**563**	598	**387**	2304	589
Penguin	6627	1705	**1367**	1212	4285	21141
Bird-fall	454	**252**	342	374	2900	**259**
Cheetah	1217	1142	**711**	1088	1225	923

three of the sequences. In Table 16.1 we report our score along with some of the recent state of the art approaches. Each channel in all the images are scaled to lie between [0.0, 1.0]. We use patches of size 7×7 centered on each pixel. In our tree model, we set λ to 0.9. We use the random forest (RF) classifier as in [341] with 16 trees, each of depth 8. Input LAB patches of 21×21 are extracted around every second pixel on both axes. We leave out border pixels in a 12 pixel band to fit all rectangular patches. We use the same kind and number of features as in [341]. The key difference is that we use the inferred *soft labels* to train the random forest (slRF). We compute the entropic information gain and the leaf node distributions (normalized histograms) by treating the data point label as a *vector* whose elements sum to unity. We note that no change was required to the entropic information gain criterion as it is convenient to use the label distribution directly to compute the entropy of the pixel labels. This is an advantage of using the random forest as compared to other classifiers.

The qualitative results are shown in Fig. 16.3 and the corresponding quantitative results are shown in Table 16.1. In five out of the six sequences we perform better or are only marginally worse than the state of the art. In the remaining case (Penguin), inference without the learned unaries outperforms the state of the art. The unaries in this case are very poor due to severe overlap between foreground and background. Fathi et al. [103] particularly design an adaptive weighting scheme to control the influence of the unaries during segmentation. The idea is to clamp highly certain labels in a few frames after inference and then adapt the contribution of the unaries based on the accuracy of their prediction of these clamped labels. Such an approach could also be incorporated into our probabilistic framework in the future albeit with an introduction of an additional parameter to control the influence of the unaries in the posterior.

Fig. 16.3 Qualitative results on the SegTrack dataset [66, 373]. Notice how our algorithm is able to cope with motion blur (**a**), large displacement (**d, j**), small sized objects (**f**). The main failure case is (**h**) due to severe overlap in appearance between the foreground and background. See Table 16.1 for quantitative results

16.5 Advantages and Drawbacks

The key advantages of our proposed approach are:

1. Our temporal tree-structured model permits exact and efficient inference of pixel labels.

2. We avoid sequential propagation of erroneous instantaneous decisions and therefore reduce false positives (see [53] for quantitative arguments).
3. We avoid the use of short time window-based processing which are currently used in several video segmentation approaches [373], quite often due to computational inefficiency.
4. We can learn unaries efficiently, using both labeled and unlabeled data, with our proposed slRF to improve segmentation accuracy.

Our approach suffers from the following drawbacks:

1. We are currently restricted to segment classes which have sizes above the patch resolution of 7×7. Using higher resolution images should alleviate this problem to a large extent or replacing patches with super-pixels.
2. The uncertainty in the pixel marginal posteriors is based on the number of pairwise cliques a patch is part of (its neighborhood connectivity), and does not include the uncertainty with which the clique was formed in the tree model. As part of future work, we would like to include this uncertainty in the model to improve performance.
3. The method is currently not applicable to real-time scenarios. It takes 3 seconds per frame for label inference and 3.0 minutes for computing the forward and backward temporal tree structure on an 8 core Intel Zeon 2.2 GHz machine. Further, the method is also memory intensive, taking up to 100 MB per frame for an image resolution of 400×320 in our unoptimized C++ implementation. Learning of the unaries took about 25 seconds per frame also with an unoptimized code.

16.6 Conclusions

This chapter has presented a novel tree-structured graphical model for video sequences and showed how to integrate a decision forest with this generative model in a bootstrapped manner. In this model, the video time-series is modeled as a temporal tree which links patches from the first frame to the last frame. The tree structure permits efficient and exact inference of pixel labels and their confidences. We demonstrated that in several cases, robust pixel unaries can be learnt directly from pixel marginal posteriors using our proposed soft label random forest and help improve segmentation. The training of the soft label random forest is identical to a standard random forest, except for the use of vector labels instead of hard scalar labels. Both training and testing times are fast which makes it suitable for interactive video segmentation in the future.

One of the other key benefits of our system is the ability to propagate label uncertainties over time using exact inference. This is in contrast to most existing approaches which use short time window-based processing and sub-optimal instantaneous decision making. As part of our future work, we envisage the use of random forests to learn the graphical model structure for a given video, in addition to the class unaries.

Chapter 17
Classification Forests for Semantic Segmentation of Brain Lesions in Multi-channel MRI

E. Geremia, D. Zikic, O. Clatz, B.H. Menze, B. Glocker, E. Konukoglu,
J. Shotton, O.M. Thomas, S.J. Price, T. Das, R. Jena, N. Ayache,
and A. Criminisi

Classification forests, as discussed in Chap. 4, present a series of advantages which make them a good choice for applications in medical image analysis. Classification forests are inherent multi-class classifiers (which allows for *e.g.* the simultaneous segmentation of different tissues), have good generalization properties (which is important as training data are often scarce in medical applications), and are able to deal with very high-dimensional feature spaces (which permits the use of long-range, context-rich features). In this chapter we demonstrate how classification forests can be used as a basic building block to develop state of the art systems for medical image analysis in two challenging applications. Given 3D multi-channel magnetic resonance images (MRI) as input we use forests for: (i) the tissue-specific segmentation of high-grade brain tumors (namely glioblastoma tumors), and (ii) the segmentation of multiple sclerosis (MS) lesions.

S.J. Price is funded by a Clinician Scientist Award from the National Institute for Health Research (NIHR).
O.M. Thomas is a Clinical Lecturer supported by the NIHR Cambridge Biomedical Research Centre.

E. Geremia (✉) · O. Clatz · N. Ayache
Asclepios Research Project, Inria, Sophia-Antipolis, France

D. Zikic · B. Glocker · E. Konukoglu · J. Shotton · A. Criminisi
Microsoft Research Ltd., Cambridge, UK

B.H. Menze
ETH Zurich, Zurich, Switzerland

O.M. Thomas · S.J. Price · T. Das · R. Jena
Cambridge University Hospitals, Cambridge, UK

A. Criminisi, J. Shotton (eds.), *Decise Forests for Computer Vision and Medical Image Analysis*, Advances in Computer Vision and Pattern Recognition, DOI 10.1007/978-1-4471-4929-3_17, © Springer-Verlag London 2013

17.1 Introduction

This chapter employs classification forests for the automatic, semantic segmentation of anomalies in 3D magnetic resonance images of the brain.

Specifically, in Sect. 17.2 we discuss a method for segmentation of the individual tissues of high-grade brain tumors, and in Sect. 17.3 we present a method for segmentation of multiple sclerosis (MS) lesions. These two methods apply decision forests for the classification of every voxel in the input, multi-channel MR scan.

From a methodological point of view, the tumor segmentation application investigates the "augmentation" of the available input image channels via the efficient estimation of approximate tissue probabilities. In contrast, the MS lesions segmentation task uses the classification forest directly, though it employs different, geometrically-inspired feature types. Further, for the MS application, we present an analysis of the effect of individual forest parameters and the discriminative power of each feature type and input channels.

Why Classification Forests for Medical Image Segmentation?   We choose to employ classification forests because of the three advantages highlighted below:

1. *The efficiency of classification forests in dealing with high-dimensional spaces* allows us to use non-local and context-aware features, which describe spatial locations based on a relatively large surrounding, and span a high-dimensional feature space. Context-aware features have two possible advantages. First, these features have the potential to successfully classify labels which usually cannot be distinguished using only a local support around a voxel (*cf.* the tumor segmentation work in [20, 205, 322, 385, 399]). Second, our experiments indicate that learning based on context-aware features has an inherent regularizing effect on the results. This regularization is not designed manually, but learned from the training data.
2. *Classification forests are inherently multi-label classifiers.* This property allows us to classify different tissues simultaneously, simplifying the modeling of the distributions of the individual classes. This is in contrast to other classifiers such as SVMs which are inherently binary classifiers [20, 385]. In order to separate multiple classes, these classifiers usually employ a certain multi-class strategy (*e.g.* hierarchical, or in the one-*vs.* -all manner). For these strategies, several classes have to be grouped together, which can make the distribution inside the aggregate group more complex than the distribution of each individual class.
3. *The good generalization ability of classification forests* is important in the medical image analysis field in general and our setting in particular, because of the inherent challenges in collecting and annotating large amounts of data for supervised learning.

17.2 Classification Forests for Segmentation of Brain Tumor Tissues

In this section, we use classification forests as our building block to perform tissue-specific segmentation of brain tumors in multi-channel MR images.[1] We focus on high-grade glioma tumors (often referred to as glioblastoma). These tumors grow rapidly, infiltrate the brain in an irregular way, and often create extensive vasculature networks. The fast growth and the high blood consumption by the active cells (AC) causes the death of the cells on the inside of the tumor, which then form the so-called necrotic core (NC). Therefore, the necrotic core is surrounded by a varyingly thick layer of active cells. Together, the necrotic core and the active cells form the gross tumor (GT). Usually, the tumor itself is surrounded by a varying amount of edema (E), in which there is an increased risk of finding isolated tumor infiltration. Due to the complexity of the bio-mechanical processes involved, high-grade gliomas have extremely irregular shape, heterogeneous appearance and varying location—for an example, please compare the Figs. 17.1 and 17.3. Also, often in the necrotic core there may be tumoral cells in a state of "suspended animation". This makes them particularly resistent to chemo- or radiotherapy, and make the prognosis of glioblastoma one of the most devastating. For further information on high-grade gliomas, please see [18].

In standard clinical routine, the diagnosis and treatment of high-grade gliomas is based on multi-sequence MR images. Each sequence (also referred to as "channel") is a 3D MR scans obtained with different protocols and settings. Multi-channel scans are used since each protocol captures different properties of the tumor. Popular MR modalities used in clinical routine are: T1, T1 after injection of gadolinium contrast agent (T1-gad), T2, and FLAIR. In the case of glioma tumors one can observe that active cells show up as bright regions in T1-gad, while T2 and FLAIR better visualize the edema (cf. Fig. 17.1). Thus, the different channels produce somewhat complementary information. Additionally, in our work, we consider two further channels from diffusion tensor imaging (DTI): the so-called DTI-p and DTI-q maps. Those channels have the potential to provide further discriminative information about the tumor structure as well as its possible reoccurrence [299]. We indicate the input multi-channel MR data by $J = (J_{\text{T1-gad}}, J_{\text{T1}}, J_{\text{T2}}, J_{\text{FLAIR}}, J_{\text{DTI-q}}, J_{\text{DTI-p}})$, where each component is a whole 3D image. Thus J could also be thought of as 4D image data.

Our goal is to segment high-grade gliomas as well as the individual tissue components automatically and reliably. This would e.g. (1) speed-up the interactive delineation of the tissue components through automatic initialization, and (2) allow direct volume measurements. Delineation of tissue components is crucial for radiotherapy and surgery planning and is currently performed manually in a labor intensive fashion. Volume measurements are critical for the evaluation of treatment [400], but are seldom performed since manual tumor segmentation is often impractical in a routine clinical setting.

---

[1]A more detailed description of our work is available in [428].

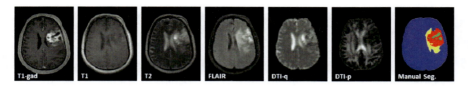

Fig. 17.1 Example of one of 40 patients in our high-grade glioma database, with tissues labeled as active cells (*red*), necrotic core (*green*), and edema (*yellow*). The figure shows a representative axial slice through 3D image volumes

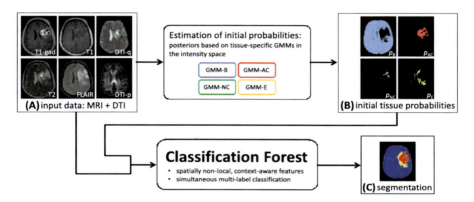

Fig. 17.2 Method overview: Given the input data (**A**), we estimate rough, initial probabilities for each tissue (**B**), based only on the intensity of each voxel. This can be thought of as augmenting the input image channels with further semantically meaningful channels. In a second step, we use both the raw input data (**A**) and the tissue probabilities in (**B**) as input features to a classification forest. Such multi-channel, context-aware forest yields high-quality semantic segmentations (**C**)

While most previous research has focused on the segmentation of gross tumor [137, 245, 399], or tumor and edema [72, 136, 297, 385], we perform the 3D delineation of three relevant tissues types: active cells (AC), necrotic core (NC), and edema (E)—as also do [20, 385]. Distinguishing between volumes of individual tissue types, especially active cells and necrotic core, is an important step for assessment of treatment response. For example, an effective drug might not change the gross tumor volume while still transforming active into necrotic cells (a desirable outcome). To detect this change, the volumes of both of these tissues must be monitored.

17.2.1 Context-Aware Voxel Classification

Our approach is based on classification forests as presented in Chap. 4. Previously, several works have applied discriminative learning techniques to tumor segmentation [20, 72, 137, 322, 385, 399]. Mostly, a learning method using comparably local features is combined with a regularization step, for example by modeling the boundary [167, 294], or by applying a variant of a random field spatial prior (MRF/CRF) [72, 137, 399].

The multi-channel MR input data we are dealing with are illustrated in Fig. 17.1. The schematic overview of our approach is given in Fig. 17.2. We adapt the standard classification forest by providing approximate tissues class probabilities as additional input features. In its effect, this step is similar to the idea of auto-context [375] or entanglement (Chap. 15). However, in auto-context the same classifier is applied repeatedly to compute increasingly refined versions of class probabilities. Here instead, the approximate, initial class probabilities are computed more readily via Gaussian mixture models (GMM) applied to each tissue. The GMM-based modeling has the advantage of faster training, at the cost of a lower test accuracy (*cf.* Fig. 17.5). This step is described in detail in Sect. 17.2.1.1.

One advantage of our auto-context-type approach is that it has an implicit regularizing effect, where the amount of regularization is not hand-designed but learned from data. In turn, this yields high-quality segmentation accuracy with low model complexity (which tends to mitigate overfitting).

Besides the use of initial tissues probabilities, the second important characteristic of our approach is that we use spatially non-local and context-aware features, with their advantages as discussed above. We describe such features in Sect. 17.2.1.2.

As mentioned in the introduction, each voxel is classified into one of four classes $C = \{B, AC, NC, E\}$ for background (B), active cells (AC), necrotic core (NC), and edema (E). Based on the tissue-specific segmentation results, we define the gross tumor as $GT = AC \cup NC$. The MR data $J = (J_{T1\text{-gad}}, J_{T1}, J_{T2}, J_{FLAIR}, J_{DTI\text{-q}}, J_{DTI\text{-p}})$ serve as input data, while the learning is based on expert voxel-wise manual annotations of the training data set.

17.2.1.1 Estimating Initial Tissue Probabilities

As the first step of our approach, we estimate the initial class probabilities for a given patient as posterior probabilities based on the likelihoods obtained by training a set of GMMs on the training data. For each tissue class $c \in C$, we train a single GMM, which captures the likelihood $p(J|c)$ of the multi-dimensional intensity for this class. For a given test data set J, the GMM-based posterior probability for the class c is estimated for each point $\mathbf{p} \in \mathbb{N}^3$ as

$$p^{GMM}(c|\mathbf{p}) = \frac{p(J(\mathbf{p})|c)p_c}{\sum_{c_j} p(J(\mathbf{p})|c_j)p_{c_j}}, \qquad (17.1)$$

with p_c denoting the prior probability for the class c. We can now use the probabilities $p_c^{GMM}(\mathbf{p}) = p^{GMM}(c|\mathbf{p})$ directly as input for the decision forests, in addition to the multi-channel MR data J. So now, the *augmented* set of channels for one patient is

$$C = \left(J_{T1\text{-gad}}, J_{T1}, J_{T2}, J_{FLAIR}, J_{DTI\text{-q}}, J_{DTI\text{-p}}, p^{GMM_{AC}}, p^{GMM_{NC}},\right.$$

$$\left. p^{GMM_E}, p^{GMM_B}\right). \qquad (17.2)$$

For simplicity, we will denote individual channels by C_j. Please note that we can use the GMM-based probabilities for maximum a posteriori classification as $c^* = \arg\max_c p^{\text{GMM}}(c|\mathbf{p})$. We will use this as a baseline for comparison in Sect. 17.2.2.

17.2.1.2 Spatial Visual Features

We employ three parametrized families of intensity-based features. These features describe a voxel based on the appearance of its (relatively large) neighborhood, defined over multiple channels.

As usual, given a 3D voxel location $\mathbf{p}$, its feature vector is $\mathbf{v}(\mathbf{p}) = (v_1, \ldots, v_d)$. With slight abuse of notation we denote the component features $v_{\text{params}}^{\text{type}}$ to highlight the associated parameters and feature type. During training, the type and parameter values for each feature are randomly drawn at every node. Also, in our notation C_j is an input channel, while $R_l(\mathbf{p})$ denotes a $\mathbf{p}$-centered and axis aligned 3D box region in C_j with edge lengths $\mathbf{l} = (l_x, l_y, l_z)$. Finally, $\boldsymbol{\delta} \in \mathbb{R}^3$ is an offset vector in 3D.

- **Feature Type 1—Intensity difference**: This feature type measures the difference between the intensity at a *reference* position $\mathbf{p}$ in channel C_{j_1}, and the intensity at a *probe* point $\mathbf{p} + \boldsymbol{\delta}$ in channel C_{j_2}

$$v_{j_1, j_2, \boldsymbol{\delta}}^{\text{probe}}(\mathbf{p}, C) = C_{j_1}(\mathbf{p}) - C_{j_2}(\mathbf{p} + \boldsymbol{\delta}). \tag{17.3}$$

- **Feature Type 2—Mean intensity difference**: This feature type measures the difference between the intensity mean within a box around $\mathbf{p}$ in C_{j_1}, and the intensity in a probe box around the point $\mathbf{p} + \boldsymbol{\delta}$ in the (in general different) channel C_{j_2}

$$v_{j_1, j_2, l_1, l_2, \boldsymbol{\delta}}^{\text{box}}(\mathbf{p}, C) = \frac{1}{|R_{l_1}|} \sum_{\mathbf{p}' \in R_{l_1}(\mathbf{p})} C_{j_1}(\mathbf{p}') - \frac{1}{|R_{l_2}|} \sum_{\mathbf{p}' \in R_{l_2}(\mathbf{p} + \boldsymbol{\delta})} C_{j_2}(\mathbf{p}'). \tag{17.4}$$

- **Feature Type 3—Intensity range along ray**: This feature type captures the intensity range along a 3D line between $\mathbf{p}$ and $\mathbf{p} + \boldsymbol{\delta}$ in one channel. This feature is designed with the intuition that structure changes can yield a large intensity change, *e.g.* NC being dark and AC bright in T1-gad.

$$v_{j, \boldsymbol{\delta}}^{\text{ray}}(\mathbf{p}, C) = \max_{\lambda}\left(C_j(\mathbf{p} + \lambda\boldsymbol{\delta})\right) - \min_{\lambda}\left(C_j(\mathbf{p} + \lambda\boldsymbol{\delta})\right) \quad \text{with } \lambda \in [0, 1]. \tag{17.5}$$

The features above capture both *appearance context* (when channels are raw input intensities) and *semantic context* (when channels are the GMM probabilities of tumor tissues), as defined in Chap. 15.

17.2.2 Evaluation

We evaluate our approach on a set of multi-channel 3D MR data for 40 patients diagnosed with high-grade glioma. All data are acquired prior to treatment on the

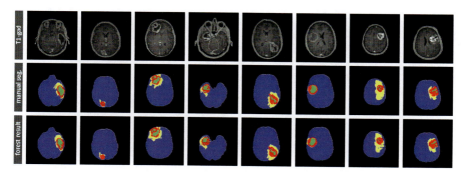

Fig. 17.3 Examples of results on eight (previously unseen) test patients. Results are obtained by a forest with MR, and DTI input, using GMM intermediate tissue probabilities, trained on 30 patients. Qualitatively, the automatic segmentation results (*bottom row*) look very similar to the manual, ground truth segmentations (*middle row*). Tissues are color coded: AC = *red*, NC = *green*, E = *yellow*. The high accuracy of our results is quantitatively confirmed in Fig. 17.4. Only representative axial slices of the multi-channel 3D scans set are shown here

same magnetic resonance scanner. For all 40 patients, a manual segmentation of the three classes of AC, NC, and E is obtained in 3D with the GeoS interactive segmentation tool in [76].

We try to keep the amount of data pre-processing at a minimum. We perform skull stripping of MR channels [350], and for each patient we register all image channels with respect to her T1-gad image, used as reference. We also avoid a full non-linear bias-field correction, and only align the mean intensities of the images within each channel via a global multiplicative factor. All these steps are fully automatic.

The evaluation reports the Dice score between the manual segmentations and the results. Besides the tissue-specific segmentation results, we also evaluate the segmentation quality for the gross tumor (with $GT = AC \cup NC$).

17.2.2.1 Experiments

We perform an extensive series of cross-validation experiments to evaluate our method. For this, the 40 patients are randomly split into non-overlapping training and testing data sets. To investigate the influence of the size of the training set and generalization properties of our method, we perform experiments with the following training/testing sizes: 10/30, 20/20, 30/10. For each of those three ratios, we perform 10 algorithm runs. Each run is applied to a randomly different training/testing data split.

To demonstrate the influence of each component of the method, we also perform tests on forests without GMMs, and compare to the results of GMM only. Finally, in order to quantify the effect of diffusion tensor channels we run all experiments: (i) with conventional MR input only (no DTI), and (ii) with MR and DTI. Overall, this results in 30 random training sets, and 600 tests for each of the six approaches.

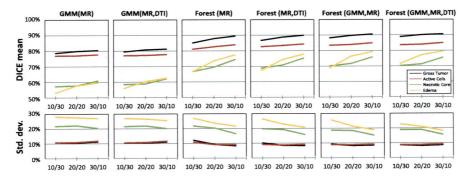

Fig. 17.4 Average mean and standard deviations of DICE scores, for experiments on 10 random folds, with training/test data set sizes of 10/30, 20/20, and 30/10. Going from left to right, the various approaches yield higher mean scores and lower standard deviations. Our approach (rightmost) shows increased robustness to amount of training data, indicating better generalization

The evaluation is performed with all images sampled to isotropic spatial resolution of 2 mm, and forests with $T = 40$ trees of depth $D = 20$. With these settings, the training of one tree takes 10–25 min, and testing 2–3 min, depending on the size of training set and the number of channels. The algorithm and feature design were done on an independent 20/20-fold.

Figure 17.3 shows qualitative results. Quantitative, comparative results for various forest configurations are presented in Fig. 17.4. The highest test accuracy is achieved by the proposed method (Forest(GMM, MR, DTI)), compared to the other variants. In particular, we observe a clear improvement of forests *vs.* GMM only. We can also see a small, but consistent improvement of accuracy when using the additional DTI channels.

Comparison to quantitative results of other approaches is difficult for a number of reasons, most prominently the different input data. To provide some indicative context, we cite results of a recent work from [20]. There, the mean and standard deviation for a leave-one-out cross-validation on 10 glioma patients, based on multichannel MR are as follows: GT: 77 ± 9, AC: 64 ± 13, NC: 45 ± 23, E: 60 ± 16. Our results compare favorably. In fact, for our 30/10-runs we get: GT: 90 ± 9, AC: 85 ± 9, NC: 75 ± 16, E: 80 ± 18, and for the more challenging 10/30-runs (less training data), we get GT: 89 ± 9, AC: 84 ± 9, NC: 70 ± 19, E: 72 ± 23.

Sensitivity to variation of parameters is assessed by varying $T \in \{15, \ldots, 40\}$ and $D \in \{12, \ldots, 20\}$, for the ten 30/10-tests. The results are summarized in Fig. 17.5. We observe robustness with respect to the selection of these values, especially T.

The algorithm presented here for the automatic segmentation of brain tumors has won the MICCAI 2012 BraTS Multimodal Brain Tumor Segmentation Challenge.[2]

---

[2]http://www2.imm.dtu.dk/projects/BRATS2012.

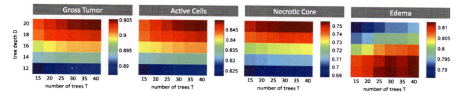

Fig. 17.5 Sensitivity to parameters is tested by varying the number of trees $T = \{15, \ldots, 40\}$ and the tree depth $D = \{12, \ldots, 20\}$. The figure shows mean Dice scores for ten random 30/10-cross-validation runs. We observe robustness with respect to the number of trees

17.3 Classification Forests for Segmentation of MS Lesions

This section presents the application of classification forests to the task of segmentating multiple sclerosis lesions in brain MR scans.[3]

Multiple sclerosis (MS) is a chronic, inflammatory and demyelinating disease that primarily affects the white matter of the central nervous system [55]. Automatic detection and segmentation of MS lesions can help diagnosis and patient follow-up. It offers an attractive alternative to manual segmentation which remains a time-consuming task and suffers from intra- and inter-expert variability. However, MS lesions show a high variability in appearance and shape which makes automatic segmentation a challenging task. In particular, MS lesions lack common intensity and texture characteristics, their shapes are variable and their location within the white matter varies across patients.

Our segmentation problem can be formalized as a binary classification of voxel samples into either background or lesions. Taking advantage of context-aware features in the classification task is key to detect the subtle differences between MS lesions and healthy brain tissue. We exploit a new geometric feature which stems from the assumption that a healthy brain is approximately symmetric with respect to the mid-sagittal plane, and that MS lesions tend to develop asymmetrically. We then show how the forest automatically selects the most discriminative channels for the task of MS lesion segmentation.

17.3.1 Data

The MICCAI 2008 Multiple Sclerosis Segmentation Grand Challenge (MSGC) [358] makes publicly available two datasets through their website: a *public* dataset of labeled MR images which can be used to train a segmentation algorithm; and a *private* dataset of unlabeled cases on which the algorithm should be tested. The public dataset contains 20 cases which are labeled by a medical expert. The private dataset contains 25 cases, each annotated by three experts. For each case, three MR

---

[3]More details can be found in [126].

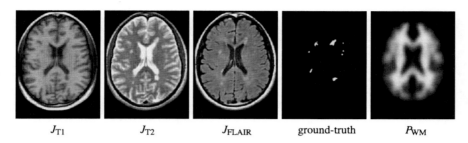

| J_{T1} | J_{T2} | J_{FLAIR} | ground-truth | P_{WM} |

Fig. 17.6 Sample case from the public Multiple Sclerosis Segmentation Grand Challenge dataset. *From left to right*: preprocessed T1-weighted (J_{T1}), T2-weighted (J_{T2}) and FLAIR MR images (J_{FLAIR}), the associated ground truth (GT) and the registered white matter atlas (P_{WM})

volumes are provided: a T1-weighted image, a T2-weighted image and a FLAIR image.

We sub-sample and crop the images so that they all have the same size, $159 \times 207 \times 79$ voxels, and the same resolution, $1 \times 1 \times 2$ mm^3. Background magnetic field inhomogeneities are corrected [300] and inter-subject intensity variations are normalized [308]. The images are then aligned on the mid-sagittal plane [301]. A spatial prior is added by registering the MNI atlas [98] to the anatomical images, each voxel of the atlas providing the probability of belonging to the white matter (P_{WM}), the gray matter (P_{GM}) and the cerebrospinal fluid (P_{CSF}). Please see also Fig. 17.6 for an illustration

As before, we have augmented the set of available input channels with priors for healthy brain tissue types. Both anatomical images and spatial priors will be treated under the unified term *channel*, and denoted $C = (J_{\mathrm{T1}}, J_{\mathrm{T2}}, J_{\mathrm{FLAIR}}, P_{\mathrm{WM}}, P_{\mathrm{GM}}, P_{\mathrm{CSF}})$.

17.3.2 Feature Types

For the segmentation of MS lesions, we compute three types of intensity-based feature. The actual feature types differ from the ones used for brain tumors in Sect. 17.2.1.2 in order to match the specifics of the magnetic resonance acquisition modality. However, it is interesting to note that the feature types for both tasks are similar in nature, and most importantly, both use the idea of spatial context-awareness.

Of the following feature types, the first one is local, measuring only the intensity of a voxel in a single channel, while the other two are non-local and context-aware.

- **Feature type 1—Local intensity**: This local feature type measures the intensity in channel C at the location $\mathbf{p}$, where C is either an MR image, or a prior channel

$$v_j^{\mathrm{loc}}(\mathbf{p}) = C_j(\mathbf{p}). \tag{17.6}$$

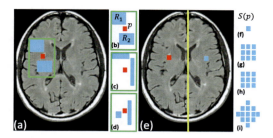

Fig. 17.7 2D illustration of context-aware features. (**a**) A context-rich feature with two regions R_1 and R_2 (*blue boxes*) offset relatively to **p** (*small red square*). (**b–d**) Three examples of randomly sampled features in an extended neighborhood. (**e**) The symmetric feature with respect to the mid-sagittal plane. (**f**) The hard symmetric constraint. (**g–i**) The soft symmetry feature considering neighboring voxels in a sphere of increasing radius

- **Feature type 2—Context-rich**: This non-local feature type compares the intensity at a reference voxel **p** with mean intensities of displaced, probe regions, in possibly different channels. More specifically, it compares the local voxel value in channel C_1 with the mean value in channel C_2 over two 3D boxes R_1 and R_2 within an extended neighborhood. Here, R_i stands for $R_{\mathbf{l}_i}(\mathbf{p} + \boldsymbol{\delta}_i)$, that is, a box with side lengths $\mathbf{l}_i$, centered around a probe point $\mathbf{p} + \boldsymbol{\delta}_i$. The feature type thus reads

$$v^{\text{cont}}_{j_1,j_2,R_1,R_2}(\mathbf{p}) = C_{j_1}(\mathbf{p}) - \frac{1}{|R_1|}\sum_{\mathbf{q}\in R_1} C_{j_2}(\mathbf{q}) - \frac{1}{|R_2|}\sum_{\mathbf{q}\in R_2} C_{j_2}(\mathbf{q}), \qquad (17.7)$$

where C_1 and C_2 can be both, intensity or prior channels. The regions R_1 and R_2 are sampled randomly in a large neighborhood of the voxel **p** (*cf.* Fig. 17.7). The sum over these regions is efficiently computed using integral volume processing [342]. This feature captures both *appearance context* (when channels are raw input intensities) and *semantic context* (when channels are healthy tissue priors), as defined in Chap. 15.

- **Feature type 3—Symmetry**: The second context-aware feature compares the voxel of interest at location **p** with its symmetric counterpart with respect to the mid-sagittal plane, denoted $\mathbf{p}'$

$$v^{\text{sym}}_j(\mathbf{p}) = C_j(\mathbf{p}) - C_j(\mathbf{p}'), \qquad (17.8)$$

where C_j is restricted to be an intensity channel. However, instead of comparing with the exact symmetric ($\mathbf{p}'$) of the voxel, we consider, respectively, its 6, 26 and 32 neighbors in a sphere $\mathcal{S}_{\mathbf{p}'}$ (*cf.* Fig. 17.7), centered on $\mathbf{p}'$. Thus, we obtain a softer version of the symmetric feature which relaxes the hard symmetric constrain and reads

$$v^{\text{sym}}_{C,\mathcal{S}_{\mathbf{p}'}}(\mathbf{p}) = \min_{\mathbf{q}\in\mathcal{S}_{\mathbf{p}'}} \left\{ C(\mathbf{p}) - C(\mathbf{q}) \right\}. \qquad (17.9)$$

Table 17.1 Average results computed by the MSGC on the private dataset and compared to the method presented in [353]. The relative mean improvement over the algorithm from [353] on the private dataset is defined as $RI = (score_{RF} - score_{Souplet})/score_{Souplet}$, as well as the p-value. The independent quantitative evaluation confirms an improvement over [353], with significant improvements in boldface. Our approach achieves a slightly higher true positive rate (TPR) and a comparable false positive rate (FPR), but with much lower volume difference (VD) and surface distance (SD) values

Rater	Metric [%]	Souplet et al. [353]	Class. Forest	RI [%]	p-value
CHB	VD	86.48 ± 104.9	52.94 ± 28.63	-38.7	0.094
	SD	$\mathbf{8.20 \pm 10.89}$	$\mathbf{5.27 \pm 9.54}$	$\mathbf{-35.7}$	$\mathbf{4.2 \cdot 10^{-6}}$
	TPR	57.45 ± 23.22	58.08 ± 20.03	$+1.0$	0.90
	FPR	68.97 ± 19.38	70.01 ± 16.32	$+1.5$	0.70
UNC	VD	55.76 ± 31.81	50.56 ± 41.41	-9.4	0.66
	SD	$\mathbf{7.4 \pm 8.28}$	$\mathbf{5.6 \pm 6.67}$	$\mathbf{-24.3}$	$\mathbf{6.1 \cdot 10^{-3}}$
	TPR	49.34 ± 15.77	51.35 ± 19.98	$+3.9$	0.54
	FPR	76.18 ± 17.07	76.81 ± 11.70	$+0.1$	0.83

17.3.3 Experiments

We train a classification forest on the whole public dataset from the MS Lesion Challenge, *i.e.* 20 labeled cases. Forest parameters are fixed to the following values: tree depth $D = 20$, number of trees $T = 30$, number of random regions $|\mathcal{T}| \simeq 950$ (fixed for all split nodes), lower bound for the information gain $I_{min} = 10^{-5}$, and the posterior threshold $\tau_{posterior} = 0.5$. Considerations that lead to these parameter values are detailed in Sect. 17.3.4.2.

The MSCG website carried out a complementary and independent evaluation of our algorithm on the previously unseen private dataset. Table 17.1 confirms a significant improvement of the results of our algorithm over [353], winner of the MICCAI MS Segmentation Challenge 2008. The presented approach achieves, on average, a slightly higher true positive rate (TPR), which is beneficial, and a comparable false positive rate (FPR), but with lower volume difference (VD) and surface distance (SD) values (see Table 17.1). Pair-sample p-values were computed for the t-test on the private dataset. Results show significant improvement over the method presented in [353] on SD, $p = 4.2 \cdot 10^{-6}$ and $p = 6.1 \cdot 10^{-3}$ for CHB and UNC raters, respectively.

17.3.4 Discussion

17.3.4.1 Interpretation of Segmentation Results

Although segmentation results include most MS lesions delineated by the expert (see Fig. 17.8), we observe that some MS lesions are missing. Missed MS lesions are located in specific locations which are not represented in the training data, *e.g.*

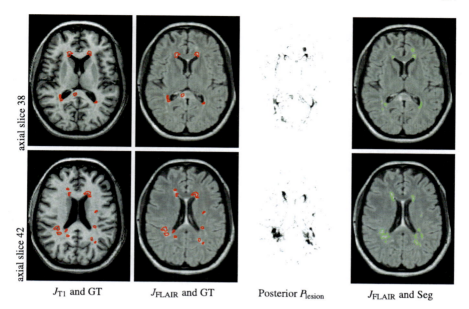

axial slice 38

axial slice 42

| J_{T1} and GT | J_{FLAIR} and GT | Posterior P_{lesion} | J_{FLAIR} and Seg |

Fig. 17.8 Segmenting Case CHB05 from the public MSGC dataset. *From left to right*: preprocessed T1-weighted (J_{T1}), T2-weighted (J_{T2}) and FLAIR MR images (J_{FLAIR}) overlayed with the associated ground truth GT, the posterior map P_{lesion} displayed using an inverted gray scale and the FLAIR sequence overlayed with the segmentation Seg = $(P_{lesion} \geqslant \tau_{posterior})$ with $\tau_{posterior} = 0.5$. Segmentation results show that most of the lesions are detected. Although some lesions are not detected, *e.g.* a lesion in the corpus callosum in slice 38, they appear enhanced in the posterior map. Moreover the segmentations of slices 38 and 42 show peri-ventricular regions, visually very similar to MS lesions, but not delineated in the ground truth

in the corpus callosum (see Fig. 17.8, slice 38). This is a limitation of the supervised approach. In this very case, however, the posterior map highlights the missed lesion in the corpus callosum as belonging to the lesion class with high uncertainty. Low confidence (or high uncertainty) reflects the incorrect spatial prior inferred from an incomplete training set. Indeed, in the training set, there are no examples of MS lesions appearing in the corpus callosum.

On the contrary, the classification forest is able to detect *suspicious regions* with high certainty. *Suspicious regions* are visually very similar to MS lesions and widely represented in the training data, but they were not delineated by the expert, *e.g.* the left frontal lobe lesion again in Fig. 17.8, slice 38. The appearance model and spatial prior implicitly learned from the training data points out that hyper-intense regions in the FLAIR MR sequence which lie in the white matter can be considered as MS lesions with high confidence.

17.3.4.2 Influence of Forest Parameters

This section aims at understanding the effect of the number of trees T and their depth D on the quality of segmentation results.

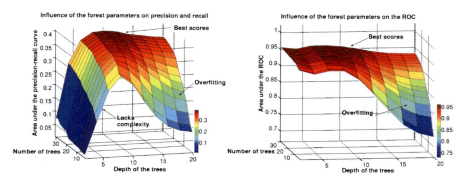

Fig. 17.9 Influence of forest parameters on segmentation results. Both curves were plotted using mean results from a 3-fold cross-validation on the public dataset. *Left*: the figure shows the influence of forest parameters on the area under the precision-recall curve. *Right*: the figure shows the influence of forest parameters on the area under the ROC curve. The ideal classifier would ensure area under the curve to be equal to 1 for both curves. We observe that: (1) for a fixed depth, increasing the number of trees leads to better accuracy; (2) for a fixed number of trees, low depth values lead to underfitting while high values lead to overfitting; (3) overfitting is reduced by increasing the number of trees, thus justifying the use of decision forests

A 3-fold cross-validation on the public dataset is carried out for each parameter combination. Segmentation results are evaluated for each combination using two different metrics: the area under the receiver operating characteristic (ROC) curve and the area under the precision-recall curve. The ROC curve plots the true positive rate (TPR) *vs.* the false positive rate (FPR) scores computed on the test data for every value of $\tau_{\text{posterior}} \in [0, 1]$. The precision-recall curve plots the positive predictive value (PPV) *vs.* TPR scores computed on the test data for every value of $\tau_{\text{posterior}} \in [0, 1]$.[4] The results are reported in Fig. 17.9. This analysis was carried out *a posteriori* using out-of-bag samples.

We observe that: (1) for a fixed depth, increasing the number of trees leads to better generalization; (2) for a fixed number of trees, low depth values lead to underfitting while high depth values lead to overfitting; (3) overfitting is reduced, in general, by increasing the number of trees. This justifies the use of a decision forest.

Forest parameters were selected in a safety-area with respect to under- and overfitting. The safety-area corresponds to a sufficiently flat region in the evolution of the areas under the ROC and precision-recall curves. We also observe that the performance of the classifier stabilizes for sufficiently large forests.

17.3.4.3 Analysis of the Relevance of Feature Types and Channels

Unlike other classifiers, classification forests provide an elegant way of ranking the employed features according to their discriminative power. In this section, we aim at

---

[4]With TP, FP, TN, and FN denoting the number of true/false positive/negatives, respectively, we have $\text{TPR} = \text{TP}/(\text{TP} + \text{FN})$, $\text{FPR} = \text{FP}/(\text{FP} + \text{TN})$, and $\text{PPV} = \text{TP}/(\text{TP} + \text{FP})$.

better understanding which are the most discriminative feature types (local, context-rich or symmetric) and input channels for the task of MS lesion segmentation.

As a first step of the analysis, we compute the statistics of how often the single feature types are selected, without taking into account the depth at which the features are chosen. We observe that local features were selected in 24 % of the nodes, context-rich features were selected in 71 % of all nodes whereas symmetry features were selected in 5 % of the nodes. This highlights the importance of contextual features. They get picked often by the training procedure as they are discriminative, they are associated with large information gain.

In the second step of the analysis, we focus on the depth at which a given feature was selected. We find that for every tree in the forest, the root node always applies a local test on the FLAIR sequence. This means that out of all available features types, with all randomly drawn parameters, v^{loc}_{FLAIR} was found to be the most discriminative. At the second level of the tree, a context-rich feature on spatial priors ($v^{cont}_{WM,GM}$) appears to be the most useful over all trees in the forest. The major effect of this feature is to discard all voxels which do not belong to the white matter.

The optimal decision sequence found while training the forest can thus be thought of as a threshold on the FLAIR MR sequence followed by an intersection with the white matter mask. Interestingly, this sequence of steps perfectly matches the first and second steps of the pipeline proposed by the winner method of the MICCAI 2008 challenge [353]. However, note that in our case, this sequence has been discovered automatically by the forest training process. Furthermore, many additional (and automatically selected) tests are carried out by the lower section of each tree in the forest.

17.4 Conclusion

This chapter has demonstrated the power of applying classification forests to the task of brain lesion delineation in 3D, multi-channel magnetic resonance scans. Specifically, we have focused on the semantic segmentation of high-grade brain tumors and multiple sclerosis lesions. Classification forests allow us to use context-rich features to perform efficient classification of all voxels into all the (healthy or diseased) tissues of interest.

For the segmentation of brain tumors, we augment forests by integrating GMM-based tissue probabilities as features, in conjunction with the original MR images themselves. This allows incorporation of "semantic context" and results in accurate segmentation of the individual sub-regions of glioma tumors (active region, necrosis and edema). This is key *e.g.* in tracking disease progression and assessing a drug's effectiveness.

For the segmentation of multiple sclerosis lesions, prior probabilities of healthy brain tissues are derived from registration with a brain atlas. The use of such priors as (augmented) input features together with the context-rich nature of forests result in one of the most accurate algorithms on the public MICCAI MS challenge dataset.

The use of long-distance voxel comparisons as tests in the forest nodes produces an implicit regularization of the output segmentation, with the amount of regularization learned from data. Therefore, we can avoid hand-designed spatial priors and regularization post-processing, resulting in a system with relatively low model complexity. Finally, detailed analysis of the learned trees and their nodes allows us to understand why forests work, how they compare to previous algorithms, and possibly how to improve their behavior.

Chapter 18
Manifold Forests for Multi-modality Classification of Alzheimer's Disease

K.R. Gray, P. Aljabar, R.A. Heckemann, A. Hammers, and D. Rueckert

Neurodegenerative disorders, such as Alzheimer's disease, are associated with changes in multiple neuroimaging and biological measures. These may provide complementary information for diagnosis and prognosis. This chapter describes a framework within which a supervised version of manifold forests is used to perform multi-modality classification of patients with Alzheimer's disease, patients with mild cognitive impairment, and elderly cognitively normal individuals. In this chapter, manifold forests are used to derive supervised similarity measures, with the aim of generating manifolds that are optimal for the task of clinical group discrimination. Embeddings are thus learned from labeled training data and used to infer the clinical labels of test data mapped into this space. Similarities from multiple (image- and non-image-based) modalities are combined to generate an embedding that simultaneously encodes information from all diverse features. Multi-modality classification is performed using coordinates from this joint embedding. Manifold forests provide consistent pairwise similarity measures for multiple modalities, thus facilitating the combination of different types of feature data.

18.1 Introduction

Alzheimer's disease (AD) is the most common cause of dementia in the elderly, with a worldwide prevalence that is expected to rise from the 26.6 million reported in 2006 to over 100 million by 2050 [47]. There is currently no disease-modifying

K.R. Gray (✉) · P. Aljabar · R.A. Heckemann · A. Hammers · D. Rueckert
Imperial College London, London, UK

P. Aljabar
King's College London, London, UK

R.A. Heckemann · A. Hammers
Fondation Neurodis, Lyon, France

A. Criminisi, J. Shotton (eds.), *Decision Forests for Computer Vision and
Medical Image Analysis*, Advances in Computer Vision and Pattern Recognition,
DOI 10.1007/978-1-4471-4929-3_18, © Springer-Verlag London 2013

therapy, but ongoing clinical trials are focused on the development of new treatments, including those aimed at lowering the risk of developing the disease or delaying its onset and progression [183]. Changes in the brain begin many years before the onset of clinical symptoms, and any disease-modifying therapy would therefore likely be of greatest benefit to asymptomatic individuals at high risk of disease development. It has been estimated that a delay of one year in both disease onset and progression would reduce the number of cases in 2050 by approximately 10 % [47]. The early identification of high-risk individuals is important to allow the recruitment of appropriate participants for clinical trials. If a successful disease-modifying therapy were to be developed, early identification would become even more important to allow targeting of patients for whom the treatment may be most effective.

Changes in multiple neuroimaging and biological measures may provide complementary information for the diagnosis and prognosis of AD. At present, clinical diagnosis is based on assessments of cognition and behavior, which start to decline in the later disease stages [243]. Recently published revisions to the diagnostic criteria incorporate suggestions that biological and neuroimaging biomarkers of structural and molecular changes in the brain may be better suited for the early detection of disease and for monitoring progression [2, 244, 354]. Automated classification of individual patients based on multiple biomarkers could provide valuable support for clinicians, when considered alongside cognitive assessment scores and traditional visual image analysis. This could be particularly useful for monitoring patients with mild cognitive impairment (MCI), who are at increased risk of developing Alzheimer's disease [289].

This chapter describes a framework within which a supervised variant of manifold forests is used to perform multi-modality classification, with the aim of distinguishing between AD patients, MCI patients, and elderly cognitively normal individuals. Manifold forests are used to derive supervised similarity measures, with the aim of generating manifolds that are optimal for the task of clinical group discrimination. Embeddings are thus learned from labeled training data and used to infer the clinical labels of test data mapped into this space. Similarities from multiple modalities are combined to generate an embedding that simultaneously encodes information from all features. Multi-modality classification is then performed using coordinates from this joint embedding. Manifold forests provide consistent pairwise similarity measures for multiple modalities, thus facilitating the combination of different types of feature. This is demonstrated by application to neuroimaging and biological data.

18.2 Background: Biomarkers for Alzheimer's Disease

Significant progress has been made in identifying the structural and molecular changes in the brain that are associated with AD. It is characterized by the abundant presence of two types of neuropathological structure: amyloid plaques and neurofibrillary tangles [86]. Disease development is thought to begin with the accumulation

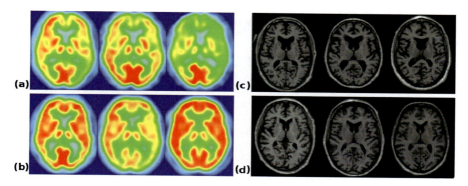

Fig. 18.1 FDG-PET and MR images depicting cerebral glucose metabolism and structure. (**a**) FDG-PET images of AD patients. (**b**) FDG-PET images of healthy individuals. (**c**) MR images of AD patients. (**d**) MR images of healthy individuals

of β-amyloid plaques in the brain, whose presence triggers the formation of tau tangles, ultimately leading to cell death and neuronal loss [329]. Surrogate measures of the levels of β-amyloid and tau in the brain may be obtained from the cerebrospinal fluid (CSF). The functional and structural changes caused by neuronal loss may be assessed using positron emission tomography (PET) and magnetic resonance imaging (MRI), respectively. These three biomarkers are briefly described in the sections that follow, along with the risk factors for disease development.

18.2.1 Cerebrospinal Fluid Measures of Neuropathology

For protection and support, the brain is surrounded by CSF, which also fills the central canal of the spinal cord. CSF may be extracted by lumbar puncture, in which a needle is inserted into the spinal CSF between the lumbar vertebrae. AD and MCI patients typically have reduced CSF β-amyloid and elevated CSF tau in comparison with healthy individuals [151, 256, 379].

18.2.2 Functional Imaging with Positron Emission Tomography

PET imaging with the radiotracer ^{18}F-fluorodeoxyglucose (FDG) can be used to assess brain function in terms of the rate of cerebral glucose metabolism. As illustrated in Fig. 18.1, AD and MCI patients typically have reduced glucose metabolism in temporo-parietal regions of the brain in comparison with healthy individuals [161, 202]. PET imaging with radiotracers for amyloid can be used to assess intracranial β-amyloid deposition. One such tracer is ^{11}C-Pittsburgh Compound B (PiB) [185]. Details about PET image acquisition can be found in [316].

18.2.3 Structural Imaging with Magnetic Resonance Imaging

The progressive structural damage caused by AD can be non-invasively assessed using MRI. As illustrated in Fig. 18.1, AD and MCI patients typically have evidence of cortical atrophy and enlarged ventricles in comparison with healthy individuals. Temporal lobe atrophy is associated with AD, and the hippocampus, amygdala and entorhinal cortex are particularly vulnerable to pathology [40]. Details about MR image acquisition can be found in [221].

18.2.4 Risk Factors for Disease Development

Age is the most significant risk factor for AD [310], but genetic factors also play a role. The ApoE gene is the only one so far shown to be associated with disease development [86]. There are three major alleles of this gene: $\varepsilon 2$, $\varepsilon 3$ and $\varepsilon 4$. The $\varepsilon 4$ allele is associated with an increased risk of disease development, and the $\varepsilon 2$ allele with a reduced risk [71]. More extensive AD pathology is generally observed in carriers of the ApoE $\varepsilon 4$ allele than in non-carriers [313]. Genetics can therefore impact the biological and neuroimaging biomarkers.

18.3 Multi-modality Classification Framework

The biomarker patterns described in the previous section are not specific to AD, and there is increasing interest in using multi-modality imaging and biological data for classification. Two independent studies using kernel combination techniques have reported that classification based on multi-modality data is superior to that based on any individual modality [162, 417]. The manifold forest-based framework described in this chapter provides an alternative multi-modality approach.

18.3.1 Manifold Forests for Multi-modality Classification

A schematic overview of the manifold forest-based multi-modality classification approach is shown in Fig. 18.2. A classification forest is applied to the feature data from each modality independently, to obtain both single-modality classification results for comparison, as well as pairwise similarity measures between subjects. These similarities are used to construct single-modality manifold representations from labeled training data and then to infer the clinical labels of test data mapped into this space. In contrast to the unsupervised manifold forests described in Chap. 7, here classification forests are applied as an intermediate step to derive *supervised* pairwise similarity measures, aiming to generate manifolds that are optimal for the

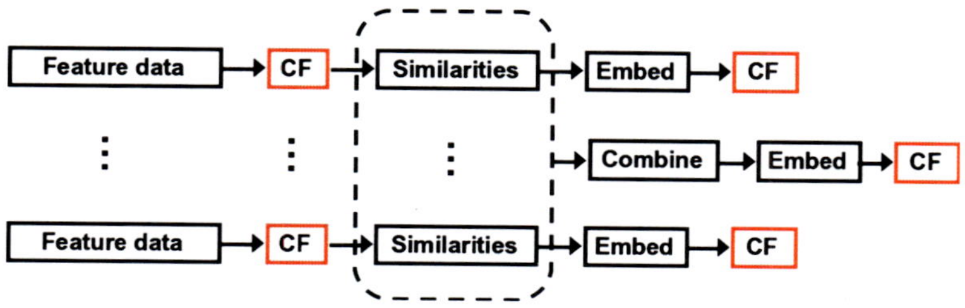

Fig. 18.2 Overview of the multi-modality classification approach. Each classification forest (CF) step provides a classification result whose performance may be reported. Classification forests are used both to derive pairwise similarity measures for each feature set, and also to perform the single- and multi-modality classification experiments

task of clinical group discrimination. Similarities from multiple modalities are then combined to generate an embedding that simultaneously encodes information from all features. Multi-modality disease classification is then performed by applying a classification forest to coordinates from this joint embedding. Our technique provides consistent pairwise similarity measures between patients, for multiple modalities. This facilitates the combination of different types of feature data, including those in which the number of features differ by several orders of magnitude.

18.3.2 Implementation Details

The multi-modality classification framework described in this chapter has been implemented using the R package for random forests. This is a port of Leo Breiman and Adele Cutler's original Fortran code, by Andy Liaw and Matthew Wiener [222].[1] There are two key differences from the decision forest model presented in Chap. 3: the randomness model, and the training objective function.

As described in Breiman's original work [44], forest randomness is injected during training by combining bootstrap aggregation (bagging) [42] with the randomized node optimization method discussed in Sect. 3.3.6. Using bagging, the training set for each individual tree in the classification forest is constructed by sampling N data points at random with replacement from S_0. As a result, approximately one third of the available N data points are not present in the training set of each tree. These are referred to as the "out-of-bag" data of the tree, for which internal test predictions can be made. By aggregating the predictions of the out-of-bag data across all trees, an internal estimate of the generalization error of the forest can be determined.

The Gini index [45] was used as the training objective function to partition the tree nodes, rather than the information gain measure discussed in Sect. 3.3.4. The Gini index, $G_j = 1 - \sum_{c \in C} p_c^2$, measures the likelihood that a data point would

---

[1] http://cran.r-project.org/web/packages/randomForest.

be incorrectly labeled if it were randomly classified according to the distribution of labels within the node. The best possible binary split is the one which maximizes the improvement in the Gini index. The relative importance of the various features for classification may also be estimated using the Gini index. In the context of a neuroimaging application, this is valuable because it allows the assessment of whether the features contributing most to the classifier correspond to regions or structures with a biologically plausible connection to pathology. A measure of the importance of an individual feature may be computed by summing the decreases in the Gini index occurring at all nodes in the forest which are partitioned based on that feature.

Other aspects of the decision forest model presented in Chap. 3 are unchanged. Axis-aligned weak learners were selected, tree predictions were combined using a simple averaging operation, and trees were fully grown without pruning. Two key parameters then remain to be selected: the forest size T, and the amount of randomness, controlled by ρ. Their selection will be described later in Sect. 18.5, along with the results of classification experiments.

In terms of the manifold learning step, there is one key difference from the manifold forests described in Chap. 7. Here, classification forests are applied to derive *supervised* pairwise similarity measures, with the aim of generating manifolds that are optimal for the task of clinical group discrimination. Manifold forests are thus applied to learn an embedding from labeled training data and then to infer the clinical labels of test data mapped into this space. A binary affinity model was used to compute the pairwise similarities between data points.

Classical multidimensional scaling (MDS) [368] was applied for manifold learning, rather than the Laplacian eigenmaps technique employed in Sect. 7.2.5. MDS is commonly used to provide low-dimensional visualizations of similarity relationships, including those derived from decision forests [154]. A detailed description of MDS can be found in [73]. Like Laplacian eigenmaps, MDS derives a coordinate embedding $\mathbf{v}'_i$ for the data points via an eigendecomposition. A goodness-of-fit parameter G, describing the extent to which the selected d' eigenvectors represent the full similarity matrix, can be useful in selecting an appropriate dimensionality for the embedding [231]. To generate an embedding that simultaneously incorporates information from multiple modalities, the similarity matrices derived from the individual modalities are additively combined, and MDS applied to the resulting joint matrix. Multi-modality classification is then performed by applying a classification forest to coordinates from this joint embedding.

18.4 Neuroimaging and Biological Data for Evaluation

The multi-modality classification framework described in the previous section is evaluated using neuroimaging and biological data from 147 participants enrolled in the Alzheimer's Disease Neuroimaging Initiative (ADNI).[2] This is a large, longitudinal, multi-center study whose primary goal has been to test whether serial MRI,

---

[2]http://adni.loni.ucla.edu.

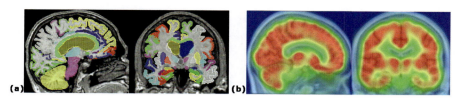

Fig. 18.3 Imaging data. (**a**) Anatomical segmentation overlaid onto the corresponding structural MRI. (**b**) Normalized FDG-PET overlaid onto a standard-space MRI

PET, other biological markers, and clinical and neuropsychological assessments can be combined to measure the progression of MCI and early AD. The participants whose clinical, neuroimaging and biological data are used for evaluation comprise 37 AD patients, 75 MCI patients, and 35 healthy controls (HC).

18.4.1 Neuroimaging features

Region-based features were extracted from the MR images based on automatic whole-brain segmentations into 83 anatomical structures. These were prepared in the native space of each MR image using multi-atlas propagation with enhanced registration (MAPER) [159]. A typical example is shown in Fig. 18.3. Regional volumes were normalized by the total intracranial volume, resulting in 83 volumetric region-based features per image.

Voxel-based features were extracted from the FDG-PET images to allow demonstration that the multi-modality classification framework can readily combine different types of feature data. The FDG-PET images were transformed into a standard template space and smoothed to a common isotropic spatial resolution. Global inter-subject variations in overall radioactivity were accounted for using a reference cluster derived from an independent dataset [406]. A typical example is shown in Fig. 18.3. A brain mask was applied to each normalized FDG-PET image to exclude background, and signal intensities were extracted from each voxel, resulting in 239,304 features per image.

Further details concerning the extraction of neuroimaging features can be found in [142], which describes the application of our multi-modality classification framework to neuroimaging data and in [143], for the Alzheimer's Disease Neuroimaging Initiative (ADNI).

18.4.2 Biological features

The ADNI Biomarker Core provides biological data for the study participants. These data include CSF measures of β-amyloid, tau and phosphorylated tau, as well as ApoE genotype information determined from a blood sample. Details of the

Table 18.1 Single-modality classification results based on the application of a classification forest to the original feature data. Balanced accuracies for each modality are expressed as mean (standard error)

	AD versus HC	MCI versus HC
CSF	76.8 (1.3)	63.8 (1.4)
MRI	81.8 (1.3)	68.9 (1.3)
FDG-PET	86.0 (1.2)	66.9 (1.3)
ApoE genotype	72.7 (1.3)	60.7 (0.9)

biofluid collection and processing are provided in [372]. The genetic feature data for each participant consist of a single categorical variable describing their ApoE genotype. This categorical genetic feature takes one of five possible values: $(\varepsilon 3, \varepsilon 3)$, $(\varepsilon 3, \varepsilon 4)$, $(\varepsilon 4, \varepsilon 4)$, $(\varepsilon 2, \varepsilon 3)$, $(\varepsilon 2, \varepsilon 4)$.

18.5 Classification Experiments and Results

Classification performance is assessed between two clinically relevant pairs of diagnostic groups: AD patients versus HC, and MCI patients versus HC. Robust estimates of classifier performance are obtained using a repeated random sampling approach. The mean balanced accuracies are evaluated over 100 runs in which 75 % of the data are randomly selected for training, with the remaining 25 % used as test data. The balanced accuracy treats both diagnostic groups with equal importance, and is computed as the average of the sensitivity and specificity. Sensitivity measures the proportion of correctly identified patients, and specificity measures the proportion of correctly identified controls.

Since the diagnostic groups are not of equal sizes, a stratified repeated random sampling method is employed in which the training and test sets are selected such that they contain examples from the two diagnostic groups in approximately equal proportions to the full dataset. This produces results with a lower variance than regular cross-validation [187].

As described in Sect. 18.3.2, the forest size T and amount of randomness, controlled by ρ, must be selected before performing classification experiments. Stable estimates of the out-of-bag classification error are consistently observed for $T \gtrsim 1,000$, and we therefore use $T = 5,000$ for all experiments in the following three sections. The value of ρ is observed to have little consistent effect on the out-of-bag classification error estimate, and we therefore use $\rho = \sqrt{d}$ for all experiments in the following three sections, following the recommendation of [222].

18.5.1 Single-Modality Classification Results

A classification forest is first applied to each set of feature data independently, and the single-modality classification results obtained are presented in Table 18.1.

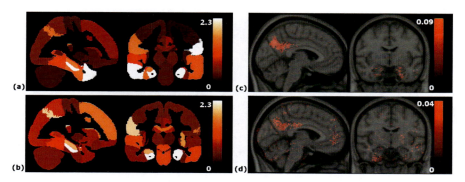

Fig. 18.4 Feature importance for distinguishing between clinical groups. (**a**) AD versus HC based on MRI. (**b**) MCI versus HC based on MRI. (**c**) AD versus HC based on FDG-PET. (**d**) MCI versus HC based on FDG-PET

Estimates of the relative importance of the high-dimensional neuroimaging features for classification are illustrated in Fig. 18.4 for both clinical group pairs. The most important features for discriminating between clinical groups correspond with those known to be visibly affected in AD on both FDG-PET and structural MR imaging [150, 284]. Important features for distinguishing between AD patients and HC are localized to affected areas, with the more challenging distinction between MCI patients and HC requiring features spread across a larger part of the brain.

18.5.2 Single-Modality Similarity-Based Classification Results

The *supervised* classification forests described in the previous section are also used to derive pairwise similarity measures for each of the four modalities, as described for the unsupervised case in Chap. 7. Examples of the resulting similarity matrices are shown in Fig. 18.5.

MDS is applied to each similarity matrix to generate a low-dimensional coordinate embedding for each modality. As described in Sect. 18.3.2, a goodness-of-fit parameter G, describing the extent to which the selected eigenvectors represent the full similarity matrix, is used to determine an appropriate dimensionality for the resulting embeddings. To reduce noise, while preserving similarity relationships, we use $G = 90$ % to determine the dimensionality of all embeddings. A classification forest is then applied to the embedded feature data from each of the four modalities independently. The single-modality classification results obtained are presented in Table 18.2.

No consistent differences are observed between the balanced accuracies based on the embedded feature data shown in Table 18.2, and those based on the original feature data shown in Table 18.1. This lack of difference in performance is expected, since a classification forest is already a non-linear classifier.

Table 18.2 Single-modality classification results based on the application of a classification forest to the embedded feature data. Balanced accuracies for each modality are expressed as mean (standard error)

	AD versus HC	MCI versus HC
CSF	76.3 (1.3)	61.7 (1.3)
MRI	82.1 (1.4)	69.1 (1.4)
FDG-PET	86.5 (1.2)	60.2 (1.2)
ApoE genotype	72.7 (1.3)	60.7 (0.9)

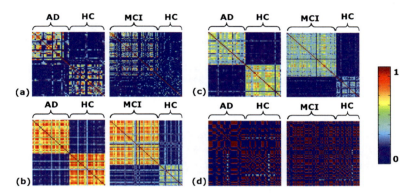

Fig. 18.5 Similarity matrices for each of the four modalities for AD patients versus HC, and MCI patients versus controls. For each modality, the matrices are symmetric, and each entry represents the similarity between a pair of subjects based on the input feature data. (**a**) CSF. (**b**) FDG-PET. (**c**) MRI. (**d**) ApoE genotype

18.5.3 Multi-modality Similarity-Based Classification Results

The supervised similarity measures derived from the individual modalities, as described in the previous section, are additively combined to generate similarities that simultaneously encode information from all features. The combination of four very different types of data is facilitated by the use of classification forests, which provide consistent pairwise similarity measures for multiple modalities. MDS is applied to the joint similarity matrix, and a goodness-of-fit value of $G = 90\%$ is again used to determine an appropriate dimensionality for the combined embedding. A classification forest is then applied to the embedded feature data, and the multi-modality classification results obtained are presented in Table 18.3. Classification based on the joint embedding constructed using information from *all* four modalities outperforms classification based on any individual modality for both experiments.

Although classification performance is commonly reported in terms of accuracy, it is reported here in terms of the *balanced* accuracy because this provides a more meaningful performance metric for diagnostic groups of unequal sizes. In terms of accuracy, 89 % classification is achieved between AD patients and HC, and 75 % between MCI patients and HC. These results are comparable with the 92 % and 93 % accuracies reported between AD patients and HC in [162] and [417], respectively, as well as the 76 % accuracy reported between MCI patients and HC in [417].

Table 18.3 Multi-modality classification results based on the application of a classification forest to the jointly embedded feature data. Balanced accuracies are expressed as mean (standard error)

	AD versus HC	MCI versus HC
CSF, MRI, FDG-PET, ApoE genotype	89.0 (1.2)	72.7 (0.8)

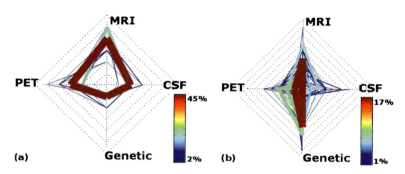

Fig. 18.6 Cobweb plots showing the distribution of parameters selected for classification. (**a**) AD patients versus HC. (**b**) MCI patients versus HC. The four spokes of each plot represent the four modalities, and each colored line connecting the four spokes represents a set of parameter values. The color and weight of each line represents the percentage of runs in which the associated parameter set is selected

The joint similarity matrix W is defined as a linear combination of the similarity matrices from each of the four modalities W_i. Each modality is assigned a weighting factor α_i, such that $W = \sum_{i=1}^{4} \alpha_i W_i$, where $\sum_{i=1}^{4} \alpha_i = 1$. To ensure the best combination of the four modalities for classification, the α_i parameters are optimized as part of the training process. This is achieved by performing a grid-search within the training data, and selecting the set of parameters resulting in the highest cross-validated accuracy. The classifier is then trained using this set of parameters, before having its performance assessed on the test data.

For both classification experiments, the distribution of parameters selected over the 100 runs is illustrated in Fig. 18.6. These visualizations provide interesting insights into the relationships among the different modalities. For example, when distinguishing between AD patients and HC, it appears that FDG-PET and MR imaging features provide the most complementary information. In this case, genetic information appears to be less useful, in comparison. However, when distinguishing between MCI patients and HC genetic information appears to have a relatively higher importance.

18.6 Conclusions

This chapter has described a framework within which manifold forests are used to perform multi-modality classification of AD patients, MCI patients, and elderly cognitively normal individuals. The approach has been evaluated using neuroimaging and biological data from a large multi-center study, including FDG-PET and MR imaging data, CSF biomarker measures, and ApoE genotype information.

Classification based on multiple modalities is shown to out-perform that based on any individual modality. This supports suggestions that there is some complementary information between the modalities which can be exploited to produce a more powerful combined biomarker for AD [201, 394]. The results are comparable with other state-of-the-art multi-modality classification methods such as multi-kernel learning. Manifold forests provide a fast and flexible alternative approach, which facilitates the combination of different types of image- and non-image-based feature. Since classification forests extend naturally to multi-class problems, the framework described in this chapter could be used for other applications, such as differential diagnosis.

Chapter 19
Entanglement and Differentiable Information Gain Maximization

A. Montillo, J. Tu, J. Shotton, J. Winn, J.E. Iglesias, D.N. Metaxas, and A. Criminisi

Decision forests can be thought of as a flexible optimization toolbox with many avenues to alter or recombine the underlying architectural components and improve recognition accuracy and efficiency. In this chapter, we present two fundamental approaches for re-architecting decision forests that yield higher prediction accuracy and shortened decision time.

The first is entanglement, *i.e.* using the learned tree structure and intermediate probabilities computed in nodes closer to the root to affect the training of other nodes deeper in the trees. Unlike more conventional classifiers which assume that all data points (even those neighboring in space or time) are IID, the entanglement approach learns semantic correlation in non IID data. To demonstrate, we build an entangled decision forest (EDF) that exploits spatial correlation in human anatomy by simultaneously labeling voxels in computed tomography (CT) scans into 12 anatomical structures.

The second contribution is the formulation of information gain as a function that is differentiable with respect to the parameters of the split node weak learner. This provides increased confidence and accuracy of maximum margin boundary localization and reduces classification time by using a few, shallow trees. We further extend the method to incorporate training label confidence, when available, into the information gain maximization. Due to bagging and random feature subset selection, we can retain decision forest virtues such as resiliency to overfitting. To demon-

A. Montillo (✉) · J. Tu
General Electric Global Research, Niskayuna, NY 12309, USA

J. Shotton · J. Winn · A. Criminisi
Microsoft Research Ltd, Cambridge, UK

J.E. Iglesias
Massachusetts General Hospital, Harvard Medical School, Boston, MA, USA

D.N. Metaxas
Rutgers, Piscataway, NJ, USA

A. Criminisi, J. Shotton (eds.), *Decision Forests for Computer Vision and Medical Image Analysis*, Advances in Computer Vision and Pattern Recognition, DOI 10.1007/978-1-4471-4929-3_19, © Springer-Verlag London 2013

strate, we build a gradient ascent decision forest (GADF) that tracks visual objects in videos. For both approaches, superior accuracy and computational efficiency is shown in quantitative comparisons with state of the art algorithms.

19.1 Introduction

As discussed in Part I of this book, decision forests are a flexible framework for addressing diverse tasks, with many avenues to alter or recombine the underlying architectural components to improve accuracy and efficiency. In this chapter, we present two fundamental approaches for re-designing the decision forest. These lead to improved prediction accuracy, increased confidence and accuracy of maximum margin boundary localization, and reduced decision time and memory requirements for real world applications including semantic segmentation of 3D medical images and tracking objects in video.

19.2 Entangled Decision Forests

Our first approach, a re-architecting of decision forests, is the *entanglement* or sharing of information between the nodes in a decision forest. In entangled decision forests, the result of the binary tests applied at each tree node depends on the results of tests applied earlier during forest growth. This concept was first presented in [252] and later refined with context selectivity [250]. This chapter presents a more general exposition than reported previously, enabling the most broad interpretation and application.

Entanglement is *the use of the learned tree structure and intermediate probabilities associated with nodes in the higher levels of a tree to affect training of split nodes in deeper levels of the forest.* In its simplest incarnation one may think of entanglement as using the class posteriors of previously trained nodes as input feature into the training of subsequent nodes in the same tree.

A traditional assumption of many classifiers is that all data points (*e.g.* pixels in an image) are independent and identically distributed (IID). However, in many applications, this assumption is incorrect; many data points are in fact highly correlated and thus non IID. Entanglement automatically learns the semantic structural pattern of this correlation and encodes it in the features chosen during decision tree training. In practice, this correlation tends to occur over time, space or both. For example, in 3D medical image segmentation, human anatomy defines a canonical 3D configuration (correlation) over 3D space. In other cases, such as 4D medical scans, the correlation can be in both space and time (the fourth dimension). In entanglement, a tree node, j, at level, ℓ, in the forest is constructed by designing *entanglement* features that exploit the uncertain partial contextual information learned (or at test time, inferred) in a correlation neighborhood by the previous $\ell - 1$ levels of the forest (already trained). We call a forest that uses such features an entangled decision forest (EDF).

As an additional contribution, we randomly sample feature types and parameters from learned, non-uniform *proposal distributions* rather than from a uniform distribution used (implicitly) in previous decision forest research [5, 44, 77, 128, 212, 341, 411]. With this modification in place, the random draws from the proposal distribution select, with greater probability, the feature types and parameters that tend to be relevant for classification. As we will demonstrate, this allows for higher accuracy for the same number of features evaluated during training. Entanglement and learned proposal distributions allow faster training, and faster, more accurate prediction.

To illustrate entanglement, we discuss an example application where we wish to automatically segment a 3D Computed Tomography (CT) scan into its anatomical components such as the aorta, pelvis, and the lungs. We cast this task as a voxel classification problem which we solve via an EDF. In this case entanglement allows the class posteriors of voxels reaching nodes deep in the tree to depend directly from the intermediate posteriors attained higher up in the same tree. This improves accuracy and captures long-range *semantic* context. Previously, segmentation constraints in the form of semantic (*e.g.* anatomical) context have been applied, but these have required either a separate random field [342] or multi-pass processing [341, 375]; EDFs achieve this in one pass with no additional methods.

19.2.1 Entanglement Feature Design

We assume we are given a set, $S = \{(\mathbf{v}, c)\}$, of voxels, $\mathbf{v} = (i, \mathbf{p})$, each consisting of its image intensity, i, (a measure of tissue density in the case of CT) voxel location $\mathbf{p}$ and ground truth label, c. This set is formed from the collection of voxels from a group of training CT scans. Our goal is to infer the probability of each label for each voxel of unseen test scans.

Following the work in [78] we construct two types of long-range, context-aware feature. The first type captures "appearance context", the latter are entangled and capture "semantic context". See also Chap. 15. Details are explained next.

19.2.1.1 Appearance Features

Using the intensity image, J, we construct intensity features for each voxel $\mathbf{v}$ that are spatially defined by (1) their position, $\mathbf{p}$, centered on the voxel to be labeled (Fig. 19.1a), and (2) one or two cuboidal probe regions, $\mathbf{F}_1$ and $\mathbf{F}_2$, offset by displacement vectors, Δ_1 and Δ_2, which can be up to 200 mm in each dimension (x, y, z). A probe region, $\mathbf{F}(\mathbf{q}; \mathbf{w})$, is the set of voxels within the region centered at $\mathbf{q}$ with side lengths, $\mathbf{w}$. We construct two variants of intensity features. The first variant consists of the mean CT intensity at a probed region, $\mathbf{F}_1$ (Fig. 19.1a, left), while the second consists of the difference in the mean intensity of regions, $\mathbf{F}_1$ and

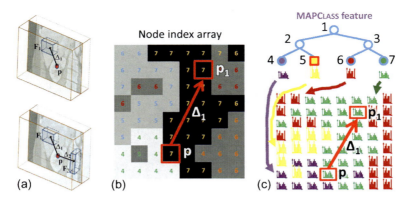

Fig. 19.1 Intensity and entanglement features. (**a**) Intensity features measure image information from regions offset from the reference voxel at **p**. (**b**) MAPCLASS feature retrieves the label that the classifier currently predicts at location $\mathbf{p}_1$ offset from **p**. We maintain a node index array which associates with each voxel the current tree node ID (represented by the number in each voxel). (**c**, *top*) The *array* allows to determine the current label posterior in the tree for the voxel at location $\mathbf{p}_1$. (**c**, *bottom*) Conceptually, the tree induces a vector image of class posteriors which we use when designing MAPCLASS and TOPNCLASSES features

$\mathbf{F}_2$ (Fig. 19.1a, right). Then split functions are defined from these as follows:

$$h_{\text{INTENSITY}}(\mathbf{v}, \boldsymbol{\theta}_j) = \left[\bar{J}\big(\mathbf{F}_1(\mathbf{p} + \boldsymbol{\Delta}_1)\big) > \tau\right], \tag{19.1}$$

$$h_{\text{INTENSITYDIFF}}(\mathbf{v}, \boldsymbol{\theta}_j) = \left[\bar{J}\big(\mathbf{F}_1(\mathbf{p} + \boldsymbol{\Delta}_1)\big) - \bar{J}\big(\mathbf{F}_2(\mathbf{p} + \boldsymbol{\Delta}_2)\big) > \tau\right]. \tag{19.2}$$

During training, each type of split function is characterized for node j by the split parameters $\boldsymbol{\theta}_j = (\boldsymbol{\phi}, \tau)$. For $h_{\text{INTENSITY}}$, $\boldsymbol{\phi}$ includes the parameters of $\mathbf{F}_1$: the offset $\boldsymbol{\Delta}_1$, the size $\mathbf{w}_1$ and an intensity threshold τ. For $h_{\text{INTENSITYDIFF}}$, $\boldsymbol{\phi}$ includes the additional parameters $\boldsymbol{\Delta}_2$ and $\mathbf{w}_2$. These parameters are sampled randomly during training for each split node. Once training has finished, the maximum information gain node test along with its optimal features are frozen and stored within the node for later use during testing.

19.2.1.2 Semantic Context Entanglement Features

We now describe an instance of our entanglement contribution. During testing on novel images, we exploit the confident voxel label predictions (peaked distributions) that can be found using early levels of the forest to aid the labeling of nearby voxels. This provides semantic context similar to auto-context [341, 375], but does so within a single forest. We define four types of long-range entanglement feature to help train the node currently being grown using knowledge learned in already trained nodes of the forest. Two features (MAPCLASS and TOPNCLASSES) are based on the posterior class distribution of the nodes corresponding to probed voxels, and two (NODEDESCENDANT and ANCESTORNODEPAIR) are based on the location of the nodes within the trees.

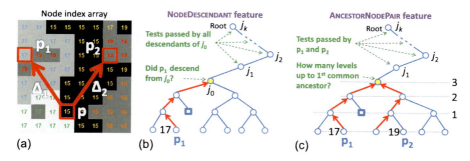

Fig. 19.2 Further entanglement features. (**a**) Node index array associates voxels with intensity and tree node indices (same format as Fig. 19.1b but for a deeper tree level). (**b**) NODEDESCENDANT feature tests whether probe voxel at $\mathbf{p}_1$ descends from a node (j_0 in this case). (**c**) ANCESTORN-ODEPAIR feature tests whether the nodes of voxels $\mathbf{p}_1$ and $\mathbf{p}_2$ have a common ancestor $< \tau$ levels away

MAPCLASS Entanglement Features   As the name suggests, this type of feature uses the maximum a posteriori label of a neighboring voxel at $\mathbf{p}_1$ to reduce uncertainty about the label at $\mathbf{p}$ (Fig. 19.1b). When such semantic context is helpful to classify the voxel at $\mathbf{p}$, the feature yields high information gain and may become the winning feature for the node during tree growth. The MAPCLASS split function tests whether the MAP class in the posterior of a probed voxel $\mathbf{p}_1 = \mathbf{p} + \boldsymbol{\Delta}_1$ is equal to a particular class $c^\star$:

$$h_{\text{MAPCLASS}}(\mathbf{v}, \boldsymbol{\theta}_j) = \left[\arg \max_c p\big(c; j(\mathbf{p}_1)\big) = c^\star \right]. \tag{19.3}$$

The parameter $\boldsymbol{\theta}_j$ includes $\boldsymbol{\phi} = (\boldsymbol{\Delta}_1, c^\star)$ while $p(c; j(\mathbf{p}_1))$ is the posterior class distribution of the node of $\mathbf{p}_1$ denoted $j(\mathbf{p}_1)$. This posterior can be retrieved from the tree because (1) we train and test voxels in breadth-first fashion, and (2) we maintain an association between voxels and the tree node ID at which they reside while moving down the tree. This association is a node index array (Fig. 19.1b).

TopNCLASSES Entanglement Features   Similarly we define features, called TopNCLASSES, where $N \in \{2, 3, 4\}$, that generalize the MAPCLASS feature. A TopNCLASSES feature tests whether a particular class $c^\star$ is in the top N classes of the posterior class distribution of the probe voxel at $\mathbf{p}_1 = \mathbf{p} + \boldsymbol{\Delta}_1$. The split function, with parameter $\boldsymbol{\theta}_j$ including $\boldsymbol{\phi} = (\boldsymbol{\Delta}_1, N, c^\star)$ is defined as

$$h_{\text{TopNCLASSES}}(\mathbf{v}, \boldsymbol{\theta}_j) = \left[c^\star \in \text{top } N \text{ classes of } p\big(c; j(\mathbf{p}_1)\big) \right]. \tag{19.4}$$

NODEDESCENDANT Entanglement Features   This type of feature tests whether a region near voxel $\mathbf{p}$ has a particular appearance. The neighboring region is centered at voxel $\mathbf{p}_1$ (Fig. 19.2a, b). The split test is whether the node currently corresponding to $\mathbf{p}_1$ descends from a particular tree node, j_0. If it does, then we know $\mathbf{p}_1$ has satisfied the appearance tests at nodes ($j_1 \ldots j_k$) above j_0 in the tree in a particular way to arrive at j_0.

ANCESTORNODEPAIR **Entanglement Features**   This type of feature tests
whether two regions near voxel **p** have passed similar appearance and semantic
tests. The neighboring regions are centered at voxels $\mathbf{p}_1$ and $\mathbf{p}_2$ (Fig. 19.2a). The
split test is whether the nodes currently corresponding to $\mathbf{p}_1$ and $\mathbf{p}_2$ have their first
common ancestor $< \tau$ tree levels above the current level (Fig. 19.2c). The threshold controls the required degree of similarity: the lower τ, the greater the required
appearance and context similarity needed to pass the test, because the lower τ, the
larger the number of tests with identical outcomes above the common ancestor.

19.2.2 Guiding Feature Selection by Learned Proposal Distributions

This section describes the use of learned proposal distributions. These distributions
aim to match the feature types and their parameters proposed at each tree node
during training to those that have proven to be most useful for classification in a
previous training run. The decision forest still chooses the winning feature, but each
node chooses from features sets that are likely to be useful based on prior experience. Specifically, we train an initial decision forest, F_{temp}, on our training data,
using a uniform proposal distribution. We then record (as histograms) the distribution of accepted feature parameters and feature types across all tree nodes in the
forest. F_{temp} is then discarded, and we then use parameter distributions as the proposal distributions in a subsequent training of the next decision forest. While this
requires additional training, it imposes no time penalty for prediction. This process
could be repeated, though in practice even just one iteration has proven sufficient
for a substantial improvement in accuracy (*e.g.* $> 5\%$).

The learned displacements tends to be Gaussian distributed and centered on the
reference voxel (Fig. 19.3 top row). Acceptance distributions of the remaining parameters, such as the thresholds τ or the choice of the MAPCLASS class $c^{\star}$, also
have non-uniform distributions (Fig. 19.3 bottom row). Similarly, the distribution
of feature types for each tree level is learned. Drawing feature types from this distribution can also improve classifier accuracy. Figure 19.4a shows how the ratio of
feature types varies with tree depth. As the tree is grown, entanglement features increasingly dominate the scene over the more conventional intensity features. The
entangled features used by the nodes in the lower part of the tree exploit semantic
context and neighborhood consistency inferred from appearance features of earlier
levels.

19.2.3 Results

We evaluate our EDF model on the task of segmenting a database of 250 varying
field of view CT scans. Each voxel in each CT scans needs be assigned one of 12
class labels from the following set of anatomical structures of interest {heart, liver,

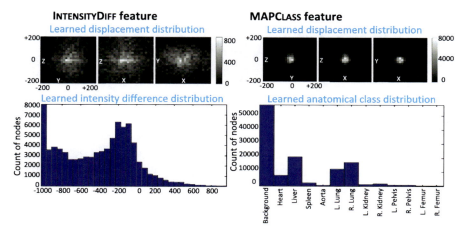

Fig. 19.3 Learned parameter distributions are clearly non-uniform. (*Left*) Learned displacement and anatomical class distributions for MAPCLASS feature. (*Right*) Displacement and intensity difference distributions for INTENSITYDIFF feature

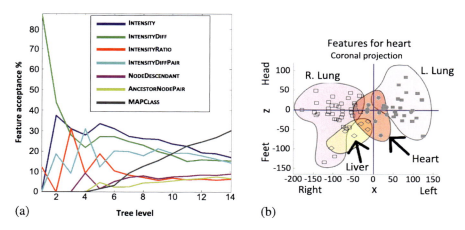

Fig. 19.4 An EDF reveals how and what it has learned. (**a**) Learned relative proportion of feature types chosen at each level of forest growth. (**b**) Location and organ class of the top 50 features used to identify heart voxels. The hand-drawn regions here group these locations for different MAPCLASS classes $c^\star$

spleen, aorta, l./r. lung, l./r. femur, l./r. pelvis, l./r. kidney} or the background class. This database has been designed to include wide variations in patient health status, field of view and scan protocol. We randomly selected 200 volumes for training and 50 for testing.

Qualitative Results   The EDF achieves a visually accurate segmentation of organs throughout the 50 test volumes. Example segmentations are shown in Fig. 19.5a where the first column is the ground truth segmentation, and the sec-

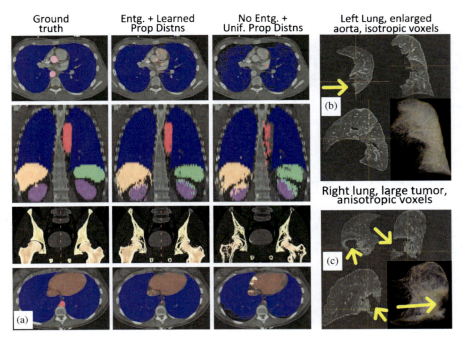

Ground truth | Entg. + Learned Prop Distns | No Entg. + Unif. Prop Distns | Left Lung, enlarged aorta, isotropic voxels

(b)

Right lung, large tumor, anisotropic voxels

(c)

(a)

Fig. 19.5 Qualitative segmentation results. (**a**) The use of entanglement and learned proposal distributions (*column 2*) improves accuracy compared to not using them (*column 3*). The *rows* show four different subjects. (**b**) EDF segmented left lung distorted by enlarged aorta; volume rendering in *lower right*. (**c**) EDF accurately segments a right lung despite a severe tumor

ond column is the EDF result. We see good agreement for the lungs (blue), liver (orange), spleen (green), kidneys (purple), femur (tan), and heart (dark brown). Column 3 shows the result using our decision forest without entanglement and with uniform proposal distributions. Entanglement with proposal distributions noticeably improves the lungs, aorta (red), kidneys, spleen, femur, and heart.

The algorithm handles many complexities commonly found in the clinic. For example, our algorithm correctly segmented the lung despite the case of a severely enlarged aorta (Fig. 19.5b) and another with a tumor (Fig. 19.5c).

Quantitative Impact of Each Contribution   For a quantitative analysis we measured segmentation accuracy across all 50 test scans using the average class Jaccard similarity coefficient [100]. The metric is the ratio of the intersection size (ground truth and predicted labels) divided by the size of their union. While EDF achieves > 97 % average voxel accuracy throughout our database, we use the Jaccard metric because we feel it is a more reliable metric of segmentation accuracy.

To understand the impact of using the acceptance distributions as proposal distributions (Sect. 19.2.2), we trained the decision forest in four different ways: (1) using uniform feature type and uniform feature parameter distributions for baseline performance (light blue curve, Fig. 19.6a), (2) using learned feature type distribution

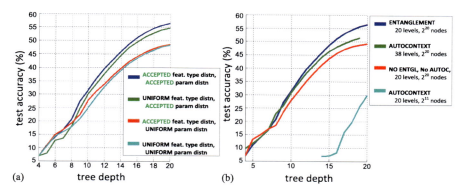

Fig. 19.6 Quantitative impact of each contribution. (**a**) Learning proposal distributions for both feature types and feature parameters increases accuracy. (**b**) Entanglement (*dark blue*) provides greater accuracy and prediction speed than auto-context (*green*). Note: the *green curve* should properly be plotted at depths 20–38, but for ease of comparison we plot it at depths 1–19

with uniform feature parameter distributions (red), (3) using uniform feature type distributions with learned feature parameter distributions (green), (4) using learned feature type and learned parameters distributions (dark blue). Learning only the feature type distribution yields a negligible improvement to baseline (red *vs.* light blue). Learning feature parameter distribution boosts accuracy significantly (green *vs.* red). Learning both yields the best performance boosting accuracy over baseline by 8 %.

We compared our method to auto-context [341, 375] by conducting four experiments. First, we trained our decision forest 20 levels deep without entanglement and without auto-context for a baseline (red, Fig. 19.6b). Second, we trained a two-round, auto-context decision forest (ADF) using 10 levels in each round (light blue). Third, we trained another ADF, but this time with an equal *modeling capacity* to the baseline by using two rounds with 19 levels each (green). Fourth, we trained the proposed EDF method as a single, 20 level deep forest using entanglement (dark blue curve). We find considerably better accuracy using the EDF method (dark blue *vs.* green). In addition to beating the performance of ADF, it reduces the prediction time by 47 % since the EDF requires 18 fewer levels (20 *vs.* 38).

Efficiency Considerations   With a parallel implementation, EDF segments volumes ($512 \times 512 \times 424$) in just 12 seconds per volume using an 8 core Xeon 2.4 GHz computer with 16 GB RAM. This speed is equal to or better than state of the art single organ methods [419], yet we segment *multiple* (12) organs simultaneously.

Inspecting the Chosen Features   Figure 19.4b shows how the MAPCLASS feature learns to segment a heart voxel located at the cross-hair. To find the top contributing semantic context features, we express information gain as a sum of the information gain from each class:

$$I(\mathcal{S}, \boldsymbol{\theta}) = \sum_{c \in \mathcal{C}} \left(-p(c|\mathcal{S}) \log p(c|\mathcal{S}) + \sum_{i \in \{L, R\}} \left(\frac{|\mathcal{S}^i|}{|\mathcal{S}|} p\left(c|\mathcal{S}^i\right) \log p\left(c|\mathcal{S}^i\right) \right) \right), \quad (19.5)$$

where $\mathcal{S}$ is the set of voxels being split into partitions $\mathcal{S}^L$ and $\mathcal{S}^R$, and c is the index over classes. We can then readily rank the learned node features based on how much they contributed to classifying the voxels of a given class (*e.g.* heart) by increasing the information gain for that class.

19.3 Differentiable Information Gain Maximization

In Sect. 19.2 we simultaneously increased classification accuracy and reduced decision time using entanglement which propagates knowledge from one part of the forest to another. In this section we achieve a similar result using a complementary approach. This second approach optimizes training by applying gradient ascent to differentiable information gain. Finding the optimum parameters for the split tests has traditionally [302] been achieved via exhaustive discrete search to find those parameters which maximize information gain. For a given computational budget, exhaustive search is limited to a small region of parameter space or a coarse quantization of a wider region.

By making information gain differentiable, we can directly find the optimal data partition for the given input subset and node feature subset. This produces more compact decision trees which in turn reduces classification (test) time and memory requirements. Through the use of random input (bagging) and feature subset selection, decision forest virtues including independent trees and resiliency to overfitting can be retained.

Using non-differentiable information gain, an optimal solution can be found by simulated annealing techniques [158, 260], though this can be computationally impractical in high dimensional feature spaces. Alternative discriminative criteria could be optimized, such as LDA [246], SVM [383], or boosting techniques [374, 413], but these may not provide the optimal data partitions when the data distributions are from many classes.

As discussed in Sect. 3.3, binary tests based on parameterized functionals (such as hyperplanes or conic sections) are stronger learner models than coordinate aligned split functions, and can have greater generalization capabilities. We show below that our differentiable information gain forest both accepts these more powerful split functions and improves their generalization power to approximate the maximum margin decision boundary (see also [80] for a detailed discussion about maximum margin behavior in decision forests). Like [173], we impose a soft split using a sigmoid function; however, we explicitly present the derivation absent in [173], and extend it to include label confidence when training data include label uncertainty. We also incorporate hyperplane and non-linear split tests in the gradient ascent framework.

We call the resulting classifier a gradient ascent decision forest (GADF) and illustrate its power in both synthetic and real-world examples. First, we investigate the impact of the GADF for a synthetic 2D classification task, and demonstrate that gradient ascent reduces classification time, increases prediction accuracy and increases confidence in the estimation of the maximum margin decision boundary, compared to the standard decision forest. Second, we implement a GADF to solve classification problems in several application domains including mass spectrometry, biomechanics, botany, image classification and 1D signal processing. We demonstrate how the GADF approach increases prediction accuracy across this application spectrum. Third, we cast visual object tracking as an iterative classification task and train a gradient ascent classifier to perform object tracking in public PET videos. We show how the approach avoids tracker drift and handles severe occlusions better than state of the art trackers.

19.3.1 Formulating Differentiable Information Gain

Given the labeled dataset $S = \{(\mathbf{v}, c)\}$ of size N, where $\mathbf{v}$ is the feature data of dimension d, and $c = \varsigma(\mathbf{v})$ is the ground truth class label of $\mathbf{v}$ (with $c \in \{1, \ldots, C\}$), the Shannon entropy of the class distribution can be computed as

$$H(S) = -\sum_{c=1}^{C} p(c|S) \log p(c|S), \tag{19.6}$$

where

$$p(c|S) = \frac{\sum_{\mathbf{v}}[\varsigma(\mathbf{v}) - c]}{N} \tag{19.7}$$

defines the data class distribution and $[\cdot]$ is the indicator function.

Given a binary split function (weak learner) $h(\cdot, \cdot)$, we can partition the data into two subsets (see Sect. 3.2.3):

$$S^{\mathrm{L}} = \{S|h = 1\} = \{(\mathbf{v}, c)|\mathbf{v} \in S, h(\mathbf{v}; \boldsymbol{\theta}) = 1\} \tag{19.8}$$

of size N^{L} and

$$S^{\mathrm{R}} = \{S|h = 0\} = \{(\mathbf{v}, c)|\mathbf{v} \in S, \bar{h}(\mathbf{v}; \boldsymbol{\theta}) = 1 - h(\mathbf{v}; \boldsymbol{\theta}) = 1\} \tag{19.9}$$

of size $N^{\mathrm{R}} = N - N^{\mathrm{L}}$. The information gain defines the entropy change before and after the split h is applied:

$$I(S|h) = H(S) - H(S|h), \tag{19.10}$$

where the entropy after partitioning is computed as

$$H(S|h) = \frac{N^{\mathrm{L}}}{N} H(S^h) + \frac{N^{\mathrm{R}}}{N} H(S^{\bar{h}}). \tag{19.11}$$

Information gain is a typical measure for selecting discriminative weak learners in decision tree training as described in Chap. 3. However, the information gain formulation is not differentiable w.r.t. the parameters $\boldsymbol{\theta}$ of h, making analytical optimization problematic.

To make $I(\mathcal{S}|h)$ in (19.10) differentiable w.r.t. the binary test h, we first define the split function h for data point $\mathbf{v}$ as a parameterized functional:

$$h_{\psi}(\mathbf{v}; \boldsymbol{\theta}) = \begin{cases} 0, & \psi(\mathbf{v}; \boldsymbol{\theta}) < 0, \\ 1, & \psi(\mathbf{v}; \boldsymbol{\theta}) \geq 0, \end{cases} \qquad (19.12)$$

where $\psi(\mathbf{v}; \boldsymbol{\theta})$ is the geometric split function of feature space with parameter set $\boldsymbol{\theta}$. The partition occurs at the boundary $\psi(\mathbf{v}; \boldsymbol{\theta}) = 0$.

We then define partition integrals for each class for all data w.r.t. h as follows:

$$U_c^{\mathcal{S}}(h) = \sum_{\mathbf{v}} h(\mathbf{v}; \boldsymbol{\theta})[\varsigma(\mathbf{v}) - c], \quad c \in \{1, \ldots, C\}, \qquad (19.13)$$

$$U^{\mathcal{S}}(h) = \sum_{\mathbf{v}} h(\mathbf{v}; \boldsymbol{\theta}), \qquad (19.14)$$

where $h(\mathbf{v}; \boldsymbol{\theta})$ can be replaced with $\bar{h}(\mathbf{v}; \boldsymbol{\theta}) = 1 - h(\mathbf{v}; \boldsymbol{\theta})$ as needed.

We can then define $N^{\mathrm{L}} = U^{\mathcal{S}}(h)$, $N^{\mathrm{R}} = U^{\mathcal{S}}(\bar{h})$, $N = N^{\mathrm{L}} + N^{\mathrm{R}}$, $p_c(\mathcal{S}^h) = \frac{U_c^{\mathcal{S}}(h)}{U^{\mathcal{S}}(h)}$ and $p_c(\mathcal{S}^{\bar{h}}) = \frac{U_c^{\mathcal{S}}(\bar{h})}{U^{\mathcal{S}}(\bar{h})}$, and the entropy after partition by h is

$$H(\mathcal{S}|h) = -\frac{1}{N}\left(\sum_c U_c^{\mathcal{S}}(h) \log U_c^{\mathcal{S}}(h) - U^{\mathcal{S}}(h) \log U^{\mathcal{S}}(h)\right.$$

$$\left. + \sum_c U_c^{\mathcal{S}}(\bar{h}) \log U_c^{\mathcal{S}}(\bar{h}) - U^{\mathcal{S}}(\bar{h}) \log U^{\mathcal{S}}(\bar{h})\right). \qquad (19.15)$$

Using the chain rule, the derivative of information gain w.r.t. $\boldsymbol{\theta}$ is

$$\frac{\partial I}{\partial \boldsymbol{\theta}} = -\frac{\partial H(\mathcal{S}|h)}{\partial \boldsymbol{\theta}}$$

$$= \frac{1}{N}\left(\sum_c U_c'^{\mathcal{S}}(h)\left(\log U_c^{\mathcal{S}}(h) + 1\right) - U'^{\mathcal{S}}(h)\left(\log U^{\mathcal{S}}(h) + 1\right)\right.$$

$$\left. + \sum_c U_c'^{\mathcal{S}}(\bar{h})\left(\log U_c^{\mathcal{S}}(\bar{h}) + 1\right) - U'^{\mathcal{S}}(\bar{h})\left(\log U^{\mathcal{S}}(\bar{h}) + 1\right)\right), \qquad (19.16)$$

where $U_c'^{\mathcal{S}}(h) = \sum_{\mathbf{v}} \frac{\partial h(\mathbf{v}; \boldsymbol{\theta})}{\partial \boldsymbol{\theta}}[\varsigma(\mathbf{v}) - c], c \in \{1, \ldots, C\}$, and $U'^{\mathcal{S}}(h) = \sum_{\mathbf{v}} \frac{\partial h(\mathbf{v}; \boldsymbol{\theta})}{\partial \boldsymbol{\theta}}$.

Information gain is not differentiable w.r.t. the binary test parameter $\boldsymbol{\theta}$ because $h_{\psi}(\mathbf{v}; \boldsymbol{\theta})$ in (19.12) is not differentiable. To make it differentiable, we approximate the weak learner h by a sigmoid function $h_{\psi}(\mathbf{v}; \boldsymbol{\theta}) = 1/(1 + e^{\frac{-\psi(\mathbf{v};\boldsymbol{\theta})}{\sigma}})$ to get:

$$\frac{\partial h_{\psi}(\mathbf{v}; \boldsymbol{\theta})}{\partial \boldsymbol{\theta}} = \frac{1}{\sigma} h_{\psi}(\mathbf{v}; \boldsymbol{\theta})\left(1 - h_{\psi}(\mathbf{v}; \boldsymbol{\theta})\right)\frac{\partial \psi(\mathbf{v}; \boldsymbol{\theta})}{\partial \boldsymbol{\theta}}. \qquad (19.17)$$

Combining (19.16) and (19.17) allows us to compute the derivative of information gain w.r.t. the binary test function parameter $\boldsymbol{\theta}$ using the chain rule. The split function $\boldsymbol{\psi}(\mathbf{v};\boldsymbol{\theta})$ can be designed according to the purpose of information gain optimization. It is worth noting that the parameter σ defines the fidelity of the binary test, and controls the smoothness of the information gain surface in the decision boundary parametric space. One may apply annealing to σ when doing gradient ascent (*i.e.* letting $\sigma \to 0$) so that the chance that the optimization reaches global maxima can be increased.

Soft Label Decision Forests   If each training data point $\mathbf{v}$ also includes a (training) class label probability measure $q_c(\mathbf{v})$, then we define a confidence score $\gamma(\mathbf{v}) \in [0, 1]$ as a function of the label log-likelihood $l(\mathbf{v}) = \log(\frac{q_c(\mathbf{v})}{1-q_c(\mathbf{v})})$ as follows:

$$\gamma(\mathbf{v}) = \frac{2}{1 + e^{-\frac{\sqrt{|l(\mathbf{v})|}-t_l}{\sigma_l}}}. \tag{19.18}$$

The intuition is that the label is less confident if the class probability ratio is too close to 1 (and thus $\sqrt{|l(\mathbf{v})|}$ approaches zero), and σ_l controls how sensitive the confidence score is to the log-likelihood-ratio score. Such class label probability measures occur naturally in tasks such as video processing. In this case an on-line model learning may be applied per frame. Given the classification model trained on-line using the previous frames, the new observations in the current frame may be labeled with likelihood confidence (soft labels), and become the training data for the on-line model updating for the current frame. In [52], such 'soft label decision forests' are used for on-line tracking in videos where labels are quantized into a histogram and a standard node training procedure is applied.

We provide an analytic solution for the soft label decision forests learning problem. By modeling the label confidence measures based on how much the label likelihood deviates from the decision threshold, we derive a differentiable information gain formulation weighted by the label confidence. Our gradient ascent optimization technique can then be applied to find the optimal data split based on the information gain criteria with respect to the known class labels. Specifically, to optimize the information gain with emphasis on data $\mathbf{v}$ labeled with high confidence, we can simply derive the differentiable information gain by weighting the terms in (19.13) with the confidence measure:

$$U_c^{\mathcal{S}}(h) = \sum_{\mathbf{v}} h(\mathbf{v};\boldsymbol{\theta})\big[\varsigma(\mathbf{v}) - c\big]\gamma(\mathbf{v}), \quad c \in \{1, \ldots, C\}, \tag{19.19}$$

$$U^{\mathcal{S}}(h) = \sum_{\mathbf{v}\in\mathcal{S}} h(\mathbf{v};\boldsymbol{\theta})\gamma(\mathbf{v}). \tag{19.20}$$

19.3.2 Split Function Design and Gradient Ascent Optimization

In training a classification forest, we solve for a decision boundary, $\boldsymbol{\psi}_{\mathrm{DF}}(\mathcal{S};\boldsymbol{\theta}_{\mathrm{DF}})$, optimally partitioning the data $\mathcal{S}$ with maximal information gain:

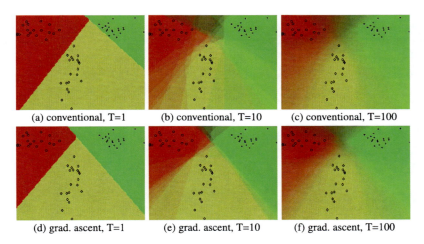

(a) conventional, T=1   (b) conventional, T=10   (c) conventional, T=100

(d) grad. ascent, T=1   (e) grad. ascent, T=10   (f) grad. ascent, T=100

Fig. 19.7 Gradient ascent can improve the location and confidence in the maximum margin decision boundary and reduce classification time. *Top row*: *discrete optimization* using: (**a**) 1 tree, (**b**) 10 trees, (**c**) 100 trees. *Bottom row*: discrete optimization followed by *gradient ascent optimization* using: (**d**) 1 tree, (**e**) 10 trees, (**f**) 100 trees

$$\boldsymbol{\theta}^*_{\mathrm{DF}} = \arg\max_{\boldsymbol{\theta}_{\mathrm{DF}}} I\big(\mathcal{S}|h(\mathbf{v};\boldsymbol{\theta}_{\mathrm{DF}})\big), \tag{19.21}$$

where $\boldsymbol{\theta}_{\mathrm{DF}}$ is the concatenated vector of the binary test parameters $\boldsymbol{\theta}$ at each tree node.

The classic decision forest [44] uses a univariate split test, which consists of a threshold τ of the kth feature element of $\mathbf{v}$. We can denote this partitioning boundary function as $\boldsymbol{\psi} = g_0(\mathbf{v};\boldsymbol{\theta}) = v_k - \tau$ with $\boldsymbol{\theta} = \boldsymbol{\theta}_0 = \{k,\tau\}$. Such a boundary is well suited for fast discrete search via maximizing I. However, the boundary coordinate alignment in feature space can require many binary tests to make the joint decision boundary $\boldsymbol{\psi}_{\mathrm{DF}}(\mathcal{S};\boldsymbol{\theta}_{\mathrm{DF}})$ approximate the maximum margin class separation boundary (as discussed in Chap. 3). An alternative is to approximate the maximal margin decision boundary using far fewer but stronger weak learner models, such as hyperplanes or conic functions, and this is especially true if differentiable information gain is used. This is vital since maximum margin fidelity is likely to endow the forest with superior generalization properties.

To illustrate, Fig. 19.7 shows synthetic 2D data points from three classes (red, yellow, green) and the resulting partitions of a 2D feature space (x_1, x_2) by different decision forests architectures. The top row shows the results of applying a conventional classification forest. The bottom row shows the results (for corresponding forest size) of a classification forest using our differentiable information gain. While it has been shown in [80] (and in Chap. 4) that when a large number of trees are used the maximum margin class boundaries can be found, in practice, a small number of trees is typically preferred for either classification runtime efficiency or memory constraints. A comparison between the two rows in Fig. 19.7 shows that our new formulation of information gain allows forests to approximate maximum margin behavior accurately even with just a few trees. In fact, in each column, showing the results on various number of trees, we see an improvement in the maximum margin boundary.

In detail, Fig. 19.7a shows the result of a decision forest with 1 tree and oriented-line weak learners. We observe that the decision boundary does not approximate well the maximum margin decision boundary. Averaging the output of 10 trees, Fig. 19.7b, starts to improve the location of the class boundary. Using 100 trees Fig. 19.7c provides a reasonable approximation to the maximum margin location and a smooth transition class posterior.

Using gradient ascent optimization yields improved location of the class boundary even for just one tree (Fig. 19.7d). Here, the method is initialized with the result from Fig. 19.7a. Figure 19.7e shows the result when the output from 10 gradient ascent trained trees are averaged. Compared to Fig. 19.7b we can see the confidence in the correct maximum margin boundary location is improved and a smoother posterior. Similarly, when the output from 100 gradient ascent trained trees are averaged in Fig. 19.7f, an improvement in the confidence of the correct maximum margin decision boundary is still observed.

The improvement in maximum margin fidelity obtained by using GADF can provide additional generalization when training data are limited, which is often the case in practice. The use of fewer trees also substantially speeds up classification time, since each gradient ascent trained tree does not require additional time to test yet provides increased accuracy. For example, the gradient ascent based result in Fig. 19.7e has similar maximum margin fidelity to the non-gradient ascent result in Fig. 19.7c yet requires 10 times fewer trees. In additional 2D synthetic tests we have also observed a large capture range (basin of convergence) for both oriented hyperplane and conic weak learners when using GADF.

With this motivation for differentiable information gain, we derive the gradient of two useful binary tests for gradient ascent as follows:

Hyperplane Partition   Binary test functionals in the form of hyperplanes for the training of decision forest can be defined as $\boldsymbol{\psi}(\mathbf{v};\boldsymbol{\theta}) = g_1(\mathbf{v};\boldsymbol{\theta}) = \boldsymbol{\theta}^\top \begin{bmatrix} \mathbf{v} \\ 1 \end{bmatrix}$ where $\boldsymbol{\theta} = \boldsymbol{\theta}_1 = [\theta^{(1)}, \theta^{(2)}, \ldots, \theta^{(d+1)}] \in \mathbb{R}^{d+1}$ may be directly incorporated into the proposed gradient ascent information gain optimization where we can show that

$$\frac{\partial \boldsymbol{\psi}}{\partial \boldsymbol{\theta}} = \begin{bmatrix} \mathbf{v} \\ 1 \end{bmatrix}. \tag{19.22}$$

Hyper-Ellipsoid Partition   Binary tests with hyper-ellipsoid split functionals in $\mathbb{R}^d$ can be defined as $\boldsymbol{\psi}(\mathbf{v};\boldsymbol{\theta}) = g_2(\mathbf{v};\boldsymbol{\theta}) = 1 - (\mathbf{v} - \mathbf{v}_0)^\top Q(\mathbf{v} - \mathbf{v}_0)$ where $\mathbf{v}_0$ is the ellipsoid center, and Q defines the semi-axes lengths and orientations. To incorporate into our gradient ascent information gain optimization, we have

$$\frac{\partial \boldsymbol{\psi}}{\partial \mathbf{v}_0} = -2(\mathbf{v} - \mathbf{v}_0)^\top Q \quad \text{and} \quad \frac{\partial \boldsymbol{\psi}}{\partial Q} = (\mathbf{v} - \mathbf{v}_0)(\mathbf{v} - \mathbf{v}_0)^\top \tag{19.23}$$

with the optimization subject to $Q > 0$.

To train each node using gradient ascent information gain optimization, an initial estimate of the split function parameters can be chosen by random guess or discrete optimization in discrete parameter space. For example, for hyperplanes we find the best simple binary test with parameter $\boldsymbol{\theta}_0^* = \{k^*, \tau^*\}$ by discrete search and then set the initial guess $\boldsymbol{\theta}_1 = [0, \ldots, 0, \theta_1^{(k^*)} = 1, 0, \ldots, -\tau^*]^\top$. Given the formulation and initial guess, we can conveniently implement the gradient ascent optimization by adopting existing off-the-shelf gradient ascent optimization toolboxes (*i.e.* `fmin-unc()` in Matlab with default options).

19.3.3 Object Tracking via Information Gain Maximization

Reliable visual tracking of a target object is difficult as many confusing factors need to be addressed including: occlusions, distractions from background clutter, and object appearance variations. We cast object tracking as an iterative classification problem [9, 11, 139, 178], and model the on-line appearance model update and tracking as a sequential process of information gain maximization that partitions the pixels in feature space (image features) and in image space (incorporating pixel coordinates as additional features) iteratively. Various decision forest based visual trackers have been proposed in the literature. A popular approach is to use classification forests to construct an appearance likelihood model that is updated on-line in the current frame and evaluated for the next frame. Tracking is achieved by finding the maxima of the confidence map for the next frame by picking the centroid. As shown in [317], the on-line decision forest model based visual tracker consistently outperformed that based on an on-line Adaboost model. In [120], the concept of Hough forests is proposed. With Hough forests, the target center is detected and tracked by the fusion of generalized Hough transforms that are based on the codebook classification of local image patches. Also, Chap. 12 and Chap. 16 provide further forest-based video tracking algorithms.

Our approach is substantially different from the previous approaches. We consider the tracking as an *information gain maximization process* (Gain-Max tracking) in pixel XY-coordinate space. By parameterizing the target shape with an ellipsoid, the tracking of the target location and scale can be achieved by maximizing the differentiable information gain via gradient ascent techniques. We note that while we train a forest for each frame, the amount of data is small and thus a forest can be trained quickly. Realtime computation can be achieved by sacrificing some model optimality (*i.e.* limiting the number of trees), or by adopting on-line decision forest learning techniques [317].

Given an image J, we define a region of interest as $\Omega(J)$ and denote the target region as $\Omega^+(J)$ and background region $\Omega^-(J)$ such that $\Omega(J) = \Omega^+(J) \cup \Omega^-(J)$. The pixel feature vector at location $\mathbf{p}$ is a d dimensional vector denoted $J(\mathbf{p}) \in \mathbb{R}^d$ where J has channels for textures, RGB colors, gradients, and wavelets. We denote target and background pixel labels as $\{F, B\}$. We use information gain maximization in two ways: first, to learn to discriminate foreground from background based on pixel appearance (feature space) and second, to track the target in the pixel XY-coordinate space (image space). These are explained next.

GainMax in Feature Space: Updating the Appearance Model   To discriminate foreground from background pixels, we train a two-category pixel classifier that assigns pixels with a label from $\{F, B\}$. When information gain maximization is achieved, solving (19.21) the classifier learns the image features that best separate the training data: $\mathcal{S}^J = \{(J(\mathbf{p}), \varsigma(\mathbf{p})) \mid \mathbf{p} \in \Omega(J), J(\mathbf{p}) \in \mathbb{R}^d, \varsigma(\mathbf{p}) \in \{F, B\}\}$ into foreground and background. The features are computed directly from the image while the target and background labels come from a prior frame (the initial frame is assumed manually labeled). For example, we can obtain the label of the pixel at location $\mathbf{p}$ as

$$\varsigma(\mathbf{p}) = \begin{cases} F & \text{if } \mathbf{p} \in \Omega^+(J), \\ B & \text{if } \mathbf{p} \in \Omega^-(J). \end{cases} \tag{19.24}$$

GainMax in Image Space: Tracking the Target   Further optimization of the foreground and background is possible if we take into consideration each pixel's XY-coordinates in image space in addition to the pixel foreground and background labels output from the previous step's two-category classifier. We denote such a training dataset as $\mathcal{S}^{\Omega(J)} = \{(\mathbf{p}, \varsigma_{\mathrm{DF}}(J(\mathbf{p}))) \mid \mathbf{p} \in \Omega(J)\}$ where $\{\varsigma_{\mathrm{DF}}(J(\mathbf{p})) \in \{F, B\} \mid \mathbf{p} \in \Omega(J)\}$. To solve, we find the optimal partition boundary $h_\psi(\mathbf{p}; \boldsymbol{\theta}^*)$ that achieves maximal information gain. Intuitively, the optimal split function $\psi(\mathbf{p}; \boldsymbol{\theta}^*) = 0$ should match the target region boundary. The solution can again be found by solving (19.21) using gradient ascent, but with the target boundary function being parameterized based on the predefined target shape model, *i.e.* a 2D ellipsoid. As $\{\varsigma_{\mathrm{DF}}(J(\mathbf{p}))\}$ is estimated by the on-line trained classification forest in feature space with probability $q_\varsigma(J(\mathbf{p}))$, we can perform tracking by optimizing the confidence weighted information gain formulation derived in (19.15) and (19.19).

19.3.4 Results

19.3.4.1 Classification of Public Machine Learning Datasets

To evaluate the gradient ascent decision forest (GADF), we compare its performance to those of commonly used classifiers including a reference standard Adaboost implementation and a decision forest with oblique hyperplanes. We denote these classifiers as follows:

Adaboost A standard Adaboost classifier that uses axis-aligned stumps as decision functions. This is used as a baseline reference for comparison.

StumpDF A standard decision forest classifier with an oblique hyperplane for the binary test. The optimal binary test is searched by randomly drawing 20 hyperplane samples in the feature space.

Table 19.1 Comparison of classification equal-error rate for **Adaboost**, **StumpDF** and **GADF** on public datasets

Dataset Name	#sample	# fea.	#Train:#Test	Adaboost	StumpDF	GADF
Arcene	200	10000	1:1	0.25	0.318	**0.240**
Vertebral Column	310	6	3:7	**0.157**	0.175	0.170
Iris	150	2	1:4	0.281	0.010	**0.000**
Cardiotocography	2126	23	3:7	0.021	0.022	**0.019**
Breast Cancer Wisconsin	569	32	1:1	0.056	0.048	**0.043**

GADF Similar to the **StumpDF**, but gradient ascent information gain optimization is also used during training, using the hyperplane with best performance of the randomly drawn 20 planes. Assuming the data are always normalized into standard deviation along each dimension, we do gradient ascent information gain optimization by gradually reducing the annealing parameter σ starting from $0.03^{\frac{1}{\sqrt{d}}}$ (where d is the feature dimension of the data) with multiplicative scaling factor 0.7. The annealing stops when the optimization converges.

We train both **StumpDF** and **GADF** with 10 trees and we train the trees by randomly sampling 90 % of the original training set. When training each tree node, we search for the optimal split parameters in a randomly sampled feature subspace with dimension number $ceil(\sqrt{d})$. We limit the maximal tree depth to 15. To evaluate the three methods, we compare their performance over a variety of different application domains using publicly available standard datasets used throughout the machine learning community [111, 377]. We select five datasets, including: Arcene (where the application is mass spectrometry), *Vertebral Column* (biomechanics), *Iris* (botany), *Cardiotocography* (1D signal processing), and *Breast Cancer Wisconsin* (cell image classification). We used the given train and test datasets when they are explicitly provided and divide the dataset into different ratios to evaluate generalization, as shown in Table 19.1, when they are not given. We also reduced *Iris* to only the first two features to make the test more challenging. The table summarizes the classification equal-error rates for the three methods, averaged over five experimental runs for each method. We observe that in nearly every case, **GADF** outperforms **StumpDF** as well as the reference standard **Adaboost**.

19.3.4.2 Object Tracking in Videos

In Sect. 19.3.3 we embedded GADF into a full-fledged tracking application. Here we compare its performance to the mean-shift tracker [69]. For the video data we used a standard object tracking PET video as the evaluation task [290]. We evaluated three variants of our GADF based tracker. For all our variants the tracker begins by learning a two-category foreground/background pixel classifier (an appearance model) using the manually delineated first frame. Characteristics of the trackers we compare are as follows:

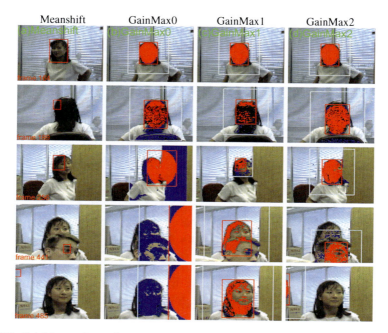

Fig. 19.8 GainMax trackers using gradient ascent information gain maximization can handle distraction and occlusions well. For the mean-shift tracker (*column 1*), the *red box* is the tracking result; for GainMax trackers 0–2 (*columns 2–4*), *red* indicates pixels correctly labeled in the ellipsoid as target (true positive), *blue* indicate false positive pixels outside of the target ellipsoid

MeanShift The standard mean-shift tracker with histogram of size 9 by 9 by 9 bins in RGB space.

GainMax0 The appearance model from the first frame is reused on all frames. Gradient ascent is used to refine the tracking boundary in image space.

GainMax1 Training data are updated to use background pixels from the previous frame and target pixels from the first frame. Then the two-category pixel classifier is retrained and the tracking boundary is refined using gradient ascent for tracking in both image and pixel feature space.

GainMax2 Training data are updated to use the previous frame's target and background pixels. Then the two-category pixel classifier is retrained and the tracking boundary is refined using gradient ascent for tracking in both image and pixel feature space.

For the three different variants of GainMax tracking, we fix the number of trees to 20, and the depth of the trees to be 10. We train the decision forest by randomly sampling 80 % of the pixels as training data for each tree, and randomly choose four features from $[r, g, b, \Delta X_x, \Delta X_y, \|\Delta X\|, \angle \Delta X]$ for the training of the binary test functionals.

Some qualitative results are shown in Fig. 19.8, in which a woman turns her head around in an office environment, and then a second person enters and occludes the

Fig. 19.9 The average
tracking/ground truth box
overlap ratio for the lady
video

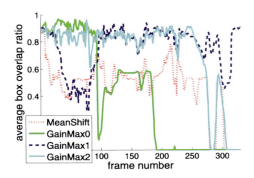

woman. Tracking is also challenging because the wall has nearly human skin color.
We observe that **Meanshift** and **GainMax0** cannot handle the substantial variations
in target appearance as they do not do model updating. They are eventually distracted and fail to track. **GainMax1** and **GainMax2** both maintain correct tracking
of the lady even over the wall because their appearance models are updated on-line
in the pixel feature space and learn to distinguish the face color from wall color.
By comparison, **GainMax2** works better when there is no occlusions. However, it
is easily distracted by the occlusion. However, **GainMax1** can resist this distraction successfully because it does not update the target pixel data, and can maintain
tracking to the end of the video.

Given the ground truth target bounding box B_g and the tracking bounding box
B_t in a frame, we can evaluate the tracking performance by their average box over-
lapping ratio w.r.t. the boxes: $R(B_g, B_t) = (\frac{\Omega(B_g \cap B_t)}{\Omega(B_g)} + \frac{\Omega(B_g \cap B_t)}{\Omega(B_t)})/2$. In Fig. 19.9
we plot the average overlap ratio of the four trackers on the *lady* video.

We can further summarize the tracker's accuracy by the percentage of frames in
which $R(B_t, B_g) > 0.5$. Figure 19.10 summarizes the performance of the four evaluated trackers on three videos commonly used for evaluation in visual tracking. Due
to substantial appearance variations, occlusions and background distractions, **Mean-
shift** and **GainMax0** get distracted easily as they do not perform model updating.
GainMax2 can achieve high tracking accuracy when there is gradual appearance
variations (as shown in Fig. 19.9), but fails to track when occlusions exist. Over all,

% ($R > 0.5$)	 *lady* [135]	 *view5* [291]	 *mall* [57]
Meanshift	0.66	0.46	0.55
GainMax0	0.43	0.47	0.42
GainMax1	0.85	0.92	1.00
GainMax2	0.82	0.47	1.00

Fig. 19.10 Robustness comparison of the visual trackers by the percentage of frames with
$R(B_t, B_g) > 0.5$

GainMax1 achieves the best robustness as it does model updating while avoiding drifting.

19.4 Discussion and Conclusion

This chapter has presented three complementary improvements to the decision forest framework presented in this book.

Entanglement propagates knowledge from one part of the forest to another which speeds learning, improves classifier generalization, and exploits long-range spatial correlations in the input data.

Differentiable information gain maximization allows the optimal data partitioning functional to be found directly through gradient ascent rather than through an exhaustive search over discrete functional parameter space.

Entanglement and differentiable information gain maximization enhance different aspects of decision forests: the use of semantic contextual features and the node optimization function, respectively; they are mutually compatible and may be combined to further enhance the forest accuracy.

The *learned proposal distributions* (Sect. 19.2.2) and differentiable information gain maximization both tackle the problem of node optimization in the presence of a high dimensional feature space. The former increases the effectiveness of brute-force feature search. The latter optimizes the information gain more directly. Since differentiable information gain requires initialization, these two methods can be combined effectively.

The fundamental enhancements presented here may be directly applied to improve results in other applications that use classification forests, including multiple sclerosis lesion segmentation [125], brain segmentation [411], myocardium delineation [212], and more generic object class segmentation tasks [342]. Here we have applied entanglement only to the task of anatomy segmentation, but it is a generic concept and may be adapted to exploit other correlations (*e.g.* over time or space). Likewise our differential information gain approach can form the basis for gradient ascent optimization with more complicated data partitioning functionals (*e.g.* differentiable shape models) based on a-priori heuristics for specific applications.

Chapter 20
Decision Tree Fields: An Efficient Non-parametric Random Field Model for Image Labeling

S. Nowozin, C. Rother, S. Bagon, T. Sharp, B. Yao, and P. Kohli

This chapter introduces a new random field model for discrete image labeling tasks, the Decision Tree Field (DTF), that combines and generalizes decision forests and conditional random fields (CRF) which have been widely used in computer vision.

In a typical CRF model the unary potentials are derived from sophisticated forest or boosting-based classifiers, however, the pairwise potentials are assumed to (1) have a simple parametric form with a pre-specified and fixed dependence on the image data, and (2) to be defined on the basis of a small and fixed neighborhood. In contrast, in DTF, local interactions between multiple variables are determined by means of decision trees evaluated on the image data, allowing the interactions to be adapted to the image content.

This results in powerful graphical models which are able to represent complex label structure.

Our key technical contribution is to show that the DTF model can be trained efficiently and jointly using a convex approximate likelihood function, enabling us to learn over a million free model parameters.

We show experimentally that for applications which have a rich and complex label structure, our model achieves excellent results.

Parts of this chapter are reprinted, with permission, from [271], © 2011 IEEE.

S. Nowozin (✉) · C. Rother · T. Sharp · P. Kohli
Microsoft Research, Cambridge, UK

S. Bagon
Weizmann Institute of Science, Rehovot, Israel

B. Yao
Stanford University, Stanford, USA

A. Criminisi, J. Shotton (eds.), *Decision Forests for Computer Vision and Medical Image Analysis*, Advances in Computer Vision and Pattern Recognition, DOI 10.1007/978-1-4471-4929-3_20, © Springer-Verlag London 2013

20.1 Introduction

In the last decade sophisticated random field models have been successfully applied
to a wide variety of computer vision problems [270]. In particular, random fields
have been used to model many problems including foreground-background (fg-bg)
segmentation [31, 38], semantic segmentation [157, 342], and a number of other
computer vision problems [363]. Many of these problems can be cast as an image
labeling problem, where we are given an image $\mathbf{x}$ and need to predict labels $\mathbf{y}$. Random fields provide a way of factorizing the joint distribution $p(\mathbf{x}, \mathbf{y})$ or the posterior
distribution $p(\mathbf{y}|\mathbf{x})$ into a product of local interactions.

In the classic Markov random field (MRF) we obtain the posterior distribution
$p(\mathbf{y}|\mathbf{x})$ by integrating a per-pixel likelihood functions with pairwise consistency potentials ensuring a smooth solution [122, 217]. One major advance in the field was
to make these smoothness costs dependent on the local image structure [38], conditioning parts of the model on the input data. In the last decade, these *conditional*
random field (CRF) models [157, 198, 361] have become popular for their improved
ability to capture the relationship between labels and the image.

A lot of research effort has been devoted to the development of efficient
algorithms for estimating the Maximum a Posteriori (MAP) solution of such
models [190, 363], and the same is true for algorithms for probabilistic inference [189, 393]. The problem of *parameter estimation* in these structured models
has likewise been addressed [361, 365, 391].

However, despite these rapid developments, (most) state-of-the-art random field
CRF models continue to suffer from the following limitations: (1) they are defined
on the basis of a fixed neighborhood structure (except the work of [191, 314]), and
(2) the potentials are assumed to have a simple parametric form with a pre-specified
and fixed dependence on the image data. While it is relatively easy to think of various ways to overcome these limitations, the key challenge is to find a model for
which efficient and high-quality training is still tractable.

This paper introduces a new graphical model, the Decision Tree Field (DTF),
which overcomes the above-mentioned limitations of existing models. We take a
simple yet radical view: every interaction in our model depends on the image, and
further, the dependence is non-parametric. It is easy to see that representing such a
model is challenging, since there are numerous ways of defining a mapping between
the image and the parameters of the interactions in the graphical model.

Our model uses *decision trees* to map the image content to interaction values. Every node of every decision tree in our model is associated with a set of parameters,
which are used to define the potential functions in the graphical model. When making predictions on a novel test instance, the leaf node of the decision tree determines
the effective weights.

There are a number of important reasons for the choice of decision trees to specify the dependence between potentials and image content. Firstly, decision trees are
non-parametric and can represent rich functional relationships if sufficient training
data are available. Secondly, the training of decision trees is scalable (see Chap. 21),
both in the training set size and in that the approach can be parallelized; recent

advances even allow training on graphics processors [333]. For most computer vision applications where an explicit physical model is unavailable, the amount of available or processable training data is the limiting factor for obtaining good predictive performance. Decision trees are scalable to large training sets, and many recent works use decision trees and their variants in the large scale setting, such as random forests [5, 44], extremely randomized trees [128], and semantic texton forests [341]. In our context, decision trees give another big advantage: they allow us to efficiently and jointly learn all parameters in the model. We achieve this by using a log-concave pseudolikelihood objective function, which is known to work well given enough training data because it is a consistent estimator and approaches the exact maximum likelihood estimate asymptotically [189].

Our contributions can be summarized as follows. (1) To the best of our knowledge, we propose the first graphical model for image labeling problems which allows all potential functions to have an arbitrary dependence on the image data. (2) We show how the dependence between potential functions and image data can be expressed via decision trees. (3) We show how the training of the DTF model, which involves learning of a large number of parameters, can be performed efficiently. (4) We empirically demonstrate that DTFs are superior to existing models such as random forest and common MRFs for applications with complex label interactions and large neighborhood structures.

20.2 Related Work

There has been relatively little work on learning image-dependent potential functions, *i.e.* the "conditional part" of a conditional random field. Most algorithms for learning the parameters of a random field try to learn a class-to-class energy table that does not depend on the image content [8, 19, 269, 365, 366]. However, there have been few attempts at learning the parameters of conditional potentials [65, 138, 296]. Gould *et al.* [138] used a multiclass logistic regression classifier on a set of manually selected features, such as the length and orientation of region boundaries to obtain an image-dependent learned model for pairwise interactions. Cho *et al.* [65] proposed a model for image restoration whose interactions were dependent on the semantic meaning of the local image content as predicted by a classifier. Unlike our work, all the above-mentioned models either target specific tasks, or assume a particular form for the dependence of the potentials on the image content. Neither of the above-mentioned approaches is able to learn a dependency model with thousands or even millions of parameters which our model can achieve.

Decision trees are popularly used to model unary interactions, *e.g.* [343]; but with two exceptions they have not been used for pairwise or higher-order interactions. The first exception is the paper of Glesner and Koller [132], where decision trees are used to model conditional probability tables over many discrete variables in a Bayesian network. The difference is that in [132] the decisions in the tree are evaluated on states of random variables, whereas in our work we evaluate the image content and thus require no change to the inference procedure.

The second exception is the "random forest random field" [287]. Despite the similarity in name, the approach is fundamentally different from ours. Instead of defining an explicit model as we do in (20.2), Payet and Todorovic [287] define the model distribution implicitly as the equilibrium distribution of a learned Metropolis–Hastings Markov chain. The Metropolis–Hastings ratio is estimated by classification trees. This is a clever idea but it has a number of limitations: (i) at test-time there is no choice between different inference methods but one is bound to using inefficient Markov Chain Monte Carlo (MCMC) (in [287] superpixel graphs of few hundred regions are used and inference takes 30 seconds despite using advanced Swendsen–Wang cuts); and (ii) the model remains *implicit*, so that inspecting the learned interactions is not possible.

In a broader view, our model has a richer representation of complex label structure. Deep architectures, such as [206] and latent variable CRFs, as in [323], have the same goal, but use hidden variables representing the presence of larger entities such as object parts. While these models are successful at representing structure, they are generally difficult to train because their negative log-likelihood function is no longer convex. In contrast, by learning powerful non-parametric conditional interactions we achieve similar expressivity but retain convexity of the training problem.

20.3 Model

We now describe the details of our model. Note that in this chapter we describe a very different model than those described in the rest of the book. This requires a different notation, defined as follows. Throughout we will refer to $\mathbf{x} \in \mathcal{X}$ as a given observed image from the set of all possible images $\mathcal{X}$. Our goal is to infer a discrete labeling $\mathbf{y} \in \mathcal{Y}$, where the labeling is per-pixel, *i.e.* we have $\mathbf{y} = (y_i)_{i \in \mathcal{V}}$, $y_i \in \mathcal{L}$, where $\mathcal{V}$ is the set of variable indices, and all variables have the same label set $\mathcal{L}$. We describe the relationship between $\mathbf{x}$ and $\mathbf{y}$ by means of an *energy function* E that decomposes into a sum of energy functions E_{t_F} over *factors* F, where F is a subsets of all variables. For example, for a pairwise factor we have $|F| = 2$. We have

$$E(\mathbf{y}, \mathbf{x}, \mathbf{w}) = \sum_{F \in \mathcal{F}} E_{t_F}(y_F, x_F, w_{t_F}). \tag{20.1}$$

By y_F we denote the collection $(y_i)_{i \in F}$, and similarly we write x_F to denote the parts of $\mathbf{x}$ contained in F. While there may be many different subsets in $\mathcal{F}$, we assume they are of few distinct *types* and denote the type of the factor F by t_F. The function E_{t_F} is the same for all factors of that type, but the variables and image content it acts upon differ. Furthermore, the function is *parametrized* by means of a weight vector w_{t_F} to be discussed below.

A visualization of a small factor graph model is shown in Fig. 20.1. It has three pairwise factor types (red, blue, and green) and two unary factor types (black and turquoise). All factors depend on the image data $\mathbf{x}$. Figure 20.2 shows the "unrolled"

Fig. 20.1 Neighborhood
structure around each pixel
with five different factor types

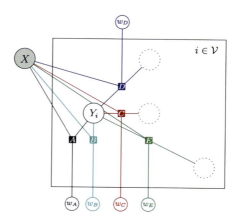

Fig. 20.2 Unrolled factor
graph (image size 4-by-3
pixels), dependencies on **x**
and **w** are not shown

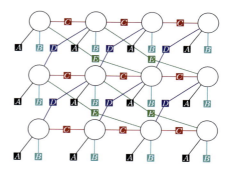

factor graph for an image of size 4-by-3 pixels, where the basic model structure
is repeated around each pixel $i \in \mathcal{V}$, and pairwise factors which reach outside the
image range are omitted. In total we have $|\mathcal{F}| = 43$ factors.

The energy (20.1) defines a conditional probability distribution $p(\mathbf{y}|\mathbf{x}, \mathbf{w})$ as

$$p(\mathbf{y}|\mathbf{x}, \mathbf{w}) = \frac{1}{Z(\mathbf{x}, \mathbf{w})} \exp\big(-E(\mathbf{y}, \mathbf{x}, \mathbf{w})\big), \qquad (20.2)$$

where $Z(\mathbf{x}, \mathbf{w}) = \sum_{\mathbf{y} \in \mathcal{Y}} \exp(-E(\mathbf{y}, \mathbf{x}, \mathbf{w}))$ is the normalizing constant. So far, our
model is in the general form of a *conditional random field* [198]. We now show how
to use decision trees for representing E_{t_F} in (20.1).

With each function E_t we associate one decision tree. To evaluate
$E_{t_F}(y_F, x_F, w_{t_F})$, we start at the root of the tree, and perform a sequence of tests
s on the image content x_F, traversing the tree to the left or right. This process is
illustrated in Fig. 20.3. When a leaf node has been reached, we collect the *path*
of traversed nodes from the root node to the leaf node. With each node q of the
tree we associate a table of energy values $w_{t_F}(q, y_F)$. Depending on the number of
variables y_F this energy function acts on, the table can be a vector (unary), a ma-

Fig. 20.3 Summation of all
energy tables along the path
of visited decision nodes
(*shaded blue*)

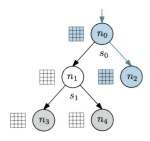

trix (pairwise), or general k-dimensional array (higher order). We *sum* all the tables
along the path taken and compute the energy as

$$E_{t_F}(y_F, x_F, w_{t_F}) = \sum_{q \in \text{Path}(x_F)} w_{t_F}(q, y_F), \qquad (20.3)$$

where $\text{Path}(x_F)$ denotes the set of nodes taken during tree evaluation. By using
weights at each node in the path we can regularize the nodes at the root of the tree
to exert a stronger influence, affecting a large number of leaves; at test-time we can
precompute the summation along each root-to-leaf path and store the result at each
leaf.

To compute the overall energy (20.1) we evaluate E_{t_F} for all factors $F \in \mathcal{F}$.
Although the type t_F might be the same, the function E_{t_F} depends on x_F through
the evaluation of the decision tree. This allows image-dependent unary, pairwise,
and higher-order interactions. The set $\mathcal{F}$ is determined by repeating the same local
neighborhood structure for each pixel, as shown in Figs. 20.1 and 20.2.

In summary, our model consists of a set of factor types. Each factor type contains:
(i) the number k of variables it acts on and their relative offsets, (ii) a single decision
tree, and (iii) for each node in the decision tree, an energy table of size $\mathcal{L}^k$. Given an
image $\mathbf{x}$, for each labeling $\mathbf{y}$ we can evaluate $E(\mathbf{y}, \mathbf{x}, \mathbf{w})$ using the above procedure.

20.3.1 Relation to Other Models

The proposed DTF generalizes a number of popular existing image labeling methods. If we ignore pairwise and higher-order interactions in (20.1), then the variables
are independent and making predictions for each pixel is the same as evaluating a
decision forests, as used in *e.g.* [341, 375]. Interestingly, as we will show in the experiments, even in this setting we still slightly outperform standard decision forests
since we learn the weights in each split node instead of using empirical histograms;
this novel modification improves predictive performance without any test-time overhead compared to conventional forests. For pairwise interactions we generalize simple CRFs with contrast-sensitive pairwise potentials such as in [31, 38], the *GrabCut
system* [315], and TextonBoost [342]. Finally, if for the pairwise interactions we use
decision trees of depth one, such that these interactions do not depend on the image
content, then our model becomes a classic Markov random field prior [217].

20.4 Learning Decision Tree Fields

Learning the model involves selecting the neighborhood structure, the decision trees, and the weights stored in the decision nodes. During learning we are given an iid set $\{(\mathbf{x}_m, \mathbf{y}_m^*)\}_{m=1,\dots,M}$ of images $\mathbf{x}_m$ and ground truth labelings $\mathbf{y}_m^*$. Our goal is to estimate the parameters $\mathbf{w}$ of our model such as to predict $\mathbf{y}_m^*$ for a given $\mathbf{x}_m$. For simplifying the derivation of the learning method, we can treat the given set of images as if it would be one large collection of pixels as is done in [361].

20.4.1 Maximum Likelihood Learning

For learning the parameters of our model, we need to elaborate on how the parameters $\mathbf{w}$ define the energy. One important observation is that for a fixed set of decision trees the energy function (20.1) can be represented such that it is linear in the parameters $\mathbf{w}$. To see this, consider a single $E_{t_F}(y_F, x_F, w_{t_F})$ function and define a binary indicator function

$$B_{t_F}(q, z; y_F, x_F) = \begin{cases} 1 & \text{if } q \in \text{Path}(x_F) \text{ and } z = y_F, \\ 0 & \text{otherwise.} \end{cases} \tag{20.4}$$

Then, we can write the energy $E_{t_F}(y_F, x_F, w_{t_F})$ as a function linear in w_{t_F},

$$\sum_{q \in \text{Tree}(t_F)} \sum_{z \in \mathcal{Y}_F} w_{t_F}(q, z) B_{t_F}(q, z; y_F, x_F). \tag{20.5}$$

The use of decision trees allows us to represent non-linear functions on $\mathbf{x}$. Although non-linear in $\mathbf{x}$, by the representation (20.5) we can parametrize this function linearly in w_{t_F}. Then, from (20.5) we see that the gradient has a simple form,

$$\nabla_{w_{t_F}(q,z)} E_{t_F}(y_F, x_F, w_{t_F}) = B_{t_F}(q, z; y_F, x_F). \tag{20.6}$$

Because (20.1) is linear in $\mathbf{w}$, the log-likelihood of (20.2) is a concave and differentiable function in $\mathbf{w}$ [189, Corollary 20.2]. This means that if computing $Z(\mathbf{x}, \mathbf{w})$ and the marginal distributions $p(y_F|\mathbf{x}, \mathbf{w})$ for all $F \in \mathcal{F}$ would be tractable, then learning the parameters by maximum likelihood becomes a convex optimization problem.

We now show how to use efficient approximate likelihood methods to learn all parameters associated with the decision trees from training data. For now we assume we are given a fixed set of factor types, including decision trees, but have to learn the weights/energies associated with the nodes of the trees. We will discuss how to learn trees later.

20.4.2 Pseudolikelihood

The pseudolikelihood [26] defines a surrogate likelihood function that is maximized. In contrast to the true likelihood function computing the pseudolikelihood is tractable and very efficient. The pseudolikelihood is derived from the per-variable conditional distributions $p(y_i | y^*_{\mathcal{V} \setminus \{i\}}, \mathbf{x}, \mathbf{w})$. By defining

$$\ell_i(\mathbf{w}) = -\log p\left(y_i | y^*_{\mathcal{V} \setminus \{i\}}, \mathbf{x}, \mathbf{w}\right) \qquad (20.7)$$

we can write the regularized negative log-pseudolikelihood $\ell_{npl}(\mathbf{w})$ as the average ℓ_i over all pixels,

$$\ell_{npl}(\mathbf{w}) = \frac{1}{|\mathcal{V}|} \sum_{i \in \mathcal{V}} \ell_i(\mathbf{w}) - \frac{1}{|\mathcal{V}|} \sum_t \log p_t(w_t), \qquad (20.8)$$

where $p_t(w_t)$ is a *prior distribution* over w_t used to regularize the weights. We will use multivariate Normal distributions $\mathcal{N}(0, \sigma_t I)$, so that $-\log p_t(w_t)$ is of the form $\frac{1}{2\sigma_t^2} \|w_t\|^2 + C_t(\sigma_t)$ and the constant $C_t(\sigma_t)$ can be omitted during optimization because it does not depend on $\mathbf{w}$. For each factor type t the prior hyperparameter $\sigma_t > 0$ controls the overall influence of the factor and we need to select a suitable value by means of a model selection procedure such as cross validation.

Function (20.8) is convex, differentiable, and tractably computable. For optimizing (20.8) we use the L-BFGS numerical optimization method [426]. To use L-BFGS we need to iteratively compute $\ell_i(\mathbf{w})$ and the gradient $\nabla_{w_t} \ell_i(\mathbf{w})$. The computation of $\ell_i(\mathbf{w})$ and $\nabla_{w_t} \ell_i(\mathbf{w})$ is straightforward and yields the expressions,

$$\ell_i(\mathbf{w}) = \sum_{F \in M(i)} E_F\left(y^*_F, \mathbf{x}, w_{t_F}\right)$$

$$+ \log \sum_{y_i \in \mathcal{Y}_i} \exp\left(- \sum_{F \in M(i)} E_F\left(y_i, y^*_{\mathcal{V} \setminus \{i\}}, \mathbf{x}, w_{t_F}\right)\right), \qquad (20.9)$$

$$\nabla_{w_t} \ell_i(\mathbf{w}) = \sum_{F \in M_t(i)} \nabla_{w_t} E_F\left(\mathbf{y}^*, \mathbf{x}, w_t\right)$$

$$- E_{y_i \sim \tilde{p}_i}\left[\sum_{F \in M_t(i)} \nabla_{w_t} E_F\left(y_i, y^*_{\mathcal{V} \setminus \{i\}}, \mathbf{x}, w_t\right)\right], \qquad (20.10)$$

where we use $M(i)$ to denote the subset of $\mathcal{F}$ that involves variable y_i, and $M_t(i)$ likewise but restricted to factors of matching type, i.e. $M_t(i) = \{F \in M(i) : t_F = t\}$. The operator $E_{y \sim p}[\cdot]$ takes the expectation of its argument over the specified distribution, and we have used the shorthand $\tilde{p}_i = p(y_i | y^*_{\mathcal{V} \setminus \{i\}}, \mathbf{x}, \mathbf{w})$. By taking the uniform average of (20.9) and (20.10) over all pixels in all images, we obtain the expressions of the overall learning objective and its gradient in the parameters, respectively.

When initializing the weights to zero we have approximately $\|\nabla_{\mathbf{w}} \ell_{npl}(\mathbf{w})\| \approx 1$. During optimization we stop when $\|\nabla_{\mathbf{w}} \ell_{npl}(\mathbf{w})\| \leq 10^{-4}$, which is the case after around 100–250 L-BFGS iterations, even for models with over a million parameters.

20.4.3 Learning the Tree Structure

Ideally, we would like to learn the neighborhood structure and decision trees jointly with their weights using a single objective function. However, whereas the weights are continuous, the set of decision trees is a large combinatorial set. We therefore propose to use a simple two-step heuristic to determine the decision tree structure: we learn the classification tree using the training samples and the *information gain* splitting criterion. This greedy tree construction is popular and known to work well on image labeling problems [341].

The key parameters are the maximum depth of the tree, the minimum number of samples required to keep growing the tree, and the type and number of split features used. As these settings differ from application to application, we describe them in the experimental section. Unlike in a normal classification tree, we store weights at every decision node and initialize them to zero, instead of storing histograms over classes at the leaf nodes only.

The above procedure is easily understood for unary interactions. We now show that it can be extended in a straightforward manner to learn decision trees for pairwise factors as well. To this end, if we have a pairwise factor we consider the product set $\mathcal{L} \times \mathcal{L}$ of labels and treat each label pair $(l_1, l_2) \in \mathcal{L} \times \mathcal{L}$ as a single class. Each training pair of labels becomes a single class in the product set. Given a set of such training instances we learn a classification tree over $|\mathcal{L}|^2$ classes using the information gain criterion. Instead of storing class histograms we now store weight tables with one entry per element in $\mathcal{L} \times \mathcal{L}$. The procedure extends to higher-order factors in a straightforward way.

Once the trees are obtained, we set all their weights to zero and optimize (20.8). During optimization the interaction between different decision trees is taken into account. This is important because the tree structures are determined independently and if we were to optimize their weight independently as well, then we would suffer from overcounting labels during training. The same overcounting problem would occur if we would want to use the class histograms at the leaf nodes directly, for example by taking the negative log-probability as an energy.

20.4.4 Complexity of Training

The complexity to compute the overall objective (20.8) and its gradient is $O(|\mathcal{V}| \cdot |\mathcal{L}| \cdot N)$, where $\mathcal{V}$ is the set of pixels in the training set, $\mathcal{L}$ is the label set, and N is the number of factors in the neighborhood structure. This complexity is the same for pairwise terms, despite pairwise terms needing $|\mathcal{L}|^2$ classes. Note that this is linear in all quantities, and independent of the order of the factors. This is possible only because of the pseudolikelihood approximation. Moreover, it is even more efficient than performing a single sweep of message passing in loopy belief propagation, which has complexity $O(|\mathcal{V}| \cdot |\mathcal{L}|^k \cdot N)$ for factors of order $k \geq 2$.

20.4.5 Making Training Efficient

Training a graphical model on millions of pixels is computationally challenging. We have two principled methods to make training efficient.

First, observe that our training procedure parallelizes in every step: we train the classification trees in parallel [333]. Likewise, evaluating (20.8) and its gradient is a large summation of independent terms, which we again compute in parallel with no communication overhead.

The second observation is that every step in our training procedure can be carried out on a subsampled training set. For classification trees we can process a subset of pixels, as in [341]. Less obvious, we can do the same thing when optimizing our objective (20.8). The first term in Eq. (20.8) takes the form of an empirical expectation $\mathsf{E}_{i \sim \mathcal{U}(\mathcal{V})}[\ell_i(\mathbf{w})]$ that can be approximated both deterministically or by means of stochastic approximation. We use a deterministic approximation by selecting a fixed subset $\mathcal{V}' \subset \mathcal{V}$ and evaluating $\ell'_{\mathrm{npl}}(\mathbf{w}) = \frac{1}{|\mathcal{V}'|} \sum_{i \in \mathcal{V}'} \ell_i(\mathbf{w}) - \frac{1}{|\mathcal{V}'|} \sum_t \log p_t(w_t)$. We select $\mathcal{V}'$ to be large enough so this computation remains efficient; typically $\mathcal{V}'$ has a few million elements. Note that when sampling $\mathcal{V}'$ uniformly at random with replacement from $\mathcal{V}$, the *law of large numbers* guarantees the asymptotic correctness of this approximation.

20.4.6 Inference

We use different inference methods during test-time. For making maximum posterior marginal predictions (MPM) we use an efficient Gibbs sampler. Because the Gibbs sampling updates use the same quantities as used for computing (20.9) we do not have to unroll the graph. For obtaining approximate MAP predictions, we use the Gibbs sampler with simulated annealing (SA), again exploiting the model structure [270]. To have a baseline comparison, we also minimize (20.1) using tree-reweighted message passing (TRW) by unrolling the factor graph and using the implementation of [190].

20.5 Experiments

We considered a broad range of applications and report experiments for multiple datasets. The aim is to show that the DTF enables improved performance in challenging tasks, where a large number of interactions and parameters need to be considered and these cannot be manually tuned. Moreover, we show that conditional pairwise interactions better represent the data and lead to improved performance. As the datasets are diverse, they also show the broad applicability of our system.

Fig. 20.4 Input (*left*),
labeling (*right*)

20.5.1 Conditional Interactions: Toy Snake Dataset

In this experiment we construct a task that has only very weak local evidence for any particular label and structural information needs to be propagated at test-time in order to make correct predictions. Moreover, this structure is not given but needs to be learned from training data.

Consider Fig. 20.4, illustrating the task. A "snake" shown on the input image is a sequence of adjacent pixels, and the color in the input image encodes the direction of the next pixel: red means "go north", yellow means "go east", blue means "go west", and green means "go south". Once a background pixel is reached, the snake ends. Each snake is ten pixels long, and each pixel is assigned its own label, starting from the head (black) to the tail (white), with the background taking its own label (green). Knowing about these rules, the labeling (Fig. 20.4, right) can be perfectly reconstructed. Here, however, these rules need to be learned from training instances.

Of course, in a real system the unary interactions typically provide strong cues [19, 342], but we believe that the task distills the limitations of noisy unary interactions: in this task, for making perfect predictions, the unary would need to learn about all possible snakes of length ten, of which there are very many.

We use a standard 4-neighborhood for both the MRF and the DTF models. The unary decision trees are allowed to look at every pixel in the input image, and therefore could remember the entire training image. We use a training set of 200 images, and a test set of 100 images.

The results obtained are shown in Table 20.1 and Fig. 20.5. Here random forests (RF), trained unary potentials (Unary), and the learned Markov random field (MRF) perform equally well, at around 91 %. Upon examining this performance further, we discovered that while the head and tail labels are labeled with perfect accuracy, towards the middle segments of the snakes the labeling error is highest, see Table 20.1. This is plausible, as for these labels the local evidence is weakest. When using conditional pairwise interactions the performance improves to an almost perfect 99.4 %. This again makes sense because the pairwise conditional interactions are allowed to

Table 20.1 Test set accuracies for the snake dataset

	RF	Unary	MRF	DTF
Accuracy	90.3	90.9	91.9	**99.4**
Accuracy (tail)	100	100	100	100
Accuracy (mid)	28	28	38	95

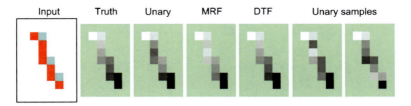

Fig. 20.5 Predictions on a novel test instance

peek at the color-codes at their neighbors for determining the directionality of the snake.

The predictions are illustrated for a single test instance in Fig. 20.5. We see that only the DTF makes a perfect prediction. To show the uncertainty of the unary model, we visualize two samples from the model.

20.5.2 Learning Calligraphy: Chinese Characters

In the previous experiment we used a standard 4-connected neighborhood structure. In this experiment we show that by using larger conditional neighborhoods we are able to represent shape. We use the KAIST Hanja2 database of handwritten Chinese characters. We occlude each character by a gray box centered on the image, but with random width and height. This is shown in the leftmost column of Fig. 20.6. We consider two datasets, one where we have a "small occlusion" and one with a "large occlusion" box. Note that most characters in the test set have never been observed in the training set, but a model that has learned about shape structure of Chinese characters can still find plausible completions of the input image. To this end we use one unary factor with a decision tree of depth 15. Additionally, we use a dense pairwise neighborhood structure of 8-connected neighbors at one and two pixels distance, plus a sparse set of 27 neighbors at $\{(-9, 0), (-9, 3), (-9, 6), (-9, 9), (-6, 0), \ldots, (9, 9)\}$. Therefore, each variable has $2 \cdot (24 + 4 + 4) = 64$ neighboring variables in the model. For the pairwise decision trees we use trees of depth one (MRF), or six (DTF).

The results for the large occlusion task are shown in Fig. 20.6. Qualitatively, they show the difference between a rich connectivity structure and conditional interactions. Observe, for example, that the MRF essentially performs only a smoothing of the results while respecting local stroke-width constraints, as apparent from the MRF MAP prediction in the first row of Fig. 20.6. In contrast, the DTF predictions hallucinate meaningful structure that may be quite different from the ground truth but bears similarity to Chinese characters. Note that we achieve this rich structure without the use of any latent variables. Because this task is an inpainting task, the quantitative assessment is more difficult since the task is truly ambiguous. We therefore report accuracies only for the small-occlusion case, where a reasonable reconstruction of the ground truth seems more feasible. We measure the per-pixel

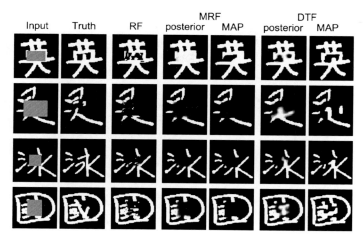

Fig. 20.6 Test set predictions for the large occlusion case

accuracy in the occluded area on the test set. For the random forest baseline we obtain 67.74 %. The MRF with dense neighborhood improves this to 75.18 % and the DTF obtains 76.01 %.

20.5.3 Body-Part Detection

We consider the task of body-part classification from depth images, as recently proposed in [343]. Given a 2D depth image, and a foreground mask, the task is to label each pixel as belonging to one of 31 different body parts, as shown in Fig. 20.7. Despite the variations in pose and body sizes [343] obtains high-quality recognition results by evaluating a classification forest for each pixel, testing local and global depth disparities. See Chap. 13 for more details. In this task, the label set has a large amount of structure, but it is not clear that a sufficiently complex unary classifier, when given the image, cannot implicitly represent this structure reasonably well. Here we show that by adding pairwise interactions we in fact improve the recognition accuracy. Moreover, once we make the interactions conditional, accuracy further improves.

The experimental setup is as follows. We use two subsets of the annotated data of [343] for training: 30 depth images, and 1500 depth images. In both cases we use a fixed separate set of 150 depth images for testing. We train four unary decision trees for all models. For the pairwise models, we use the following neighborhood sizes: (i) "+1" for adding a 4-neighborhood one pixel away, (ii) "+5" for an 8-neighborhood five pixels away, and (iii) "+20" when adding an 8-neighborhood 20 pixels away. In the "+1,5,20" configuration, each variable has $4 + 8 + 8 = 20$ neighbors. For each of the pairwise interactions we train two trees of depth six. We measure the results using the same mean per-class accuracy score as used in [343].

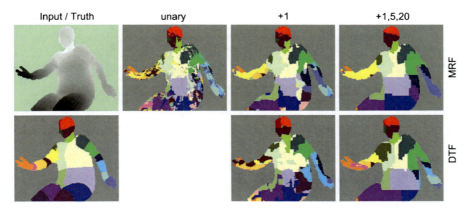

Fig. 20.7 Test set recognition results on the training set of 30 images. We show MRF (*top*) and DTF (*bottom*) results

Table 20.2 Body-part recognition results: mean per-class accuracy, training time (4 cores, 8 threads), and number of parameters. (*) We did not obtain reliable run times for the 1500 image runs, as multiple jobs have been running in parallel on the machines used

Training set	Measure	[343]	unary	MRF			DTF		
				+1	+1,20	+1,5,20	+1	+1,20	+1,5,20
30 images	Average accuracy	14.8	21.36	21.96	23.64	24.05	23.71	25.72	**27.35**
	Run time	1m	3m18	3m38	10m	10m	5m16	17m	22m
	Model parameters	–	176k	178k	183k	187k	438k	951k	1.47M
1500 images	Average accuracy	34.4	36.15	37.82	38.00	39.30	39.59	40.26	**41.42**
	Run time	6h34	*	*	*	(30h)*	*	*	(40h)*
	Model parameters	–	6.3M	6.2M	6.2M	6.3M	6.8M	7.8M	8.8M

The results for 30 and 1500 training images are shown in Table 20.2 and one instance is shown in Fig. 20.7. Even without adding pairwise interactions, our learned unary weights already outperform the classification forest [343]. When adding more interactions ($+1$, $+1,20$, $+1,5,20$), the performance increases because dense pairwise interactions can represent implicit size preferences for the body parts. Likewise, when adding conditionality (MRF to DTF), the performance improves. The best performing model is our DTF with large structure ($+1,5,20$) and almost 1.5 million free parameters. It is trained in only 22 minutes and achieves 27.35 % mean per-class accuracy. For the same setup of 30 and 1500 training images, the original work [343] reports mean per-class accuracies of 14.8 % (30 train) and 34.4 % (1500

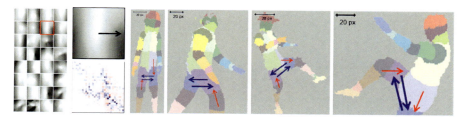

Fig. 20.8 Illustrating one learned horizontal interaction (20 pixels apart): The *left figure* shows the average depth-normalized silhouette reaching each of the 32 leaf nodes in the learned decision tree. We select one leaf (marked *red box*, enlarged) and show the corresponding effective 32×32 weight matrix obtained by summing the learned weights along the path from the root-to-leaf node. The conditional interaction can be understood by visualizing the most attractive (*in blue*) and most repulsive (*in red*) elements in the matrix. We superimpose arrows for the two most attractive and repulsive interactions on test images (*right*). The first and second pose exemplify how left and right upper parts of the legs can appear 20 pix to the right of each other in a way that matches the pattern of the leaf. While the configuration shown in the third and fourth pose is plausible, it does not fit the leaf pattern and thus the interaction is not active

train), but reports an impressive 56.6 % with 900k training images, trained for a day on a 1000 core cluster.

An example of a learned pairwise interaction is shown in Fig. 20.8, demonstrating that the improved performance of the DTF can be attributed to the more powerful interactions that are allowed to take the image into account.

20.6 Conclusion

We have introduced Decision Tree Fields as flexible and accurate models for image labeling tasks. This accuracy is achieved by being able to represent complex image-dependent structure between labels. Most importantly, this expressiveness is achieved without the use of latent variables and therefore we can learn the parameters of our model efficiently by minimizing a convex function.

The source code for the decision tree field implementation will be made available at the authors' homepages.

Part III
Implementation and Conclusion

Part III discusses implementation details and 'tricks of the trade' to be kept in mind when implementing decision forests. Details of the freely available research code library *Sherwood* are also described. Finally, we offer some closing remarks.

Chapter 21
Efficient Implementation of Decision Forests

J. Shotton, D. Robertson, and T. Sharp

This chapter describes a variety of techniques for writing efficient, scalable, and general-purpose decision forest software. It will cover:

- algorithmic considerations, such as how to train in depth first or breadth first order;
- optimizations, such as cheaply evaluating multiple thresholds for a given feature;
- designing for multi-core, GPU, and distributed computing environments; and
- various 'tricks of the trade', including tuning parameters and dealing with unbalanced training sets.

21.1 Introduction

A useful property of decision forests is their simplicity: basic forest training and test algorithms can be implemented using fewer than 50 lines of code. However, straightforward implementations may run too slowly in some applications, *e.g.* where a large quantity of training data is required or where many trees or tree levels are used. Fortunately, decision forest training and test times can be significantly reduced by high- and low-level code optimization and parallelization. Furthermore, this benefit can, with care, be achieved without sacrificing code readability or flexibility. This chapter describes several practical techniques for implementing fast, efficient, scalable, and reusable software for decision forest training and inference. The insights presented here are gleaned from years of practical experience using forests, and we hope they will save considerable time and effort on the part of future practitioners.

J. Shotton (✉) · T. Sharp
Microsoft Research Ltd., Cambridge, UK

D. Robertson
Redimension Ltd., Cambridge, UK

A. Criminisi, J. Shotton (eds.), *Decision Forests for Computer Vision and Medical Image Analysis*, Advances in Computer Vision and Pattern Recognition, DOI 10.1007/978-1-4471-4929-3_21, © Springer-Verlag London 2013

One of the most crucial lessons we have learned about efficient decision forest implementation is that *everything depends on the data*. For example, the most effective strategy for parallelizing decision forest training across multiple processors or processor cores will typically depend on the quantity of training data (*e.g.* whether or not it will all fit in available RAM) and whether the best test accuracy will necessitate many shallow trees or few deep trees. As you read this chapter, keep in mind the properties of your data and the problem you are addressing.

The chapter is structured as follows. The next section explains the difference between depth first and breadth first tree training, and explains advantages and limitations of these two approaches. It goes on to describe some techniques for making training more efficient, including how multiple candidate thresholds can be evaluated cheaply for a given feature response function, and gives some advice on designing data structures for cache utilization efficiency. It then describes various techniques for parallelizing decision forest training and test for multi-core, GPU, and distributed computing environments. Finally, we discuss parameter tuning and present a few miscellaneous 'tricks of the trade'. Most of the following discussion will focus on the implementation of single decision *trees*, as the extension to forests is usually trivial.

The next chapter, Chap. 22, describes the software library that accompanies this book ('Sherwood'). This library includes a reusable and easy-to-understand implementation of a basic decision forest training algorithm. It does not employ all the techniques described in this chapter, but it may provide a useful basis for implementing your own decision forest software.

21.1.1 Notation

This chapter's emphasis on implementation details means that we will need to use a slightly expanded form of the notation introduced in Part I. Specifically, we will expand the definition of a weak learner as follows (*cf.* Eqs. (3.5) and (3.6)):

$$\underbrace{h(\mathbf{v}, \boldsymbol{\theta})}_{\text{weak learner response}} = [\ \underbrace{f(\mathbf{v}, \boldsymbol{\phi})}_{\text{feature response}} \geq \underbrace{(\tau)}_{\text{threshold}}\ ], \qquad (21.1)$$

where $[\cdot]$ is the 0–1 indicator function, $\mathbf{v}$ represents a data point, and $\boldsymbol{\theta} = (\boldsymbol{\phi}, \tau)$ comprises the weak learner parameters $\boldsymbol{\phi}$ (the feature parameters) and τ (the feature response threshold). As usual, the weak learner partitions the training data points into left and right subsets, $\mathcal{S}^{\mathrm{L}}$ and $\mathcal{S}^{\mathrm{R}}$. A function $I(\mathcal{S}, \mathcal{S}^{\mathrm{L}}, \mathcal{S}^{\mathrm{R}})$ will then compute statistics over the labels of these subsets in order to compute the information gain. For example, in a classification forest, the statistics are a histogram over the class labels, and the information gain uses the entropy of the left and right histograms. For the purposes of this chapter, we will treat $\mathbf{v}$ as an *indirect* representation of the

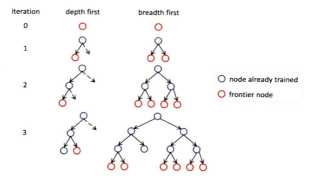

Fig. 21.1 Depth first *vs.* breadth first training. In depth first training a single node is trained at a time. This is typically implemented using a recursive function. In breadth first training, a 'frontier' set of leaf nodes is trained together as a single iteration. The frontier is typically the set of all leaf nodes at a particular depth in the tree. This means that the total number of tree nodes can potentially double at each iteration. The text discusses various trade-offs between these two training schedules

training point, *e.g.* the index of a pixel in a particular image, or a point in time for a temporal sequence.

21.2 Depth First and Breadth First Training

One of the most important decisions to make about implementing decision tree training is whether to use depth first or breadth first training. The two approaches are illustrated in Fig. 21.1, and pseudocode implementations are given in Algorithms 21.1 and 21.2. Please note that, for clarity of exposition, the pseudocode implementations do not include training termination criteria other than fixing a maximum tree depth D.

21.2.1 Depth First Training

In depth first training, tree nodes are trained one at a time, starting at the root node. For each node, the goal is to select the weak learner that will be used to assign incoming data points to the left or right child. Many candidate weak learners are tested and the one associated with the largest information gain over candidate partitions of the training data points is selected. Then this weak learner is used to partition the set of training points S into left and right subsets, and the algorithm *recurses* for the left and right child nodes. This recursive program structure results in a depth first tree traversal ordering. A pseudocode implementation of this algorithm is given in Algorithm 21.1. Depth first training is used within Sherwood, the code library that accompanies this book (see Chap. 22).

Algorithm 21.1 Depth first training algorithm

// $\mathcal{S}$: set of training points
// d: depth of current node in tree
Require: `TrainDepthFirst`$(\mathcal{S}, d)$

  1: *// Check for termination. D is max tree depth.*
  2: **if** $d > D$ **then**
  3:     **return** LeafNode(`TrainPredictor`$(\mathcal{S})$)

  4: *// Search over weak learners for best information gain*
  5: $I^\star \leftarrow -\infty, \boldsymbol{\theta}^\star \leftarrow \emptyset$
  6: **for** $i = 1 \rightarrow |\mathcal{T}|$ **do**
  7:     $\boldsymbol{\theta} \leftarrow$ `SampleWeakLearner`()
  8:     $(\mathcal{S}^{\mathrm{L}}, \mathcal{S}^{\mathrm{R}}) \leftarrow$ `PartitionData`$(\mathcal{S}, \boldsymbol{\theta})$
  9:     $I \leftarrow I(\mathcal{S}, \mathcal{S}^{\mathrm{L}}, \mathcal{S}^{\mathrm{R}})$ *// Compute information gain*
10:     **if** $I > I^\star$ **then** $I^\star \leftarrow I, \boldsymbol{\theta}^\star \leftarrow \boldsymbol{\theta}$

11: *// Recurse on left and right subsets*
12: $(\mathcal{S}^{\mathrm{L}}, \mathcal{S}^{\mathrm{R}}) \leftarrow$ `PartitionData`$(\mathcal{S}, \boldsymbol{\theta}^\star)$
13: LeftChild $\leftarrow$ `TrainDepthFirst`$(\mathcal{S}^{\mathrm{L}}, d + 1)$
14: RightChild $\leftarrow$ `TrainDepthFirst`$(\mathcal{S}^{\mathrm{R}}, d + 1)$
15: **return** SplitNode$(\boldsymbol{\theta}^\star, \text{LeftChild}, \text{RightChild})$

21.2.2 Breadth First Training

Breadth first training differs from depth first training in that a whole 'frontier' of leaf nodes are split at each iteration. The frontier may be any subset of all the leaf nodes in the tree.[1] The tree can therefore potentially double in size at each iteration.

At each iteration, a set of statistics are initialized for each frontier node and for each candidate setting of the weak learner parameters $\boldsymbol{\theta}$. The set of *all* training points is then iterated over. For each training point, the leaf node on the frontier that it reaches is found. This can be computed on demand by traversing the existing tree from the root to a leaf node (or cached from a previous iteration). An inner loop over the candidate weak learners is then performed, and according to the binary left/right decision made for each training point, the relevant frontier node's statistics are incremented. After all training points have been seen, the choice of weak learner parameters that gave the best information gain can be computed for each frontier node based on the aggregated sets of statistics. Pseudocode for breadth first training is given in Algorithm 21.2.

---

[1]The frontier can comprise all the leaf nodes or only a subset. It might contain leaf nodes from different levels in the tree. Some leaf nodes might not be on the frontier; for example, those nodes for which no candidate weak learner could improve the information gain at a previous iteration of breadth first training.

Algorithm 21.2 Breadth first training algorithm

// $\mathcal{S}$: set of training points
// RootNode: root node of tree
// $\mathcal{F}$: set of frontier leaf nodes
Require: `TrainBreadthFirstLevel`$(\mathcal{S}, \text{RootNode}, \mathcal{F})$

  1: *// Initialize*
  2: call $\mathcal{I}_{ij} = $ `InitializeStatistics`$()$ for all $i \in \{1, \ldots, |\mathcal{T}|\}$ and $j \in \mathcal{F}$
  3: call $\boldsymbol{\theta}_i = $ `SampleWeakLearner`$()$ for all $i \in \{1, \ldots, |\mathcal{T}|\}$

  4: *// Aggregate statistics across all training points*
  5: **for** $(\mathbf{v}, \mathbf{y}) \in \mathcal{S}$ **do**
  6:     $j \leftarrow$ `TraverseTreeToLeaf`$(\text{RootNode}, \mathbf{v})$ *// $j \in \mathcal{F}$*
  7:     **for** $i = 1 \rightarrow |\mathcal{T}|$ **do**
  8:         $h \leftarrow h(\mathbf{v}, \boldsymbol{\theta}_i)$ *// Did $\mathbf{v}$ go left or right?*
  9:         `UpdateStatistics`$(\mathcal{I}_{ij}, h, \mathbf{y})$

10: *// Choose best weak learner at each frontier node*
11: **for** $j \in \mathcal{F}$ **do**
12:     compute $\boldsymbol{\theta}^\star \leftarrow \arg\max_i$ `ComputeInformationGain`$(\mathcal{I}_{ij})$
13:     `ConvertToSplitNode`$(j, \boldsymbol{\theta}^\star, \mathcal{I}_{ij})$ *// This also trains predictors at new child leaf nodes*

// $\mathcal{S}$: set of training points
Require: `TrainBreadthFirst`$(\mathcal{S})$

  1: RootNode $=$ LeafNode$()$
  2: **for** $d = 0 \rightarrow D$ **do**
  3:     $\mathcal{F} \leftarrow$ `GetAllLeaves`(RootNode)
  4:     `TrainBreadthFirstLevel`$(\mathcal{S}, \text{RootNode}, \mathcal{F})$
  5: **return** RootNode

21.2.3 Properties

Depth first and breadth first training have very different properties:

- In depth first training, the outer loop is over candidate weak learners and the inner loop is over training points. In breadth first training, this order is reversed.
- Depth first training requires the training points to be recursively partitioned many times over. Breadth first training requires at most D (maximum tree depth) linear sweeps through the training points.
- Depth first training can be implemented to use a constant amount of memory for candidate weak learner statistics. A straightforward implementation of breadth first training requires $O(2^D)$ memory for the weak learner statistics.
- Depth first is easier to implement.

These properties mean that implementations of the two algorithms will have very different computational characteristics and use cases. Breadth first is the natural choice when it is expensive to randomly access the data. This might happen, for example, when the training data are too big to fit in memory and must be streamed from disk, or when it is more efficient to compute feature responses sequentially for the pixels of an image due to cache coherency. It is also easier to parallelize and distribute the breadth first training over multiple CPU or GPU cores (see Sects. 21.5.1, 21.5.2, and 21.5.3 below).

However, breadth first uses a very large amount of memory when the tree gets deep. To avoid this, a sensible 'hybrid' strategy might be to train the first few levels with breadth first and then switch to depth first for the lower levels. Alternatively, one can 'batch up' either the frontier nodes or the candidate weak learners to maintain a constant memory usage with breadth first training.

Of course, as we have mentioned before, the efficiency of any implementation depends heavily on your particular data and application.

21.3 Weak Learner Implementation

In this section, we discuss two implementation issues relating to computing the weak learner response (21.1): when to compute the feature responses $f(\mathbf{v}, \boldsymbol{\phi})$, and how we can evaluate multiple candidate feature response thresholds τ per candidate feature parameters $\boldsymbol{\phi}$.

21.3.1 Computing Responses on the Fly

Many traditional machine learning algorithms treat the feature responses $f(\mathbf{v}, \boldsymbol{\phi})$ as a pre-computed matrix $F = f_{ij} = f(\mathbf{v}_i, \boldsymbol{\phi}_j)$ for all possible settings of the weak learner parameters $\boldsymbol{\phi}_i$ and for all training points $\mathbf{v}_i$. By pre-computing matrix F, the learning algorithm can simply look up feature response values as needed. However, storing the full matrix of feature responses may be needlessly memory inefficient. This is especially true when there is a very large search space of parameters $\boldsymbol{\phi}$, *e.g.* in the case of the depth difference features used in Chap. 13. Even if sufficient memory is available, it is possible that poor cache utilization will result in inefficient training.

One of the attractions of randomized decision forests is that they positively encourage a simple alternative: computing the feature responses $f(\mathbf{v}, \boldsymbol{\phi})$ on the fly. The random choice of feature parameters $\boldsymbol{\phi}$ at each node allows the learning to explore a huge number of features. The feature function f is allowed to compute *any* function of the original data. For example, if the training point $\mathbf{v}$ is used to index a pixel in a particular image, then $f(\mathbf{v}, \boldsymbol{\phi})$ could compute any function of the image at, *or in the surrounding neighborhood of*, the pixel. Sometimes pre-processing (such

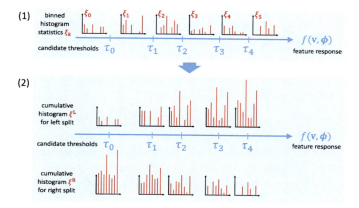

Fig. 21.2 Efficient evaluation of multiple candidate thresholds τ per feature parameters ϕ. In step (1), statistics are aggregated across a set of training points. These statistics are binned by the candidate thresholds τ_k. In step (2), a linear sweep is sufficient to compute the cumulative left and right statistics, and thereby the information gain, for all candidate thresholds. While this illustration deals with classification forests where the statistics are unnormalized class count histograms, the approach generalizes to any additive statistics, *e.g.* sum and sum of squares for a Gaussian

as edge-detection or integral imaging) might be used; then $f(\mathbf{v}, \phi)$ could compute any function of that pre-processed data too. It is particularly appropriate to compute responses on the fly when the response is a trivial function of existing data, for example the difference of image pixel intensities, or temporal differences in a sequence.

21.3.2 Multiple Candidate Thresholds per Feature

A related implementation question is how to convert from the real-valued scalar feature response f into the binary weak learner response h representing the 'branch left or right' decision (see (21.1)). In other words, how can we choose a sensible threshold value τ? The simplest solution is to sample the weak learner parameter vector $\theta = (\phi, \tau)$ from some sensible distribution. However, a cheaper alternative may be to evaluate several candidate thresholds τ for each setting of ϕ. In this case, one need only compute f once (a relatively costly operation) to obtain multiple possible values of h. This strategy therefore works well when computing feature responses on the fly, as discussed in the previous section. If you have sufficient training data to avoid overfitting, this strategy may result in a more accurate decision forest for less training computation.

Figure 21.2 illustrates the algorithm, which has two steps. The first step aggregates binned statistics across a set of training points as follows. Given the sampled feature parameters ϕ, an ordered set of candidate thresholds $\{\tau_k\}_{k=0}^{K-1}$ is sampled. After the feature response $f(\mathbf{v}, \phi)$ is computed for a particular data point $\mathbf{v}$, the relevant bin $k \in \{0, \dots, K\}$ is found as

$$
k = \begin{cases}
0 & \text{if } f < \tau_0, \\
1 & \text{if } \tau_0 \leq f < \tau_1, \\
\dots & \\
K & \text{if } \tau_{K-1} \leq f.
\end{cases} \tag{21.2}
$$

Note that there are thus $K + 1$ bins for K thresholds. If the thresholds are uniformly spaced, then bin number k can be computed trivially. Alternatively, binary or linear search may be used to find k reasonably efficiently. The statistics for bin k are then updated for the data point $\mathbf{v}$. This is done for all data points, giving statistics ξ_k (*e.g.* unnormalized class count histograms) for $k = 0, \dots, K$.

The second step performs a linear sweep through the candidate thresholds to compute the associated information gains in $O(K)$ time, as follows. First, the statistics are accumulated for all training points by aggregating all binned statistics; let us call this $\xi^R \leftarrow \bigcup_k \xi_k$. Let also $\xi^L \leftarrow \emptyset$ initially. Then a linear sweep is performed through the candidate thresholds τ_k from $k = 0, \dots, K - 1$. At each bin k the statistics are updated as

$$
\xi^L \leftarrow \xi^L \cup \xi_k, \tag{21.3}
$$

$$
\xi^R \leftarrow \xi^R \setminus \xi_k. \tag{21.4}
$$

After each such update, the statistics ξ^L and ξ^R contain exactly the left and right statistics needed to compute the information gain I given weak learner parameters $\theta = (\phi, \tau_k)$.

With care, this approach can be used with both depth first and breadth first tree training. It can also be generalized efficiently to evaluate weak learners of the form $h(\mathbf{v}, \theta) = [\tau_1 \geq f(\mathbf{v}, \phi) \geq \tau_2]$ with two thresholds τ_1 and τ_2.

21.3.3 Efficient Threshold Selection

The previous section explains how multiple feature response thresholds τ can be efficiently evaluated for a single candidate feature response function $f(\mathbf{v}, \phi)$. However, a remaining question is how to choose candidate thresholds τ that are likely to give good information gain. One method is simply to fix these in advance, based on some expected range of sensible thresholds. Another method (see Chap. 19) is to train a forest once, compute the distribution over the chosen thresholds, and then re-train the forest by drawing random threshold values from that distribution. However, the main limitation of both of these methods is that it is impossible to know in advance whether the response values associated with training data reaching a *particular* node will conform to the fixed range or the observed distribution.

An interesting alternative is to perform two passes over the feature responses for each node: first to determine a set of sensible threshold values by inspecting the distribution of feature response values, and second to accumulate the statistics given that range. Sensible thresholds values might be chosen *e.g.* by dividing the range of response values into equal parts, or by using percentiles using the cumulative distribution (the latter approach is taken by the Sherwood software library described in the next chapter). While this does require two passes through the data, (i) it may be sufficient to use only a subset of feature response values to approximate the range or distribution, and (ii) the feature responses can be cached when using the depth first training schedule. Further, even with breadth first, it is possible that the increased relevance of the thresholds tested will result in a forest that is more accurate, even when fewer thresholds are evaluated. This technique will likely increase the strength of the weak learners, and so, as usual, care is needed to avoid overfitting.

21.4 Data Structures

In general, the use of compact data structures and a contiguous memory layout helps to ensure efficient cache utilization. How data structures such as trees are represented in computer memory can have an important impact on the performance of decision forest training and test algorithms.

21.4.1 Tree Memory Organization

Traditionally, trees are stored in computer memory by referencing a root node. Each node in turn contains a pointer or reference to its child nodes, and optionally to its sibling and parent nodes. New nodes can be appended simply by allocating additional memory and fixing up the pointers accordingly. However, while this kind of structure may be convenient for growing trees during training, this is not necessary during test. Since tree nodes will be accessed successively and repeatedly, we would prefer them to be stored in nearby memory locations to improve cache performance. Therefore we recommend using a contiguous array structure, at least at test time.

One possibility is to store all the nodes of the tree in a contiguous array structure (see Fig. 21.3a and b), where each element of the array represents one tree node, with the first element corresponding to the root node. Because the trees used here are binary, the indices of a node's two (left and right) children can always be determined simply as follows:

$$\text{leftChildIndex} = 2 \times \text{parentNodeIndex} + 1, \qquad (21.5)$$

$$\text{rightChildIndex} = 2 \times \text{parentNodeIndex} + 2. \qquad (21.6)$$

These relationships allow tree nodes to be represented compactly, since no memory is used to encode the relationship between parent and child nodes. Provided that trees are approximately balanced (all leaf nodes at the same depth), this permits both memory-efficient tree representation and time-efficient random access to

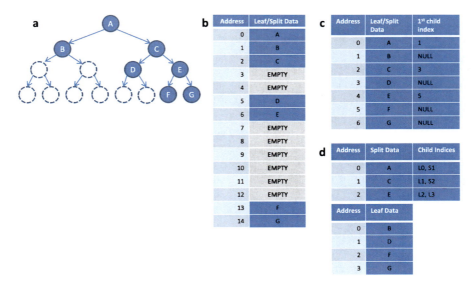

Fig. 21.3 Options for memory organization. (**a**) A toy decision tree. (**b**) The data associated with the nodes may be stored in a linear array, organized so that the indices of a node's child or parent nodes an be simply computed from the node's index. (**c**) If the tree is unbalanced, it may be more efficient to store the index of the first child for each parent node (or NULL for leaf nodes). (**d**) Since split and leaf nodes have different data storage requirements, it may be more efficient to store them in separate arrays. An extra boolean variable (prefix S or L) is needed to distinguish split and leaf nodes

nodes. However, where the tree is unbalanced (*e.g.* Fig. 21.3a), the node array will contain empty elements. It is memory inefficient to store very unbalanced trees in this way.

An alternative is to store at each array element the index (or offset) of the left and right children (Fig. 21.3c). We can adopt the convention that left and right siblings are always contiguous and we therefore require only one offset to be stored with each element. Since we will only be traversing the tree in top-down order, it is not necessary to store references to parent or sibling elements. Storing indices (or offsets) rather than explicit pointers has the benefit of being invariant to serialization and deserialization.

21.4.2 Split and Leaf Node Representation

Another consideration is how to represent split (interior) nodes and leaf nodes. At split nodes we must store the parameters of the weak learner, and be able to navigate to child nodes. Conversely, leaf nodes do not have associated weak learners nor child nodes; instead we must be able to retrieve statistics that are associated with the leaf during training. The different data requirements for split and leaf nodes suggest that they be treated differently. This is particularly true when the amount of memory used by the forest is an issue: unnecessarily storing feature parameters for all leaf nodes is likely to double the amount of memory used.

A simple way to implement this is to store split nodes and leaf nodes separately, each in their own contiguous array (Fig. 21.3d). When storing child node indices in the split nodes (as described above) we can use one bit of this index to indicate whether the child is another split node or instead a leaf node. When this bit is set, we know that the child is a leaf rather than a split node, and can then look up the statistics in the leaf array. Additional memory might also be saved with this approach by quantizing the leaf statistics and sharing the leaf elements across the tree, or indeed across the whole forest.

21.5 Parallelization

Modern computer architectures are becoming increasingly parallel with the rise of multi-core CPUs, graphics processing units (GPUs), and distributed compute clusters. Thankfully decision forests offer numerous ways to parallelize their training. We have explored some possible parallel implementations in [333] on the GPU, and in [51] for multi-core and distributed environments. Decision forests can also be implemented in hardware, for example on FPGAs [272]. As usual, the optimal parallelization is likely to depend on your particular scenario, but we will try to give some high-level guidance here.

Important considerations when parallelizing decision forests include:

- Is training time important? For large training problems especially, being able to train in a reasonable amount of time has many practical advantages, such as being able to iteratively investigate different variants.
- Over which dimension(s) should you parallelize? You might choose the different trees in the forest, the weak learners, the tree nodes, or the training points. The right choice here can ensure a steady high-compute load with minimal synchronization time. The depth and breadth first schedules presented above will of course need to be adapted appropriately. Parallelizing over trees in the forest can of course only give a substantial benefit if you have more trees than compute cores.
- How many data do you have? With a large amount of data, you might consider distributing batches of it to different compute nodes and processing the batches in parallel.

The following sections discuss how to implement decision tree training and software for specific computational architectures: multi-core CPU (Sect. 21.5.1), GPU (Sect. 21.5.2), and distributed computing environments (Sect. 21.5.3).

21.5.1 Multi-core CPU Implementation

Modern computer architectures are increasingly parallel devices: as power consumption limits the clock speed of individual processors, computing power is more efficiently increased by adding additional processing units. But parallelism in hardware can only be effectively utilized by corresponding parallelism in multi-threaded software. Thus for efficient computation it is essential to have both parallel algorithms and the appropriate programming constructs to implement them. Fortunately, for decision forest training and inference, we have no shortage of options for dividing the computing load into independent tasks that can be performed in parallel.

21.5.1.1 Parallel-For

A foundational component in implementing parallel workloads is the *parallel-for* loop. Whereas the traditional 'for' loop iterates over each element in turn, the 'parallel-for' loop divides the elements of the loop between all available processors and allows them to proceed simultaneously. So, unlike the traditional 'for' loop, 'parallel-for' implies and assumes that each iteration of the loop is independent of all others since they may be processed in any order.

In the C++ programming language, the 'parallel-for' loop can be accessed in a number of ways. C++ compilers that support OpenMP allow the programmer to insert a #pragma statement before a 'for' loop to indicate that it should be run in parallel. However, newer compilers that support lambda functions allow for a better option: libraries such as Intel's Thread Building Blocks and Microsoft's Parallel Patterns Library (part of Visual C++) allow the 'parallel-for' loop to be invoked directly in code.

In the C♯ programming language and other .NET languages, the Parallel.For routine in the System.Threading.Tasks namespace provides the same functionality.

21.5.1.2 Parallel Training

When approaching a parallel implementation of forest learning, the most pressing question is over which dimension(s) will we choose to parallelize? This choice will have consequences for memory use, data access patterns and overall performance. There are options to parallelize over the trees of the forest, over the weak learners, over the leaf nodes of a tree, or over the training data points. The right choice will be determined partly by the size of the problem (such as the amount of training data and the number of trees required), and partly by the available hardware. The choice is also closely linked with the choice of a breadth first or depth first training schedule (Sect. 21.2).

One option is to parallelize over the trees in a forest. This is trivial to do, but is not recommended on a single machine unless all the training data fits into memory: since each thread is required to be working on different input data, data-loading bandwidth can easily be saturated and the shared cache is not well utilized. Instead, with large training data sets, we prefer schemes that can process the input data systematically to maximize the load throughput and cache coherency.

For example, consider the breadth first approach of Algorithm 21.2. Simply parallelizing the inner loop over weak learners, we can keep all cores busy processing the same batch of training data, reducing the need for disk bandwidth and improving cache coherency. As the depth of the tree increases, one can limit the number of leaf nodes considered to be part of the 'frontier' to keep the required memory constant (Sect. 21.2.2). This is recommended.

Alternatively, when the depth first approach is preferred, perhaps because training data is already loaded into system memory, a worthwhile option is to parallelize both over the weak learners and over the leaf nodes of the tree. The reason for this is that at the higher levels of the tree, there is not much opportunity to parallelize over nodes whereas there are many weak learners to process for each node. However, at the lower levels of the tree, the converse is true. Parallelizing over the weak learners is again achieved through the simple use of the 'parallel-for' loop. Parallelizing over the leaf nodes can be easily achieved by replacing the recursive function calls in Algorithm 21.1 with the use of a concurrent stack data structure. Worker threads pop from this stack to process each newly available leaf.

In the end, the best strategy depends on the problem at hand: the number of trees, training data points, weak learners and processor cores. However, in a good multi-threading programming environment it should be straightforward to compare the merits of different strategies if it is not initially clear which to pursue.

21.5.1.3 Parallel Inference

One of the main benefits of using decision forests is the speed at which inference can be performed at test time. Performing inference simply requires a handful of feature tests to be evaluated, and this can be done independently at each data point.

A typical strategy is to form an outer loop over data points and for each data point to loop over the trees in the forest. An inner loop then evaluates feature tests on the data point, descending through the nodes of a tree until reaching a leaf, whereupon the leaf statistics are aggregated for that data point. If there are many more data points than trees, as is often the case, it makes sense to parallelize the outer loop over the data points. This is trivial as each data point can be processed independently.

For details about data structures for efficient navigation of the tree, see Sect. 21.4.

21.5.1.4 Multi-threading Considerations

Care must be taken when executing code in a multi-threaded scenario. Although it is safe for multiple threads to access the same data if all the accesses are read-only, any simultaneous non-atomic read/write access can cause race conditions. An easy way to avoid problems is to ensure that each thread writes to a different area of output memory. For example, this is handled naturally during inference if each data point is tested in parallel to produce its own output value that is written to an array.

Training randomized decision forests makes extensive use of random sampling. One must take care with random number generators which contain state and are typically not thread-safe. If, for example, two threads attempt to sample from the same random number generator, a race condition may occur whereby the random number generator ends up in an indeterminate state. This can give rise to subtle bugs, such as highly correlated samples and forests that therefore generalize poorly.

21.5.2 GPU Implementation

When there is sufficient parallelism, GPU computation can be many times faster than CPU computation. In addition to having many more cores, GPUs also have impressive memory bandwidth and a large texture cache.

GPU programming can be achieved through a number of different technologies. Traditional graphics APIs like Direct3D and OpenGL allow the programmer to write custom pixel shaders that can be used to process data points. In [333], an implementation of this kind is discussed in detail. More modern, general-purpose APIs such as CUDA, OpenCL and C++ AMP instead do not require the programmer to deal with graphics primitives but allow for generic computation kernels to be launched on the GPU device. This is a far more convenient paradigm for GPU programming. (One should be aware, however, that CUDA software can only be executed on nVidia GPUs.)

When implementing forest training or inference for the GPU, the considerations of the preceding section on multi-core CPU implementations are equally relevant. A few additional considerations are also appropriate.

A GPU can have hundreds of cores—many times more cores than CPUs. A high degree of parallelism is required to take full advantage of this compute power. For training, typically only the breadth first approach will be appropriate for GPUs. For inference, evaluation on the GPU is ideal when there is a significant number of data points to process. In particular, the GPU is a great choice for parallelizing the inference across pixels in an image. To minimize the amount of data that must be read back from the GPU, it also makes sense to implement any post-processing on the GPU if possible. An example of such post-processing would be to compute at each pixel the most likely class from the resulting distribution.

To represent the trees on the device memory, we recommend storing them in 1D or 2D texture memory to benefit from the texture cache. The trees can be stored as described above in Sect. 21.4. Data points are read-only and can be stored in texture memory too.

To be able to use a GPU for your application, it must be possible to implement your particular choice of feature within the limits of GPU programming. Fortunately, GPUs are well suited to on-the-fly computation of many standard image features (see Sect. 21.3.1), such as the pixel difference features used in Chap. 13. In this case, the raw images would be stored as textures, and the GPU kernel function would compute the relevant feature responses by reading from the image textures.

Finally, note that it is best to avoid *branching* in the kernels (*i.e.* the use of 'if' statements) since the GPU executes multiple kernels in lock-step, and if different kernels take different code paths, this *thread divergence* can reduce performance dramatically. To eliminate thread divergence, note that the jump to a left or right child in the tree can be computed using arithmetic rather than logical expressions.

21.5.3 Distributed Computing Implementation

When the amount of computation required for forest training is very high, for example because there is a large amount of training data, achieving acceptably rapid training may necessitate distributing the training computation over multiple machines in a cluster.

One of the simplest ways of doing this is to duplicate all the training data over several machines and train several trees in parallel, one tree per machine. However, if the amount of training data is large, it may not be convenient to accommodate all of it in a single machine's RAM. Despite continuing rapid growth in RAM sizes, volumetric data, perhaps from medical scans, will rapidly fill all available memory. In any case, training even a single tree may still take too long. A partial solution to the problem of having too little memory is to leave the training data on disk until it is needed, using a breadth-first training schedule to ensure that data are accessed sequentially with each training front so as to minimize disk I/O. However, this will likely cause even further reduction in speed. Another possible solution is to use bagging to reduce the amount of data that needs to be stored on each machine. However, bagging reduces the amount of data that is available to each tree, which may reduce generalization (Sect. 4.4.4).

An alternative is to distribute the training of a single tree across multiple machines. The training algorithm can be parallelized in multiple dimensions: (i) partition the data space (individual data units), (ii) partition the search space (the nodes of the decision tree), and (iii) partition the feature space.

One particular implementation is discussed in [51]. In their implementation, the computation proceeds breadth first, in rounds. At each round, breadth first training processes all nodes at depth d in the decision tree and generates a new frontier at depth $d + 1$. Each round has three phases, which comprise a large number of parallel tasks.

1. In Phase 1 each task operates on one data unit, one partition of the feature space and the entire tree from the previous round. This phase processes each example, builds a four-dimensional histogram, indexed by (node; feature; class; left/right).
2. In Phase 2 each task operates on one (node; feature) partition of the histogram, and computes the best feature in that partition for splitting each node in that partition (each task is responsible for a subset of nodes and features).
3. Finally, Phase 3 aggregates the information produced by Phase 2, producing a new tree frontier by selecting the best overall feature for splitting each node, and generating its left and right children.

This implementation, built for Kinect's body part recognition system (see Chap. 13), demonstrated that one can effectively distribute the training of decision trees. However, the efficiency (measured in computer core hours per training image) was considerably lower than a single machine implementation due to network and disk overheads.

In summary, a distributed implementation can allow you to scale training up considerably further than would be possible on a single CPU or GPU. However, even with modern tools such as DryadLINQ [51], writing a distributed implementation is a considerable engineering effort, and so should be approached with caution.

21.6 Parameter Tuning

Decision forest training algorithms have several parameters, and achieving good test accuracy will require some tuning of these parameters.[2] Next, we summarize the important parameters, and try to give some insight into how they should be tuned to best effect.

21.6.1 Maximum Tree Depth, D

Trees must be trained sufficiently deeply to capture a nuanced model of the training data, but not so deep as to model sampling noise. In other words, training too many decision levels quickly gives rise to overfitting, but too few to underfitting (see Part I). Sometimes tree depth is constrained by simply limiting the number of decision levels applied. In practice, this solution may be suboptimal if different branches of the tree model differing proportions of the training set. An alternative way of constraining tree depth is to supply an appropriate training termination criterion. Typically the termination criterion would prevent further training of a branch when none of the candidate weak learners yields appreciable information gain. Training depth can thus be adapted automatically to the training data. With such a termination criterion, a specified maximum tree depth is still useful, but mainly as a means of limiting the size of the tree.

21.6.2 Number of Trees in the Forest, T

As discussed in Part I, increasing the number of trees in a decision forest can increase generalization accuracy, but typically only at the expense of test time performance. Usually we have found that generalization accuracy increases sublinearly with the number of trees in a forest, whilst performance decreases linearly. With this observation in mind, it is usually sufficient to test a few different forest sizes

---

[2]Of course, for rigorous testing, you should always use a hold-out validation set when optimizing these parameters: optimizing on the test set will lead to misleadingly inflated accuracy scores.

and pick the size that gives an acceptable trade-off between generalization accuracy and performance. Sometimes using a few trees proves sufficient, although it is also not unusual to find an appreciable improvement in generalization accuracy with hundreds of trees. Experience suggests that optimal values for other tree parameters depend only relatively weakly on the number of trees in the forest.

21.6.3 Number of Candidate Weak Learners

This parameter must be chosen so as to achieve the right trade-off between modeling the variability of the training data and randomness (which is essential to generalization accuracy). If the space of candidate weak learners is explored too exhaustively at training time, the danger is that the forest training procedure will produce duplicate trees for a given set of input data. Conversely, if too few candidate weak learners are considered, then the resulting trees may be ineffective at capturing the variability of the data. In practice, the dimensionality of the space of available weak learners is an important factor in this decision. For the toy examples in Part I (which use 1D and 2D data) and linear weak learners, using 10–20 candidates has been found to be appropriate. However, for higher dimensional feature spaces (such as features computed in the local vicinity of pixels in an image), it may be necessary to explore a much greater number of candidate weak learners.

21.6.4 Number of Candidate Response Thresholds per Feature

Section 21.3.2 describes an algorithm for efficiently evaluating multiple thresholds for each candidate feature response function. But how many threshold should be tested? When candidate thresholds are selected by using quantiles computed over a sample of response values, we have typically found that approximately 10 candidate thresholds per candidate feature response yield improved test accuracy and reduced training time.

21.7 Tricks of the Trade

Finally, we describe some miscellaneous 'tricks of the trade'. We hope these may prove useful to other practitioners.

21.7.1 In-place Partitioning of Training Data

During depth first training, we need to keep account of which data points reach which tree nodes so that we can proceed to train the next child or sibling. A simple solution is to store lists of the indices of the data points that arrive at each node. However, building many such lists is inefficient because or repeated allocation and deallocation of memory. Because the number of training data points does not change during training, a better solution is to keep all the indices in a single array that is reordered during tree training by a sequence of *in-place partition* operations. When training commences the array is in arbitrary order. At the root decision node, the array is partitioned into two parts, one containing the samples that descend to the left child, the other containing the samples that descend to the right child. Then each descendent split node operates on one contiguous section of the array, further partitioning it into sub-parts. In-place partitioning can be achieved by simply swapping pairs of data point indices like in the *Quicksort* algorithm.

21.7.2 Retrospective Tuning of Maximum Tree Depth

So as to avoid the need to re-train the forest for multiple values of the maximum tree depth D, we allow the tree depth to be specified at *test* time independently of the maximum tree depth specified at training time. This necessitates larger memory consumption as we need to store training data statistics in *all* nodes in the tree, not just the leaf nodes. However, this trick allows for much faster experimentation with varying values of D, essential for research applications. Once the ideal tree depth has been found, a post-processing step can be used to build a more compact version of the tree for which weak learner parameters are only stored for split nodes and training data statistics are only stored for leaf nodes.

21.7.3 Dealing with Unbalanced Datasets

In some applications, one may have an unbalanced distribution of classes in the training set, *e.g.* the number of negative examples may dominate positive examples. Two commonly used heuristics for dealing with this problem are: (i) resample the training data to have roughly the same number of positive and negative examples, and (ii) weight the contribution of each class by its inverse frequency when computing information gain at each split node.

21.7.4 Bagging and Leaf Predictors

Bagging [42] can be a powerful randomization technique to help reduce overfitting. It works by training the forest on only a subset of the training examples. We have two practical tips here:

- Firstly it can be much better to bag across independent samples. For example, it is better to bag across *images* from a training set than across pixels within those images. This ensures that each tree really does see independent samples.[3]
- Overfitting is most likely to occur when the weak learners become too strong. Our second tip is therefore that it can sometimes be beneficial to perform bagging when learning the tree structure, but to then fix the structure and re-estimate the leaf node predictors with *all* the training examples. We have observed modest improvements in generalization using this technique.

21.7.5 Augmenting Your Training Set

A common way to improve generalization is to encode specific desirable invariances directly into the training data. In images, photometric (such as affine intensity changes) and geometric (such as rotations or scale changes) transformations are common ways to improve matters. In temporal sequences, time warping can be applied.

21.7.6 Sampling Weak Learner Parameters

We have seen in this book many examples of how decision forests are able to select good weak learners from a large space of candidates. Part of this success is due to the random sampling of a candidate set of features at each node; roughly speaking, over the whole tree, each 'good' feature is likely to be seen somewhere. However, as discussed further in Chap. 19 and [344], one can do better by sampling the candidates in a more informed manner. In particular, a good heuristic is the following. First, train a forest using a uniform sampling distribution for the features. Next, learn the distribution of the features chosen across the nodes in the forest, optionally as a function of depth. Finally, use that learned distribution as the sampling distribution for training a new forest. In practice we have observed this to give modest improvements in accuracy, as it makes it more likely that 'good' features will be tested during training.

21.7.7 Reducing Correlation Between Trees in a Forest

To reduce correlation between the trees in a forest, beyond simply bagging the training examples, one could reduce the number of candidate features or thresholds near

---

[3]A similar strict separation is even more important to ensure truly independent training and test sets.

the root of the tree. Totally randomized trees [128] take this idea to the limit by choosing the features and thresholds completely at random. No node optimization is necessary here, and thus training is extremely efficient. For certain applications this may improve generalization.

21.8 Conclusion

We have seen how decision forests can be trained and evaluated efficiently. We hope these techniques prove useful to the reader and spur further progress in large scale learning with forests.

Chapter 22
The Sherwood Software Library

D. Roberston, J. Shotton, and T. Sharp

This chapter describes *Sherwood*, the code library that accompanies this book. This library is available in both C# and C++ versions and includes both (i) a general purpose, object-oriented software framework for solving decision forest inference problems, and (ii) example code in the form of a command line demo (which is required to complete the exercises at the end of several of the chapters in Part I). Here we describe the library's important design features and explain how the object-oriented framework can be applied to new inference tasks.

22.1 Introduction

Sherwood is the code library designed to accompany this book. It comprises two important components:

- a general purpose, object-oriented software framework for applying decision forests to a wide range of inference problems; and
- example code in the form of a command line demo that shows how this framework can be applied to several of the problems described in Part I.

We hope that the reader will use this code library to gain insight into how decision forests work and how they can be implemented. The accompanying example code shows how the general purpose framework can be applied to a variety of toy problems including (i) supervised classification of 2D data, (ii) 1D-1D regression, (iii) 2D density estimation, and (iv) semi-supervised classification of 2D data. The

D. Roberston (✉)
Redimension Ltd., Cambridge, UK

J. Shotton · T. Sharp
Microsoft Research Ltd., Cambridge, UK

A. Criminisi, J. Shotton (eds.), *Decision Forests for Computer Vision and Medical Image Analysis*, Advances in Computer Vision and Pattern Recognition, DOI 10.1007/978-1-4471-4929-3_22, © Springer-Verlag London 2013

command line demo (which may be called from Matlab) can be used with the supplied data to reproduce many of the figures in Part I. It is also needed to complete the exercises at the end of the early chapters.

The object oriented framework that forms the heart of Sherwood could also serve as a useful basis for applying decision forests to new inference tasks. To this end, it has been written so as to be easily adaptable. It can support *e.g.* different types of training data, different weak learners, and different information gain metrics. Whilst the code has been written mainly with simplicity and ease of use in mind, it is nonetheless sufficiently fast for use in non-trivial real world applications.

22.2 Getting Started

You can download Sherwood from:

http://research.microsoft.com/projects/decisionforests.

To use the command line demo on the Windows platform, it will be helpful to add the directory containing the precompiled binary executable to your path. The simplest way of doing this is by using the `path` command at the command prompt. For example, assuming you have copied the library to the directory `c:\temp\sherwood`, you would type:

```
path = %PATH%;c:\temp\sherwood\bin
```

and to check that the demo tool is working, just type a command, *e.g.*:

```
sw help
```

which gives more information on the available command line modes.

You can also build the library from source for both the Windows and Linux platforms. This is necessary if you wish to use the demo on Linux or if you want to use the software as the basis of your own decision forest inference solution. Sherwood is available in both C++ and C# versions, which are implemented very similarly. These can be found in the `cpp\` and `csharp\` subdirectories of the distribution. Feel free to use whichever version you are most comfortable with. For detailed instructions on building the library for Windows (with Visual Studio or Visual Studio Express) or Linux (with gcc or Mono), please refer to the file `ReadMe.txt` in the root directory.

22.3 Architectural Overview

In implementing the object-oriented software framework that forms the basis of Sherwood, the most important goal was code reuse. A key concern was to make effective use of abstraction, *i.e.* to represent the interaction between the general purpose training code and application-specific training tasks by generic interfaces. This

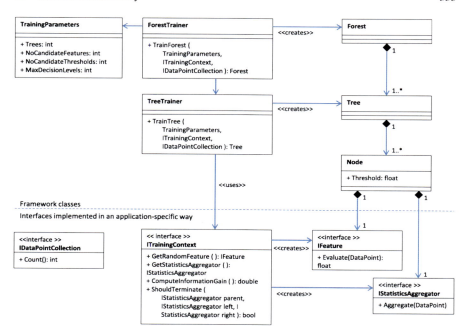

Fig. 22.1 UML diagram to illustrate the architecture of the Sherwood library. To facilitate code reuse, the general purpose forest and tree training classes interact with the training data only via abstract interfaces `ITrainingContext`, `IStatisticsAggregator` and `IFeatureResponse`. Note that some members and classes have been omitted for clarity

approach is possible mainly because typical decision forest implementations have much in common. It is testament to the flexibility of decision forests that a single framework (containing only a few hundred lines of code) can be applied so easily to so many different inference problems.

Figure 22.1 illustrates the architecture of the Sherwood library using a UML diagram. This diagram shows the relationships between the classes that participate in forest training and test. Within the library decision forests are represented by the `Forest`, `Tree`, and `Node` classes. Naturally, a `Forest` contains one or more `Tree` instances, and each `Tree` contains one or more `Node` instances. A `Node` can represent either a split node or a leaf node. Both split nodes and leaf nodes have a set of training sample statistics (an `IStatisticsAggregator`). Additionally, split nodes have an associated weak learner, *i.e.* the feature response function selected during the forest training procedure (an `IFeatureResponse`) and an associated decision threshold.

Decision forest training is the responsibility of the `ForestTrainer` class. So that the training framework can be simply reused across problem domains, training tasks are represented by abstract interfaces that need to be implemented within client code. These interfaces abstract out what is common amongst decision forest training implementations, such as the computation of information gain over candidate partitions of a set of data points, or how to decide when to stop training a branch of the tree. The important interfaces are as follows:

- `IDataPointCollection`. This class represents a collection of data points. In Part I, data points **v** were considered to be vectors of feature values. In principle, however, a data point could represent anything for which a scalar feature response can be computed, *e.g.* an image, or a pixel in an image. Since data points can have various forms, the training framework interacts with collections of data points only via the `IDataPointCollection` abstraction.
- `IStatisticsAggregator`. This class is responsible for aggregating statistics over subsets of the training data points. During training, these statistics are used both (i) to compute information gain over partitions of the data resulting from the application of candidate weak learners, and (ii) to decide when to stop training a particular tree branch. At test time, statistics computed during training are used for inference. Which statistics should be aggregated depends on the problem at hand. For example, when training a classification tree, we would typically aggregate histograms over the data points' class labels.
- `IFeatureResponse`. This class is responsible for computing feature responses $f(\mathbf{v}, \boldsymbol{\phi})$ on incoming data points, *i.e.* for mapping data points to scalar values. Combined with a threshold τ, feature response functions form the basis of the weak learners used to form binary partitions over sets of data points (see (21.1)). In Sherwood, feature response function parameters $\boldsymbol{\phi}$ are generated at random by the client code. For illustration, a simple weak learner might partition data points in $\mathbb{R}^d$ by splitting them by a plane; in this case the feature response function might be parameterized by the plane normal.
- `ITrainingContext`. This is the main interface by which the general purpose training framework interacts with the training data. At training time, application-specific implementations of `ITrainingContext` are responsible for random generation of candidate feature response functions (`IFeatureResopnse` instances), for creating `IStatisticsAggregator` instances, and for the computation (based on statistics computed over parent and child nodes) of the information gain associated with each candidate weak learner.

22.4 Performance Considerations

An important concern for implementors of decision forest algorithms is performance. Chapter 21 describes a variety of advanced techniques for efficient implementation of decision forest algorithms, for example, by using breadth first training to increase cache coherence. Because the Sherwood library was designed with simplicity and readability in mind, we have implemented only the simpler depth first training algorithm and stopped short of a multithreaded (parallel) implementation. However, we have endeavored to write reasonably efficient code nonetheless. Next, we will draw attention to some important performance considerations:

- At training time, we keep account of which data points reach which node by simply reordering a single array of data point indices. See Sect. 21.7.1.
- The nodes that comprise each tree are stored in simple, linear arrays (see Fig. 21.3b). Because the trees used here are binary, the indices of a node's two (left and right) children can always be determined simply using Eqs. (21.5) and (21.6). One limitation of this approach is that it may be memory inefficient to store very unbalanced trees in this way.
- Because value types are used to represent tree nodes, feature response functions, and training data statistics, trees can be stored contiguously in memory, *i.e.* in simple linear arrays. Avoiding many small memory allocations increases performance by reducing the amount of work for the memory manager and increasing cache coherence.
- Weak learners comprise a feature (which maps input data points to floating point response values) and an associated threshold value (see Chap. 21). During forest training, the parameters (ϕ, ψ) of the feature response function f (21.1) are chosen at random but for each candidate feature response function, Sherwood performs a search over candidate thresholds so as to find thresholds that are effective in partitioning the data. For a given feature response function, response values computed over the training data points at the node being split are used to determine the range over which to search for candidate thresholds.

22.5 Application Illustration: Supervised Classification

As an illustration of how the Sherwood library can be applied to a specific inference problem, we describe how it has been adapted to the supervised classification task described in Chap. 4. A similar approach has been used to adapt the framework to other inference tasks described in Part I, such as the density estimation, regression, and semi-supervised classification.

The steps required are:

1. Implement the abstract interfaces by which the training framework interacts with the training data. These are: `IDataPointCollection`, `IFeatureResponse`, `IStatisticsAggregator`, and `ITrainingContext`.
2. Use the `ForestTrainer.TrainForest()` method to create a new `Forest`.
3. Optionally serialize the trained forest to a binary file for later deserialization and use.
4. Apply the trained forest to test data: tune parameters on a validation set, and then apply the forest to a previously unseen test set.

Next, we discuss each of these steps in turn, with particular reference to the supervised classification task. Given labeled training data points, the goal here is to assign a probability distribution over class labels to previously unseen test data points.

22.5.1 Implementing Interfaces

The first step is to write application-specific implementations of the interfaces by which the training framework interacts with the training data. These are dealt with in turn below:

IDataPointCollection. Implementations of this interface store collections of data points. Implementations of IFeatureResponse and IStatisticsAggregator collaborate with implementations of IDataPointCollection to evaluate feature responses and aggregate statistics over sets of training data points. All of the toy examples in the Sherwood library use the same basic IDataPointCollection implementation, DataPointCollection. This simple class stores vector data points of arbitrary dimension and provides functionality for feature vectors (and associated class labels) to be read from disk.

IFeatureResponse. The purpose of the IFeatureResponse implementations is to assign a floating point feature response to incoming data points. In combination with a selected response threshold, which is stored by the containing node, an IFeatureResponse instance forms the weak learner that is used at split nodes to partition incoming data points between its child nodes. A simple feature response is obtained computing the dot product of the feature vector with a unit vector chosen at random. In our 2D feature space, thresholding this feature response gives rise to a straight line decision boundary (as illustrated in Fig. 3.2b). The toy examples within Sherwood use the LinearFeature2d class (a concrete implementation of IFeatureResponse) to compute such a feature response for 2D data points.

IStatisticsAggregator. The purpose of IStatisticsAggregator instances is to aggregate statistics over subsets of the training data points. In the context of our classification task, we aggregate histograms over the training data points' class labels. This is the role of the HistogramAggregator class (a concrete implementation of the IStatisticsAggregator interface). This class maintains a vector of class label counts, which are incremented inside the Aggregate() method. HistogramAggregator also implements a method GetEntropy() for computation of entropy over the histogram—this is used within ClassificationTrainingContext (see below) to compute the information gain obtained using a candidate partition function.

ITrainingContext. Finally, ITrainingContext implementations are responsible for (i) computing information gain over sets of data points and (ii) deciding when to stop training each branch. For classification tasks, we define information gain in terms of the reduction in entropy associated with the distributions over class labels at the child nodes compared to the entropy associated with the distribution at the parent node (4.2). At training time, this metric is used by the framework (via the ComputeInformationGain() method) to select the optimal weak learner at each split node. ITrainingContext also defines the termination criterion used by the framework to decide when to stop training a particular branch (the ShouldTerminate() method). For simple classification problems a sufficient termination criterion is when the information gain is less than some threshold, *e.g.* 0.01.

22.5.2 *Training the Forest*

Having implemented the application-specific interfaces by which the training framework interacts with the training data, the next step is to train the forest. The following C# code fragment (taken from `ClassificationDemo.cs`) illustrates how we can load training data, define the forest training parameters, and run training. Closely equivalent C++ code can be found in `ClassificationDemo.cpp`.

```csharp
// Load 2D training data for 2 class classification problem.
DataPointCollection trainingData = DataPointCollection.Load (
    path,
    2,
    DataDescriptor.HasClassLabels );

// The framework interacts with the training data via an
//    ITrainingContext instance
ITrainingContext trainingContext = new
    ClassificationTrainingContext (
    trainingData.CountClasses() );

// We will a train a forest with T=10 trees of maximum depth
//    D=8
TrainingParameters parameters = new TrainingParameters
{
    MaxDecisionLevels = 8,
    NumberOfCandidateFeatures = 30,
    NumberOfCandidateThresholdsPerFeature = 20,
    NumberOfTrees = 10
};

// Initiate training
ForestTrainer<LinearFeature2d> trainer = new
    ForestTrainer<LinearFeature2d>();
Forest<LinearFeature2d> forest = trainer.TrainForest (
    parameters, trainingContext, trainingData );
```

22.5.3 *Serialization and Deserialization*

Having trained a forest, the Sherwood library provides the capability to save the tree to a binary file for later use. This is useful if training is very time-consuming. The `Forest.Serialize()` method serialize a binary representation of a forest to a binary stream; the `Forest.Deserialize()` method instantiates a new forest based on a previously created binary file.

22.5.4 Testing

Having trained our classification forest, the final step is to apply it to previously unseen test data. The following code fragment shows how this is achieved. First, the
forest is applied to the test data using a call to `Forest.Apply()`. This returns an
array of indices that describes which leaf nodes were reached by the data points for
each tree. Next, a posterior class label distribution for each test data point is computed by combining the training data statistics from the leaf nodes reached by that
data point in each tree. In the context of supervised classification, this is achieved
simply by aggregating the histograms computed over the training data points' class
labels and stored at each leaf. Optionally, we could save the posterior distributions
to file or use them for measuring accuracy on a validation set.

```
// Load 2D test data.
DataPointCollection testData = DataPointCollection.Load (
        path,
        2,
        DataDescriptor.Unadorned );

// Load a trained forest saved previously to binary file
   (from forestPath)
Forest<LinearFeature2d> forest =
    Forest<LinearFeature2d>.Deserialize ( forestPath );

// Apply the forest to the test data
int[][] leafIndicesPerTree = forest.Apply(testData);

int nClasses =
    forest.GetTree(0).GetNode(0).
    TrainingDataStatistics.BinCount;
HistogramAggregator[] result = new
    HistogramAggregator[testData.Count()];

for (int i = 0; i < testData.Count(); i++)
{
    // Aggregate statistics for this sample over all leaf
       nodes reached
    result[i] = new HistogramAggregator(nClasses);
    for (int t = 0; t < forest.TreeCount; t++)
    {
        int leafIndex = leafIndicesPerTree[t][i];
        var leafStats =
            forest.GetTree(t).GetNode(leafIndex).
            TrainingDataStatistics;
        result[i].Aggregate(leafStats);
    }
}
```

22.6 Other Applications

In addition to the supervised classification task, the Sherwood library contains example code to show how decision forests can be applied to several of the other inference tasks described in Part I. Whilst this example code will not be described in so much detail as that for supervised classification, it will be useful to draw the reader's attention to the following implementation details:

Density Estimation   Density estimation works by fitting a Gaussian model to the training data points at each tree node (see Chap. 6). During training, weak learners are selected that partition the training data so as to achieve maximum information gain. However, simplistic maximum likelihood estimation of Gaussian parameter values can easily result in overfitting for small numbers of training data points (so that the resulting Gaussians exhibit artificially high correlations between the data dimensions). A possible solution is to enforce a minimum number of data points at each node, perhaps explicitly or perhaps as a by-product of limiting the maximum number of tree levels D. However, the example code adopts the more elegant solution of defining a simple prior on the Gaussian parameter estimation, similar to the Wishart prior [28]. This has the property that when the number of observations is small, the prior model tends to dominate; conversely when the number of observations is large, the data tends to dominate. The prior has two *hyperparameters*, which can be specified as parameters to the command line demo that accompanies Sherwood. These hyperparametres reflect (i) the number of 'effective' prior observations (*i.e.* the relative significance assigned to the prior and the data), and (ii) the covariance matrix of these prior observations (which is assumed for simplicity to be isotropic).

1D-1D Regression   The purpose of the toy 1D-1D regression example is to show how a regression forest can be used to learn a mapping from a 1D input space to a 1D output space. Using 1D training data labeled with 1D target values, the forest is trained to predict 1D output values for arbitrary 1D input values. Regression trees work by fitting a piecewise linear model to the input data, in which each component is described by line offset and gradient parameters. These parameters are estimated using Bayesian linear regression, which enables us to predict not only a single output value for a given input, but a Gaussian probability distribution over possible output values. This has the important benefit that output values are less confidently predicted for regions of the input space that contain less training data.

Semi-supervised Classification   Semi-supervised classification works by propagating class labels to unlabeled training data points from the 'nearest' labeled training data points. The distance between each unlabeled data point and each labeled data point is computed using the geodesic distance defined in (8.6). As in Chap. 8, we model the training data density at each node of the classification tree using Gaussians. The position of a data point is considered to be the mean of the Gaussian associated with the leaf node that contains it, and pairwise distances between each pair of leaf nodes can be computed using the symmetric Mahalanobis distance defined in (8.7). Then the geodesic distance between all pairs of leaf nodes can then be found efficiently using *e.g.* the *Floyd–Warshall* algorithm [110].

22.7 Summary

This chapter has described *Sherwood*, the free research code library that accompanies this book. The reader is encouraged to download and use this library. We hope that it will provide a means of gaining insight into how decision forests work and how they can be implemented. The Sherwood library should also provide a useful basis for applying decision forests to new inference tasks not discussed in this book.

Chapter 23
Conclusions

A. Criminisi and J. Shotton

This book has discussed decision forests and their use in many computer vision and medical imaging applications. A number of tutorial experiments, illustrations and exercises have guided the reader in understanding properties and nuances of forests both in theory and practice.

23.1 Summary

Part I introduced the theoretical underpinnings and discussed the properties of decision forests through toy illustrations and exercises. The flexibility of forests has been demonstrated via their use for: classification, regression, density estimation, manifold learning, semi-supervised learning, and active learning.

Part II illustrated various real uses of decision forests in computer vision and medical image analysis. The range of practical application goes from tracking people in security cameras, to domestic entertainment, assisted driving and diagnosis and treatment of tumors.

Part III provided useful suggestions on how to implement forests efficiently. Also, research code has been made available for free in the form of the Sherwood software library.

Together with being a tutorial on decision forests, this book has also explored some relatively new ideas such as the use of forests for density estimation, manifold learning and semi-supervised learning. Some of these concepts are less mature than others and require more experimentation in practical applications in order to be thoroughly understood and assessed. However, it is encouraging to see how the same underlying model can be applied to so many diverse learning tasks.

A. Criminisi (✉) · J. Shotton
Microsoft Research Ltd., 7 J.J. Thomson Avenue, Cambridge CB3 0FB, UK

A. Criminisi, J. Shotton (eds.), *Decision Forests for Computer Vision and Medical Image Analysis*, Advances in Computer Vision and Pattern Recognition, DOI 10.1007/978-1-4471-4929-3_23, © Springer-Verlag London 2013

23.2 Successes and Challenges

Success Stories   In the past few years, computer vision has reached a new level of maturity which has been reflected in a number of practical, commercial applications. For instance: Automatic number plate recognition (ANPR) has been used successfully for many years, *e.g.* in the United Kingdom. Face detection technology [389] is now present in almost every webcam and in compact photo cameras. Automatic panorama stitching[1] can be run from your own smartphone. Microsoft Kinect [247] has demonstrated how vision technology can be deployed to millions of people and change the way they interact with machines, from the comfort of their sofa. GrabCut for interactive image segmentation [315] ships as part of Microsoft Office 2010.[2] Other commercial realities include Metail[3] for on-line garment shopping, Oxford Metrics[4] for motion capture, automatic road surveying, movie post-production and "moment capture" photography, and Mobileye and Seeing Machines for assisted driving[5], to name just a few.

Remaining Challenges   However, despite these successes, much research is still necessary to build reliable tools that can "understand" all types of images and videos, in *all* conditions. This may necessitate being able to train on millions if not billions of images. How can we acquire the necessary labeled training data? Or, perhaps, with better models of the visual world, which capture its variability efficiently, we could achieve accurate recognition with small amount of supervision. Being able to handle millions of categories is an unsolved problem. How easily can forests or alternative techniques scale to those levels?

Can we ever achieve perfectly accurate automatic face identification despite variations in hair style, beard, lighting, head-wear *etc.*? Can we photograph a plant or animal and automatically return its scientific name with perfect accuracy? Can we detect suspicious behavior in crowded airports with sufficient accuracy to make this tool a worth-while investment? Can we develop fully autonomous, cheap and lightweight visual navigation systems for the blind, or for driverless cars? Can we build automatic, accurate medical screening machines which would alert patients of possible anomalies and suggest the optimal course of action? Can we automatically identify every single cancerous region in histopathological images, or radiology scans and help doctors defeat cancer? Can automatic computer vision ever surpass human vision? Think of all the depth-, infra-red- and xray-sensing devices out there. If those "cameras" could be augmented with the level of effortless semantic interpretation that humans have then they would really surpass human visual capabilities.

---

[1] *E.g.* Photosynth http://photosynth.net/.

[2] http://office.microsoft.com/.

[3] http://www.metail.com/.

[4] http://www.omgplc.com/.

[5] http://www.mobileye.com/, http://www.seeingmachines.com.

23.3 Conclusion

The work presented here has only scratched the surface of what will be possible in the future. We are still far from solving the challenges above. However, we truly hope that this book has excited the reader as much as it has excited its authors. We hope that this structured description of decision forests has helped the reader to make sense of what they are and what they can do. Certainly, writing this book has helped the authors learn more about the different fields of machine learning, various existing algorithms, how they relate to one another, and their practical nuances. We also hope that the theory, practical algorithms, and code provided in this book can serve as a springboard for future research to advance the state of the art in automatic image understanding, for all those applications that are still waiting to be invented.

Further Material   The web site below presents further learning material in the form of PowerPoint slides, animations, experiments, the Sherwood software library and other resources that will be made available in the future. http://research. microsoft.com/projects/decisionforests.

References

1. Agarwal S, Awan A, Roth D (2004) Learning to detect objects in images via a sparse, part-based representation. IEEE Trans Pattern Anal Mach Intell 26(11)
2. Albert MS, DeKosky ST, Dickson D, Dubois B, Feldman HH, Fox NC, Gamst A, Holtzman DM, Jagust WJ, Petersen RC, Snyder PJ, Carrillo MC, Thies B, Phelps CH (2011) The diagnosis of mild cognitive impairment due to Alzheimer's disease: recommendations from the National Institute on Ageing-Alzheimer's Association workgroups on diagnostic guidelines for Alzheimer's disease. Alzheimer's Dement 7(3)
3. Amit Y (2002) 2D object detection and recognition. MIT Press, Cambridge
4. Amit Y, Geman D (1994) Randomized inquiries about shape; an application to handwritten digit recognition. Technical Report 401, Dept of Statistics, University of Chicago, IL, Nov 1994
5. Amit Y, Geman D (1997) Shape quantization and recognition with randomized trees. Neural Comput 9(7)
6. Amit Y, Geman D, Wilder K (1997) Joint induction of shape features and tree classifiers. IEEE Trans Pattern Anal Mach Intell 19
7. Andriluka M, Roth S, Schiele B (2008) People-tracking-by-detection and people-detection-by-tracking. In: Proc IEEE conf computer vision and pattern recognition (CVPR)
8. Anguelov D, Taskar B, Chatalbashev V, Koller D, Gupta D, Ng A (2005) Discriminative learning of Markov random fields for segmentation of 3D scan data. In: Proc IEEE conf computer vision and pattern recognition (CVPR)
9. Avidan S (2001) Support vector tracking. In: Proc IEEE conf computer vision and pattern recognition (CVPR), vol 1
10. Avidan S (2005) Ensemble tracking. In: Proc IEEE conf computer vision and pattern recognition (CVPR)
11. Avidan S (2007) Ensemble tracking. IEEE Trans Pattern Anal Mach Intell 29(2)
12. Babenko B, Yang M-H, Belongie S (2011) Robust object tracking with online multiple instance learning. IEEE Trans Pattern Anal Mach Intell
13. Badrinarayanan V, Galasso F, Cipolla R (2010) Label propagation in video sequences. In: Proc IEEE conf computer vision and pattern recognition (CVPR)
14. Bai X, Wang J, Simons D, Sapiro G (2009) Video SnapCut: robust video object cutout using localized classifiers. In: ACM SIGGRAPH
15. Ballard DH (1981) Generalizing the Hough transform to detect arbitrary shapes. Pattern Recognit 13(2)
16. Barinova O, Lempitsky VS, Kohli P (2010) On detection of multiple object instances using Hough transforms. In: Proc IEEE conf computer vision and pattern recognition (CVPR)
17. Barinova O, Lempitsky VS, Kohli P (2012) On detection of multiple object instances using Hough transforms. IEEE Trans Pattern Anal Mach Intell

A. Criminisi, J. Shotton (eds.), *Decision Forests for Computer Vision and Medical Image Analysis*, Advances in Computer Vision and Pattern Recognition, DOI 10.1007/978-1-4471-4929-3, © Springer-Verlag London 2013

18. Barnett GH (ed) (2007) High-grade gliomas. Springer, Berlin
19. Batra D, Sukthankar R, Chen T (2008) Learning class-specific affinities for image labelling. In: Proc IEEE conf computer vision and pattern recognition (CVPR)
20. Bauer S, Nolte L-P, Reyes M (2011) Fully automatic segmentation of brain tumor images using support vector machine classification in combination with hierarchical conditional random field regularization. In: Fichtinger G, Martel A, Peters T (eds) Proc medical image computing and computer assisted intervention (MICCAI). LNCS, vol 6893. Springer, Berlin
21. Beis J, Lowe DG (1997) Shape indexing using approximate nearest-neighbour search in high-dimensional spaces. In: Proc IEEE conf computer vision and pattern recognition (CVPR)
22. Belkin M, Niyogi P (2003) Laplacian eigenmaps for dimensionality reduction and data representation. Neural Comput
23. Belkin M, Niyogi P (2008) Towards a theoretical foundation for Laplacian-based manifold methods. J Comput Syst Sci 74(8)
24. Belongie S, Malik J, Puzicha J (2002) Shape matching and object recognition using shape contexts. IEEE Trans Pattern Anal Mach Intell 24
25. Benfold B, Reid I (2011) Unsupervised learning of a scene-specific coarse gaze estimator. In: Proc IEEE intl conf on computer vision (ICCV), Barcelona, Spain
26. Besag J (1977) Efficiency of pseudolikelihood estimation for simple Gaussian fields. Biometrika
27. Bibby C, Reid I (2008) Robust real-time visual tracking using pixel-wise posteriors. In: Proc European conf on computer vision (ECCV). Springer, Berlin
28. Bishop CM (2006) Pattern recognition and machine learning. Springer, New York
29. Bishop CM, Svensen M, Williams CKI (1998) GTM: the generative topographic mapping. Neural Comput
30. Bjoerck A (1996) Numerical methods for least squares problems. Society for Industrial and Applied Mathematics (SIAM), Philadelphia
31. Blake A, Rother C, Brown M, Perez P, Torr PHS (2004) Interactive image segmentation using an adaptive GMMRF model. In: Pajdla T, Matas J (eds) Proc European conf on computer vision (ECCV), Prague, Czech Republic, May 2004. LNCS, vol 3021. Springer, Berlin
32. Blockeel H, De Raedt L, Ramon J (1998) Top-down induction of clustering trees. In: Proc intl conf on machine learning (ICML)
33. Boland MV, Murphy RF (2001) A neural network classifier capable of recognizing the patterns of all major subcellular structures in fluorescence microscope images of HeLa cells. Bioinformatics 17
34. Boland MV, Markey MK, Murphy RF (1998) Automated recognition of patterns characteristic of subcellular structures in fluorescence microscopy images. Cytometry 33
35. Borenstein E, Ullman S (2002) Class-specific, top-down segmentation. In: Proc European conf on computer vision (ECCV). LNCS, vol 2351. Springer, Berlin
36. Bosch A, Zisermann A, Muñoz X (2007) Image classification using random forests and ferns. In: Proc IEEE intl conf on computer vision (ICCV)
37. Bourdev L, Malik J (2009) Poselets: body part detectors trained using 3D human pose annotations. In: Proc IEEE intl conf on computer vision (ICCV)
38. Boykov Y, Jolly M-P (2001) Interactive graph cuts for optimal boundary and region segmentation of objects in N-D images. In: Proc IEEE intl conf on computer vision (ICCV), Vancouver, Canada, July 2001, vol 1
39. Boykov Y, Veksler O, Jolly M-P (1999) Fast approximate energy minimization via graph cuts. In: Proc IEEE intl conf on computer vision (ICCV), Kerkyra, Corfu, Greece, September 1999, vol 1
40. Braak H, Braak E (1998) Evolution of neuronal changes in the course of Alzheimer's disease. J Neural Transm Suppl 53
41. Bregler C, Malik J (1998) Tracking people with twists and exponential maps. In: Proc IEEE conf computer vision and pattern recognition (CVPR)
42. Breiman L (1996) Bagging predictors. Mach Learn 24(2)
43. Breiman L (1999) Random forests. Technical Report TR567, UC Berkeley

44. Breiman L (2001) Random forests. Mach Learn 45(1)
45. Breiman L, Friedman J, Stone CJ, Olshen RA (1984) Classification and regression trees. Chapman and Hall/CRC, London
46. Brook A, El-Yaniv R, Isler E, Kimmel R, Meir R, Peleg D (2008) Breast cancer diagnosis from biopsy images using generic features and SVMs. Technical Report CS-2008-07, Technion, Israel
47. Brookmeyer R, Johnson E, Ziegler-Grahamm K, Arrighi HM (2007) Forecasting the global burden of Alzheimer's disease. Alzheimer's Dement 3(3)
48. Brostow GJ, Shotton J, Fauqueur J, Cipolla R (2008) Segmentation and recognition using structure from motion point clouds. In: Proc European conf on computer vision (ECCV). Springer, Berlin
49. Brox T, Malik J (2010) Object segmentation by long term analysis of point trajectories. In: Proc European conf on computer vision (ECCV). Springer, Berlin
50. Brubaker MA, Fleet DJ, Hertzmann A (2010) Physics-based person tracking using the anthropomorphic walker. Int J Comput Vis
51. Budiu M, Shotton J, Murray D, Finocchio M (2011) Parallelizing the training of the Kinect body parts labeling algorithm. In: Advances in neural information processing systems (NIPS). BigLearn workshop
52. Budvytis I, Badrinarayanan V, Cipolla R (2010) Label propagation in complex video sequences using semi-supervised learning. In: Proc British machine vision conference (BMVC)
53. Budvytis I, Badrinarayanan V, Cipolla R (2011) Semi-supervised video segmentation using tree structured graphical models. In: Proc IEEE conf computer vision and pattern recognition (CVPR)
54. Burr A (2010) Active learning literature survey. Technical Report 2010-09-14, Univ Wisconsin Madison, Computer Sciences Technical Report
55. Calabresi P (2007) Multiple sclerosis and demyelinating conditions of the central nervous system. In: Cecil medicine. Saunders Elsevier, Philadelphia
56. Caruana R, Karampatziakis N, Yessenalina A (2008) An empirical evaluation of supervised learning in high dimensions. In: Proc intl conf on machine learning (ICML)
57. CAVIAR04. http://homepages.inf.ed.ac.uk/rbf/CAVIARDATA1/
58. Cayton L (2005) Algorithms for manifold learning. Technical Report CS2008-0923, University of California, San Diego
59. Cehovin L, Kristan M, Leonardis A (2011) An adaptive coupled-layer visual model for robust visual tracking. In: Proc IEEE intl conf on computer vision (ICCV)
60. Chandna P, Deswal S, Pal M (2010) Semi-supervised learning based prediction of musculoskeletal disorder risk. J Ind Syst Eng
61. Chapelle O, Schölkopf B, Zien A (2006) Semi-supervised learning. MIT Press, Cambridge
62. Chen Y, Kim T-K, Cipolla R (2011) Silhouette-based object phenotype recognition using 3D shape priors. In: Proc IEEE intl conf on computer vision (ICCV), Barcelona, Spain
63. Cheung V, Frey BJ, Jojic N (2005) Video epitomes. In: Proc IEEE conf computer vision and pattern recognition (CVPR), June 2005, vol 1
64. Chipman H, George EI, Mcculloch RE (1997) Bayesian CART model search. J Am Stat Assoc 93
65. Cho TS, Joshi N, Zitnick CL, Kang SB, Szeliski R, Freeman WT (2010) A content-aware image prior. In: Proc IEEE conf computer vision and pattern recognition (CVPR)
66. Chockalingam P, Pradeep N, Birchfield S (2009) Adaptive fragments-based tracking of nonrigid objects using level sets. In: Proc IEEE intl conf on computer vision (ICCV)
67. Chum O, Zisserman A (2007) An exemplar model for learning object classes. In: Proc IEEE conf computer vision and pattern recognition (CVPR)
68. Cohn DA, Ghahramani Z, Jordan MI (1996) Active learning with statistical models. J Artif Intell Res 4
69. Comaniciu D, Meer P (2002) Mean shift: a robust approach toward feature space analysis. IEEE Trans Pattern Anal Mach Intell 24(5)

70. Cootes TF, Ionita MC, Lindner C, Sauer P (2012) Robust and accurate shape model fitting using random forest regression voting. In: Proc European conf on computer vision (ECCV)

71. Corder EH, Saunders AM, Strittmatter WJ, Schmechel DE, Gaskell PC, Small GW, Roses AD, Haines JL, Pericak-Vance MA (1993) Gene dose of apolipoprotein E type 4 allele and the risk of Alzheimer's disease in late onset families. Science 261(5123)

72. Corso JJ, Sharon E, Dube S, El-saden S, Sinha U, Yuille A (2008) Efficient multilevel brain tumor segmentation with integrated Bayesian model classification. Trans Med Imaging 27(5)

73. Cox TF, Cox MAA (2001) Multidimensional scaling. Chapman and Hall, London

74. Crammer K, Singer Y (2001) On the algorithmic implementation of multi-class SVMs. J Mach Learn Res

75. Cremers D, Funka-Lea G (2006) Dynamical statistical shape priors for level set based tracking. IEEE Trans Pattern Anal Mach Intell

76. Criminisi A, Sharp T, Blake A (2008) GeoS: geodesic image segmentation. In: Proc European conf on computer vision (ECCV). Springer, Berlin

77. Criminisi A, Shotton J, Bucciarelli S (2009) Decision forests with long-range spatial context for organ localization in CT volumes. In: MICCAI workshop on probabilistic models for medical image analysis (PMMIA)

78. Criminisi A, Shotton J, Robertson D, Konukoglu E (2010) Regression forests for efficient anatomy detection and localization in CT studies. In: MICCAI workshop on medical computer vision: recognition techniques and applications in medical imaging, Beijing. Springer, Berlin

79. Criminisi A, Shotton J, Konukoglu E (2011) Online tutorial on decision forests. http://research.microsoft.com/projects/decisionforests

80. Criminisi A, Shotton J, Konukoglu E (2012) Decision forests: a unified framework for classification, regression, density estimation, manifold learning and semi-supervised learning. Found Trends Comput Graph Vis 7(2–3)

81. Csurka G, Dance CR, Fan L, Willamowski J, Bray C (2004) Visual categorization with bags of keypoints. In: ECCV intl workshop on statistical learning in computer vision

82. Cuingnet R, Prevost R, Lesage D, Cohen L, Mory B, Ardon R (2012) Automatic detection and segmentation of kidneys in 3D CT images using random forests. In: Proc medical image computing and computer assisted intervention (MICCAI)

83. Dalal N, Triggs B (2005) Histograms of oriented gradients for human detection. In: Proc IEEE conf computer vision and pattern recognition (CVPR), June 2005, vol 2

84. Dantone M, Gall J, Fanelli G, van Gool L (2012) Real-time facial feature detection using conditional regression forests. In: Proc IEEE conf computer vision and pattern recognition (CVPR)

85. Danuser G (2011) Computer vision in cell biology. Cell 147(5)

86. Dawbarn D, Allen SJ (eds) (2007) Neurobiology of Alzheimer's disease, 3rd edn. Oxford University Press, New York

87. De Porte J, Herbst BM, Hereman W, van Der Walt SJ (2008) An introduction to diffusion maps. Techniques

88. Dempster A, Laird N, Rubin D (1977) Maximum likelihood from incomplete data via the EM algorithm. J R Stat Soc Ser B Methodol 39

89. Denison DGT, Mallick BK, Smith AFM (1998) A Bayesian CART algorithm. Biometrika 85

90. Deselaers T, Moller H, Clough P, Ney H, Lehmann TM (2007) The CLEF 2005 automatic medical image annotation task. Int J Comput Vis 74

91. Devroye L (1986) Non-uniform random variate generation. Springer, New York

92. Domingos P, Pazzani M, Provan G (1997) On the optimality of the simple Bayesian classifier under zero-one loss. Mach Learn

93. Donida Labati R, Piuri V, Scotti F (2011) ALL-IDB: the acute lymphoblastic leukemia image database for image processing. In: Proc IEEE intl conference on image processing (ICIP), September 2011

94. Driessens K, Reutemann P, Pfahringer B, Leschi C (2010) Using weighted nearest neighbour to benefit from unlabelled data. In: Advances in knowledge discovery and data mining. 10th Pacific-Asia conference

95. Duchateau N, De Craene M, Piella G, Frangi AF (2011) Characterizing pathological deviations from normality using constrained manifold learning. In: Proc medical image computing and computer assisted intervention (MICCAI)

96. Dumont M, Marée R, Geurts P, Wehenkel L (2009) Fast multi-class image annotation with random subwindows and multiple output randomized trees. In: Proc intl conference on computer vision theory and applications (VISAPP)

97. Elkan C (2003) Using the triangle inequality to accelerate k-means. In: Proc intl conf on machine learning (ICML)

98. Evans AC, Collins DL, Mills SR, Brown ED, Kelly RL, Peters TM (1993) 3D statistical neuroanatomical models from 305 MRI volumes. In: IEEE-nuclear science symposium and medical imaging conference

99. Everingham M, van Gool L, Williams C, Winn J, Zisserman A (2007) The Pascal visual object classes (VOC) challenge. http://www.pascal-network.org/challenges/VOC/voc2007/workshop/index.html

100. Everingham M, van Gool L, Williams C, Winn J, Zisserman A (2010) The Pascal visual object classes (VOC) challenge 2010. Int J Comput Vis 88

101. Fan J, Shen X, Wu Y (2010) Closed-loop adaptation for robust tracking. In: Proc European conf on computer vision (ECCV). Springer, Berlin

102. Fanelli G, Gall J (2011) Real time head pose estimation with random regression forests. In: Proc IEEE conf computer vision and pattern recognition (CVPR)

103. Fathi A, Balcan M, Ren X, Rehg JM (2011) Combining self training and active learning for video segmentation. In: Proc British machine vision conference (BMVC)

104. Fei-Fei L, Perona P (2005) A Bayesian hierarchical model for learning natural scene categories. In: Proc IEEE conf computer vision and pattern recognition (CVPR)

105. Felzenszwalb P, Girshick R, McAllester D, Ramanan D (2010) Object detection with discriminatively trained part based models. IEEE Trans Pattern Anal Mach Intell

106. Fenchel M, Thesen S, Schilling A (2008) Automatic labeling of anatomical structures in MR FastView images using a statistical atlas. In: Proc medical image computing and computer assisted intervention (MICCAI)

107. Fergus R, Perona P, Zisserman A (2003) Object class recognition by unsupervised scale-invariant learning. In: Proc IEEE conf computer vision and pattern recognition (CVPR)

108. Feulner J, Zhou SK, Seifert S, Cavallaro A, Hornegger J, Comaniciu D (2009) Estimating the body portion of CT volumes by matching histograms of visual words. In: Pluim JPW, Dawant BM (eds) Proc Intl society for optical engineering (SPIE) medical imaging

109. Fischler MA, Bolles RC (1981) Random sample consensus: a paradigm for model fitting with applications to image analysis and automated cartography. Commun ACM 24

110. Floyd RW (1962) Algorithm 97: shortest path. Commun ACM 5(6)

111. Frank A, Asuncion A (2010) UCI machine learning repository

112. Freund Y, Schapire RE (1997) A decision theoretic generalization of on-line learning and an application to boosting. J Comput Syst Sci 55(1)

113. Freund Y, Schapire RE (1998) Discussion of the paper "Arcing classifiers" by Leo Breiman. Processing 26(3)

114. Freund Y, Dasgupta S, Kabra M, Verma N (2007) Learning the structure of manifolds using random projections. In: Advances in neural information processing systems (NIPS)

115. Friedman J (2001) Greedy function approximation: a gradient boosting machine. Ann Stat 2(28)

116. Friedman JH, Fayyad U (1997) On bias, variance, 0/1-loss, and the curse-of-dimensionality. Data Min Knowl Discov 1

117. Gall J, Lempitsky V (2009) Class-specific Hough forests for object detection. IEEE Trans Pattern Anal Mach Intell

118. Gall J, Lempitsky VS (2009) Class-specific Hough forests for object detection. In: Proc IEEE conf computer vision and pattern recognition (CVPR)
119. Gall J, Razavi N, van Gool L (2010) On-line adaption of class-specific codebooks for instance tracking. In: Proc British machine vision conference (BMVC)
120. Gall J, Yao A, Razavi N, van Gool LJ, Lempitsky VS (2011) Hough forests for object detection, tracking, and action recognition. IEEE Trans Pattern Anal Mach Intell 33(11)
121. Ganapathi V, Plagemann C, Koller D, Thrun S (2010) Real time motion capture using a single time-of-flight camera. In: Proc IEEE conf computer vision and pattern recognition (CVPR). IEEE, New York
122. Geman S, Geman D (1984) Stochastic relaxation, Gibbs distributions, and the Bayesian restoration of images. IEEE Trans Pattern Anal Mach Intell 6
123. Geman G, Jedinak B (1996) An active testing model for tracking roads from satellite images. IEEE Trans Pattern Anal Mach Intell 18(1)
124. Gerber S, Tasdizen T, Joshi S, Whitaker R (2009) On the manifold structure of the space of brain images. In: Proc medical image computing and computer assisted intervention (MICCAI)
125. Geremia E, Menze B, Clatz O, Konukoglu E, Criminisi A, Ayache N (2010) Spatial decision forests for MS lesion segmentation in multi-channel MR images. In: Proc medical image computing and computer assisted intervention (MICCAI). Springer, Berlin
126. Geremia E, Clatz O, Menze BH, Konukoglu E, Criminisi A, Ayache N (2011) Spatial decision forests for MS lesion segmentation in multi-channel magnetic resonance. NeuroImage
127. Geurts P (2002) Contributions to decision tree induction: bias/variance tradeoff and time series classification. PhD thesis, University of Liège, Belgium, May
128. Geurts P, Ernst D, Wehenkel L (2006) Extremely randomized trees. Mach Learn 36(1)
129. Geurts P, Marée R, Wehenkel L (2006) Segment and combine: a generic approach for supervised learning of invariant classifiers from topologically structured data. In: Proc of the machine learning conference of Belgium and The Netherlands (Benelearn)
130. Geurts P, Wehenkel L, d Alché-Buc F (2006) Kernelizing the output of tree-based methods. In: Proc intl conf on machine learning (ICML)
131. Girshick R, Shotton J, Kohli P, Criminisi A, Fitzgibbon A (2011) Efficient regression of general-activity human poses from depth images. In: Proc IEEE intl conf on computer vision (ICCV)
132. Glesner S, Koller D (1995) Constructing flexible dynamic belief networks from first-order probabilistic knowledge bases. In: ECSQARU
133. Glocker B, Feulner J, Criminisi A, Haynor DR, Konukoglu E (2012) Automatic localization and identification of vertebrae in arbitrary field-of-view CT scans. In: Proc medical image computing and computer assisted intervention (MICCAI)
134. Glocker B, Pauly O, Konukoglu E, Criminisi A (2012) Joint classification-regression forests for spatially structured multi-object segmentation. In: Proc European conf on computer vision (ECCV). Springer, Berlin
135. Godec M, Roth PM, Bischof H (2011) Hough-based tracking of non-rigid objects. In: Proc IEEE intl conf on computer vision (ICCV)
136. Gooya A, Pohl KM, Bilello M, Biros G, Davatzikos C (2011) Joint segmentation and deformable registration of brain scans guided by a tumor growth model. In: Proc medical image computing and computer assisted intervention (MICCAI)
137. Gorlitz L, Menze BH, Weber M-A, Kelm BM, Hamprecht FA (2007) Semi-supervised tumor detection in magnetic resonance spectroscopic images using discriminative random fields. In: Proc annual symposium of the German association for pattern recognition (DAGM)
138. Gould S, Fulton R, Koller D (2009) Decomposing a scene into geometric and semantically consistent regions. In: Proc IEEE intl conf on computer vision (ICCV)
139. Grabner H, Grabner M, Bischof H (2006) Real-time tracking via on-line boosting. In: Proc British machine vision conference (BMVC)
140. Grabner H, Leistner C, Bischof H (2008) Semi-supervised on-line boosting for robust tracking. In: Proc European conf on computer vision (ECCV). Springer, Berlin

141. Grauman K, Darrell T (2005) The pyramid match kernel: discriminative classification with sets of image features. In: Proc IEEE intl conf on computer vision (ICCV)
142. Gray KR, Aljabar P, Heckeman RA, Hammers A, Rueckert D (2011) Random forest-based manifold learning for classification of imaging data in dementia. In: Proc medical image computing and computer assisted intervention (MICCAI)
143. Gray KR, Aljabar P, Heckemann RA, Hammers A, Rueckert D (2013) Random forest-based similarity measures for multi-modal classification of Alzheimer's Disease. Neuroimage 65:167–175
144. Grest D, Woetzel J, Koch R (2005) Nonlinear body pose estimation from depth images. In: Proc annual symposium of the German association for pattern recognition (DAGM)
145. Grossberg S (1987) Competitive learning: from interactive activation to adaptive resonance. Cogn Sci
146. Grundmann M, Kwatra V, Han M, Essa I (2010) Efficient hierarchical graph based video segmentation. In: Proc IEEE conf computer vision and pattern recognition (CVPR)
147. Gueld MO, Kohnen M, Keysers D, Schubert H, Wein BB, Bredno J, Lehmann TM (2002) Quality of DICOM header information for image categorization. In: SPIE storage and retrieval for image and video databases, San Diego
148. Gupta SS (1963) Probability integrals of multivariate normal and multivariate t. Ann Math Stat 34(3)
149. Hamm J, Ye DH, Verma R, Davatzikos C (2010) GRAM: a framework for geodesic registration on anatomical manifolds. Med Image Anal 14(5)
150. Hampel H, Burger K, Teipel SJ, Bokde AL, Zetterberg H, Blennow K (2008) Core candidate neurochemical and imaging biomarkers of Alzheimer's disease. Alzheimer's Dement 4(1)
151. Hansson O, Zetterberg H, Buchlave P, Londos E, Blennow K, Minthon L (2006) Association between CSF biomarkers and incipient Alzheimer's disease in patients with mild cognitive impairment: a follow-up study. Lancet Neurol 5(3)
152. Hardle W (1990) Applied non-parametric regression. Cambridge University Press, Cambridge
153. Hartley R, Zisserman A (2003) Multiple view geometry in computer vision, 2nd edn. Cambridge University Press, Cambridge
154. Hastie T, Tibshirani R, Friedman J (2001) The elements of statistical learning. Springer, Berlin
155. Hastie T, Tibshirani R, Friedman J, Franklin J (2005) The elements of statistical learning: data mining, inference and prediction. Math Intell 27(2)
156. Hastings WK (1970) Monte Carlo sampling methods using Markov chains and their applications. Biometrika 57
157. He X, Zemel RS, Carreira-Perpiñán MÁ (2004) Multiscale conditional random fields for image labeling. In: Proc IEEE conf computer vision and pattern recognition (CVPR), June 2004, vol 2
158. Heath D, Kasif S, Salzberg S (1993) Induction of oblique decision trees. J Artif Intell Res 2(2)
159. Heckemann RA, Keihaninejad S, Aljabar P, Gray KR, Nielsen C, Rueckert D, Hajnal JV, Hammers A, The Alzheimer's Disease Neuroimaging Initiative (2011) Automatic morphometry in Alzheimer's disease and mild cognitive impairment. NeuroImage 56(4)
160. Hegde C, Wakin MB, Baraniuk RG (2007) Random projections for manifold learning—proofs and analysis. In: Advances in neural information processing systems (NIPS)
161. Herholz K, Salmon E, Perani D, Baron JC, Holthoff V, Frolich L, Schonknecht P, Ito K, Mielke R, Kalbe E, Zundorf G, Delbeuck X, Pelati O, Anchisi D, Fazio F, Kerrouche N, Desgranges B, Eustache F, Beuthien-Baumann B, Menzel C, Schroder J, Kato T, Arahata Y, Henze M, Heiss WD (2002) Discrimination between Alzheimer dementia and controls by automated analysis of multicenter FDG PET. NeuroImage 17(1)
162. Hinrichs C, Singh V, Xu G, Johnson SC, The Alzheimer's Disease Neuroimaging Initiative (2011) Predictive markers for AD in a multi-modality framework: an analysis of MCI progression in the ADNI population. NeuroImage 55(2)

163. Hinton GE (2002) Training products of experts by minimizing contrastive divergence. Neural Comput 14
164. Hinton GE (2010) Learning to represent visual input. Philos Trans R Soc B 365
165. Ho TK (1995) Random decision forests. In: Proc intl conf on document analysis and recognition
166. Ho TK (1998) The random subspace method for constructing decision forests. IEEE Trans Pattern Anal Mach Intell 20(8)
167. Ho S, Bullitt E, Gerig G (2002) Level-set evolution with region competition: automatic 3-D segmentation of brain tumors. In: Proc intl conf on pattern recognition (ICPR)
168. Hoiem D, Sukthankar R, Schneiderman H, Huston L (2004) Object-based image retrieval using the statistical structure of images. J Mach Learn Res 02
169. IEEE-IMS Workshop on Information Theory and VA Statistics, Alexandria, Oct 1994
170. Isgum I, Staring M, Rutten A, Prokop M, Viergever MA, van Ginneken B (2009) Multi-atlas-based segmentation with local decision fusion: application to cardiac and aortic segmentation in CT scans. Trans Med Imaging 28(7)
171. Javed O, Ali S, Shah M (2005) Online detection and classification of moving objects using progressively improving detectors. In: Proc IEEE conf computer vision and pattern recognition (CVPR)
172. Joachims T (1999) Making large-scale SVM learning practical. In: Schölkopf B, Burges C, Smola A (eds) Advances in kernel methods—support vector learning. MIT Press, Cambridge
173. John GH (1995) Robust linear discriminant trees. In: Fifth intl workshop on artificial intelligence and statistics
174. Jojic N, Frey BJ, Kannan A (2003) Epitomic analysis of appearance and shape. In: Proc IEEE intl conf on computer vision (ICCV), Nice, France, October 2003, vol 1
175. Jolliffe IT (1986) Principal component analysis. Springer, Berlin
176. Julesz B (1981) Textons, the elements of texture perception, and their interactions. Nature 290(5802)
177. Jurie F, Triggs B (2005) Creating efficient codebooks for visual recognition. In: Proc IEEE intl conf on computer vision (ICCV), vol 1
178. Kalal Z, Matas J, Mikolajczyk K (2010) P-N learning: bootstrapping binary classifiers by structural constraints. In: Proc IEEE conf computer vision and pattern recognition (CVPR)
179. Kannan A, Winn J, Rother C (2006) Clustering appearance and shape by learning jigsaws. In: Advances in neural information processing systems (NIPS)
180. Kelm BM, Mittal S, Zheng Y, Tsymbal A, Bernhardt D, Vega-Higuera F, Zhou KS, Meer P, Comaniciu D (2011) Detection, grading and classification of coronary stenoses in computed tomography angiography. In: Proc medical image computing and computer assisted intervention (MICCAI)
181. Keysers D, Dahmen J, Ney H (2001) Invariant classification of red blood cells: a comparison of different approaches. In: Bildverarbeitung fur die Medizin'01
182. Kim TK, Stenger B, Woodley T, Cipolla R (2010) Online multiple classifier boosting for object tracking. In: Online learning for computer vision workshop
183. Klafki H-W, Staufenbiel M, Kornhuber J, Wiltfang J (2006) Therapeutic approaches to Alzheimer's disease. Brain 129(11)
184. Klein S, Staring M, Murphy K, Viergever MA, Pluim JP (2010) Elastix: a toolbox for intensity-based medical image registration. Trans Med Imaging 29
185. Klunk WE, Engler H, Nordberg A, Wang YM, Blomqvist G, Holt DP, Bergstrom M, Savitcheva I, Huang GF, Estrada S, Ausén B, Debnath ML, Barletta J, Price JC, Sandell J, Lopresti BJ, Wall A, Koivisto P, Antoni G, Mathis CA, Långström B (2004) Imaging brain amyloid in Alzheimer's disease with Pittsburgh compound-B. Ann Neurol 55(3)
186. Knoop S, Vacek S, Dillmann R (2006) Sensor fusion for 3D human body tracking with an articulated 3D body model. In: Proc IEEE intl conf on robotics and automation (ICRA)
187. Kohavi R (1995) A study of cross-validation and bootstrap for accuracy estimation and model selection. In: 14th intl joint conference on artificial intelligence (IJCAI), vol 2

188. Kohli P, Torr PHS (2005) Efficiently solving dynamic Markov random fields using graph cuts. In: Proc IEEE intl conf on computer vision (ICCV), Beijing, China, October 2005, vol 2

189. Koller D, Friedman N (2009) Probabilistic graphical models: principles and techniques. MIT Press, Cambridge

190. Kolmogorov V (2006) Convergent tree-reweighted message passing for energy minimization. IEEE Trans Pattern Anal Mach Intell 28(10)

191. Kolmogorov V, Boykov Y (2005) What metrics can be approximated by geo-cuts, or global optimization of length/area and flux. In: Proc IEEE intl conf on computer vision (ICCV)

192. Kontschieder P, Rota Buló S, Bischof H, Pelillo M (2011) Structured class-labels in random forests for semantic image labelling. In: Proc IEEE intl conf on computer vision (ICCV), Barcelona, Spain

193. Konukoglu E, Criminisi A, Pathak S, Robertson D, White S, Haynor D, Siddiqui K (2011) Robust linear registration of CT images using random regression forests. In: Proc intl society for optical engineering (SPIE) medical imaging

194. Konukoglu E, Glocker B, Zikic D, Criminisi A (2012) Neighborhood approximation forests. In: Proc medical image computing and computer assisted intervention (MICCAI)

195. Kristan M, Skocaj D, Leonardis A (2008) Incremental learning with Gaussian mixture models. In: Computer vision winter workshop (CVWW), Moravske Toplice, Slovenia

196. Kumar S, Hebert M (2003) Discriminative random fields: a discriminative framework for contextual interaction in classification. In: Proc IEEE intl conf on computer vision (ICCV), October 2003, vol 2

197. Kwon JS, Lee KM (2009) Tracking of a non-rigid object via patch-based dynamic appearance modeling and adaptive Basin Hopping Monte Carlo sampling. In: Proc IEEE conf computer vision and pattern recognition (CVPR)

198. Lafferty J, McCallum A, Pereira F (2001) Conditional random fields: probabilistic models for segmenting and labeling sequence data. In: Proc intl conf on machine learning (ICML)

199. Lampert CH (2008) Kernel methods in computer vision. Found Trends Comput Graph Vis 4(3)

200. Lampert C, Blaschko M, Hofmann T (2008) Beyond sliding windows: object localization by efficient subwindow search. In: Proc IEEE conf computer vision and pattern recognition (CVPR)

201. Landau SM, Harvey D, Madison CM, Reiman EM, Foster NL, Aisen PS, Petersen RC, Shaw LM, Trojanowski JQ, Jack CR Jr., Weiner MW, Jagust WJ (2010) Comparing predictors of conversion and decline in mild cognitive impairment. Neurology 75(3)

202. Langbaum JBS, Chen K, Lee W, Reschke C, Bandy D, Fleisher AS, Alexander GE, Foster NL, Weiner MW, Koeppe RA, Jagust WJ, Reiman EM, The Alzheimer's Disease Neuroimaging Initiative (2009) Categorical and correlational analyses of baseline fluorodeoxyglucose positron emission tomography images from the Alzheimer's disease neuroimaging initiative (ADNI). NeuroImage 45(4)

203. Laptev I, Marszalek M, Schmid C, Rozenfeld B (2008) Learning realistic human actions from movies. In: Proc IEEE conf computer vision and pattern recognition (CVPR)

204. Lazebnik S, Schmid C, Ponce J (2006) Beyond bags of features: spatial pyramid matching for recognizing natural scene categories. In: Proc IEEE conf computer vision and pattern recognition (CVPR)

205. Lee CH, Wang S, Murtha A, Brown M, Greiner R (2008) Segmenting brain tumors using pseudo-conditional random fields. In: Proc medical image computing and computer assisted intervention (MICCAI)

206. Lee H, Grosse R, Ranganath R, Ng AY (2009) Convolutional deep belief networks for scalable unsupervised learning of hierarchical representations. In: Proc intl conf on machine learning (ICML)

207. Lee YJ, Kim J, Grauman K (2011) Key-segments for video object segmentation. In: Proc IEEE intl conf on computer vision (ICCV)

208. Leibe B, Schiele B (2003) Interleaved object categorization and segmentation. In: Proc British machine vision conference (BMVC), vol II
209. Leibe B, Leonardis A, Schiele B (2004) Combined object categorization and segmentation with an implicit shape model. In: ECCV'04 workshop on statistical learning in computer vision, May 2004
210. Leibe B, Leonardis A, Schiele B (2008) Robust object detection with interleaved categorization and segmentation. Int J Comput Vis 77(1–3)
211. Leistner C, Saffari A, Santner J, Bischoff H (2009) Semi-supervised random forests. In: Proc IEEE intl conf on computer vision (ICCV)
212. Lempitsky V, Verhoek M, Noble A, Blake A (2009) Random forest classification for automatic delineation of myocardium in real-time 3D echocardiography. In: Workshop on functional imaging and modelling of the heart (FIMH). Springer, Berlin
213. Lepetit V, Fua P (2006) Keypoint recognition using randomized trees. IEEE Trans Pattern Anal Mach Intell
214. Lepetit V, Lagger P, Fua P (2005) Randomized trees for real-time keypoint recognition. In: Proc IEEE conf computer vision and pattern recognition (CVPR)
215. Lezama J, Alahari K, Sivic J, Laptev I (2011) Track to the future: spatio-temporal video segmentation with long-range motion cues. In: Proc IEEE conf computer vision and pattern recognition (CVPR)
216. Lezoray O, Elmoataz A, Cardot H (2003) A color object recognition scheme: application to cellular sorting. Mach Vis Appl 14
217. Li SZ (1995) Markov random field modeling in computer vision. Springer, Berlin
218. Li J, Allinson N (2008) A comprehensive review of current local features for computer vision. Neurocomputing 71
219. Li L-J, Fei-Fei L (2007) What, where and who? Classifying events by scene and object recognition. In: Proc IEEE intl conf on computer vision (ICCV)
220. Li Y, Sun J, Shum H-Y (2005) Video object cut and paste. ACM Trans Graph 24
221. Liang Z-P, Lauterbur PC (1999) Principles of magnetic resonance imaging: a signal processing perspective. IEEE Press/Wiley, New York
222. Liaw A, Wiener M (2002) Classification and regression by random forest. R News 2
223. Lin Y, Jeon Y (2002) Random forests and adaptive nearest neighbors. J Am Stat Assoc
224. Lindner C, Thiagarajah S, Wilkinson JM, arcOGEN Consortium, Wallis GA, Cootes TF (2012) Accurate fully automatic femur segmentation in pelvic radiographs using regression voting. In: Proc medical image computing and computer assisted intervention (MICCAI)
225. Lowe DG (2004) Distinctive image features from scale-invariant keypoints. Int J Comput Vis 60(2)
226. Ma J (2008) Dixon techniques for water and fat imaging. J Magn Reson Imaging
227. MacQueen JB (1967) Some methods for classification and analysis of multivariate observations. In: Proc of 5th Berkeley symposium on mathematical statistics and probability. University of California Press, Berkeley
228. Maji S, Malik J (2009) Object detection using a max-margin Hough transform. In: Proc IEEE conf computer vision and pattern recognition (CVPR)
229. Malik J, Belongie S, Leung T, Shi J (2001) Contour and texture analysis for image segmentation. Int J Comput Vis 43(1)
230. Malisievicz T, Gupta A, Efros AA (2011) Ensemble of exemplar-SVMs for object detection and beyond. In: Proc IEEE intl conf on computer vision (ICCV), Barcelona, Spain
231. Mardia KV, Kent JT, Bibby JM (1979) Multivariate analysis, 5th edn. Academic Press, London
232. Marée R (2012) Towards generic image classification an extensive empirical study. Technical report, University of Liège
233. Marée R, Geurts P, Visimberga G, Piater J, Wehenkel L (2003) An empirical comparison of machine learning algorithms for generic image classification. In: Coenen F, Preece A, Macintosh AL (eds) Proc of the 23rd SGAI intl conference on innovative techniques and

applications of artificial intelligence, research and development in intelligent systems XX. Springer, Berlin

234. Marée R, Geurts P, Piater J, Wehenkel L (2004) A generic approach for image classification based on decision tree ensembles and local sub-windows. In: Proc Asian conf on computer vision (ACCV), vol 2

235. Marée R, Geurts P, Piater J, Wehenkel L (2005) Random subwindows for robust image classification. In: Proc IEEE conf computer vision and pattern recognition (CVPR), vol 1. IEEE, New York

236. Marée R, Geurts P, Wehenkel L (2007) Content-based image retrieval by indexing random subwindows with randomized trees. In: Proc Asian conf on computer vision (ACCV). LNCS, vol 4844. Springer, Berlin

237. Marée R, Geurts P, Wehenkel L (2007) Random subwindows and extremely randomized trees for image classification in cell biology. Data Mining Inf 8(S1). BMC Cell Biology supplement on Workshop of Multiscale Biological Imaging, July 2007

238. Marée R, Geurts P, Wehenkel L (2009) Content-based image retrieval by indexing random subwindows with randomized trees. IPSJ Trans Comput Vis Appl 1(1) (open-access)

239. Marée R, Stevens B, Geurts P, Guern Y, Mack P (2009) A machine learning approach for material detection in hyperspectral images. In: Proc 6th IEEE workshop on object tracking and classification beyond and in the visible spectrum (CVPR09). IEEE, New York

240. Marée R, Denis P, Wehenkel L, Geurts P (2010) Incremental indexing and distributed image search using shared randomized vocabularies. In: Proc 11th ACM intl conference on multimedia information retrieval (MIR), March 2010. ACM Press, New York

241. Marée R, Stevens B, Rollus L, Rocks N, Moles-Lopez X, Salmon I, Cataldo D, Wehenkel L (2012) A rich Internet application for remote visualization and collaborative annotation of digital slide images in histology and cytology. In: BMC diagnostic pathology, proc 12th European congress on telepathology and 5th intl congress on virtual microscopy

242. Matthews L, Ishikawa T, Baker S (2004) The template update problem. IEEE Trans Pattern Anal Mach Intell

243. McKhann G, Drachman D, Folstein M, Katzman R, Price D, Stadlan EM (1984) Clinical diagnosis of Alzheimer's disease—report of the NINCDS-ADRDA work group under the auspices of department of health and human services task force on Alzheimer's disease. Neurology 34(7)

244. McKhann GM, Knopman DS, Chertkow H, Hyman BT, Jack CR Jr., Kawas CH, Klunk WE, Koroshetz WJ, Manly JJ, Mayeux R, Mohs RC, Morris JC, Rossor MN, Scheltens P, Carrillo MC, Thies B, Weintraub S, Phelps CH (2011) The diagnosis of dementia due to Alzheimer's disease: recommendations from the National Institute on Aging-Alzheimer's Association workgroups on diagnostic guidelines for Alzheimer's disease. Alzheimer's Dement 7(3)

245. Menze BH, Leemput KV, Lashkari D, Weber M-A, Ayache N, Golland P (2010) A generative model for brain tumor segmentation in multi-modal images. In: Proc medical image computing and computer assisted intervention (MICCAI)

246. Menze B, Kelm BM, Splitthoff DN, Koethe U, Hamprecht FA (2011) On oblique random forests. In: Proc European conf on machine learning (ECML/PKDD)

247. Microsoft Corporation Kinect for Windows and Xbox 360

248. Mikolajczyk K, Schmid C (2004) Scale and affine invariant interest point detectors. Int J Comput Vis 60(1)

249. Mikolajczyk K, Tuytelaars T, Schmid C, Zisserman A, Matas J, Schaffalitzky F, Kadir T, van Gool L (2005) A comparison of affine region detectors. Int J Comput Vis 65(1/2)

250. Montillo A (2011) Context selective decision forests and their application to lung segmentation in CT images. In: MICCAI workshop on pulmonary image analysis

251. Montillo A, Ling H (2009) Age regression from faces using random forests. In: Proc intl conf on image processing (ICIP)

252. Montillo A, Shotton J, Winn J, Iglesias J, Metaxas D, Criminisi A (2011) Entangled decision forests and their application for semantic segmentation of CT images. In: Proc information

processing in medical imaging (IPMI). Springer, Berlin

253. Moosmann F, Triggs B, Jurie F (2006) Fast discriminative visual codebooks using randomized clustering forests. In: Advances in neural information processing systems (NIPS)

254. Moosmann F, Nowak E, Jurie F (2008) Randomized clustering forests for image classification. IEEE Trans Pattern Anal Mach Intell 30(9)

255. Moreno-Noguer F, Sanfeliu A, Samaras D (2008) Dependent multiple cue integration for robust tracking. IEEE Trans Pattern Anal Mach Intell

256. Motter R, Vigopelfrey C, Kholodenko D, Barbour R, Johnsonwood K, Galasko D, Chang L, Miller B, Clark C, Green R, Olson D, Southwick P, Wolfert R, Munroe B, Lieberburg I, Seubert P, Schenk D (1995) Reduction of beta-amyloid peptide(42) in the cerebrospinal fluid of patients with Alzheimer's disease. Ann Neurol 38(4)

257. Müller J, Arens M (2010) Human pose estimation with implicit shape models. In: ARTEMIS

258. Müller A, Nowozin S, Lampert CH (2012) Information theoretic clustering using minimum spanning trees. In: Proc annual symposium of the German association for pattern recognition (DAGM)

259. Murphy RF (2011) An active role for machine learning in drug development. Nat Chem Biol 7

260. Murthy SK, Kasif S, Salzberg S (1994) A system for induction of oblique decision trees. arXiv:cs/9408103

261. Mutch J, Lowe DG (2006) Multiclass object recognition with sparse, localized features. In: Proc IEEE conf computer vision and pattern recognition (CVPR)

262. Nadler B, Lafon S, Coifman RR, Kevrekidis IG (2005) Diffusion maps, spectral clustering and eigenfunctions of Fokker-Plank operators. In: Advances in neural information processing systems (NIPS)

263. Neal RM (2001) Annealed importance sampling. Stat Comput 11

264. Nejhum SM, Ho J, Yang M-H (2008) Visual tracking with histograms and articulating blocks. In: Proc IEEE conf computer vision and pattern recognition (CVPR)

265. Nelder JA, Mead R (1965) A simplex method for function minimization. Comput J 7(4)

266. Nistér D, Stewénius H (2006) Scalable recognition with a vocabulary tree. In: Proc IEEE conf computer vision and pattern recognition (CVPR)

267. Nowak E, Jurie F, Triggs B (2006) Sampling strategies for bag-of-features image classification. In: Proc European conf on computer vision (ECCV). Springer, Berlin

268. Nowozin S (2012) Improved information gain estimates for decision tree induction. In: Proc intl conf on machine learning (ICML)

269. Nowozin S, Lampert CH (2009) Global connectivity potentials for random field models. In: Proc IEEE conf computer vision and pattern recognition (CVPR)

270. Nowozin S, Lampert CH (2011) Structured learning and prediction in computer vision. Found Trends Comput Graph Vis 6(3–4)

271. Nowozin S, Rother C, Bagon S, Sharp T, Yao B, Kohli P (2011) Decision tree fields. In: Proc IEEE intl conf on computer vision (ICCV)

272. Oberg J, Eguro K, Bittner R, Forin A (2012) Random decision tree body part recognition using FPGAs. In: Proc 22nd int conf on field programmable logic and applications (FPL)

273. O'Hara S, Draper BA (2012) Scalable action recognition with a subspace forest. In: Proc IEEE conf computer vision and pattern recognition (CVPR)

274. Ojala T, Pietikainen M, Harwood D (1996) A comparative study of texture measures with classification based on featured distributions. Pattern Recognit 29

275. Okada R (2009) Discriminative generalized Hough transform for object detection. In: Proc IEEE intl conf on computer vision (ICCV)

276. Oliva A, Torralba A (2006) Building the gist of a scene: the role of global image features in recognition. Vis Percept Prog Brain Res 155(1)

277. Opelt A, Pinz A, Zisserman A (2008) Learning an alphabet of shape and appearance for multi-class object detection. Int J Comput Vis

278. Orlov N, Shamir L, Macura T, Johnston J, Eckley DM, Goldberg I (2008) WND-CHARM: multi-purpose image classification using compound transforms. Pattern Recognit Lett 29(11)

279. Ozuysal M, Fua P, Lepetit V (2007) Fast keypoint recognition in ten lines of code. In: Proc IEEE conf computer vision and pattern recognition (CVPR), June 2007
280. Ozuysal M, Calonder M, Lepetit V, Fua P (2010) Fast keypoint recognition using random ferns. IEEE Trans Pattern Anal Mach Intell 32(3)
281. Pang J, Huang Q, Jiang S (2008) Multiple instance boost using graph embedding based decision stump for pedestrian detection. In: Proc European conf on computer vision (ECCV). Springer, Berlin
282. Parzen E (1962) On estimation of a probability density function and mode. Ann Math Stat 33
283. Pathak S, Criminisi A, White S, Munasinghe I, Sparks B, Robertson D, Siddiqui K (2011) Automatic semantic annotation and validation of anatomy in DICOM CT images. In: Proc intl society for optical engineering (SPIE) medical imaging
284. Patwardhan MB, McCrory DC, Matchar DB, Samsa GP, Rutschmann OT (2004) Alzheimer disease: operating characteristics of PET—a meta-analysis. Radiology 231(1)
285. Pauly O, Mateus D, Navab N (2010) ImageCLEF 2010 working notes on the modality classification subtask. Technical report, Technische Universitat Munchen
286. Pauly O, Glocker B, Criminisi A, Mateus D, Martinez Möller A, Nekolla S, Navab N (2011) Fast multiple organs detection and localization in whole-body MR Dixon sequences. In: Proc medical image computing and computer assisted intervention (MICCAI), Toronto
287. Payet N, Todorovic S (2010) $(RF)^2$—random forest random field. In: Advances in neural information processing systems (NIPS)
288. Percannella G, Foggia P, Soda P Contest on HEp-2 cells classification. http://mivia.unisa.it/hep2contest/index.shtml
289. Petersen RC (2004) Mild cognitive impairment as a diagnostic entity. J Intern Med 256(3)
290. PETS. http://www.cvg.rdg.ac.uk/slides/pets.html
291. PETS10. http://www.cvg.rdg.ac.uk/PETS2010/a.html
292. Plackett RL (1954) A reduction formula for normal multivariate integrals. Biometrika 41
293. Plagemann C, Ganapathi V, Koller D, Thrun S (2010) Real-time identification and localization of body parts from depth images. In: Proc IEEE intl conf on robotics and automation (ICRA)
294. Popuri K, Cobzas D, Murtha A, Jägersand M (2011) 3D variational brain tumor segmentation using Dirichlet priors on a clustered feature set. Int J Comput Assisted Radiol Surg
295. Porikli FM (2005) Integral histogram: a fast way to extract histograms in Cartesian spaces. In: Proc IEEE conf computer vision and pattern recognition (CVPR), vol 1
296. Prasad M, Zisserman A, Fitzgibbon AW, Kumar MP, Torr PHS (2006) Learning class-specific edges for object detection and segmentation. In: ICVGIP
297. Prastawa M, Bullitt E, Ho S, Gerig G (2004) A brain tumor segmentation framework based on outlier detection. Med Image Anal
298. Predictions Workshop. Models, Computing. 31st Symp on the Interface: Computing Science, and IL. Statistics. Schaumburg, Jun 1999
299. Price SJ, Peña A, Burnet NG, Jena R, Green HAL, Carpenter TA, Pickard JD, Gillard JH (2004) Tissue signature characterisation of diffusion tensor abnormalities in cerebral gliomas. Eur Radiol 14
300. Prima S, Ayache N, Barrick T, Roberts N (2001) Maximum likelihood estimation of the bias field in MR brain images: investigating different modelings of the imaging process. In: Proc medical image computing and computer assisted intervention (MICCAI). LNCS, vol 2208. Springer, Berlin
301. Prima S, Ourselin S, Ayache N (2002) Computation of the mid-sagittal plane in 3D brain images. Trans Med Imaging 21(2)
302. Quinlan JR (1993) C4.5: programs for machine learning. Morgan Kaufmann, San Mateo
303. Rabinovich A, Vedaldi A, Galleguillos C, Wiewiora E, Belongie S (2007) Objects in context. In: Proc IEEE intl conf on computer vision (ICCV)
304. Ram P, Gray AG (2011) Density estimation trees. In: Proc ACM SIGKDD intl conf on knowledge discovery and data mining (KDD)

305. Rasmussen CE, Williams C (2006) Gaussian processes for machine learning. MIT Press, Cambridge
306. Razavi N, Gall J, Van Gool L (2010) Backprojection revisited: scalable multi-view object detection and similarity metrics for detections. In: Proc European conf on computer vision (ECCV). Springer, Berlin
307. Ren X, Malik J (2007) Tracking as repeated figure/ground segmentation. In: Proc IEEE conf computer vision and pattern recognition (CVPR)
308. Rey D (2002) Détection et quantification de processus évolutifs dans des images médicales tridimensionnelles : application à la sclérose en plaques. Thèse de sciences, Université de Nice Sophia-Antipolis, October (in French)
309. Roberts MG, Cootes TF, Adams JE (2012) Automatic location of vertebrae on DXA images using random forest regression. In: Proc medical image computing and computer assisted intervention (MICCAI)
310. Rocca WA, Hofman A, Brayne C, Breteler MMB, Clarke ML, Copeland JRM, Dartigues J-F, Engedal K, Hagnell O, Heeren TJ, Jonker C, Lindesay J, Lobo A, Mann AH, Mls PK, Morgan K, O'Connor DLW, da Silva Droux A, Sulkava R, Kay DWK, Amaducci L (1991) Frequency and distribution of Alzheimer's disease in Europe: a collaborative study of 1980–1990 prevalence findings. Ann Neurol 30(3)
311. Rogez G, Rihan J, Ramalingam S, Orrite C, Torr PHS (2008) Randomized trees for human pose detection. In: Proc IEEE conf computer vision and pattern recognition (CVPR)
312. Rosenberg C, Hebert M, Schneiderman H (2005) Semi-supervised self-training of object detection models. In: 17-th IEEE workshop on applications of computer vision
313. Roses AD, Saunders AM (1997) ApoE, Alzheimer's disease, and recovery from brain stress. Cerebrovasc Pathol Alzheimer's Dis 826
314. Roth S, Black MJ (2007) Steerable random fields. In: Proc IEEE intl conf on computer vision (ICCV)
315. Rother C, Kolmogorov V, Blake A (2004) GrabCut—interactive foreground extraction using iterated graph cuts. ACM Trans Graph 23(3)
316. Rudin M (2005) Molecular imaging: basic principles and applications in biomedical research. Imperial College Press, London
317. Saffari A, Leistner C, Santner J, Godec M, Bischoff H (2009) On-line random forests. In: ICCV workshop on on-line learning for computer vision
318. Santner J, Leistner C, Saffari A, Pock T, Bischof H (2010) PROST: parallel robust online simple tracking. In: Proc IEEE conf computer vision and pattern recognition (CVPR)
319. Saul LK, Jordan MI (1996) Exploiting tractable substructures in intractable networks. In: Advances in neural information processing systems (NIPS)
320. Schapire RE (1990) The strength of weak learnability. Mach Learn 5(2)
321. Schindler G, Brown M, Szeliski R (2007) City-scale location recognition. In: Proc IEEE conf computer vision and pattern recognition (CVPR), Minneapolis, June 2007
322. Schmidt M, Levner I, Greiner R, Murtha A, Bistriz A (2005) Segmenting brain tumors using alignment-based features. In: ICMLA
323. Schnitzspan P, Roth S, Schiele B (2010) Automatic discovery of meaningful object parts with latent CRFs. In: Proc IEEE conf computer vision and pattern recognition (CVPR)
324. Schroff F, Criminisi A, Zisserman A (2008) Object class segmentation using random forests. In: Proc British machine vision conference (BMVC)
325. Schulter S, Leistner C, Roth PM, van Gool L, Bischof H (2011) On-line Hough forests. In: Proc British machine vision conference (BMVC)
326. Seber GAF, Wild CJ (1989) Non linear regression. Wiley, New York
327. Seemann E, Schiele B (2006) Cross-articulation learning for robust detection of pedestrians. In: Proc annual symposium of the German association for pattern recognition (DAGM)
328. Seifert S, Barbu A, Zhou SK, Liu D, Feulner J, Huber M, Sühling M, Cavallaro A, Comaniciu D (2009) Hierarchical parsing and semantic navigation of full body CT data. In: Pluim JPW, Dawant BM (eds) Proc intl society for optical engineering (SPIE) medical imaging
329. Selkoe DJ (1991) The molecular pathology of Alzheimer's disease. Neuron 6(4)

330. Settles B (2010) Active learning literature survey. Technical report, Computer Sciences Technical Report 1648, University of Wisconsin Madison

331. Shamir L, Macura T, Orlov N, Eckely DM, Goldberg IG (2008) IICBU 2008—a benchmark suite for biological imaging. In: 3rd workshop on bio-image informatics: biological imaging, computer vision and data mining

332. Shamir L, Delaney J, Orlov N, Eckley DM, Goldberg IG (2010) Pattern recognition software and techniques for biological image analysis. PLoS Comput Biol 6(11)

333. Sharp T (2008) Implementing decision trees and forests on a GPU. In: Proc European conf on computer vision (ECCV). Springer, Berlin

334. Shawe-Taylor J, Cristianini N (2004) Kernel methods for pattern analysis. Cambridge University Press, Cambridge

335. Shi T, Horvath S (2006) Unsupervised learning with random forest predictors. J Comput Graph Stat 15

336. Shi J, Malik J (1997) Normalized cuts and image segmentation. In: Proc IEEE conf computer vision and pattern recognition (CVPR), Washington, DC, USA

337. Shimizu A, Ohno R, Ikegami T, Kobatake H (2006) Multi-organ segmentation in three-dimensional abdominal CT images. Int J Comput Assisted Radiol Surg 1

338. Shotton J, Winn J, Rother C, Criminisi A (2006) TextonBoost: Joint appearance, shape and context modeling for multi-class object recognition and segmentation. In: Proc European conf on computer vision (ECCV). Springer, Berlin

339. Shotton J, Blake A, Cipolla R (2008) Efficiently combining contour and texture cues for object recognition. In: Proc British machine vision conference (BMVC)

340. Shotton J, Blake A, Cipolla R (2008) Multiscale categorical object recognition using contour fragments. IEEE Trans Pattern Anal Mach Intell 30(7)

341. Shotton J, Johnson M, Cipolla R (2008) Semantic texton forests for image categorization and segmentation. In: Proc IEEE conf computer vision and pattern recognition (CVPR)

342. Shotton J, Winn JM, Rother C, Criminisi A (2009) TextonBoost for image understanding: multi-class object recognition and segmentation by jointly modeling texture, layout, and context. Int J Comput Vis 81(1)

343. Shotton J, Fitzgibbon AW, Cook M, Sharp T, Finocchio M, Moore R, Kipman A, Blake A (2011) Real-time human pose recognition in parts from a single depth image. In: Proc IEEE conf computer vision and pattern recognition (CVPR)

344. Shotton J, Girshick R, Fitzgibbon A, Sharp T, Cook M, Finocchio M, Moore R, Kohli P, Criminisi A, Kipman A, Blake A (2012) Efficient human pose estimation from single depth images. IEEE Trans Pattern Anal Mach Intell

345. Siddiqui M, Medioni G (2010) Human pose estimation from a single view point, real-time range sensor. In: CVCG at CVPR

346. Sigal L, Bhatia S, Roth S, Black MJ, Isard M (2004) Tracking loose-limbed people. In: Proc IEEE conf computer vision and pattern recognition (CVPR)

347. Silverman BW (1986) Density estimation. Chapman and Hall, London

348. Sivic J, Zisserman A (2003) Video Google: a text retrieval approach to object matching in videos. In: Proc IEEE intl conf on computer vision (ICCV)

349. Skilling J (2010) Maximum entropy and Bayesian methods. Kluwer Academic, Dordrecht

350. Smith SM (2002) Fast robust automated brain extraction. Hum Brain Mapp

351. Smola AJ, Scholkopf B (2003) A tutorial on support vector regression. Technical report, Statistics and Computing

352. Sonnenburg S, Rätsch G, Schäfer C, Schölkopf B (2006) Large scale multiple kernel learning. J Mach Learn Res 7

353. Souplet J-C, Lebrun C, Ayache N, Malandain G (2008) An automatic segmentation of T2-FLAIR multiple sclerosis lesions. In: The MIDAS journal—MS lesion segmentation (MICCAI 2008 workshop)

354. Sperling RA, Aisen PS, Beckett LA, Bennett DA, Craft S, Fagan AM, Iwatsubo T, Jack CR Jr., Kaye J, Montine TJ, Park DC, Reiman EM, Rowe CC, Siemers E, Stern Y, Yaffe K, Carrillo MC, Thies B, Morrison-Bogorad M, Wagster MV, Phelps CH (2011) Toward defining

the preclinical stages of Alzheimer's disease: recommendations from the National Institute on Aging-Alzheimer's Association workgroups on diagnostic guidelines for Alzheimer's disease. Alzheimer's Dement 7(3)

355. Statnikov A, Wang L, Aliferis CA (2008) A comprehensive comparison of random forests and support vector machines for microarray-based cancer classification. BMC Bioinf

356. Stern O, Marée R, Aceto J, Jeanray N, Muller M, Wehenkel L, Geurts P (2011) Automatic localization of interest points in zebrafish images with tree-based methods. In: Proc 6th IAPR intl conference on pattern recognition in bioinformatics. Lecture notes in bioinformatics. Springer, Berlin

357. Strecha C, Fransens R, van Gool L (2006) Combined depth and outlier estimation in multiview stereo. In: Proc IEEE conf computer vision and pattern recognition (CVPR)

358. Styner M, Lee J, Chin B, Chin MS, Commowick O, Tran H, Markovic-Plese S, Jewells V, Warfield SK (2008) 3D segmentation in the clinic: a grand challenge II: MS lesion segmentation. MIDAS J

359. Sudderth EB, Jordan MI (2008) Shared segmentation of natural scenes using dependent Pitman-Yor processes. In: Advances in neural information processing systems (NIPS)

360. Sun M, Kohli P, Shotton J (2012) Conditional regression forests for human pose estimation. In: Proc IEEE conf computer vision and pattern recognition (CVPR)

361. Sutton C, McCallum A (2006) An introduction to conditional random fields for relational learning. MIT Press, Cambridge. Chap 4

362. Szekely GJ, Rizzo ML (2004) Testing for equal distributions in high dimensions. Interstat, Nov 2004.

363. Szeliski R, Zabih R, Scharstein D, Veksler O, Kolmogorov V, Agarwala A, Tappen ML, Rother C (2008) A comparative study of energy minimization methods for Markov random fields with smoothness-based priors. IEEE Trans Pattern Anal Mach Intell 30(7)

364. Szummer M, Jaakkola T (2001) Partially labelled classification with Markov random walks. In: Advances in neural information processing systems (NIPS)

365. Szummer M, Kohli P, Hoiem D (2008) Learning CRFs using graph cuts. In: Proc European conf on computer vision (ECCV). Springer, Berlin

366. Taskar B, Chatalbashev V, Koller D, Guestrin C (2005) Learning structured prediction models: a large margin approach. In: Proc intl conf on machine learning (ICML)

367. Tenenbaum JB, deSilva V, Langford JC (2000) A global geometric framework for nonlinear dimensionality reduction. Science 290(5500)

368. Torgerson WS (1952) Multidimensional scaling: I. Theory and method. Psychometrika 17(4)

369. Torralba A, Murphy KP, Freeman WT, Rubin MA (2003) Context-based vision system for place and object recognition. In: Proc IEEE intl conf on computer vision (ICCV), Nice, France, October 2003, vol 2

370. Torralba A, Murphy KP, Freeman WT (2004) Sharing features: efficient boosting procedures for multiclass object detection. In: Proc IEEE conf computer vision and pattern recognition (CVPR), vol 2

371. Torralba A, Murphy KP, Freeman WT (2007) Sharing visual features for multiclass and multiview object detection. IEEE Trans Pattern Anal Mach Intell 19(5)

372. Trojanowski JQ, Vandeerstichele H, Korecka M, Clark CM, Aisen PS, Petersen RC, Blennow K, Soares H, Simon A, Lewczuk P, Dean R, Siemers E, Potter WZ, Weiner MW, Jack CR Jr., Jagust W, Toga AW, Lee VM-Y, Shaw LM (2010) Update on the biomarker core of the Alzheimer's disease neuroimaging initiative subjects. Alzheimer's Dement 6(3)

373. Tsai D, Flagg M, Rehg JM (2010) Motion coherent tracking with multi-label MRF optimization. In: Proc British machine vision conference (BMVC)

374. Tu Z (2005) Probabilistic boosting-tree: learning discriminative models for classification, recognition, and clustering. In: Proc IEEE intl conf on computer vision (ICCV), Beijing, China, October 2005, vol 2

375. Tu Z, Bai X (2010) Auto-context and its application to high-level vision tasks and 3D brain image segmentation. IEEE Trans Pattern Anal Mach Intell 32(10)

376. Tuytelaars T, Schmid C (2007) Vector quantizing feature space with a regular lattice. In: Proc IEEE intl conf on computer vision (ICCV)
377. UCI Machine Learning Repository. http://archive.ics.uci.edu/ml/datasets.html
378. Urtasun R, Darrell T (2008) Local probabilistic regression for activity-independent human pose inference. In: Proc IEEE conf computer vision and pattern recognition (CVPR)
379. Vandermeeren M, Mercken M, Vanmechelen E, Six J, Vandevoorde A, Martin JJ, Cras P (1993) Detection of tau proteins in normal and Alzheimer's disease cerebrospinal fluid with a sensitive sandwich enzyme-linked immunosorbent assay. J Neurochem 61(5)
380. Vapnik V (2000) The nature of statistical learning theory. Springer, Berlin
381. Varma M, Zisserman A (2005) A statistical approach to texture classification from single images. Int J Comput Vis 62(1–2)
382. Vazquez-Reina A, Avidan S, Pfister H, Miller E (2010) Multiple hypothesis video segmentation from superpixel flows. In: Proc European conf on computer vision (ECCV). Springer, Berlin
383. Vedaldi A, Blaschko M, Zisserman A (2011) Learning equivariant structured output SVM regressors. In: Proc IEEE intl conf on computer vision (ICCV)
384. Verbeek J, Triggs B (2007) Region classification with Markov field aspect models. In: Proc IEEE conf computer vision and pattern recognition (CVPR)
385. Verma R, Zacharaki EI, Ou Y, Cai H, Chawla S, Lee A-K, Melhem ER, Wolf R, Davatzikos C (2008) Multi-parametric tissue characterization of brain neoplasm and their recurrence using pattern classification of MR images. Acad Radiol 15(8)
386. Vezhnevets A, Ferrari V, Buhmann JM (2012) Weakly supervised structured output learning for semantic segmentation. In: Proc IEEE conf computer vision and pattern recognition (CVPR)
387. Villamizar M, Moreno-Noguer F, Andrade-Cetto J, Sanfeliu A (2010) Efficient rotation invariant object detection using boosted random ferns. In: Proc IEEE conf computer vision and pattern recognition (CVPR)
388. Viola P, Jones MJ (2001) Rapid object detection using a boosted cascade of simple features. In: Proc IEEE conf computer vision and pattern recognition (CVPR), December 2001, vol 1
389. Viola P, Jones MJ (2004) Robust real-time face detection. Int J Comput Vis 57(2)
390. Viola P, Jones MJ, Snow D (2003) Detecting pedestrians using patterns of motion and appearance. In: Proc IEEE intl conf on computer vision (ICCV)
391. Vishwanathan SVN, Schraudolph NN, Schmidt MW, Murphy KP (2006) Accelerated training of conditional random fields with stochastic gradient methods. In: Proc intl conf on machine learning (ICML)
392. Vitter JS (1985) Random sampling with a reservoir. ACM Trans Math Softw 11(1)
393. Wainwright MJ, Jordan MI (2008) Graphical models, exponential families, and variational inference. Found Trends Mach Learn 1(1–2)
394. Walhovd KB, Fjell AM, Dale AM, McEvoy LK, Brewer J, Karow DS, Salmon DP, Fennema-Notestine C (2010) Multi-modal imaging predicts memory performance in normal aging and cognitive decline. Neurobiol Aging 31(7)
395. Wang J (2007) On transductive support vector machines. In: Prediction and discovery. American Mathematical Society, Providence
396. Wang RY, Popović J (2009) Real-time hand-tracking with a color glove. In: Proc ACM SIGGRAPH
397. Wang C, Gorce M, Paragios N (2009) Segmentation, ordering and multi-object tracking using graphical models. In: Proc IEEE intl conf on computer vision (ICCV)
398. Wang Y, Fan Y, Bhatt P, Davatzikos C (2010) High-dimensional pattern regression using machine learning: from medical images to continuous clinical variables. NeuroImage
399. Wels M, Carneiro G, Aplas A, Huber M, Comaniciu D, Hornegger J (2008) A discriminative model-constrained graph-cuts approach to fully automated pediatric brain tumor segmentation in 3D MRI. In: Proc medical image computing and computer assisted intervention (MICCAI)

400. Wen PY, Macdonald DR, Reardon DA, Cloughesy TF, Sorensen AG, Galanis E, Degroot J, Wick W, Gilbert MR, Lassman AB, Tsien C, Mikkelsen T, Wong ET, Chamberlain MC, Stupp R, Lamborn KR, Vogelbaum MA, van den Bent MJ, Chang SM (2010) Updated response assessment criteria for high-grade gliomas: response assessment in neuro-oncology working group. Am J Neuroradiol

401. Williams B, Klein G, Reid I (2007) Real-time SLAM relocalisation. In: Proc IEEE intl conf on computer vision (ICCV)

402. Winder S, Brown M (2007) Learning local image descriptors. In: Proc IEEE conf computer vision and pattern recognition (CVPR)

403. Winn J, Shotton J (2006) The layout consistent random field for recognizing and segmenting partially occluded objects. In: Proc IEEE conf computer vision and pattern recognition (CVPR)

404. Winn J, Criminisi A, Minka T (2005) Categorization by learned universal visual dictionary. In: Proc IEEE intl conf on computer vision (ICCV), Beijing, China, October 2005, vol 2

405. Xiong C, Johnson D, Xu R, Corso JJ (2012) Random forests for metric learning with implicit pairwise position dependence. In: Proc of ACM SIGKDD intl conf on knowledge discovery and data mining

406. Yakushev I, Hammers A, Fellgiebel A, Schmidtmann I, Scheurich A, Buchholz HG, Peters J, Bartenstein P, Lieb K, Schreckenberger M (2009) SPM-based count normalization provides excellent discrimination of mild Alzheimer's disease and amnestic mild cognitive impairment from healthy aging. NeuroImage 44(1)

407. Yan R, Yang J, Hauptmann A (2003) Automatically labeling video data using multi-class active learning. In: Proc IEEE intl conf on computer vision (ICCV)

408. Yao C, Wada T, Shimizu A, Kobatake H, Nawano S (2006) Simultaneous location detection of multi-organ by atlas-guided eigen-organ method in volumetric medical images. Int J Comput Assisted Radiol Surg 1

409. Yao A, Gall J, van Gool L (2010) A Hough transform-based voting framework for action recognition. In: Proc IEEE conf computer vision and pattern recognition (CVPR)

410. Yao B, Khosla K, Fei-Fei L (2011) Combining randomization and discrimination for fine-grained image categorization. In: Proc IEEE conf computer vision and pattern recognition (CVPR), Springs, USA, June 2011

411. Yi Z, Criminisi A, Shotton J, Blake A (2009) Discriminative, semantic segmentation of brain tissue in MR images. In: Proc medical image computing and computer assisted intervention (MICCAI). Springer, Berlin

412. Yin Z, Collins R (2009) Shape constrained figure-ground segmentation and tracking. In: Proc IEEE conf computer vision and pattern recognition (CVPR)

413. Yin P, Criminisi A, Winn J, Essa I (2007) Tree based classifiers for bilayer video segmentation. In: Proc IEEE conf computer vision and pattern recognition (CVPR)

414. Zhan Y, Zhou X-S, Peng Z, Krishnan A (2008) Active scheduling of organ detection and segmentation in whole-body medical images. In: Proc medical image computing and computer assisted intervention (MICCAI)

415. Zhang Q, Souvenir R, Pless R (2006) On manifold structure of cardiac MRI data: application to segmentation. In: Proc IEEE conf computer vision and pattern recognition (CVPR), Los Alamitos, CA, USA

416. Zhang J, Marszałek M, Lazebnik S, Schmid C (2007) Local features and kernels for classification of texture and object categories: a comprehensive study. Int J Comput Vis 73(2)

417. Zhang D, Wang Y, Zhou L, Yuan H, Shen D, The Alzheimer's Disease Neuroimaging Initiative (2011) Multimodal classification of Alzheimer's disease and mild cognitive impairment. NeuroImage 55(3)

418. Zheng F, Webb GI (2005) A comparative study of semi-naïve Bayes methods in classification learning. In: Australasian data mining conference

419. Zheng Y, Georgescu B, Comaniciu D (2009) Marginal space learning for efficient detection of 2D/3D anatomical structures in medical images. In: Proc information processing in medical imaging (IPMI). Springer, Berlin

420. Zhou SK, Comaniciu D (2010) Shape regression machine and efficient segmentation of left ventricle endocardium from 2D B-mode echocardiogram. Med Image Anal

421. Zhou SK, Georgescu B, Zhou X, Comaniciu D (2005) Image-based regression using boosting method. In: Proc IEEE intl conf on computer vision (ICCV)

422. Zhou SK, Zhou J, Comaniciu D (2007) A boosting regression approach to medical anatomy detection. In: Proc IEEE conf computer vision and pattern recognition (CVPR)

423. Zhu Y, Fujimura K (2007) Constrained optimization for human pose estimation from depth sequences. In: Proc Asian conf on computer vision (ACCV)

424. Zhu X, Ghahramani Z (2002) Learning from labeled and unlabeled data with label propagation. Technical Report CMU-CALD-02-107, Carnegie Mellon University

425. Zhu X, Goldberg A (2009) Introduction to semi-supervised learning. Synthesis lectures on artificial intelligence and machine learning. Morgan and Claypool Publishers, San Rafael

426. Zhu C, Byrd RH, Lu P, Nocedal J (1997) Algorithm 778: L-BFGS-B: Fortran subroutines for large-scale bound-constrained optimization. ACM Trans Math Softw 23(4)

427. Zien A, Ong CS (2007) Multiclass multiple kernel learning. In: Proc intl conf on machine learning (ICML)

428. Zikic D, Glocker B, Konukoglu E, Criminisi A, Demiralp C, Shotton J, Thomas OM, Das T, Jena R, Price SJ (2012) Decision forests for tissue-specific segmentation of high-grade gliomas in multi-channel MR. In: Proc medical image computing and computer assisted intervention (MICCAI)

Index

A

Active learning, 1, 7, 95, 96, 102, 106, 230, 232, 233, 343
Alzheimer's disease, 261, 262, 266, 267
Anatomy detection, ix, 26, 194–196, 202–204, 209, 307

B

Brain
   lesion, xi, 1, 26, 245, 246, 253, 254, 256, 257, 259
   tumor, 245, 247, 252, 254, 259

C

Car detection, 153
Classification, 1, 2, 7, 13, 16, 25, 26, 28, 31, 47, 95, 102, 111, 112, 114, 120, 137, 146, 149, 150, 160, 186, 187
Computed tomography, ix, 193, 198, 202, 273, 275
Context, viii, 99, 112, 118, 120, 123, 129–131, 134, 138, 140, 144, 147, 150, 163, 197–199, 201, 203, 209, 217, 219, 241, 252, 266, 274, 278, 297, 338, 340
   appearance, 147, 197, 219, 250, 253, 255, 275, 278
   semantic, 144, 211, 213, 219, 222, 250, 255, 259, 275–278, 281

D

Decision forest, viii, ix, xi, 4, 5, 8, 21, 23, 26, 43, 48, 51, 57, 59, 75, 80, 81, 96, 105, 111, 113, 115, 117, 120, 121, 130–132, 134–136, 140, 143, 144, 149, 153, 164, 176, 177, 179, 180, 185, 209, 212, 213, 229, 231, 233, 239, 241, 242, 244, 258, 265, 266, 273–275, 278, 280–283,
286–289, 291, 293, 295, 297, 298, 307, 313, 314, 319, 321, 324, 328, 332, 334–336, 343
Decision tree, vii, 4, 8–12, 16, 17, 21, 49, 84, 104, 131, 185, 211, 213, 273, 296, 299, 300, 306, 322, 327
Decision tree field, 295, 296, 300, 301, 304, 306, 308, 309
Deformable objects, 156, 160–162, 169, 241
Density estimation, viii, xi, 1, 5, 7, 16, 59, 60, 67, 68, 73–75, 77, 81, 83, 95, 98, 333, 337, 341, 343
Depth images, 175–178, 189, 192, 307
Dimensionality reduction, 79–82, 84, 89, 90

E

Entangled forests, 273, 274
Entanglement, 219, 249, 273–278, 280–282, 293
Extremely randomized trees, 115, 131, 132, 135, 136, 140, 297

H

Hough forest, 143–148, 150–154, 156, 157, 164, 166, 183, 288
Human pose, xi, 26, 147, 175, 176, 178, 189, 191, 192, 307

I

Image, vii, 7, 9–11, 112, 113, 117, 122, 126–130, 132, 135, 138–140, 150–152, 155, 164, 177, 179, 196, 197, 204, 208, 212, 216, 218, 220, 224, 226, 231, 246–248, 296, 300, 306, 307, 336
   annotation, 123, 125, 126, 132
   categorization, 125, 146, 211–213, 215–221, 224, 227

A. Criminisi, J. Shotton (eds.), *Decision Forests for Computer Vision and Medical Image Analysis*, Advances in Computer Vision and Pattern Recognition, DOI 10.1007/978-1-4471-4929-3, © Springer-Verlag London 2013

Image (*cont.*)

  classification, 2, 7, 25, 48, 95, 125, 126, 134–137, 141, 144, 175, 262, 283, 288, 290, 307

  retrieval, 118, 125, 132, 134, 135, 140

  segmentation, xi, 1, 7, 26, 28, 80, 134, 139, 141, 144, 146, 150, 177, 211–213, 215, 227, 229, 230, 232, 246, 274, 296, 344

Implementation, 115, 124, 147, 149, 157, 163, 173, 176, 205, 216, 217, 220, 244, 304, 309, 314, 315, 317–319, 323, 326–328, 338

  distributed, 186, 313, 323, 327, 328

  GPU, 157, 176, 186, 323, 326

  parallel, 176, 281, 323, 324, 327, 336

Information gain, 3, 11, 13, 14, 16–19, 27, 28, 37, 39, 42, 51, 52, 61, 97, 98, 101, 116, 132, 149, 163, 185, 200, 214, 229, 241, 242, 256, 259, 273, 276, 277, 281–289, 293, 314–316, 319, 320, 328, 330, 335, 336, 338, 341

K

Keypoint recognition, 2, 112, 113, 116, 117

Kinect, viii, 1, 2, 176, 327, 344

M

Magnetic resonance, 7, 193, 197, 198, 206, 245, 246, 251, 254, 263, 264

Manifold learning, viii, xi, 1, 5, 7, 79–83, 87, 90, 93, 266, 343

Maximum-margin, 26, 37, 39–43, 273, 274, 282, 283, 286, 287

Multiple sclerosis, 245, 246, 253, 254, 256, 257, 259, 293

P

Pedestrian detection, 2, 145

Proposal distribution, 275, 278, 293

R

Random ferns, 117, 120, 121, 134, 162, 164, 168, 208, 209

Regression, viii, ix, xi, 1, 2, 5, 7, 13, 16, 22, 26, 28, 47–59, 62, 64, 67, 95, 96, 126, 132, 137–139, 147, 149, 150, 176–179, 181, 183, 184, 186, 187, 190–199, 201, 202, 206, 208, 209, 297, 333, 337, 341, 343

S

Semantic texton forest, 211–215, 217, 219, 220, 224, 227, 297

Semi-supervised classification, xi, 5, 95, 96, 101, 104, 105, 333, 337, 341

Semi-supervised learning, 1, 7, 93, 95, 96, 161, 230, 343

Shannon entropy, 17, 18, 149, 186, 200, 229, 283

Sherwood, 45, 57, 66, 75, 77, 106, 311, 314, 315, 321, 333–339, 341–343, 345

Software library, xi, 1, 8, 43, 66, 106, 314, 321, 343, 345

T

Tracking, ix, xi, 2, 26, 137, 146, 147, 159–164, 166–173, 176, 179, 184, 193, 230, 241, 242, 259, 274, 283, 285, 288–292, 343

V

Video segmentation, 229–234, 239, 244